WOMEN AND THE LAW

The Unfinished Revolution

LEO KANOWITZ

WOMEN
and the
LAW

The Unfinished Revolution

UNIVERSITY OF NEW MEXICO PRESS
ALBUQUERQUE

Chapters 1, 2, 3 and 7, © by *Saint Louis University Law Journal,*
1967; chapters 4 and 5 © by *Hastings Law Journal,* 1968.

 14

© Leo Kanowitz, 1969. Manufactured in the United States of America
by the University of New Mexico Printing Plant. Library of Congress
Catalog Card No. 70-78551. *Second printing,* 1970.

TO LIBBY, CARRIE, TONI AND MIGNONNE,
THE WOMEN IN MY LIFE

Preface

Between the end of the Civil War and the historic desegregation decision of the United States Supreme Court in 1954, the struggle for racial justice in the United States was waged with varying degrees of intensity, passion and commitment. But after *Brown v. Board of Education,* that struggle became an overriding issue in our national life, directly affecting all Americans, black and white alike.

The intensification of the quest for racial justice in the United States since 1954 is of course partly attributable to a variety of other factors, such as the growing importance of foreign opinion in a shrinking world, the strategic significance of the emergent African states, the secularization of American religious organizations, and the increased militancy of the victims of injustice themselves. At the same time, the heightened tempo of recent civil rights activity on the racial front is largely, perhaps ultimately, traceable to the courtroom success in the *Brown* case and its progeny and to the new federal and state equal opportunity legislation enacted in their wake.

The fact is that for some complex sociological reason, successful attacks upon the legal aspects of social injustice, rather than dampening the desire for reform, can often stimulate fresh concern and renewed activity beyond the strictly legal sphere.

It is with this phenomenon in mind that the present book has been written. Though we have been amply informed in recent years about the disparities in the condition of men and women in American society, no widespread passionate commitment to the elimination of these disparities has developed. Perhaps an awareness of the many areas of sex-based legal discrimination, whose continued existence this book seeks to identify, will stimulate, first, courtroom and legislative attacks upon those disparities or injustices, then, a much-needed national examination of the respective roles of the sexes in every sphere of American life, and finally, the active and continuing participation of all Americans in bringing about the needed changes. That, at least, is the primary goal of this book and the hope of its author.

Many people have contributed their time, energy and ideas toward making this book as meaningful and useful as possible. Whatever merit the book has is largely due to their encouragement, stimulation, and suggestions—although its faults are entirely my own. Among those to whom a debt of gratitude is due are Professors Michael I. Sovern, Kent Greenawalt, Charles Szladits, Frank Grad and Tom Farer of the Columbia University School of Law, Professor Frederick Hart of the University of New Mexico School of Law, and Manuel Nestle of the California Continuing Education of the Bar. I would also like to thank John Hollis of the New Mexico Bar and Theodore Parnall of the New York Bar for their technical assistance, and Sandra Kruzich, Carolina Le Blanc and Janet Cox for their efficient typing of much of the manuscript.

There are four people, however, to whom a special debt of gratitude is owed. One is my colleague, Professor Henry Weihofen of the University of New Mexico School of Law, who read most of the manuscript and made many useful suggestions for its improvement. Another is Professor Walter Gellhorn of the Columbia University School of Law. Despite an exacting schedule and frequent trips away from New York City, he rarely missed an opportunity to send me local newspaper clippings on the status of women, whether they appeared in Oxford, Mississippi or Los Angeles, California. Still another is Dean Monrad G. Paulsen of the University of Virginia School of Law who, during most of the time this book was in preparation, was Professor of Law at the Columbia Law School. It was Dean Paulsen, more than any other person, who continually inspired me with his vision of the potential importance of a work on this subject and who contributed his ideas and comments in numerous ways. The fourth is my wife, Libby Kanowitz. Her patience and understanding during the many months I worked on this book (while writing another at the same time) were indispensable to its completion. As a woman, a wife, and a mother, deeply concerned with world affairs, music, politics, literature, art, architecture and gardening, among other matters, she has constantly exemplified this book's underlying premise—that women, despite their special attributes for which we may all be grateful, are, above all, people.

Portions of this book have previously appeared in volumes 11 and 12 of the *Saint Louis University Law Journal,* volume 2 of the *Family Law Quarterly,* volume 20 of the *Hastings Law Journal,* and volume 48 of the *Nebraska Law Review.* Permission of those journals to publish herein is gratefully acknowledged.

Leo Kanowitz
Albuquerque, New Mexico

Contents

CHAPTER 1

Introduction

"The Female equally with the Male I sing."
Walt Whitman, *Leaves of Grass*

It will not come as a surprise to anyone even cursorily acquainted with the work of courts and legislatures to be told that the law has often accorded markedly different treatment to men and women solely because of sex. Voting rights, jury service, right to a separate domicile, causes of action for loss of consortium, capacity to enter into binding agreements and to sue and be sued, change in citizenship upon marriage to an alien, change of name upon marriage, age of attaining majority—these are only a few of the many areas in which a person's sex has at times made the sole difference in the treatment he or she would receive under the law in the United States and other countries.

What is more, sexually discriminatory rules of law are by no means relics of the past, mere historical curiosities. Despite the removal of legal barriers to the right to vote by American women in 1920, despite the passage of Married Women's Property Acts throughout the United States in the latter half of the nineteenth century, and despite the prohibition against sex discrimination in employment contained in the Civil Rights Act of 1964,[1] sex-based legal inequality continues to be a fact of life both here and abroad.

In most of the cantons of Switzerland and in Afghanistan, Iraq, Jordan, and other countries, the fundamental right to vote was, as of 1964, still withheld from women.[2] In France, as recently as 1965, jurists and nonjurists alike were heatedly debating government proposals aimed at eliminating major instances of legal discrimination against French women.[3] And in the United States, as a result of piecemeal legislative enactments, the interpretive role of judges reared in the tradition of "natural male dominance,"[4] and the existence of other complex factors to be examined hereafter, separate rules of law for men and women continue to regulate numerous areas neither contemplated nor affected by the Married Women's Property Acts.[5]

Remarkably, the persistence of legal inequality between the sexes has in recent years engendered little excitement among Americans. In marked contrast to the spirit of the suffragist movement, still within living memory,[6] and the current drive of American Negroes toward equal legal status with white persons,[7] no Americans have recently marched, picketed, sat-in, or otherwise dramatically demonstrated their opposition to legal expressions of sex discrimination.[8]

At the same time, Americans have not been unaware of social differences between the sexes. The commercial success in the United States of books by Simone de Beauvoir,[9] Betty Friedan,[10] and Phyllis McGinley[11] suggests widespread concern with the male-female relationship in American society. But these authors have largely concerned themselves with the subtler aspects of that relationship: the social and psychological obstructions to woman's fulfillment as a human being, the joys and sorrows of "housewifery," and the issue of freedom and equality in the sphere of sexual conduct. For the most part, they have passed over the continued existence of sex-based inequities, supported, perpetuated and often aggravated by the organized might of domestic and foreign legal systems.

Some groups concerned with the general status of women have, of course, not ignored the strictly legal aspects of that status. The League of Women Voters and the National Woman's Party have over the years urged fundamental changes in American law aimed at promoting legal equality between the sexes.[12] The United States President's Commission on the Status of Women,[13] the Women's Bureau of the United States Department of Labor,[14] and the United Nations Commission on the Status of Women[15] have also been active in this field. These groups have issued periodic reports, describing in general terms the legal situation of women in today's world.[16] Yet none appear to have fired the imagination or engaged the militancy of ordinary American women. With the exception of an intellectual elite or those who have inherited or retained the feminist tradition, most American women do not appear to be greatly exercised by the persistence of inequities in their legal status.

Several explanations can no doubt be advanced to account for this relative calm among American women over the continuance of sex-based legal inequality. One, founded upon the teachings of the modern existentialist philosophers, is proffered by Simone de Beauvoir in her remarkable book, *The Second Sex*.[17] According to that theory, women have been conditioned by life and history to look upon themselves as "the Other." They have, as a result, lost their desire to achieve full equality with men—socially, legally, or on any other level.

A second, somewhat more prosaic, explanation may lie in the nature of the laws that discriminate on the basis of sex. Though legal rules often discriminate between the sexes, they do not always favor men over women. In certain areas, women appear to be the beneficiaries rather than the victims of the law's discrimination. Examples include protective labor laws that limit the weights to be lifted[18] and the hours to be worked by women,[19] the frequently encountered statutory[20] or judicial[21] preference for a divorced mother over the father as legal custodian of a child of tender years,[22] the exclusive liability of males for military service and conscription,[23] the general rule imposing the primary responsibility for family support upon a husband rather than a wife,[24] and the influence of that rule upon the questions of alimony,[25] child support,[26] and property distributions[27] when marriages are dissolved by divorce.

Fear of losing these and other legal "protections" as the *quid pro quo* for achieving full legal equality may also partly explain the decline of women's concern with their legal status since the adoption of the Nineteenth Amendment.

Finally, American women's apathy in regard to sex-based legal discrimination may merely reflect a lack of information about the extent to which such discrimination still exists. Knowing that past struggles have been fought and won, and suspecting that their legal status is more advanced than that of women in other Western countries or in non-Western countries,[28] women have seemingly adopted the view that discrimination under the law has become a thing of the past.

But sex-based discrimination in the United States is far from dead. In this connection, the dual meaning of the word "discrimination," as used throughout this essay, should be kept in mind.

When, in the following pages, the sex discriminatory aspects of various statutory, judicial and administrative rules of law are identified and analyzed, the primary concern will be whether those rules "make a difference in treatment or favor on a class or categorical basis in disregard of individual merit."[29] In particular, the inquiry will be whether the designated legal rules discriminate against females by according them less favorable treatment than they would receive if they were males.

At other times, however, attention will be focused on whether the rules in question fall within the secondary meaning of the word "discrimination"; *i.e.,* whether they "mark or perceive the distinguishing or peculiar features of . . . recognize as being different from others . . . distinguish between or among . . . make a distinction."[30]

Though such rules may not result in less favorable or even in different treatment for females than for males, the mere fact that they contain language—whether embodied in statutes or judicial opinions—that emphasizes irrelevant differences between men and women cannot help influencing the content and the tone of the social, as well as the legal, relations between the sexes. For the relationship between law and society is probably more intimate and reciprocally influential in this area of human affairs than in most others. Not only do legal norms tend to mirror the social norms that govern male-female relationships; they also exert a profound influence upon the development and change of those social norms. Rules of law that treat of the sexes *per se* inevitably produce far-reaching effects upon social, psychological and economic aspects of male-female relationships beyond the limited confines of legislative chambers and courtrooms.[31] As long as organized legal systems, at once the most respected and most feared of social institutions, continue to differentiate sharply, in treatment or in words, between men and women on the basis of irrelevant and artificially created distinctions, the likelihood of men and women coming to regard one another primarily as fellow human beings and only secondarily as representatives of another sex will continue to be remote. When men and women are prevented from recognizing one another's essential humanity by sexual prejudices, nourished by legal as well as social institutions, society as a whole remains less than it could otherwise become.[32]

As thus defined and as will be demonstrated in the following pages, numerous instances of sex-based legal discrimination are still to be found in American legislation and judicial decisions. At times, as in the areas of marriageable age[33] and jury service,[34] the fact of discrimination is obvious; statutes or decisions simply prescribe one rule for males, another for females. At other times, as in the principle of inter-spousal immunity in tort[35] and the criminal abortion laws,[36] discrimination is present but obscured. For here, though the language of the rule seems to apply equally to both male and female, social realities outside of the courtroom have often caused the burden of the rule to fall upon the sexes unevenly.

It will also be seen that many of the rules that differentiate on the basis of sex at the present time stem from a sincere desire on the part of lawmakers to "protect" women, rather than from an openly avowed belief in the principle of "natural male dominance" so characteristic of much official thinking in the not-too-distant past.[37] But, as California's Justice Traynor has pointed out in another context, women may very well have become the "victims of protection."[38]

This is not to suggest that women do not need the law's special assistance in many areas; differences in physique and other biological factors hardly need to be labored.[39] But often the law "protects" women in areas of activity where the need arises not from biological factors but from a constellation of cultural, sociological and legal conditions—all products of a long prior history of open subjugation of women by men.

Many recent students of women's social condition have stressed the similarities between the situation of women in a male-dominated society and that of Negroes in a white-dominated society— noting the particular plight of those who are at the same time both female and Negro. Though recognition of such similarities is an aid to understanding women's past and present legal condition, fundamental differences in both the legal and social situation of Negroes and women in the United States should not be overlooked. With that important qualification, the observation of Simone de Beauvoir, in comparing the paternalism evinced by a male-dominated society toward women with the paternalism of white persons toward Negroes, is particularly useful. "In both cases," she writes, "the dominant class bases its argument on a state of affairs that it has itself created."[40] Nowhere is this principle better demonstrated than in the rules of law that "protect" women from imprudent economic transactions because of their assumed lack of proficiency in matters of this kind.[41] To the extent such lack now exists, it is the result of previously lost educational opportunities[42] and the continuous belief, enforced by legal institutions, that woman's highest if not sole life's work is that of wife and mother.

Laws that discriminate on the basis of sex raise obvious constitutional questions of a "due process" or "equal protection" character. Though the United States Supreme Court and lower federal and state courts have in the past upheld the constitutionality of sex-discriminatory laws, there are portents that, with regard to at least some of these laws, the tide may be turning.[43] Consideration of these matters, however, has been reserved for a later chapter. The present concern is to identify certain representative areas of the law in which sex-based discrimination has been or is now present, and to examine the sociological conceptions and misconceptions underlying that legal discrimination.

Finally, at the risk of stating the obvious, it should be emphasized that neither the method of analysis nor the viewpoint expressed in this essay are in any manner intended to deny the existence of important biological, psychological, and other differences between men and women. No contradiction is involved, however, in endorsing the French declaration, *"Vive la différence!"* while, at the same time, insisting that despite those differences women are, after all, people. Some rules of law that tend to ignore this simple fact will now be examined.

CHAPTER 2

Law and the Single Girl[1]

> "Woman is the lesser man."
> Alfred Lord Tennyson, *Locksley Hall*, line 151.

> "Though woman never can be man
> By change of sex and a' that,
> To social rights, 'gainst class and clan
> Her claim is just, for a' that."
> William Lloyd Garrison, *An Autograph*

AGE OF MAJORITY

TODAY, as in the past, the law denies children the right to engage in many types of activities normally permitted to adults. Minors, for example, may not directly engage in property transactions, contract with others, or sue and be sued. For these purposes, it is generally provided that a guardian must be appointed for the child. In contrast to similar disabilities imposed upon married women by the common law, which were based on the fiction of the unity of husband and wife, the legal disabilities of children are the products of logical social and factual premises. Commercial and property transactions being complex and children simply not having lived long enough to have become educated in the ways of the business world, it is not unreasonable to require that for their own protection these matters be handled for them by adults who are better suited to the task.

Though some children undoubtedly mature more quickly than others, the common law did not permit a special inquiry to be made into the actual understanding and capabilities of particular young persons in deciding whether they should be freed of their legal disabilities. Instead, the uniform age of twenty-one years was established as the age of majority for all children. Whether they were male or female, children were considered by the common law to remain children until they reached the age of twenty-one. At that time, and only then, did they legally become adults.[2]

7

The common law rule, which prescribes the same age of majority for male and female, has been preserved in the statutes or decisions of most states.[3] At times, however, some states have prescribed different ages of majority for males and females. Often, these differences have been established without regard to the marital status of the individual. In Illinois, for example, even today, the statutory age of majority for most purposes is twenty-one for all males and eighteen for all females. "[U]ntil those ages are attained, they [are] considered minors."[4] Though similar statutes were formerly found in many other states, most of these have been amended in recent years to reestablish the common law parity between the male's and female's age of majority. Generally, this has been achieved by raising the female's age of majority to twenty-one years rather than by lowering the male's age to eighteen.[5]

In other states, while unmarried females as well as males remained minors until they reached the age of twenty-one, a sex-based difference in the age of majority often obtained in the event of marriage. Thus, in those states, married females who were at least eighteen years old were considered to have attained the age of majority, while their husbands remained minors until they reached the age of twenty-one. Here, too, many statutes have been amended to reestablish a uniform age of majority for married males and females. In contrast to the equalization trend with regard to the age of majority of single persons, parity has generally been achieved between married persons by reducing the married male's age of majority, rather than by raising the married female's. In Alabama, California and Minnesota, for example, married males formerly did not attain majority until they reached the age of twenty-one years. Their wives, however, were unburdened of their disabilities as minors if they had attained the age of eighteen. Today, these states provide that males, as well as females, who are at least eighteen years old attain majority upon marriage.[6]

Legal tampering with the age of majority of the male and female presents an interesting example of the law's conceptualism. On the one hand, there are the common law disabilities of married women.[7] While those disabilities were originally justified by the fiction of the husband's and wife's theoretical identity, their preservation beyond the era of fictions was no doubt based in part upon the premise that women, not having been trained in the ways of the business world, were in need of protection comparable to that given to children. On the other hand, there is the countervailing public policy generally permitting females to be married at a younger age than males. Somehow the married state bespeaks maturity and wisdom.[8]

In line with these concepts, married persons have been deemed to have attained the age of majority upon marriage—provided that they were not so young as to leave no doubt that they were still children in fact. Thus, married females were often held to attain majority at eighteen, though males had to wait until they were twenty-one. And in many states, though they were not yet married, the fact that they could be married without their parents' permission at an earlier age than males led to rules that permitted girls to reach majority at an earlier age than boys, without regard to their marital status.

At the same time, in the realm of sexual behavior, other social conceptions concerning the proper conduct of males and females produced uneven laws for the sexes with regard to such crimes as statutory rape, seduction and enticement.[9] Universally, the young female, but not the male, has been considered to be incapable of consenting to sexual relations, though for all other purposes—contracts, property ownership, capacity to sue and be sued—she might reach the age of majority years before the male.

Such inconsistencies are inevitable once separate minimum ages for various types of activities for males and females are established. They reflect the irrationality of many sex-based legal distinctions. Their ultimate rationalization requires our legal system to begin treating people as people, without reference to their sex. Especially with regard to the age of majority, there is no reason why the same rules should not be prescribed for males and females in all instances.

MARRIAGE QUALIFICATIONS

Although the recent United States Supreme Court decision[10] invalidating on constitutional grounds a state "antimiscegenation" law, which prohibits marriages between persons of different races, has cast some doubt upon the propriety of state regulation of marriageability on other grounds, such as age, health and prior familial relationship,[11] the latter type of marriage regulation has long been recognized. In some of these areas, different rules have frequently been prescribed for men and women. An examination of those differences and their reasons can, perhaps, illuminate some aspects of the law-society relationship in this field.

Marriageable Age

Only eleven states prescribe the same minimum age for marriage for males and females, where parental consent is not required.[12] The remaining thirty-nine states permit girls to be married from two to three years earlier than boys, the most frequent arrangement being a twenty-one-year minimum for boys and eighteen for girls. Even at the lower ages where parental consent is necessary, statutes maintain a comparable differential between irreducible marriage ages of the sexes, with only four states (Connecticut, Maine, Missouri and Tennessee)[13] prescribing a uniform age for boys and girls under these circumstances.

The historical basis for sex-based differences in minimum marriageable age requirements may be found in the early English legal presumptions of differences in physical capacity to produce children.[14] As a result of these presumptions, and at a time when parental arrangement of marriages between infants was not unusual, the common law set fourteen years as the age of consent for males and twelve years for females.[15] Much evidence can be found to demonstrate that, physically, females in fact develop more rapidly than males.

As Anglo-American law developed, prescribed minimum ages for marriage were gradually increased, though the law generally still permitted girls to be married earlier than boys.[16] But in place of the "physical development" rationale for the minimum-age differential, important roles began to be assigned to new factors: e.g., whether "boys and girls under the designated ages [were] normally or generally possessed of sufficient stability, logic, or experience, to reasonably understand the full significance or responsibilities of the marital status."[17] Here again, much biological and psychological data can be adduced to support the reasonableness of the classification, at least as against constitutional attacks on "equal protection" grounds—although as demonstrated in Chapter 6, it is by no means a foregone conclusion that the disparity in minimum-age requirement would, today, survive a constitutional challenge.

In any event, the female's more rapid emotional, as well as physical, maturation is no doubt also demonstrable.

The question remains whether on a policy basis such sex-based minimum-age differentials for marriage should be preserved.[18] It is submitted that without regard to the constitutionality of such distinctions, intelligent, humanitarian and realistic social policies would require their elimination. The establishment of a uniform minimum marriageable age for both girls and boys in each of the fifty states would assist tremendously in the task of ameliorating male-female relationships in American society.

While the fundamental vice in the marriageable age distinctions has lain dormant in all previous stages of legal development in this area, it has become particularly acute in the modern era. That vice lies in two sociological presumptions that accompany the aforementioned legal presumptions of earlier physical and emotional maturity in the female. One is that the married state is the only proper goal of womanhood. The other is that the male, and only the male, while not to be denied the benefits of marriage, should also be encouraged to engage in bigger, better and more useful pursuits.

Recognizing that early marriage impedes preparation for meaningful extra-family activities, society has decreed that males should not be permitted this digression from life's important business at too early an age. Since women's participation in meaningful activities outside the home was until recently socially inconceivable, no great harm was seen in permitting females to follow their biological inclination and to marry earlier than males.

In modern times, however, early marriage for women often results in great social waste. It can lead to premature removal from socially productive enterprise or lost educational opportunities.[19] Those opportunities have been achieved in the United States, as elsewhere, only after long and difficult struggles.[20] With early marriage, however, comes the likelihood of early pregnancy, the effects of which obviously fall more heavily upon the wife than upon the husband. One result is a higher frequency of interruptions in educational pursuits among females than among males. A further consequence is the perpetuation of past social stratifications and divisions of social functions between the sexes.

Even if agreement could be reached on the desirability of a uniform minimum age requirement for marriage without parental consent,[21] an additional problem would remain to be solved, namely, what should that uniform age be? Should the usual eighteen-year minimum age in girls be raised, or the twenty-one-year age for boys be lowered? Among the various possibilities, the Hawaiian system, which prescribes the minimum age of twenty years for both males and females,[22] may strike some people as the most desirable. A compromise solution, the twenty-year uniform age does not defer marriage so long as to create emotional problems, yet defers it long enough to enable both males and females to complete between two and three years of higher education before marriage. In the era of the "knowledge explosion," few will question the desirability of making educational opportunities beyond the secondary school level available to all. While neither boys nor girls will normally have finished all work for a baccalaureate degree at age twenty, the likelihood that their studies will be continued until completion is much greater at this point than if marriage is permitted at an earlier age.

On the other hand, experience since the Second World War has demonstrated that many young people can successfully pursue a program of higher education while married. Indeed, a stable marriage relationship may have spurred a large percentage of post-World War II male college students to greater levels of educational achievement than they would have attained if unmarried. Many young people, moreover, are neither desirous of nor suited for higher education. For them, early marriage may be the best step to take. If the problem is viewed with this group in mind, equal treatment of the sexes might appropriately be achieved by lowering the minimum marriageable age of males to correspond with the age at which girls are permitted to marry.

The complex problems raised by the sex-based disparity in minimum-age requirements for marriage obviously do not admit of facile solutions. Further exploration and reflection is needed in this area before firm recommendations for change can be made. The foregoing tentative analysis, however, indicates the existence of an important area of human relations in which discrimination, as defined earlier, is highly visible. Here, certain indefensible factors of sexual bias—culturally created conceptions of the relative "places" of male and female in society—combine with other less indefensible reasons—more rapid physical development among females than among males—to produce different rules for male and female in an otherwise comparable situation.

Health

Reflecting advances in scientific knowledge, statutes have increasingly required a medical certificate or an affidavit from the parties to be married, establishing freedom from venereal disease as a condition precedent to the issuance of a marriage license.[23] Almost universally, such "proof" of health in regard to syphilis and gonorrhea has been required for the prospective bride as well as the groom. At one time, however, in many of the states, only the male has had to furnish proof of freedom from those diseases. And even today, the state of Washington requires the male but not the female to submit an affidavit declaring "that such male is not affected with any contagious venereal disease."[24]

The validity of the present Washington requirement has apparently never been litigated. In 1914, however, a group of physicians attacked a similar Wisconsin statute in *Peterson v. Widule*.[25] That statute, which was later modified to apply to females as well,[26] prohibited county clerks from issuing a marriage license unless the male filed a certificate setting forth that he was "free from acquired venereal disease so nearly as can be determined by physical examination and by application of the recognized clinical and laboratory tests of scientific search"; the statute also set a $3.00 limit on the fee that doctors could charge a prospective groom for an examination and certificate.

Though the plaintiff doctors in the *Peterson* case were primarily troubled by the fee limitation, they also asserted that the law was void because of an unreasonable, arbitrary, and discriminatory classification. There was, said the physicians, "no substantial differences which suggest the propriety of different legislative treatment between men who are about to marry and women who are about to marry." To which the court replied:

> Theoretically the argument is strong. Women who marry and transmit a loathsome disease to their husbands do just as much harm as men who transmit such a disease to their wives. If women were in fact doing this thing as frequently or any-

where near as frequently as men the argument could hardly be met. The medical evidence in the case, however, corroborates what we suppose to be common knowledge, namely that *the great majority of women who marry are pure,* while a considerable percentage of men have had illicit sexual relations before marriage, and consequently that the number of cases where newly married men transmit a venereal disease to their wives is vastly greater than the number of cases where women transmit the disease to their newly married husbands.[27]

The greater frequency of venereal disease among men than women was probably a valid social fact at the time of *Peterson v. Widule.* Its present validity is more questionable, especially in view of the "new morality." But even in 1914 and the years since then, the number of women who contracted a venereal disease prior to marriage and transmitted it to their new husbands was undoubtedly substantial.[28] The Wisconsin and Washington legislatures could easily have required females as well as males to prove their good health in this regard as they are required to do in many other states.

One cannot help suspecting that the separate treatment of the sexes in this situation reflects more than the traditional legislative course of dealing with less than the whole of a problem. Consciously or unconsciously, the legislators here appear to be basing this classification not only on a belief that "the great majority of women who marry are pure," but also on the assumption that single women, as opposed to single men, are expected to remain "pure." Viewed somewhat differently, the lawmakers are saying here in effect: "To require women to submit such proof is to admit the possibility that they have engaged in pre-marital sex relations. But, as we all know, only 'good' girls or 'pure' girls are the ones who marry."

Such thinking was of course consistent with the frequently encountered legal enshrinement of a double moral standard. A Maryland statute, for example, contained a provision which remained in effect until its repeal in 1939,[29] giving to a husband but not to a wife a ground for divorce

> when the *woman* before marriage has been guilty of illicit carnal intercourse with another man, the same being unknown to the husband at the time of the marriage, and when such

carnal connection shall be proved to the satisfaction of the court.[30]

Similar statutes were at one time found in at least fourteen states.[31] And in the Texas case of *McAllister v. McAllister*[32] the court stated: "Wisely or not, our statutes do not make occasional acts of adultery on the part of the husband a cause of divorce, when sought by the wife; otherwise, when the husband asks divorce from the wife taken in adultery."[33]

At the present time, Washington appears to be the only state that exempts the female from the duty to furnish proof of freedom from venereal disease. That exemption is a subtle, albeit indirect, reflection of law's acquiescence in separate standards of morality for male and female, and should be amended to apply to women as well as men. Though the particular problem is now limited to one state and has, therefore, lost its former vital significance, it continues to be of interest as another example of the American legal system's endorsement of society's double standard of sexual morality—an endorsement which, as we shall see hereafter, appears in less subtle form in many other areas of legal regulation.

CRIMINAL LAW

Prostitution

In Oakland, California, it was reported recently,[34] two women have appealed their convictions for prostitution on the grounds of sexual bias, claiming that they were discriminated against "because the male customers who were with them when they were arrested were released without charge."

Farfetched? It is difficult to say without knowing all the details of the case—which are not available at this writing. The case does point up, however, a significant area of the law in which public officials, under the influence of society's now-traditional double standard of sexual morality, have often adopted or applied sexually discriminatory legal standards in deciding whether to punish certain modes of sexual behavior.

Frequently referred to with euphemistic delicacy as "the social evil,"[35] prostitution in the United States has been controlled at various times by methods of "reglementation, segregation and repression."[36] In the present century, however, state as well as national policies have been directed toward "absolute suppression of prostitution."[37] At common law, prostitution was not a specific crime, having been dealt with originally as an ecclesiastical offense.[38] In modern times it has been variously defined as "the practice of a female in offering her body to an indiscriminate intercourse with men for money or its equivalent;"[39] "indiscriminate sexual intercourse with males for compensation;"[40] or "common lewdness of a woman for gain."[41] The obvious vice of such definitions is that they make criminal the conduct of only one party—the woman—to an act which, with the possible exception of certain aberrational cases not relevant here,[42] necessarily requires the participation of a male second party. Indeed, it has been held that under the terms of such a statute a male cannot be a prostitute or an inmate of a house of prostitution.[43]

With the American legal system's characteristic lack of uniformity, however, a number of jurisdictions make possible in theory at least the punishment of men for patronizing a prostitute. Some do so directly.[44] In others, males may be punished for "aiding and abetting" prostitution,[45] which crime can apparently be committed by patronizing a prostitute.[46] And, provided that transportation in interstate or foreign commerce is involved, the Federal White Slave Act, or Mann Act,[47] would appear to permit successful prosecution of a prostitute's male customer—since it has been frequently held to apply to situations having nothing to do with the control of prostitution, such as the taking of a mistress along on a trip[48] or the interstate transportation of a female in order to maintain an adulterous relationship.[49]

In most states, males cannot be directly punished for patronizing a prostitute. But, if their conduct happens to fall within the terms of certain collateral crimes, e.g., fornication, lewdness, solicitation, or associating with a prostitute, they may be indirectly dealt with by the law. Such crimes do not exist in all states, however.[50] And even in those states where such crimes do exist, restrictive interpretations have often led to the exoneration of male customers of prostitutes. Thus, it has been held that resorting to a house of ill fame for an isolated act of intercourse does not warrant conviction for "open and gross lewdness;"[51] that a statute penalizing persons who "solicit" another for prostitution does not apply where the solicitation is for the personal gratification of the solicitor;[52] and that a statute prohibiting "adultery or fornication" is not violated by occasional intercourse not accompanied by any pretense of the parties living together.[53]

More important than the rules of statutes and decisions in this area are those developed by lower echelon administrators of the criminal law, such as police officials and prosecuting attorneys. As a result of these officials' exercise of discretion, though a prostitute's male customer may theoretically be prosecuted, this rarely occurs.

The Oakland ladies may indeed have a valid point. As observed by one authority, arrests of male "customers are made in most instances with no expectation that an actual criminal prosecution will be carried through, but only as an inducement to the male to cooperate in convicting the woman."[54] The invocation of the collateral "statutes is less likely to be designed to punish the male or control his future activities than it is to coerce him to cooperate with the prosecuting authorities by testifying against the woman."[55]

It is of course possible to argue that unequal treatment in this situation is not the result of sexual bias, but stems from factors that distinguish the respective roles of male and female when prostitution occurs; *e.g.*, the indiscriminate and more frequent intercourse of the prostitute[56] increases the likelihood of communicating venereal disease; the commercial aspects of her enterprise distinguish it from the male's, and so forth.[57] The fact remains that female prostitutes simply could not exist without male customers. Ultimately, if attempted solution of the "social evil" is to continue along the lines of suppression rather than reglementation, vigorous legal and social measures against male participants should also be taken.

In this regard, the Soviets, despite their shifting policies in the "easy-versus-hard-divorce" controversy, have had remarkable success in the suppression of prostitution.[58] At one point in their antiprostitution campaign, they decreed that:

> Whenever officers raided a place of vice—whether it was a house, a tavern, or simply a dark street—they were to take down the names, addresses and place of employment of all men found there. The customers were not to be arrested. But on the following day, and for a specified period, those men would have their names and identifying information posted in a public place, under the heading "Buyers of the Bodies of

Women." These lists were to be prominently displayed outside public buildings or on factory bulletin boards.[59]

While such measures may not be in keeping with present conceptions in American society, they suggest that many aspects of our own treatment of this problem reflect sexual bias. Discriminatory law enforcement in this area is by no means a new development in the history of legal institutions.[60] But if the progress that American law has made in the last two centuries in rejecting the theory of male superiority is to be completed, women should no longer bear the entire burden of an offense that involves both sexes.[61] As proposed by Abraham Flexner, one of the early students of the problem, in 1914: "The stigma and consequence of crime must . . . be either removed from the woman or affixed to the man."[62]

Statutory Rape and Related Crimes

The sexual assault of a man by a woman is not an inconceivable occurrence. But given the basic anatomical differences between male and female, variations in the threshold of their sexual appetites, and the fact that most women who wish to engage in indiscriminate sexual intercourse can normally find an obliging male partner, the incidence of women forcing men to engage in sexual relations is rare indeed. Not surprisingly, therefore, the crime of rape is universally defined in terms of a male's forcible sexual violation of a woman and no provision is made for the situation in which the woman is the aggressor and the man the victim.

Where sexual intercourse between male and female is *voluntary,* however, the likelihood that the female initiated the event is not as remote as in the case of the above-posited forcible attack by a female. Despite this fact, the criminal law distinguishes sharply between male and female in many situations in which they appear to be similarly situated. In most states, for example, it is a crime for a male to have sexual intercourse with a female, not his wife, who is below a certain age—generally ranging from 14 to 21 years—though to all appearances, no force, guile or threats are employed by the male. These crimes are often set forth in the same statutes that define the crime of forcible rape, and penalties for their commission are frequently severe. At the same time, it is rarely a special crime and never a case of "statutory rape"—as sexual intercourse with a female below the statutory age of consent is called—for women to engage in sexual relations with young males who are within those same age groupings.[63]

So strongly have legislatures and courts felt about this rule that almost universally the male's good faith belief that the female was older than the statutory age has not been a defense to the crime,[64] although it has no doubt been a significant factor in the sentencing process. Only recently, in fact, has the California Supreme Court been the first to permit a defendant to introduce evidence of his reasonable and bona fide belief that the prosecutrix was over the statutory age as a defense to the charge of statutory rape.[65]

In an effort to reconcile the concepts of statutory and forcible rape, courts have consistently talked of the legal incapacity of a female below the statutory age to give a meaningful consent to the intercourse—a rationalization that is reminiscent of the general contractual incapacity of minors and the formerly general common law disabilities of married women. As a result, though the participation in the act of intercourse appears to be consensual, the event has been assimilated to forcible rape by holding that an apparent consent to intercourse by a female within the specified age categories is not a true consent at all.[66] Since adult women do not commit the crime of statutory rape when they engage in intercourse with boys of fourteen to twenty-one years, lawmakers presumably believe that, unlike girls, boys of that age are capable of meaningfully consenting to sexual intercourse.[67]

In only a few states do other statutes seem to provide special penalties for an adult female who engages in sexual intercourse with a young boy. In Massachusetts, for example, a statute provides that "Whoever induces *any person* under eighteen of chaste life to have unlawful sexual intercourse shall be punished as provided in the preceding section."[68] The use of the phrase "any person" in this statute, as compared with the specification of female victims in "the preceding section,"[69] suggests that it could be used, and may have been intended to be used, to prosecute an adult female for having sexual relations with a boy below the age of eighteen. This type of law is rare, however, and is by no means a deliberate effort to establish the crime of statutory rape by a female.

Another statutory crime under which, in theory at least, a female could be prosecuted for having sexual relations with an underage

male is that of "contributing to the delinquency of a minor."[70]
Again, emphasis must be placed upon the theoretical availability
of such statutes to prosecute a woman for engaging in sexual relations with, let us say, a seventeen year old boy. A review of anno-
tations to a typical "contributing to the delinquency of a minor"
statute[71] reveals that in an overwhelming majority of prosecutions
under its provisions the minor victim is a female. In the relatively
infrequent cases in which the minor victim is a male, the usual
offense charged is that of making available to the minor whiskey
or some other alcoholic beverage.[72]

Judicial rationalization of the statutory rape statutes in terms of
a young girl's incapacity to consent to an act of intercourse, while
ingenious, does not accurately reflect the underlying social reasons
for sex-based discrimination in this area. As will be demonstrated
hereafter, the prime motivation for modern statutory rape laws
can once again be found in the pervasive double standard of sexual
morality.

Statutory rape laws can be divided into two broad categories:
1) those requiring as an element of the crime the previous chaste
character of the victim; and 2) those defining statutory rape as an
unlawful carnal knowing of a female below the designated age,
without regard to the victim's previous chastity. Among the first
group of statutes are those in the District of Columbia,[73] Florida,[74]
Massachusetts,[75] and Mississippi.[76] Unlike the others, the Mississippi Code also provides that "In the trial of all [statutory rape]
cases . . . it shall be *presumed* that the female was previously of
chaste character, and the burden shall be upon the defendant to
show that she was not. . ."[77]

States that do not make the victim's previous chaste character an
essential element of the crime of statutory rape include Illinois,[78]
Connecticut,[79] Indiana,[80] Iowa,[81] Maryland,[82] and Missouri.[83]

Though American jurisdictions are divided on whether the previous chastity of the "victim" is an essential element of the crime of
statutory rape, they are in agreement that it is an indispensable
part of another offense which in purpose and goals is not unrelated
to the concept of statutory rape—namely, the crime of "seduction."
Here, too, with the exception of the Massachusetts statute previously cited,[84] the male is uniformly the offender, the female the
victim. The crime of seduction is generally defined in terms of a

male having deceived a female to engage in sexual intercourse by means of a false promise of marriage.[85] In some states, any other "subtle device," such as a promise of a gift to a young girl by an old man, may constitute a criminal deception.[86] In contrast to the victim of statutory rape, however, the victim of the crime of seduction may often be any unmarried female, regardless of age.[87] A second distinction is that all seduction statutes require the victim to have been of previous chaste character.[88] Seduction statutes, in contrast to the statutory rape laws, also frequently provide that the defendant's marriage to the victim before judgment on an indictment[89] or before a jury is sworn[90] bars further prosecution for the crime. And, apart from criminal prosecution, a civil remedy for damages for seduction is often provided for the victim or her parent.[91]

In addition to statutory rape and seduction, another crime, "enticement," is also closely related in purpose and intent. Enticement is generally defined in terms of a male persuading a female below a designated age to leave her father's home and to accompany him for purposes of effecting a clandestine marriage without the consent of her parent or guardian.[92] Once again, the victim must be a female, the defendant male.[93] Indeed, all three offenses—statutory rape, seduction, and enticement—generally involve a male offender and a female victim and rarely, if ever, the reverse.

As indicated earlier, the states are not in agreement as to the female's age of consent with regard to the crime of statutory rape. In Georgia and Maine, for example, the age of consent is fourteen.[94] In Massachusetts and Indiana it is sixteen.[95] And in Florida, Minnesota and California it is eighteen.[96] In Tennessee, statutory rape may be committed by having sexual intercourse with a female below the age of *twenty-one*![97] In most states the statutory age limit has steadily risen over the years. In California, for example, "it was increased from ten to fourteen years in 1889, to sixteen years in 1897, and to eighteen years in 1913."[98] In Mississippi, it is also eighteen years, but the crime cannot be committed unless the female victim is of previous chaste character and the defendant is older than she.[99] In the District of Columbia, the age of consent is twenty-one years where there is a special relationship between the defendant and the victim. There, any male teacher, superintendent or tutor in a public or private school, seminar or other institution, who is himself over the age of twenty-one, may be imprisoned be-

tween one and ten years if he is convicted of having "sexual intercourse with any female under twenty-one years of age . . . with her
consent, while under his instruction during the term of his en-
gagement as superintendent, tutor, or teacher. . . ."[100]

Concern with the age of the accused in addition to that of the
victim is not an uncommon feature of statutory rape laws—as exemplified by the last-mentioned District of Columbia statute. This circumstance sheds some light on the reasons for making such conduct
subject to criminal prosecution. We have seen, for example, that
the Mississippi law requires the defendant to be older than the
victim in order to sustain a prosecution.[101] In Maryland, statutory
rape simply cannot be committed by any male person under the
age of eighteen years.[102] And in the Iowa law of statutory rape may
be found one of the most interesting variations on this theme.
There, the age of the defendant is crucial in determining the victim's age of consent. Under the Iowa statute, carnally knowing and
abusing "any female child under the age of sixteen years" is statutory rape if committed by "any person" (meaning any male person). But if the victim is over sixteen and below the age of seventeen, it will also be statutory rape if it is committed by "any person
over the age of twenty-five years."[103] Like the District of Columbia
statute with regard to teachers and a Kansas rule that provides special penalties for statutory rape where it is committed by a guardian or "any other person to whose care and protection [the] female
shall have been confided,"[104] the Iowa provision—by referring to
the age of the male accused to fix the female's age of consent on a
sliding scale—proceeds on the apparent assumption that the persuasiveness of the male may be more difficult to resist under some
circumstances than under others.[105] Consistently with the overall
policy of the statutory rape rules, however, no corresponding presumption is indulged in with reference to young males "victimized"
by the blandishments of adult females—whether those females be
guardians, teachers, superintendents or simply women over the age
of twenty-five years.

What, then, of the discriminatory aspects of these rules of law
that provide penalties for males and not for females in comparable
situations? Before detailed consideration, one point should be emphasized. By no means is it intended here to suggest that the laws
on statutory rape, seduction and enticement are in themselves use-

less, harmful, or in need of repeal. Obviously there are many activities, especially in the sexual realm, in which young people do not stand on an equal footing with adults and require the protective arm of the law to ward off disastrous consequences of unwise conduct. The point, however, is that if sexual intercourse is objectively harmful for persons of tender years, then it should be equally harmful for young males as well as young females. Certainly, where the female "victim" is already unchaste, there would seem to be little reason for the laws on statutory rape to distinguish between the sexes.

This is not to ignore the fact that beyond legal regulation of sexual conduct, society at large often imposes greater penalties upon the young female who transgresses in matters sexual than it does upon the male who does so. In providing special penalties where the young victim of sexual transgression is a female rather than a male, law may perhaps be regarded as providing protection where protection is needed. At the same time, one cannot overlook the fact that the extra-legal sanctions of social disfavor, ostracism and lessened attractiveness on the marriage market imposed upon the female transgressor are the clear results of society's double standard of sexual behavior, which allows males great sexual freedom and imposes severe restrictions where females are concerned. Laws that provide special penalties for male offenders in this area effectively lend their support to those social sanctions and ultimately to the perpetuation of the hypocritical double moral standard upon which they are based.[106]

As suggested earlier, courts have rationalized the concept of statutory rape in terms of the young female's legal incapacity to give her consent to intercourse. Like the general contractual incapacity of minors, this in turn is based on the presumption that, though there is consent in fact, legal recognition should be withheld because of the minor's presumed inability to appreciate the consequences of the agreement into which she has apparently entered. In the case of the general contractual incapacity of minors, however, the age of majority at common law was twenty-one years for both sexes. Only recently in the United States have some states prescribed different ages of majority for male and female, a trend that now seems to be in the process of reversing itself.[107] Even when sex-based differences in the age of majority have appeared, however, they have uniformly been lower for females than for males. As a result, a female in some states may enter into a valid and binding commercial contract at the age of eighteen, though a male cannot do so until he has attained the age of twenty-one.[108] Moreover, as we have already seen, females are generally allowed to marry and thus permitted—nay, required—to engage in sexual intercourse at a younger age than males. It is anomalous, therefore, for laws to restrain females below a certain age from consenting to sexual intercourse, while males of the same age, though not positively encouraged to engage in such conduct, are not prevented from doing so by making the conduct of their adult female sexual partners a special crime.

At the risk of delving into the realm of the Freudian subconscious, another possible explanation may be offered to account for the discriminatory aspects of the statutory rape laws. Despite intellectual recognition of the pleasurableness of sexual relations, the notion is still very much abroad that the act of intercourse necessarily represents an assault by the male upon the female. This attitude is reflected, among other ways, in the secondary meaning of the epithet that contains the tabooed four-letter word, followed by the word "you." No notion of pleasurable sexual intercourse is intended when that phrase is used. Instead, a threat of physical injury is implicit in the expletive. Though attitudes on this question undoubtedly vary among social strata, the idea of sexual intercourse as synonymous with the infliction of physical injury by the male upon the female may, subconsciously at least, be shared by much of mankind. To this extent, rules of law that penalize the perpetrator of an act resulting in physical injury (the male defendant in a statutory rape trial), but do not punish the one who is injured (the adult female who engages in sexual intercourse with the young male) are logically consistent. Needless to say, any equation of the act of sexual intercourse with the infliction of physical injury, whether entertained consciously or subconsciously, is highly debatable.

Previous reference has been made to the division among American jurisdictions between those that require the female victim of statutory rape to have been of previous chaste character and those that do not. We have also seen that all states that proscribe the crime of seduction make the female victim's previous chastity an essential element of the crime. There are obvious similarities between loss of a woman's chastity and suffering physical injury. To this extent there may be some rational basis for distinguishing between the sexes under these statutes. The unequal burden of a possible pregnancy may also account for the law's one-sidedness here. But the impregnation of the female is in no state an essential element of statutory rape, criminal seduction or enticement. And, as we have seen, many jurisdictions—perhaps most—define statutory rape in terms which do not include the female victim's previous chaste character.

"The protection of society, of the family, and of the infant" are the goals that one court has ascribed to the statutory rape laws.[109] Undoubtedly these goals are also implicit in the seduction and enticement statutes. By limiting the definitions of those crimes to situations in which the offender is a male and the victim a female, those statutes are providing only an incomplete and unsatisfactory protection. At the same time, they are lending their support to society's pernicious and hypocritical double standard of sexual morality.

Criminal Abortion

Every person who provides, supplies, or administers to any woman, or procures any woman to take any medicine, drug, or substance, or uses or employs any instrument or other means whatever, with intent thereby to procure the miscarriage of such woman, unless the same is necessary to preserve her life, is punishable by imprisonment in the State prison not less than two nor more than five years.

So declared California's "criminal abortion" statute[110] which, prior to its liberalization in 1967,[111] had been described as being "similar in substance to statutes in forty-one other jurisdictions in the United States."[112]

Under these statutes abortion is a crime unless it is necessary to save the life of the mother. In addition, as of 1958, six states permitted therapeutic abortion to save the life of the unborn child, two to prevent serious or permanent bodily injury, two to preserve the life or health of the mother, and fourteen "on medical advice as well as the peril of necessity."[113]

But "the abortion problem," as Professors Packer and Gampell have observed, "exhibits a dramatic variation between a legal norm and social fact."[114] On the one hand, many non-clandestine abortions are performed to protect a woman's health, as opposed to her life, which is generally not an excuse under most abortion laws.[115] More important is the fact that the felt need to submit to abortion is so great that a vast abortion black market thrives throughout the entire United States. Leavy and Kummer, criticizing our criminal laws on the subject, estimate that over a million abortions a year take place in the United States, and that between five thousand and ten thousand women die as a result.[116]

Contrary to what might be expected, most illegal abortions are performed upon married women with children.[117] They are often sought for reasons of economic hardship, psychological stress and apprehensions as to general health. Some women may seek an abortion if they have been impregnated as a result of forcible rape or an act of incest. Many abortions are no doubt sought to ward off the social stigma and practical difficulties imposed upon mothers of illegitimate children. Regardless of the underlying reasons, the significant fact is that every year vast numbers of women run the risk of criminal prosecution, [118] serious injury or death in order to be aborted.

The sex-discriminatory aspects of criminal abortion laws are not as readily apparent as in some other rules of criminal law discussed above. Unlike lawmaking and enforcement practices with regard to prostitution, statutory rape, seduction and enticement, legal regulation of abortion does not present the prospect of one law for males and another for females. True, women who solicit an abortifacient or submit to an abortion are at times singled out for punishment.[119] But childbearing still being the exclusive function of the female, such laws neither shock nor surprise. On the other hand, punishment for performing an abortion or for "procuring" any woman to take any medicine, drug or substance intending to produce a miscarriage is generally applicable to "every person," whether male or female. The male who fathers an unwanted child, whether he is the woman's husband or not, is undoubtedly one of the intended targets of such provisions—provided that he participates in the efforts to procure an abortion.

But sex discrimination is nevertheless inherent in the criminal abortion laws. Ultimately, it stems from the tremendous gap between legal rules and social mores in this area. Regardless of the potential risks of punishment under the criminal law, there are obviously many circumstances under which women feel the need to be aborted to be irresistibly compelling. Most legitimate physicians and surgeons, however, are considerably less willing to risk criminal prosecution. The effect of generally restricting the reasons for legal abortions to cases in which they are necessary to preserve the life of the mother is devastating. Many women are virtually forced to seek abortions from illegal abortionists or else, bewildered and frightened by their own pregnancies, to resort to self-abortion. In either case, such illegal abortions are performed hastily, under unsanitary conditions, and without the safeguards normally present in hospital surgical wards. These facts undoubtedly account for the large number of women—between five thousand and ten thousand every year—who lose their lives as a result of abortion. Though in many cases the desire to have the pregnant woman aborted is shared by her husband or lover, and though the latter are also subject to criminal prosecution for their participation in procuring an abortion, the criminal abortion laws have not caused those males to lose their lives.

The criminal abortion laws are another instance of legal rules that do not by their terms discriminate between the sexes, but whose practical effects fall much more heavily upon women than upon men. Though very few people would urge the legalization of all abortions, the principle of legal equality of the sexes is an additional reason for extending the circumstances under which therapeutic abortions should be legally justified.

POLITICAL RIGHTS

The Right to Vote

The Nineteenth Amendment to the United States Constitution was ratified less than 50 years ago. It stated simply:

> The rights of citizens of the United States to vote shall not be denied or abridged by the United States or by any State on account of sex.
> Congress shall have power to enforce this article by appropriate legislation.

That women in the United States should have an equal right to vote with men is probably now regarded as a self-evident truth by most Americans, regardless of sex. This fact is a striking example of law's powerful role as the shaper of social attitudes. Prior to the adoption of the Nineteenth Amendment, following a long and arduous struggle,[120] opposition to granting women voting rights at times reached ferocious proportions—always stopping short, however, of outright bombings and killings, the not uncommon responses to recent striving of American Negroes for an equal right to vote.

Although many opponents of women's suffrage were motivated by utilitarian and economic considerations rather than by strongly held ideological convictions in the preservation of a male-dominated society,[121] the arguments adduced in opposition to women's suffrage were more often than not based upon openly professed beliefs in the rightness, if not the holiness, of male superiority.

Those arguments were proved to be ultimately unsuccessful. But despite their success in overcoming legal obstacles to their right to vote,[122] women have not yet achieved full equality with men in regard to political rights, as will be seen below.

Jury Service

"Jury service is a form of participation in the processes of government, a responsibility and a right that should be shared by all citizens, regardless of sex." So declared a three-judge federal district court in *White v. Crook*,[123] decided on February 7, 1966, and holding that Alabama's statutory exclusion of women from jury service violated the Fourteenth Amendment's equal protection clause.

Whether the views expressed in *White* are now shared by all courts, including the United States Supreme Court, is uncertain.[124] At early English common law, however, it is clear that the court's words in *White* would have fallen on deaf ears. For at that time juries were composed exclusively of men except in two special situations involving the question of pregnancy of a female before the court.[125] In 1898 Utah became the first of the United States to permit women to serve on juries.[126]

At the present time, women's eligibility to serve as jurors varies according to whether the federal or state courts are involved. By virtue of the Civil Rights Act of 1957,[127] women may now sit on all federal juries, state rules no longer controlling as they did before 1957.[128] Many federal district courts, however, have lagged in implementing the 1957 Act.[129] As a result, the Committee on Civil and Political Rights of the President's Commission on the Status of Women as well as the Judicial Conference and the Department of Justice have endorsed legislative proposals[130] aimed at speeding up equality in regard to federal jury service.[131]

In the state courts, the eligibility of women for jury service presents a somewhat more complicated picture. As of August 1, 1962, only 21 states permitted women to serve on juries on the same basis as men.[132] Of 14 other states recognizing child care problems as special grounds for exemptions from jury service, only 5 allowed the exemption to both sexes, the remaining 9 making it available to women only.[133] In 15 states, women were allowed an exemption on the basis of their sex alone. In 3 other states women could be exempted for reasons not available to men, such as the nature of the crime in a criminal proceeding or the unavailability of adequate courthouse facilities to accommodate women jurors.[134] In 3 states, women could serve only if they registered with the clerk of the court[135]—an arrangement that is similar to the automatic exemption on the basis of sex alone, but one that obviates the necessity of appearing at the courthouse if a woman chooses not to volunteer her services for jury duty. Finally, in addition to Alabama, two other states, Mississippi and South Carolina, excluded women from jury service entirely,[136] a practice declared unconstitutional in *White v. Crook.*

If the decision in *White v. Crook* is permitted to stand, women will become *eligible* to serve as jurors in all states. Even if it should be reversed at some later date, the fact that only 3 states now exclude women entirely from jury service limits the significance of the eligibility problem—although it would still merit legislative attention in those 3 states. The most important problem at the moment is to discover the considerations lawmakers should be guided by in determining whether women, though eligible for jury service, should be permitted to be excused for reasons and by means not available to men.

In *Hoyt v. Florida,*[137] the Supreme Court expressed one view of the problem. There, the Court upheld the constitutionality of a Florida statute which, while it made women eligible to serve on juries, did not require them to serve unless they "registered with the clerk of their court [their] desire to be placed on the jury list."[138]

Recognizing that Florida's men could not be excused on the basis of their sex alone and that even if they were entitled to some other exemption they were, unlike women, included on jury lists unless they filed a written claim of exemption, the Court held the statute to be constitutional both on its face and as applied,[139] stating:

> In neither respect can we conclude that Florida's statute is not "based on some reasonable classification," and that it is thus infected with unconstitutionality. Despite the enlightened emancipation of women from restrictions and protections of bygone years, and their entry into many parts of community life formerly considered to be reserved to men, *Woman is still regarded as the center of home and family life*. We cannot say that it is constitutionally impermissible for a State, acting in pursuit of the general welfare, to conclude that a woman should be relieved from the civic duty of jury service unless she herself determines that such service is consistent with her own special responsibilities.[140]

The fact is, however, that neither men nor women have ever flocked to the courthouse to volunteer for jury service. Indeed, in the *Hoyt* case itself, the Court conceded that "women, like men, can be expected to be available for jury service only under compulsion."[141] But this argument was rejected as being "beside the point."[142] Yet it is somewhat anomalous to permit women to determine that jury service is "consistent with [their] own special responsibilities," and not permit men to do so. The special responsibilities of men include their need to hold a job and to earn a living for themselves as well as their families. Fees received for jury service are notoriously low. Except for cases where employers, voluntarily or under the compulsion of a collective bargaining agreement, pay their employees the difference between their jury fees and what they would otherwise have earned on their jobs, jury service frequently involves considerable sacrifice for men as well as women.

In describing women as "the center of home and family life," the Supreme Court in the *Hoyt* case also implies that both would suffer if women were required to perform jury service on the same basis as men. Both the Court and the states whose policies it has confirmed seem to have in mind the common situation in which a husband is gainfully employed and the wife is at home with the children, although neither the Florida statute in the *Hoyt* case nor other similar statutes require that there be children in the family to excuse women from jury service; their mere status as women is sufficient. Neither the Court nor those states, however, appear to be unduly troubled by possible injury to children and families resulting from a husband's reduced income during his period of jury service. In their view, such economic loss to the family as a whole seems to be permissible. Yet, if a family were to spend a sum equal to a husband's lost earnings, this would in most cases be more than sufficient to enable a mother called for jury service to pay a third party to take care of her children for the necessary period.

In this era of working mothers, child care centers, nursery schools and "baby-sitters," making such arrangements would not present insurmountable difficulties. As for the welfare of the children, they will have benefited in the long run from their mother's intimate participation in an important aspect of the nation's political processes. To be sure, sacrifice would be involved; but sacrifice is inevitable under present schemes of compensation for jury service. The ultimate solution to that part of the problem requires reimbursement to both men and women for lost income or child care costs, whatever the case may be. That reimbursement could come from public funds or, where appropriate, from employers of large numbers of people who would finance the cost of their employees' jury service as an additional cost of doing business.

Constitutional questions aside, laws that permit women to be excused from jury service on the basis of their sex alone or not to serve unless they volunteer freeze the position of women as second-class citizens in the field of political rights. Like the generally lower marriageable age for girls as compared with boys, though such laws reflect certain valid policies, they also express present day vestiges of male supremacy doctrines.

WOMEN IN EMPLOYMENT

Laws that regulate the employment situation of women are of a three-fold character: 1) Those which, in the exercise of the police power and purporting to recognize differences in physical capacity and family functions of the sexes, require employers to treat their women employees differently from their men employees. Such laws, for example, place limits on weights to be lifted by women workers,[143] prohibit night-time employment of women,[144] or prescribe the maximum daily and weekly hours they may work,[145] without making comparable provision for male workers similarly situated. 2) Other laws, based in part on social conceptions of "ladylike" and "unladylike" activities, restrict the type of work women may engage in—the most frequently encountered prohibition being directed at the employment of female bartenders.[146] 3) Finally, rather than requiring women workers to be treated differently from male workers, a third set of laws, enacted in a more recent period, has aimed at equality of treatment and specifically sought to correct employment abuses stemming from sexual bias in hiring practices or as expressed in sex-based wage differentials.

Amendment of the Fair Labor Standards Act by the Equal Pay Act of 1963[147] has partially met the problem of the sex-based wage differential. Under that Act, women workers may not be paid less than male workers doing similar work.[148] Because of the limited jurisdictional applicability of the Fair Labor Standards Act, however, many women workers are still unaffected by the law. And even in the twenty-two states which, as of October, 1963, had their own equal pay laws, not all women workers were in covered employment.[149]

Some legislative enactments have sought to remove barriers to equal employment opportunity for women by penalizing employers who refuse unreasonably to hire women workers for jobs they are capable of performing. The most important of these are the equal employment opportunity provisions of the Civil Rights Act of 1964.[150] By the middle of 1965, ten states and the District of Columbia also had laws prohibiting sex-based discrimination in employment.[151]

Because the subject of legal regulation of women's employment will be examined in later chapters only a few features of that regulation are noted here: First, these various types of legal regulation of women's employment do exist. Second, in this area statutes and decisions frequently express contradictory goals and conceptions of women's role in American society. And third, there is an important jurisprudential question whether, in the absence of "equal employment opportunity" legislation, "law" can be said to discriminate in setting different standards for hiring males and females for various occupations, or whether the blame rests exclusively on non-legal social institutions. Stated differently, the question is whether a legal system's failure to prohibit private discrimination based upon sex, race, religion or any other factor equals legal affirmance of such discriminatory practices and attitudes.

In contrast to the problem posed above, law's active role in confirming societal prejudices cannot be doubted where statutes affirmatively prohibit women from engaging in certain occupations, such as professional wrestling,[152] or bartending.[153] In *Goesart v. Cleary*,[154] the United States Supreme Court upheld the constitutionality of the latter type of statute, though it made an exception for the wives and daughters of the owners of liquor establishments. "[B]artending by women," stated the Court, "may, in the allowable legislative judgment, give rise to moral and social problems against which it may devise preventive measures [and] the legislature need not go to the full length of prohibition if it believes that as to a defined group of females other factors are operating which either eliminate or reduce the moral and social problems otherwise calling for prohibition."[155]

Occupational restrictions of the kind involved in *Goesart* appear to be motivated by at least two considerations: 1) the need to counteract a specific type of anti-social conduct, such as the "B-Girl" type of problem; and 2) a general purpose of "protecting" women. As for the first, other types of legal regulation—civil as well as criminal—appear to be sufficient for the purpose. As for the second goal of such statutes, it should be first recalled that there is no restriction on women working as waitresses—where they come in much closer contact with the clientele—in establishments that dispense alcoholic beverages. It is only where they serve drinks from behind a bar that the restrictions generally prevail. Except for possible pressures from special interest groups such as bartenders' labor unions,[156] it would appear therefore that these statutes, to the extent that they are motivated by the desire to "protect" women, are sadly misguided. Adult women, unlike children who are the objects of special child labor law protection, are generally capable of making their own determinations of the extent of the dangers or risks such employment might entail and whether they are willing to undertake them. The net effect of the statutory occupational restrictions is merely to deprive women of the opportunity of earning their living in some ways that are open to men.

Justice Frankfurter's opinion for the majority in the *Goesart* case also contained the following interesting language:

> The fact that women may now have achieved the virtues that men have long claimed as their prerogatives and now indulge in vices that men have long practiced, does not preclude the States from drawing a sharp line between the sexes, certainly in such matters as the regulation of the liquor traffic. . . . *The Constitution does not require legislatures to reflect sociological insight, or shifting social standards, any more than it requires them to keep abreast of the* latest *scientific standards.*[157]

The *Goesart*-type statute can, therefore, withstand constitutional attack—at least as of the moment. Whether it can also stand up against the equal employment opportunity provisions of the 1964 Civil Rights Act is doubtful. Those provisions outlaw all sex-based employment discrimination, whether it is practiced by employers, employment agencies or labor organizations.[158] The only exception permitted by the law is where sex is a "bona fide occupational qualification reasonably necessary to the normal operation of [a] particular business or enterprise."[159]

Detailed discussion of the 1964 Civil Rights Act will be undertaken in later chapters. However, it should be noted that a statute forbidding women from being licensed as bartenders would be difficult to sustain on the grounds that sex was a "bona fide occupational classification reasonably necessary to the normal operation of the particular business or enterprise"—unless it could be shown that a primary duty of bartenders was not only to serve drinks but also to "bounce" unruly patrons.[160] In the light of the 1964 Civil Rights Act, comparable questions may also arise with regard to the continued validity of state laws that subject the working hours, conditions and wages of women to special regulation.[161]

CHAPTER 3

Law and the Married Woman

> "And Adam said, this is now bone of my bones, and flesh of
> my flesh; she shall be called Woman, because she was taken
> out of man. Therefore shall a man leave his father and his
> mother, and shall cleave unto his wife and they shall be one
> flesh."
>
> *Genesis,* ii, 22-23

> *"Hamlet:* Farewell, dear mother.
> *King:* Thy loving father, Hamlet.
> *Hamlet:* My mother: father and mother is man and wife,
> man and wife is one flesh, and so, my mother."
>
> *Hamlet,* IV, 3, 53-5

THE DOCTRINE OF COVERTURE: ORIGINS AND ANTECEDENTS

At COMMON LAW, unmarried females were subject to
oppressive sexually discriminatory rules of law principally in the
public sphere—as in the denial of the right to vote or to serve on
juries on the same basis as men. In the areas of contracts and property, however, except for their disqualification under a system of
primogeniture during the time it prevailed in England,[1] single
women enjoyed almost equal legal status with single males. If they
were not under age, they could contract with other persons, sue
and be sued, manage and control their lands and chattels, reduce
to possession all their choses in action and retain the proceeds.
When single women married, however, these and other rights were
lost or suspended.[2]

The theoretical basis for the married woman's loss of legal rights
was the feudal doctrine of coverture. Based in part upon biblical
notions of the unity of flesh of husband and wife, the doctrine was
described by Blackstone as follows:

> By marriage, the husband and wife are one person in law; that
> is, the very being or legal existence of the woman is suspended
> during the marriage, or at least is incorporated and consoli-
> dated.[3]

35

In modern times, the doctrine has been described with greater candor as resting "on the old common-law fiction that the husband and wife are one . . . [which] has worked out in reality to mean . . . the one is the husband."[4]

As a result of the doctrine of coverture, or unity of husband and wife, a married woman incurred both substantive and procedural disabilities. Substantively, she lost control and management of her real property to her husband; he did not have to account to her for the rents and profits, although he could not alienate them.[5] In respect to her leasehold interests, she suffered an even worse fate; not only did her husband gain control of them upon marriage, but he could alienate them and keep the proceeds for himself.[6] All of her chattels she owned at the time of marriage and those she acquired later became her husband's absolutely.[7] And though her choses in action[8] did not become her husband's until he reduced them to possession, they were effectively taken from the wife, since only her husband could so reduce them while the marriage lasted.[9] Only if the marriage ended before the husband had reduced his wife's choses in action to possession did they revert to her.

In addition, as a result of her marriage a woman lost her power to transfer her own real property by an ordinary conveyance[10] and, except in certain special cases,[11] to contract with either her husband or third parties.[12] In the field of criminal law, marriage also produced special consequences. Thus, owing to the concept of the unity of husband and wife, it was held at an early date that a husband and wife could not be guilty of conspiring together,[13] or of stealing one another's property,[14] and that acts of the wife, committed in her husband's presence, which would otherwise be deemed misdemeanors, were presumed to be done under the husband's command, relieving the wife of criminal responsibility for her conduct.[15]

Procedurally, as a result of coverture, wives could neither sue nor be sued at law unless they were joined with their husbands,[16] and, according to Blackstone,[17] the doctrine of coverture also produced the rule that a husband and wife were not permitted to give evidence for or against one another.[18]

At the same time, marriage did not represent a matter of all economic gain and no loss, for the husband. For one thing, the wife, immediately upon marriage, became entitled to inherit a life estate in one-third of all lands of which her husband was seised at any time during the marriage and which her issue might have inherited.[19] Though this was a right of inheritance, it vested in the wife upon marriage and thus reduced the husband's estate; it also tended to restrict the alienability of the husband's property during his lifetime, potential purchasers normally insisting upon the wife's relinquishment of her dower rights, as they were called.[20] Moreover, the husband upon marriage acquired the obligation to support his wife and family.[21] While this duty may have arisen partly in consideration of the wife's property acquired by the husband upon marriage,[22] it was also in keeping with the concept of the husband's role as head and master of the family. The persistence of that concept no doubt accounts in part for the continuance of the husband's universal basic support obligation, notwithstanding the general emancipation of married women in the areas of property and contract rights. In addition, as a result of marriage, the husband became liable for all of his wife's premarital contracts[23] and all the torts she committed before[24] or during the marriage.[25] As a counterpart to the wife's immunity from criminal liability for certain acts committed in the husband's presence, the husband also "became subject to indictment for a crime committed by his wife in his presence, without any evidence of any complicity or knowledge on his part."[26]

Explanation of the married woman's position at common law involves consideration of many complex sociological and historical factors. Max Radin has attributed one of its principal causes to the character of feudal tenures,

> the chief duties of which, suit and service, were by their nature not readily performed except by men. Whatever lands a woman held, the feudal implications made it normal to assume that it would be a man and not a woman who appeared to represent the tenant, whoever it was, and representation was a familiar concept to the feudal system.[27]

According to that explanation, the married woman's inferior legal position at common law was the result primarily of practical rather than ideological considerations. However that may be, the feudal theory of "natural male dominance," as Radin himself has acknowledged elsewhere,[28] was also a fundamental cause of the married woman's position at common law. That theory, in turn, supported itself upon the fiction, inherited from an earlier period, of the unity of flesh between husband and wife. Because the "one" was always the husband, the dominance of the male was assured. Above all, the position of married women at common law both resulted from and contributed to a failure of men and women to see themselves essentially as human beings rather than as representatives of another sex.

EQUITY TO THE RESCUE?

In an effort to alleviate the rigors of the common law rules governing the contract and property rights of married women, the English Court of Chancery early developed devices and practices which, for some married women at least, counteracted the financial disadvantages of marriage. The principal device was the concept of the trust, which developed in time into the institution of the wife's separate equitable estate.

The wife's separate equitable estate could arise in two ways. The first was by the wife's agreement with her husband—either before or during marriage—or by a gift, conveyance, devise or bequest to her from her husband or third persons,[29] in which it clearly appeared that the wife should take and the husband should not.[30] Under such an agreement or document, though no trustee was named, equity would nevertheless treat the property as the wife's separate estate, "and hold the husband as trustee of his legal interest for her."[31]

The second method for creating the wife's separate estate in equity was contingent upon the husband's, or one claiming in his right, invoking the assistance of a court of equity to reduce the wife's choses in action to possession. When that occurred the court could condition its aid upon the petitioner's making a suitable settlement to maintain the wife and children.[32]

The principal benefit of the equitable separate estate was that a married woman could hold it as a *feme sole,* or single woman, free from her husband's control and regardless of whether it consisted of real or personal property, or both.[33] She could dispose of her equitable separate estate by will, gift, transfer or conveyance, as long as the instrument creating the estate did not expressly prevent her from doing so.[34] Though it was not expressly conferred by the instrument creating the estate, the English Court of Chancery held this power to be a necessary incident of the estate.[35] In England and in most of the American states, the concept of the wife's equitable separate estate also gave rise to a rudimentary contractual capacity for married women. Thus, "unless the power was excluded in the creation of the estate,"[36] a married woman could charge that estate by contract, even though the contract was not for the benefit of the estate or "for the benefit of the wife generally."[37] At the same time, the power to obligate her equitable separate estate by contract did not permit a married woman to bind herself personally by contract.[38]

As for its effect upon the general relationship of the sexes, the institution of the wife's equitable separate estate suffered from many shortcomings. In the early days of American law, some states had no court of chancery.[39] Often, where they existed, those courts had limited equity jurisdiction.[40] The result was that no forum was available to which a wife could apply for recognition or enforcement of her rights to a separate equitable estate. Second, if a husband or his agent could manage to reduce a wife's choses in action without resorting to a court of equity, no occasion would arise for a court to condition its aid upon the making of an appropriate settlement for the wife and family. Third, equitable relief was not a reality for women of limited financial means or limited education and intellect.[41] In many respects the concept of the wife's separate equitable estate was designed to assist the rich who were troubled lest the property they had transferred to their daughters would fall into the hands of undeserving husbands.[42] Fourth, equitable remedies were confined to the area of the wife's rights to property and, in a more limited sense, to contract. They did not reflect any fundamental social change in attitudes toward women. The old prejudices were reflected in the continued restrictions in other areas, such as jury service and voting. They were also expressed in the persistence of the fiction of the unity of husband and wife as the basis for special rules of criminal, tort, evidence and family law.

Above all, there was the profound, albeit subtle, effect of purporting to protect married women's property rights by means of the equitable trust—a device which, until its application to married women, had been associated with the protection of infants and idiots. Admittedly, women, like idiots and children, needed judicial protection. But though equitable relief helped, as far as it went, to adjust unfair legal property relations between married women, their husbands, and third persons, it also reinforced the conception of women as "the Other," widened the gulf between men and women, and dramatically emphasized irrelevant differences between the sexes. These differences were not the result of any natural endowments or limitations of either sex. They were, rather, the historical products of past social attitudes, themselves produced by the concept of "natural male dominance."

The Married Women's Property Acts

First enacted in Mississippi in 1839,[43] some form of the Married Women's Act or—as it was often called—the Married Women's Property Act was soon adopted by all American jurisdictions. By 1882 it had also become law in England[44]—the nation that had bestowed upon the United States the complex of rules establishing the married woman's inferior legal position.

Though the precise wording and scope of these statutes varied from state to state, they were all products of conscious and deliberate legislative efforts to redress property and contract relations between wives and husbands and to remove previous procedural disabilities of married women. Responding in great part to the rising tide of individual[45] and organizational[46] protest against the married woman's status of legal subjugation to her husband, these laws generally granted married women the right to contract, to sue and be sued without joining their husbands, to manage and control the property they brought with them to the marriage, to engage in gainful employment without their husbands' permission, and to retain the earnings derived from the employment.

Despite the great strides toward full legal equality for married women achieved by these Acts, emancipation is by no means complete. In the early period following the enactment of such legislation, the interpretive role of judges reared in the tradition of "natural male dominance"[47] and the rule of strict construction of statutes in derogation of the common law both limited the practical gains for married women.[48] In addition, many areas of the law in which married women received different or less favorable treatment than their husband were neither contemplated nor affected by those Acts.

Those areas, and the remaining pockets unaffected by the Married Women's Acts, will be explored in the following sections.

A MARRIED WOMAN'S NAME

Mary Smith married John Brown. Despite having lived her life before her marriage as Miss Smith, having been known in social and business circles by that name, and perhaps having brothers and sisters with the same name, her marriage causes her to lose her own surname and to acquire that of her husband. Henceforth, she will be known as Mary Brown. Her new husband, on the other hand, will retain the name by which he has been known all along. And, upon birth, their children will also acquire the husband's surname—now the wife's also—as their own.

The probable effects of this unilateral name change upon the relations between the sexes, though subtle in character, are profound. In a very real sense, the loss of a woman's surname represents the destruction of an important part of her personality and its submersion in that of her husband. Notwithstanding legislative rejection in the Married Women's Acts of the theory of the husband and wife's legal unity in other spheres, this name change is consistent with the characterization of coverture as "the old common-law fiction that the husband and wife are one . . . [which] has worked out in reality to mean that the one is the husband."[49] Particularly significant is that, unlike other changes wrought by the marriage, the change of name occurs as soon as the marriage takes place and both husband and wife are immediately aware of it.

The loss of a married woman's maiden surname and the acquisition of her husband's is of course firmly rooted in Anglo-American social custom. If, as has been suggested, the change of a woman's name upon marriage represents the destruction of a major facet of her personality, women for the most part submit to that destruction knowingly and willingly. The reasons for their acquiescence are varied. Once custom has been established, regardless of its underlying reasons, departures entail serious difficulties—possible questions concerning the legitimacy of children of the marriage, suspicions raised among neighbors and acquaintances as to whether "wife" and "husband" have been married in accord with legal formalities, and the like. In addition, strong psychological factors also operate here. For many women the name change must symbolize a merger in fact of their own personalities in that of their husbands. Given the social setting of relations between the sexes, that merger may strike them as a highly desirable state of affairs.

On the other hand, social custom in this regard, even in the "Western" world, is by no means uniform. In such non-common law jurisdictions as Denmark[50] and France,[51] both custom and law permit a married woman to retain her maiden name. By contrast, in the United States, the change in a woman's name upon marriage is not only consistent with social custom; it also appears to be generally required by law.

Many American judicial decisions have denied women's requests that they be permitted to be known by their maiden names after marriage. Thus, in *Chapman v. Phoenix National Bank of the City of New York*,[52] the court stated: "For several centuries by the common law among all English speaking people, a woman upon marriage takes her husband's surname. That becomes her *legal* name, and she ceases to be known by her maiden name."[53]

In *People v. Lipsky*,[54] a state law required every "registered voter who changes his, or her name by marriage or otherwise . . . to register anew and authorize the cancellation of the previous registration."[55] Petitioner, a married woman, sought mandamus to require the Board of Election Commissioners to permit her to vote though she had not re-registered under her married name. Reversing the trial court's grant of mandamus, the Illinois Appellate Court based its decision upon

> the long-established custom, policy and rule of the common law among English-speaking peoples whereby a woman's name is changed by marriage and her husband's surname becomes *as a matter of law* her surname.[56]

Similarly, in *Bacon v. Boston Electric Railway Co.*,[57] failure of a woman to re-register her automobile under her married name led to a holding that the automobile "was not legally registered and was a nuisance on the highway."[58] As a result, she was precluded from bringing an action for injuries sustained when her automobile was struck by defendant's train. And in *In re Kayaloff*[59] a federal court held that a certificate of naturalization should not be issued to a married woman in her maiden name although, as a professional musician, she was well-known by that name.

At first blush, these cases seem difficult to reconcile with the common law rule that an individual who has no fraudulent purpose may change his name merely by adopting and using a different one. Though lacking the approval of a court of law, this new name becomes his legal name for all purposes.[60] This common law rule has usually been stated in general terms—without exceptions based upon the sex or marital status of the person purporting to change his or her name by the simple expedient of adopting a new one. There is strong reason to believe, however, that this rule has never in the past and would not now permit a married woman to adopt a surname other than her husband's if he should object.[61] One court, for example, has qualified the common law rule that anyone may change his or her name at will by saying that it has "been approved for certain conditions and stations in life."[62] Moreover, apart from the requirement that the informal name change not be made for a fraudulent purpose, third persons have always been able, by obtaining an injunction, to prevent such a change if it would cause them injury. Fathers, for example, have at times been granted an injunction restraining their divorced wives from enrolling their children at a school under a surname other than their own.[63]

A review of the cases does not reveal whether the precise question has ever arisen in any judicial proceeding. Nevertheless, present law would appear to permit a husband's prevention, by injunction proceedings, of his wife's attempt to change her name informally.

Most states, for example, have statutes that prescribe formal procedures for changing one's name, and thus a means of obtaining an official record of the change. Many of them expressly exempt married women from their provisions. The Iowa law, for example, permits a formal name change to be granted by a court to "any person, under no civil disabilities, who has attained his or her majority *and is unmarried, if a female* . . ."[64] (It also provides that the new surname of the petitioner "shall become the legal surname of *the wife and minor children* of such person.")[65] Similarly, the

Kentucky law provides that "Any person at least twenty-one years of age, *who is not a married woman,* may have his name changed by the county court of the county in which he resides."[66]

Under other statutes, though a married woman is not expressly precluded from changing her surname to one that is different from her husband's, that rule may be implied. In Colorado, for example, "every person [is allowed] to change *his or her* name by petition to and order of the Court . . . [if the] . . . judge is satisfied that the desired change would be proper, *and not detrimental to the interests of any other person.*"[67] Under this principle, a Colorado judge could refuse to change a married woman's surname if her husband objected. The rule that a change of name should not be permitted if it would be "detrimental to the interests of any other person" has always been part of the common law. A judge, therefore, could enjoin a married woman from using a surname that is different from her husband's—if the husband requested the injunction. The husband's right in this matter would no doubt be regarded as similar to his right as a father that his children continue to bear his surname, unless he has forfeited that right by his misconduct.

Sex-based discrimination is apparent in still another area involving the change of a married woman's surname. Since a married woman acquires her husband's surname upon marriage, it is provided generally that if she is granted a divorce, the court may upon her request permit her to assume her maiden name, a former married name, or some other name altogether. But the express wording of some statutes appears to permit a judicial record of such change only if the married woman is the successful complainant and not where she is the defendant in a divorce action.[68] Though such limitations may be the result of a draftsman's oversight, they more likely express a legislative policy which, once again, reflects sexual bias. Under such a rule, a woman not only acquires her husband's surname upon marriage; she is also denied the right to receive a judicial decree restoring her maiden name if her husband successfully procures a divorce from her. In addition to other penalties for her misconduct leading to her husband's divorce, she is "punished" by being required to bear her husband's name until she remarries and thus submerges that name in that of a new husband.

In contrast to these statutes, Michigan permits a court, when granting a decree of divorce, to restore the maiden name of the wife, or the name she legally bore prior to her marriage to her husband in the divorce suit, or to decree that she may be known by some other name, at the request "of the woman, *whether* [she is] *complainant or defendant*."[69] Despite this attempt at equalizing the situation, the Michigan statute contains another provision—also found in the laws of some other states—that represents an even more serious expression of sex discrimination. That provision states "that when there is a minor child or children, issue of the marriage, this act shall not apply."[70] The interest of the minor children of the marriage in retaining their father's surname, even when they are not living with their mother under the custody provisions of a divorce decree,[71] is apparently so favored that their mother is not permitted to resume her maiden name until the children have reached majority or, presumably, until she has remarried.[72] At that time, at least so far as her legal name is concerned, she can once more become subservient to a man—her new husband. His interest in this respect will prevail over her children's. In both instances, her rights and her interest in selecting a surname are secondary.

The right of children to select a name prevails over their mother's corresponding right in still another situation under Michigan law. In the ordinary formal change of name proceedings, not involving a divorce, the petition may be brought by "any person."[73] But

> when such petitioner is the husband or head of the family, in its order changing the name of such petitioner, the court *shall* include the name of the wife of such petitioner and *may* also in its discretion include the name of such minor children of whom the petitioner has legal custody. Provided, however, that the written consent to the change of name of any child over the age of sixteen years signed by said child in the presence of the court shall be filed with the court before the court shall include such child in its order.[74]

Three sex-based discriminatory principles are discernible in this Michigan statute: 1) The husband's change of name automatically results in the wife's change of name (which is generally true elsewhere); 2) Though the statute does not expressly give the wife the right to petition for a change of name without the husband's joinder, no provision is made for a corresponding change in the husband's name, which suggests very strongly that the wife does not have this right; 3) Though a wife may not contest the change of her own name resulting from the change in her husband's, their minor children over the age of sixteen may do so.

As suggested earlier, American women are not clamoring for the right to be known by their maiden names after marriage or for the right to change their names without their husbands' approvals. However, in those instances where for some reason or another married women have expressed a desire to do this the courts have uniformly rejected the effort. Despite the common law rule, which does not appear to differentiate between the rights of married men and their wives to change their names in an informal manner, no cases can be found in which the wife has been permitted to do this over the husband's objection. In addition, under many of the statutes that prescribe formal procedures for changing one's name, the right to do so has been either expressly or impliedly denied to married women. No comparable restriction has been imposed upon married men. Finally, the law, once more either expressly or by implication, generally requires that a change in the husband's surname produce a corresponding change in that of his wife, but never the reverse.

Married Women's Domiciles

To most non-lawyers, the word "domicile" conveys the idea of a home. In legal contemplation, while "home" and "domicile" are often synonymous, the latter word has a more technical meaning. *The Restatement of the Conflict of Laws* defines domicile as a "place where a person has a settled connection for certain legal purposes, either because his home is there *or because it is assigned to him by law*."[75] Elsewhere domicile has been described as "a relationship which the law creates between an individual and a particular locality or country."[76]

The distinction between "residence" and "domicile" is also important. A person's domicile may be in one state or territory and his actual residence in another.[77] In effect, a domicile is the place where a person lives and has his true, permanent home, to which, whenever he is absent, he has an intention of returning.[78] The question of a person's domicile is largely one of intent.[79]

The areas of law in which a person's domicile may be important are many and varied. Domicile of a party or a decedent often determines whether a court has jurisdiction to hear and decide certain kinds of legal questions: *e.g.,* divorce suits,[80] probate matters,[81] and guardianship proceedings.[82] In other types of cases, though the parties' domiciles may not affect the court's basic jurisdiction (*i.e.,* its power or authority to hear a particular case), it may be of importance in determining whether the court should nevertheless entertain the action (the question of venue).[83] The availability of many rights and privileges of citizenship also depend upon a person's domicile. These include the right to vote,[84] to hold and, therefore, to run for public office,[85] to receive welfare assistance,[86] or to qualify for free or limited tuition at state-operated educational institutions.[87] Some obligations of citizenship—*e.g.,* jury duty and the taxability of personal and intangible property—are also determined by the juror's[88] or taxpayer's[89] domicile, respectively.

From the foregoing, it should be evident that the location of a person's domicile may have important practical, as well as legal, consequences. Ideally, free choice of domicile should be possible. For the most part, that has in fact been the situation. Adult women who are unmarried and adult men, regardless of their marital status, have the legal right to establish or change a former domicile freely. This type of domicile—not surprisingly called a "domicile of choice"[90]—can be acquired by those who are authorized to do so by actually residing in a particular locality and, at the same time, intending to remain there.[91]

Where married women are concerned, however, the rule is otherwise. Though exceptions have been carved out in recent years, the general rule persists that a wife's domicile follows that of her husband.[92] This means that by operation of law, when a woman marries, she "loses her domicile and acquires that of her husband, no matter where she resides, or what she believes or intends."[93] In choosing the domicile of his family and wife, the husband must of course act reasonably. He cannot, for example, insist that the only place for his wife to live is in his parents' home.[94] As long as his selection of a domicile is a reasonable one, however, that choice is his to make, and his wife is legally bound to abide by it.

This rule can cause much hardship. If a married woman owns

personal property in State X, it may be taxed at the higher rate of State Y, her husband's domicile, though she is residing in State X with her husband's consent. Similarly, where a married woman is, for any reason, living in a different state from her husband (a not uncommon situation in this day and age), her right to vote or run for public office may be rendered meaningless by the rule that attributes her husband's domicile to her.

Apart from these practical problems, the continued enshrinement into law of a rule that accords to only one of the spouses, the husband, the right to decide a question of such intimate concern to both husband and wife is obviously inconsistent with the spirit and intent of the Married Women's Acts.

In recognition of the difficulties created by the traditional rule, four states (Arkansas, Delaware, Hawaii and New Hampshire) permit married women to acquire an independent domicile for all purposes.[95] A married woman may also acquire a separate domicile in 42 states if she is living apart from her husband for cause.[96] This exception is justified by some courts on the ground that the general rule is founded upon the concept of a unified marriage relationship. That unity having been destroyed by the husband's misconduct amounting to grounds for divorce or separation, the wife is allowed to acquire a domicile of her own.[97] Where husband and wife are living apart by mutual agreement, however, or if the husband consents to the separation, only 18 of the last-mentioned 42 states permit a married woman to acquire a separate domicile.[98]

In all states, married women are permitted to acquire a separate domicile for the purpose of instituting divorce proceedings.[99] Having done so, they may then claim the same separate domicile for other purposes—*e.g.*, to establish their citizenship in a particular state in order to sustain federal court jurisdiction based upon the parties' "diversity of citizenship" though the action is for tort damages only.[100] Finally, in addition to the four states previously mentioned as permitting married women to acquire separate domiciles for all purposes, some states allow married women to establish their own domicile for limited purposes only: 15 states for purposes of voting, 6 for election to public office, 5 for jury service, 7 for taxation, and 5 for probate.[101]

The Committee on Civil and Political Rights of the President's Commission on the Status of Women has noted the unfairness of the traditional married women's domicile rule and its incompatibility with the modern "partnership principle" of marriage.[102] In apparent deference to the complexities of our federal system, however, the Committee, in an ambiguously worded recommendation, seems to suggest that the basic rule be left intact or, at most, that it be the subject of further study.[103] Recommendations for positive reform are limited to the specific problems of "voting, holding public office, jury service, taxation, and probate."[104]

Though the suggested improvements in the designated areas are unobjectionable, the total abandonment of the basic rule itself would also appear to be warranted. That rule, as will be demonstrated hereafter, is impractical, regressive, and unworkable. In the context of modern social and legal facts, it is an inglorious fiction, serving no useful social purpose and causing much unnecessary social harm.

American courts have in recent times assigned various reasons to justify the traditional rule which forces a husband's domicile upon his wife. Some have frankly acknowledged its origins in the theoretical identity of husband and wife at common law.[105] Recognizing, perhaps, that this fiction was supposed to have been rejected by the passage of the married women's acts, these courts have at times urged additional policy reasons of a more logical nature in support of the rule. Thus, in *Estate of Wickes,* the California Supreme Court stated:

> The subjection of the wife to the husband *was not the only reason for the rule.* Parties marrying contract to live together. The husband obligates himself to furnish a proper home for his wife and to maintain her there in a degree of comfort authorized by his circumstances, and they mutually agreed to live there together. It is a matter of great public concern that this should be so. In this association there can be no majority vote, and the law leaves the ultimate decision to the husband.[106]

Similarly, describing the reasons for the common law rule, the Tennessee Supreme Court, in *Younger v. Gianotti,* stated:

> The rule of the common law that the domicile of the wife follows that of the husband was based on (1) the doctrine of marital unity, and (2) that public policy demanded that the

family unity be protected by allowing one family to have only one domicile.[107]

Other courts have completely denied the part played by the common law fiction of the unity of husband and wife in the development of the rule. Instead, they have sought to assign allegedly modern social reasons as its only basis. Thus, in *Carlson v. Carlson*,[108] the Arizona Supreme Court offers as "sound reasons" for the rule the following:

> The law imposes upon the husband the burden and obligation of the support, maintenance and care of the family and almost of necessity he must have the right of choice of the situs of the home. There can be no decision by a majority rule as to where the family home shall be maintained, and a reasonable accompaniment of the imposition of the obligations is the right of selection. The violation of this principle tends to sacrifice the family unity, the entity upon which our civilization is built. *The principle is not based on the common law theory of the merger of the personality of the wife with that of the husband; it is based on the theory that one domicile for the family home is still an essential way of life.*[109]

Whether presented as additional or substituted arguments for the common law fictional unity of the spouses, these "policy reasons" are, in the light of modern day sociological and legal conditions, specious and unrealistic.

At one time in Anglo-American legal history, when divorces were virtually impossible to procure,[110] the married woman's domicile rule was no doubt an effective determinant when questions of the family home's location arose within the family itself. If the spouses could not agree, the husband decided where he and his wife and his children should live. If the wife was unhappy with the decision she could protest. But if he insisted, she went along. Legally, there was nothing she could do to alter the decision.

Today—now that divorces are relatively simple to procure[111]—the husband's unilateral right to choose the family domicile has practical significance only with reference to third parties, such as creditors who seek to sue the wife. And, of course, it affects the wife's rights with regard to the matters discussed earlier. As for resolving the question of the family domicile within the family itself, however, the rule, as a practical matter, can have no meaningful influence at all.

Documentation on this point is, of course, difficult to come by.[112] Nevertheless, one may safely suggest that contemporary decisions concerning the location of the family home are commonly made jointly—by husband and wife together. Sometimes they may even involve the participation of the children in the family. Though an important factor in this decision is undoubtedly the husband's employment situation (or the wife's), other considerations are also relevant. Climate, cultural opportunities, presence of friends or relatives may also influence the family's choice of its domicile.

The selection of a family home generally rests upon family consensus. When consensus cannot be reached and if their individual preferences do not stem from factors the husband and wife consider to be critical, the matter may be resolved by either spouse deferring to the wishes of the other. But where differences of opinion are strongly held, the husband's assertion of his legal right unilaterally to decide the question would have a relatively short-lived effect. If he should so decide, the wife's behavior, and then the husband's, would no doubt soon become such as to constitute sufficient grounds for the other to procure a divorce somewhere in the United States. When courts say, therefore, that the husband has the right to choose the domicile of the family, they are talking about a right that is meaningless in the light of present day realities.

What of the frequently encountered phrase in these cases that a "majority vote" is impossible in this situation? This theme runs through many judicial and statutory rules that discriminate on the basis of sex. It assumes that for marital partners to pull in opposite directions on certain matters would be intolerable. The power to make important decisions is therefore given to only one of the spouses. Yet consistently the one who is given this power is always the husband, never the wife.

Various reasons have been urged in support of this arbitrary allocation of decision-making power. In the *Carlson* case, the court invokes the husband's support obligation as justifying his unilateral right to decide matters of family domicile. Aside from the fact that the almost exclusive obligation of the husband to support the family may have become in modern America an impediment to true legal equality of the sexes,[113] the argument assumes the primacy of economic considerations in the marriage relationship. As suggested earlier, however, other factors may be equally important in deciding where a family should make its home.

The suggestion in the cases that a family should have one home only under all circumstances also overlooks the frequency of family separations caused by a husband's military service. Somehow marriages survive and often thrive under these conditions. This is by no means to suggest that as a general rule husband and wife should live apart from one another. But husbands and wives live together because they want to, and not because the law tells them that they must. Certainly, where spouses decide, amicably and for whatever reasons, that each should maintain a separate domicile, the law should allow them this choice. More than a "majority vote," such a choice by husband and wife would in fact constitute a "unanimous vote." As indicated above, however, only 18 states permit such an arrangement—which means that 32 states do not. So used have lawmakers become to the mechanical statement of the rule that the wife's domicile follows her husband's that they have lost sight of the major reason ("no majority vote is possible"), however erroneous, they themselves have given for the rule in the first place.

Despite judicial efforts to dress up the old common law rule in modern garb, it has become useless as an influence within the family. Its most important practical effects are to deprive wives of certain governmental benefits they would otherwise have and to create technical legal difficulties for third parties. The cases in which the issue is raised typically do not involve the resolution of a dispute between spouses in an ongoing marriage. The rule should be dropped entirely. Its retention serves only to evoke bygone images of the husband as master and the wife as obedient servant. These images need to be replaced by others that are in greater harmony with present notions of human dignity.

MARRIED WOMEN'S CONTRACTS

United States v. Yazell, decided by the United States Supreme Court in 1966,[114] involved a possible conflict between a state law and federal policy in a federal court lawsuit. Only incidentally did the case also bring into focus some vestiges of married women's contractual incapacity within the United States.

Commentators on the *Yazell* decision have so far concerned themselves with the state-federal conflict.[115] For the most part, they have shunned the substantive question of the continued incapacity of married women to contract as freely as married men. The *Yazell* case, however, provides an excellent starting point for examining the basic injustice of the married woman's formerly general contractual incapacity. It also permits assessment of the present extent of state judicial and legislative rules that still deny married women the same degree of contractual freedom accorded to married men.

Trouble for Mr. and Mrs. Yazell, residents of Lampasas, Texas, began on May 12, 1957, when the town was struck by a disastrous flood, seriously damaging a children's clothing shop owned and operated by them. Shortly thereafter, the federal Small Business Administration opened a Disaster Loan Office in Lampasas. The Yazells applied for and were granted a loan of $12,000. In return for the loan, Mr. and Mrs. Yazell, doing business as "Yazell's Little Ages," signed a note and executed a mortgage on their merchandise and store fixtures to secure repayment.

At the time the loan was made, Texas law provided that a married woman could not bind her separate property—Texas being a community property state[116]—unless she had first obtained a court decree removing her disability to contract.[117] Though this provision was subsequently amended by the Texas legislature in 1963,[118] removing the married woman's former contractual incapacity, it was in force at all times relevant to the *Yazell* case.

Some time after the loan had been made the Yazells defaulted on the note, causing the government to foreclose on the mortgage. The amount realized upon foreclosure being less than the Yazells' debt, the government later sought a deficiency judgment against Mr. and Mrs. Yazell in a federal district court. Judgment was obtained against Mr. Yazell and he failed to appeal.

Mrs. Yazell, however, defended the government's suit on the ground that she was a married woman. Though she had personally signed the note, she asserted, no personal judgment and no judgment affecting her separate estate could be rendered against her because her disability to bind her separate estate by contract had not been removed by court decree as required by Texas law. The United States Government countered by insisting that an important federal interest was involved—namely, the collection by the government of money loaned by it. Therefore, argued the government, federal law should be fashioned to override the state coverture law.

Distinguishing other cases in which a strong federal interest had justified the rejection of state law where it would otherwise apply,[119] a majority of the Court affirmed two lower court decisions and held that in the absence of specific congressional action, the implementation of federal interests did not require the overriding of the particular state rule involved in *Yazell*. "Each State," declared the majority in an opinion by Mr. Justice Fortas, "has its complex of family and family-property arrangements. There is presented in this case no reason for breaching them. We have no federal law relating to the protection of the separate property of married women. We should not here invent one and impose it upon the States, despite our personal distaste for coverture provisions such as those involved in this case."[120]

As a result, Mrs. Yazell, who had benefited from the money borrowed from the Small Business Administration and had personally signed the note for the loan, was permitted unilaterally to revoke her promise to repay the money to the extent that her separate property was involved. Married men in Texas could not, of course, insist upon the same treatment—as exemplified by Mr. Yazell's own fate. Sex-based legal inequality is, therefore, clearly involved in such a rule. But the question remains why any woman should object to a legal principle, which, in effect, permits her to contract with others, retain the benefits of the contract, and then invoke the aid of the courts to prevent the promisee from recovering his share of the bargain. We shall return to the question shortly.

Mr. Justice Fortas' "strong personal distaste for coverture provisions" has already been noted.[121] Elsewhere in the opinion, he referred to the "quaint doctrine of coverture,"[122] and at another point characterized the Texas law involved in *Yazell* as dealing with "the protection (whether or not it is up-to-date or even welcome) of married women."[123] At the same time, the issue in *Yazell* did not strike Justice Fortas as a "summons to do battle to vindicate the rights of women."[124] Rather, for him, the fundamental question in the case was whether the federal government could enter into a contract with an individual, knowing that such individual's contractual capacity and liability was limited by state law, and then insist upon disregarding such limitation when attempting to collect.

Mr. Justice Black, joined by Mr. Justices Douglas and White, disagreed. Adopting Judge Prettyman's dissenting opinion in the Circuit Court of Appeals[125] ("A loan from the Federal Government is a federal matter and should be governed by federal law."),[126] Justice Black also emphasized that the Texas law of coverture was based upon the old common law fiction of the unity of husband and wife. This, in turn, rested on what he had supposed was "today a completely discredited notion that a married woman, being a female, is without capacity to make her own contracts and do her business."[127] From its context, it is clear that the word "capacity" as used by Justice Black is intended to refer to intellectual, physical and emotional capacity, rather than to capacity in a legal sense. In any event, he concluded, "It seems at least unique to me that this Court in 1966 should exalt this archaic remnant of a primitive caste system to an honored place among the laws of the United States."[128]

The Texas law of coverture which gave rise to the *Yazell* case has since been repealed.[129] However, though all states have enacted married women's property statutes, in at least eleven states the capacity of married women is still limited to some degree.[130] Michigan, for example, still has a coverture rule which closely resembles the one repealed in Texas. Under it, Michigan wives are granted "the power and capacity . . . to bind and make themselves jointly liable with their husbands."[131] But enforcement of that liability is limited to property owned by husband and wife as tenants by the entirety or otherwise jointly held;[132] the wife's separate property is exempted from liability for debts she jointly assumes with her husband.

Other states that still place some types of restrictions on married women's contractual capacity are Alabama, Arizona, California, Florida, Georgia, Idaho, Indiana, Kentucky, Nevada and North Carolina. Under Kentucky law, for example, though a married woman generally has full contractual capacity, she is, with some exceptions, prohibited from being a "joint maker on a note or a surety on any bond or obligation of another" unless her husband joins with her.[133] No restriction is imposed, however, upon her power to make a note together with her husband or from becoming a surety on his bond or obligation.[134] In contrast with the Kentucky rule that permits a married woman to be a surety for her husband's debt but not for the debts of others, Georgia law provides that a married woman "may not bind her separate estate by *any* contract of suretyship or by an assumption of the debts of her husband."[135] Any sale of a wife's separate estate, made to a creditor of her husband in extinguishment of his debts, is declared to be "absolutely void."[136] Similarly, an Alabama statute provides that "The husband and wife may contract with each other, but all contracts into which they enter are subject to the rules of law as to contracts by and between persons standing in confidential relations."[137] This has been interpreted as preserving the wife's original disability as to contracts of suretyship.[138]

Some states continue to limit the wife's contractual capacity with regard to contracts to convey, encumber, or lease her separate real property. Generally, these states require that a deed, encumbrance or lease of the wife's real property must be executed by the husband as well as the wife in order to be valid.[139] As for the husband's conveyance, etc. of his own real property, the wife's joinder is not a condition of validity. These laws should be distinguished from those found in other states which have either preserved the common law estates of dower and curtesy or have substituted some other nonbarrable interests in their place.[140] In those states, a conveyance by either spouse of his or her separate property does not defeat inheritance rights of the other unless there is joinder. Generally, such laws apply to husbands and wives impartially and are substantially different from statutes that require the husband to join in the wife's conveyance, mortgage or lease of her own property as a condition of validity.

There are still other vestiges of the married woman's common law disabilities in the laws of other states. In Utah, for example, there is a limitation upon the married woman's right to serve in a position of trust.[141] Maryland limits her right to sue or be sued in her own name.[142] Several states still severely restrict the married woman's right to engage in a separate business. Five states (California,[143] Florida,[144] Nevada,[145] Pennsylvania,[146] and Texas[147]) require court approval before a wife may engage in an independent business. These laws, called "free dealer" or "sole trader" statutes, though presumably aimed once more at "protecting" married women, are—to say the least—demeaning. The Florida "free dealer" law, for example, requires the married woman's petition to set forth her name and age "and her character, habits, education and mental capacity for business, and briefly set out the reasons why such disabilities [to engage in her own business] should be removed."[148] She must either procure her husband's consent or serve him with a copy of the petition.[149] Only if the judge is "satisfied that the removal of the disabilities of such married woman will be for her permanent interest or benefit [will he] make a decree removing her disabilities of marriage and authorizing such married woman to assume the management and control of all her own estate and property and to become a free dealer . . ."[150]

Returning now to the question posed earlier, we ask once more why married women should object to laws which insulate them from personal liability. Part of the answer may be found in a reading of the above-cited Florida "free dealer" statute, which is similar in important respects to the laws of some other states. Under its provisions, a married woman, no matter how extensively she has been educated or how great her intellect, is put to the burden of establishing her right to engage in a separate business. No comparable burden is imposed upon married men, whether, in individual cases, they are totally uneducated or, indeed, congenital idiots.

Under such laws and others insulating married women from liability, "protection" or a "preference" is granted only on the assumption that women are virtually biologically incapable of exercising the same wisdom and intelligence as men in the business and commercial spheres. Like the illusory "preference" shown toward women in exempting them from jury service, such benefits are purchased at the high price of accepting the status of second-class citizens or second-class members of the human race.

Similarly, those states that still limit the wife's capacity to serve as a guarantor of her husband's or a third party's debts are out of touch with the times in several important respects. For one thing, they necessarily assume that all women are ill-equipped to make an intelligent decision in this area. No corresponding assumption is made of course with respect to the husband's judgment in these matters; no state, as far as can be determined, has ever imposed any restrictions upon a married man's capacity to guarantee the debts of his wife or of strangers.[151]

A further anachronism can also be seen in those rules that preserve the common law restrictions upon the wife's ability to guarantee her husband's debts. In holding fast to such a rule some states may merely be recognizing the practical effects of the legal system's designation of the husband as the head and master of the family—a position he appears to enjoy in all of the United States. Given that law-buttressed role for the husband, a wife may find it difficult, if not impossible, to resist a husband's request, entreaty or command that she expose her separate funds to a potential liability by acting as his surety or guarantor. But experience in the overwhelming majority of states that have removed the wife's disability to act as her husband's or a third party's surety or guarantor does not reveal the rise of any special problems or abuse. A wife's incapacity in this realm, moreover, is highly inconsistent with the entire scheme of legal regulation of marriage—a scheme which in almost every detail is aimed at fostering a mutual respect between husband and wife, at least to the extent that legal regulation is capable of achieving such ends. To impose an arm's-length type of relationship between the spouses, even when limited to the narrow question of the wife's capacity to guarantee her husband's debts, flies in the face of the American legal system's basic presuppositions with respect to the nature of the marital relationship. This legal ideal is demonstrably ever-present notwithstanding the social reality that many husbands do exert an undue influence upon their wives with respect to these questions—a fact that may be dealt with by many devices short of restricting the wife's contractual capacity.

When it is compared with most of the other legal areas explored in this essay, the persistence of some aspects of the married woman's common-law contractual disabilities in some of the states does not represent an overriding problem in American jurisprudence. By and large, the legal emancipation of American women has gone further in the sphere of contract rights and obligations than in most others. Nevertheless, it should be clear from the above brief description of some vestiges of married women's contractual incapacity in the United States that the extent to which the emancipatory process had progressed was probably overstated when Professor Currie, writing in 1958, suggested that

> The practical importance of the specific problem [married women's contracts in the Conflict of Laws] is no doubt approaching the vanishing point as a result of the progressive removal of restrictions on the capacity of married women to contract.[152]

PROPERTY RIGHTS OF MARRIED WOMEN IN THE COMMON LAW STATES

As one would surmise from their titles, the Married Women's Property Acts were designed to eliminate the basic injustices of the common law rules governing the property rights of married women. Though the precise words and effects of these statutes varied from state to state, the following Minnesota statute may be regarded as a typical example of many that were adopted throughout the United States in the second half of the nineteenth century:

> All property, real, personal and mixed, and all choses in action, owned by any woman at the time of her marriage, shall continue to be her separate property, notwithstanding such marriage; and any married woman, during coverture, may receive, acquire, and enjoy property of every description, and the rents, issues and profits thereof, and all avails of her contracts and industry, free from the control of her husband, and from any liability on account of his debts, as fully as if she were unmarried.[153]

Despite these reforms, isolated pockets of legal discrimination in the area of married women's property rights can still be found in some of the 42 common law marital property states.[154] In five states, for example, wives cannot make a valid conveyance of real property unless they are joined by their husbands.[155] Occasionally, a decision can also be found in which a court imposes a property disability upon a wife, despite the enactment of a married women's property law within that state. Thus, in the Georgia case of *Childs v. Charles*,[156] it was held that though a wife might own the property that she and her husband occupied as their home, the husband's position as head of the family authorized him to contract to board another in that home and to make contracts in his own right for working the property. For the most part, however, it is fair to say that the legal emancipation of married women has progressed further in the sphere of property rights than in most other areas of legal regulation.

Other features of present-day regulation of married women's property rights in the common law states are discussed in the preceding section ("Married Women's Contracts")[157] and in the following section ("Property Rights of Married Women in the Community Property States").[158] In the latter section, various features of the community property system and the common law marital property system are compared and evaluated—and the conclusion presented that the property rights of married women under both systems are not fundamentally dissimilar.[159]

Apart from the reasons offered in that section to support that conclusion, another may be added here. Many laymen believe that the rights of married women in the community property states are superior to those in the common law marital property states because, in the former, the earnings of the husband are classified as the spouses' community property, whereas in the common law states, the husband's earnings are his separate property. Though this is a correct statement of the law, there are at least three reasons why it does not support the conclusion that married women are therefore better off in the community states. They are: 1) Though his earnings are community property, the husband has the exclusive right to manage and control that property in the community property states;[160] 2) Where his wife is employed outside the home, her earnings are also community property;[161] and 3) By contrast, in the common law property states, though a wife does not have a present interest in the husband's earnings, her earnings are her separate property.[162]

In its recommendation concerning the property rights of married women under the two systems, the Committee on Civil and Political Rights of the President's Commission on the Status of Women has concluded:

> that during marriage each spouse should have a legally defined and substantial right in the earnings of the other spouse and in the real and personal property acquired as a result of such earnings, as well as in the management of such earnings and property. . . .[163]

The effectuation of such a policy—which is eminently sound in the light of modern views of the marital relationship—would require the legislatures of both systems to adopt laws giving husbands and wives joint rights in the earnings of the other and in their management and control. Despite the general progress of the law in the area of married women's property rights, the married woman's lack of any legal interest in her husband's earnings in the common law states or in their management and control in the community property states represents a serious shortcoming which, one would hope, will be remedied by prompt legislative action in all of the affected jurisdictions.

PROPERTY RIGHTS OF MARRIED WOMEN IN THE COMMUNITY PROPERTY STATES

Unlike the situation that prevailed under the common law, the legal system that developed over a large part of continental Europe did not dictate the submersion of the wife's legal personality into that of her husband at the time of marriage.[164] No fiction of the "unity of husband and wife" is found in continental law or in its progeny in other parts of the world.[165] Moreover, on the European continent, a special approach to regulating the husband's and wife's ownership and control over marital property was developed. In modern times, such organization of marital property rights has come to be called the "community property system."

In the United States, there are now eight states—Arizona, California, Idaho, Louisiana, Nevada, New Mexico, Texas and Washington—in which, with some variations, a type of community property system prevails. Under these systems, and in contrast to the philosophical premises of the common law marital property regimes, the marriage relationship is regarded as a type of partnership. Though not possessed of the rights and liabilities of ordinary business partners, each spouse is regarded as contributing his or her efforts (either within the home or outside, by a combination of both) to the economic and financial well-being of the marital enterprise.[166] As a result, these systems emphasize the respective rights of the spouses to share equally in the property acquired by their joint efforts although this principle, as will be demonstrated hereafter, is honored as often in the breach as in the observance.

Community property rules are generally directed at crucial

periods of the marriage relationship: *i.e.*, its beginning, its continuous life, and its dissoluton by death or divorce. They furnish guidelines for distinguishing community property from the individual spouse's separate property, define the respective rights of husband and wife to manage and control the community property, and determine the method of its distribution upon the community's dissolution. Generally, in the American community property states, the separate property of the husband and wife includes all property each owned before marriage, property acquired after marriage by gift, bequest, devise, or descent, and, in California, the rents, issues and profits of separate property.[167] All other property acquired after marriage by either husband or wife (with some exceptions) is community property.[168]

Aside from the present eight community property states, several others (Oregon, Oklahoma, Michigan, Pennsylvania, Nebraska and the territory of Hawaii) temporarily adopted community property systems during the 1930's and 1940's. Solicitude for the property rights of married women, however, was not the primary stimulus for these enactments. Rather, they were passed to gain for their own residents the income-splitting advantages that married residents of community property states had previously been allowed under the federal income tax laws.[169]

Fearful lest the new system unduly upset existing marital property relationships, the Oklahoma and Oregon legislatures at first allowed married couples to choose whether to be governed by a community property system.[170] In effect, this permitted husbands to decide whether the tax advantages to be derived from converting to a community property status outweighed the benefits they enjoyed under the existing system. Ironically, this optional feature of the legislation proved its undoing. The United States Supreme Court in 1932 denied income-splitting rights to Oklahoma residents on the ground that the state's community property system was "not a system, dictated by State policy, as an incident of matrimony," but was based upon a contract between the spouses.[171]

In any case, when the Revenue Act of 1948 permitted married couples to file joint federal income tax returns, regardless of the marital property regimes of the states in which they lived,[172] these hastily enacted community property statutes were soon repealed.[173]

Most of the eight states that now have community property systems derived their basic structures from the law of Mexico, following the Mexican-American War which ended in 1848. Transplanted to Mexico by its Spanish colonizers who, in turn, had acquired its basic format from the Visigothic occupiers of 5th century Spain,[174] a community property system prevailed over the Mexican territory ceded to the United States at the end of the war. Eventually, this territory was carved into the states of New Mexico, Arizona, Nevada and California—Texas having established its independence in 1836 and having retained the community property system in 1840. In 1867 and 1869, the territorial legislatures of Idaho and Washington, respectively, adopted community property statutes.[175] These were based upon the California model.[176] Spanish law thus influenced the community property systems of those seven states. Louisiana, the remaining original community property state, received its system from the laws of Spain and France.[177]

California, which we have chosen as a typical community property state for purposes of describing the effects of the system upon the status of married women,[178] also acquired the framework of its community property system from Mexico under the 1848 Treaty of Guadalupe Hidalgo, following the Mexican-American War. Under Article VIII of that treaty, property of Mexican residents and non-residents in the territory ceded to the United States was to be "inviolably respected."[179] To avoid the confusion that would result from the simultaneous existence of two marital property systems, the community property system was soon adopted for all married persons in California, Mexicans or not.[180]

From that time on, the system has prevailed in California, living, as in the other community property states (except Louisiana), as an institutional civil law stranger in a common law environment.[181] Partly as a result of this fact and also because of changing social concepts concerning the family roles of husband and wife the California community property system has received more than its due share of legislative surgery since its original adoption.

To many laymen, the community property system represents the crowning point of women's legal emancipation. In popular periodicals and newspapers, it is frequently read that, in contrast to the non–community property states, a wife divorced in California "gets everything," the husband "gets nothing," and that while the marriage is ongoing, the rule is "share-and-share-alike."

As in other areas of the law, the reality is markedly different from popular misconceptions about the situation. True, piecemeal legislative correctives have over the years tended toward establishing an equitable balance between the respective interests of husband and wife in California community property. The result has been a patchwork of laws reminiscent of the federal Internal Revenue Code. Despite these legislative efforts, however, the community property rights of married women under California law are still substantially inferior to those of their husbands.

A review of historical developments in this area should confirm this last statement. Before Section 172 of the California Civil Code was amended in 1891 to forbid husbands from making a gift of community property without the wife's consent in writing, California law vested in the husband all the elements of absolute ownership of the community property to the exclusion of the wife.[182] Despite the equality-of-sharing philosophy of community property law, the California wife's interest in the community property was characterized as a "mere expectancy."[183] This meant that in the event of a divorce or of the husband's death before the wife's, she was entitled to receive a designated share of the community property, provided, of course, that the community property had not been previously dissipated by the husband. If the wife died before her husband, however, without having in the meantime obtained a decree of separate maintenance or divorce, all the community property belonged to the husband. The wife had no right to will any portion of it to others.

The husband was, in addition, vested with the absolute power of management and control of the community property during the marriage. This power extended to all of the community property, regardless of its source. It included the wife's earnings and other real and personal property that had been acquired with, or whose value had been increased by, those earnings.[184] Translated into everyday terms, the husband's power of management and control permitted him to make a gift of the community property or to convey community real property without the wife's consent or joinder. It meant also that the husband could invest the community property in wise or unwise business ventures without regard to his wife's wishes.[185] He was limited only by the requirement that he deal with the property in good faith and that he not have an intention to defraud his wife.

Today, the husband in California is still vested with the basic right to manage and control the community property.[186] By statute, he is also declared to be "the head of the family."[187] As a result, he may choose any reasonable place or mode of living, and the wife must comply with his choice.[188]

Beginning in 1891, The California legislature has steadily increased the wife's interest in the community property, thereby limiting, but by no means ending, the husband's basic statutory right of management and control. In 1891, a restriction of the husband's power to manage and control was effected by prohibiting gifts of community property without the wife's consent in writing.[189] In 1901, the wife's written consent was also required for the sale, conveyance, or encumbrance of the household furnishings or of the wife's or minor children's clothing.[190] In 1917, the legislature required the wife to join with the husband in any instrument by which the community real property, or any interest in it, was leased for more than a year or was sold, conveyed, or encumbered.[191] And in 1927, the legislature declared both spouses' interest in the community property to be "present, existing and equal, although still under the management and control of the husband," as elsewhere provided in the Civil Code.[192]

In addition to limiting the husband's power of management and control, California has over the years increased the wife's. Before 1923, if the husband predeceased the wife, she would automatically be entitled to half of the community property. The husband could dispose of the other half by will. When the wife died first, however, she had no right of testamentary disposition over any part of the community property. The entire community property passed to the husband. In 1923 the wife was given for the first time the power of testamentary disposition of one-half of the community property if she died before her husband.[193] Only as recently as 1951 was the wife permitted to manage and control community property earned by her.[194] Until then, even her personal earnings were subject to the absolute management and control of her husband.[195]

Despite California's legislative attempts to improve the wife's position with regard to the community property, that position is still far from ideal.[196] For one thing, because of a line of decisions only now being questioned by the California courts,[197] the rule had been established that legislative enactments changing the spouses' respective interests in community property could be applied prospectively only. This meant that such enactments could not affect property acquired prior to the legislative change. Nor could those legislative changes apply to property acquired after their enactment, if the ultimate source of that property was "traceable" to pre-change property.[198]

As a result of this rule the respective interests of husbands and wives in much California community property, as well as their respective rights to manage and control it, are still subject to earlier modes of regulation. Since the husband's former position was virtually supreme and the wife's decidedly second-class, the present disparities supported by the rule are incongruous indeed.

Further, the continued legal position of the husband as head of the household[199] and the rule vesting in him the fundamental powers of management and control suggest that much ground needs to be covered before California wives will have achieved equal legal status with their husbands with respect to their community property.

In some areas the discriminatory treatment of married women continues in a direct sense, or has only recently been ended. Although married women in California may generally sue and be sued,[200] a husband must bring all actions that concern the community property, unless express statutory exceptions permit the wife to bring such action.[201] Nor need a married woman be named a party defendant in any suit involving the community property.[202]

In the California inheritance tax laws sex discrimination has only recently stopped. Before 1961, if a wife died, the community property passing to her husband was not subject to California inheritance taxation. If, however, the husband was the first to die, one-half of the community property (*i.e.*, the portion passing to the wife) was subject to such tax.

Based in part upon the husband's superior statutory rights to manage and control the community property, this rule also proceeded upon the assumption that the community property had been acquired by the husband.[203] While this assumption may have been valid in the past, it had become increasingly less so in times that had seen more and more married women gainfully employed outside the home. The assumption also ignored some fundamental principles of the community property system: that the wife's work at home had a monetary value that could equal the income earned by the husband away from home, and that marriage was in certain important respects a type of partnership.

Legislative changes in 1961 still left important differences between the inheritance tax treatment the wife and husband received upon the death of the other. From 1961 to 1965, community property that passed to the wife as a surviving spouse was subject to inheritance taxation if she received a power of appointment in connection with that property. When such property passed to the husband, however, it was not subject to the inheritance tax laws of the state. Only in 1965 did such obviously discriminatory treatment come to an end.[204] Even today, when the husband dies with or without a will, all the community property is subject to administration and payment of debts. But if the wife dies, not even her share of the community property that passes to the husband need be administered if she leaves no will.[205]

What, then, of the popular belief that women have achieved ideal legal status under community property regimes? The myth is no doubt based in large part upon the power of divorce courts to divide the community property. In actions for divorce or separate maintenance, if the decree is rendered on the ground of adultery, incurable insanity or extreme cruelty, California law requires the community property to be assigned to the husband and wife "in such proportions as the court, from all the facts of the case, and the condition of the parties may deem just."[206] This has been interpreted as requiring the court to award more than one-half of the community property to the prevailing spouse in divorce actions based upon the designated grounds.[207] In all other cases of divorce, community property must be equally divided between husband and wife.[208]

If the patterns of property distributions upon divorce in the common law and community property states are compared, the following picture emerges. In common law states, where property acquired by the spouses during the marriage stands in the name of the husband alone, courts either cannot dispose of it in the divorce action or, if they have the power to do so, may not be as generous as California courts are required to be under the statutes discussed above.[209] In those states, however, the husband's retention upon divorce of property that was acquired during the marriage will often lead a court to award to a wife a larger sum for support than she would otherwise have received.[210] In many states, moreover, married couples take title to property as joint tenants or as tenants in common. In some ways, their respective rights in such property exceed those they would have in community property (*e.g.,* the right to bring an action for partition at any time).[211] On this score at least, the supposed advantage of wives in community property states over those in common law jurisdictions is more illusory than real.

As for rights of succession to marital property, community property states again do not afford wives a much better situation than exists in non-community property states. California, for example, like many common law jurisdictions, has abolished the common law estates of dower and curtesy.[212] But the right of a California spouse to succeed to a one-half interest in the community property upon the death of the other,[213] or to the entire community property in the event of the other's intestacy,[214] is in effect the community property substitute for those common law estates.

Outside the community property states, however, the institution of the "spouse's nonbarrable share" also furnishes a large measure of protection to the wife upon the death of her husband. That institution generally requires that upon the death of one spouse, the survivor is entitled to receive a designated share of the decedent's property—usually a third or a half. The concept of the "non-barrable" or "forced" share is remarkably widespread among the common law marital property states. Indeed, it has been noted that of the non-community property states, "only two leave the testator unfettered . . . while thirty-nine . . . permit the surviving spouse to claim a share in the estate of the deceased spouse."[215]

Professor Marsh, basing his conclusion upon a systematic comparison between succession rights of wives in the community property and common law marital property states, has offered the "qualified generalization" that "the wife's interest in the so-called statutory 'separate' property of the husband in a majority of the common law states is afforded a protection nearly equal to that given to her interest in the community property jurisdictions."[216]

In spite of the fact that the protections afforded wives' survivorship interests in marital property under the community property and common law systems are not fundamentally dissimilar, the community property regime still appears superior in important respects—most important being its potential effects upon the total content of the daily relationships (of a property and non-property character alike) between husbands and wives.

As Professor Sayre has suggested, the "notion of community property has many elements of equality for husband and wife and other factors that give dignity and separate protection to the wife far beyond the legal notions of dower and right to support that the common law conceded to married women."[217]

The same can no doubt be said when comparing the community property concept to the principle of the spouse's nonbarrable share which, as we have seen, has generally replaced the common law estates of dower and curtesy. Though often abused in its application, the community property regime and the partnership principle of marriage upon which it is based are in greater accord with modern and enlightened views of the husband-wife relationship.

Married Women and the Law of Support

The details of the legal rules governing the financial support obligations and rights of husband and wife are as complex as those in any other field of law.[218] Their basic principles, on the other hand, are relatively simple. Except for some states that impose a duty upon the wife to support the husband "under certain circumstances,"[219] the universal rule is that the primary obligation to provide financial support to the family rests upon the husband.[220]

This fundamental rule finds expression in a variety of situations. First, it has meaning—although precisely what that meaning is may often be difficult to determine[221]—with regard to the relations between husband and wife in an ongoing marriage. Secondly, the rule is important to creditors, *i.e.,* those who have supplied goods or money on credit to the husband, the wife, or to the family as a single entity. And thirdly, the rule plays a decisive role in fixing the nature, extent, and allocation of financial obligations when marriages are disrupted by judicial separation or dissolved by divorce.

Failure to distinguish these various functions served by rules about support may account in part for what commentators have generally agreed are their anachronistic character. In the light of fundamental changes in the husband-wife relationship worked by the Married Women's Acts and other emancipatory legislation, the legal rules about support often appear to have been left behind by social developments.[222]

The effects of the basic rule upon the marital relationship itself are complex. In common law marital property jurisdictions, the husband's legal obligation to support the family is not an unmixed blessing for the wife. That obligation has been cited, for example, as justifying his right to choose the family home.[223] It has no doubt also played an important part in solidifying his legal role as head and master of the family. For in according the husband this position within the family, the law often seems to be applying on a grand scale the modest principle that "he who pays the piper calls the tune." However, even in the community property states, in which a wife's services in the home are theoretically viewed as being equal to or exceeding in monetary value the husband's earnings outside of the home, husbands have generally been given the rights to manage and control the community property, along with other superior rights and interests in it.[224]

Not unlike the rules that accord the husband the right to choose the family home, those requiring him to support his wife may have only limited practical significance in an ongoing marriage. True, a husband's willful failure to satisfy that obligation may in almost all jurisdictions constitute a crime.[225] But though the wife's institution of criminal proceedings can lead, indirectly, to her receiving money from the husband (as where he is placed on probation on condition that he make certain payments to her),[226] such a course of action, like the husband's insistence upon his right to locate the family home, would in most instances soon lead to a complete dissolution of the marriage by divorce.[227] Similarly, if a wife should rely upon her husband's failure to support her as a reason for leaving him or divorcing him[228]—which she may do almost everywhere —this too would, by definition, be something altogether different from the fulfillment of the husband's support obligation while the spouses are living together. Indeed, as Professor Paulsen has demonstrated,

[A] wife living with her husband has almost no remedy to *enforce* her right to support except her personal persuasiveness.
. . . "[A]lmost" because both self help and pledging the husband's credit for necessaries are, theoretically, means of enforcing a wife's rights against a spouse with whom she lives.[229]

The precise nature of the husband's legal duty to support his wife is, therefore, rarely ever articulated while the marriage is in progress and the spouses are living together. In fact, its exact details are normally spelled out by the law only in cases of marital breakdown[230]—when the marriage has been disrupted or dissolved by a judicial separation, a decree of annulment, an interlocutory or final decree of divorce, or a preliminary proceeding relative thereto. Not until one of these events has occurred does a court usually decide how much support a husband (or more accurately, in most cases, a former husband) is required to contribute for the maintenance of his spouse (or former spouse), and issue an effective order assuring a wife that the power of the state will be applied on her behalf in collecting the payments ordered.

One explanation for the lack of definition or enforceability of the husband's support liability while the spouses are living together has been proffered by Blanche Crozier.[231] In her view, the "peculiar" rule that the husband has the legal duty to support the wife was founded upon the concept that the wife was, in many important respects, the husband's property. Though the sweeping nature of this generalization renders it of doubtful validity, it is clear that at common law, the wife's labor, at least, was owned by the husband.[232] For Blanche Crozier, however, the wife's status as the husband's property accounted for her inability to get a court to enforce the husband's support obligation while they were living together.[233] "This is precisely the situation in which property finds itself," she wrote, "it may be overworked and underfed, or it may be petted and fed with cream, *and that is a matter for the owner to decide.*"[234]

A more satisfactory explanation of this principle may lie in the fact that the law, in applying it, appears to be giving at least tacit recognition to some obvious facts of life: 1) that marriage is based upon mutual affection; 2) that husband and wife abide by "legal" obligations toward each other not because the law tells them that they must but because they wish to do so; and 3) that if those obligations require enforcement by the courts, the marriage in all likelihood consists of not much more than an empty shell. These, in fact, may be implicit in Professor Paulsen's analysis of the rules about support, when he suggests that those rules "often give a kind of reality to cherished myth."[235]

Still another explanation for the rules about support can be found in the field of cultural anthropology. George Murdock, the American anthropologist, has described the functions and relations of the "nuclear family" (presumably without regard to time or place) in the following terms:

> By virtue of their primary sex differences, a man and a woman make an exceptionally efficient cooperating unit. Man, with his superior physical strength, can better undertake the more strenuous tasks, such as lumbering, mining, quarrying, land clearance, and housebuilding. Not handicapped, as is woman, by the physiological burdens of pregnancy and nursing, he can range farther afield to hunt, to fish, to herd, and to trade. Woman is at no disadvantage, however, in lighter tasks which can be performed in or near the home, e.g. the gathering of vegetable products, the fetching of water, the preparation of food, and the manufacture of clothing and utensils. *All known human societies have developed specialization and cooperation between the sexes roughly along this biologically determined line of cleavage.* It is unnecessary to invoke innate psychological differences to account for the division of labor by sex; the indisputable differences in reproductive functions suffice to lay out the broad lines of cleavage.[236]

Thus, if Murdock's view were adopted the biological differences between the sexes, and especially the incapacitating effects of pregnancy upon women, would account in large part for the universal division of labor between the sexes in all societies.

There is no doubt that ideas of a natural division of labor between husband and wife have played a significant part in shaping our legal rules about the rights and duties of support within the family. Still, it is important to distinguish those factors that are strictly biological and that can scarcely be altered in the foreseeable future from others that are primarily of a cultural or sociological character. That it is the wife rather than the husband, for example, who actually gives birth to the child is, for the moment, a controlling circumstance militating in favor of social and legal policies imposing the exclusive or primary support obligation upon a husband rather than a wife. But the fact that homemaking has in the past been such a time-consuming occupation has no doubt also contributed to the development of those policies. In an era of technological revolution, however, the time may not be far off—and in some families may have already arrived—when homemaking functions (including child care) can be dispatched with a minimum of effort and in a very short time. The prospect of new labor-saving inventions, along with the greater employability of women resulting from changed social patterns and the availability of law-enforced penalties for those who would discriminate against women in hiring,[237] may require American lawmakers to begin devising new modes of regulating support rights and duties within the family.

That the time has not yet arrived for such a restructuring of family support rights and duties may explain the qualified position on this question assumed by the Committee on Civil and Political Rights of the President's Commission on the Status of Women. Though a doctrinaire feminism or a fascination with symmetry might lead some persons to insist that the principle of true equality of the sexes requires that, at the very least, both husband and wife should now share equally in the obligations of family support, the Committee has refused to take such a stand.[238] Instead, it has limited its action on the problems of family support to the following recommendation:

> The husband should continue to have the primary responsibility for the support of his wife and minor children, but in line with the partnership view of marriage, the wife should be given some legal responsibility for sharing in the support of herself and the children to the extent she has sufficient means to do so.[239]

While this recommended rule would, in some instances, affect the spouses in an ongoing marriage (as where the wife was possessed of a substantial estate at the time she was married), it is clear that in the vast majority of cases, the rule would be much more important to third parties, such as creditors of the family, than to the spouses themselves. Significantly, the recommendation does not require the wife to acquire "sufficient means" in order to be able to share in the support of herself and the children. It is by no means suggested, for example, that she must seek gainful employment—which, after all, is the most common way for a married woman to acquire separate funds. Only where the wife has already done this is she given some responsibility for family support.

But this rule would be generally superfluous—at least to the extent that only the spouses themselves are concerned. It is the rare marriage in which a wife uses her separate earnings for purposes entirely unrelated to family needs. If adopted, therefore, the rule's major effect would be to create an additional fund to which family creditors could look for satisfaction of outstanding obligations.

That creditors may need such assistance is not unlikely. Though in a few states, family expense statutes render a wife liable for certain family items furnished on credit,[240] in most states it is the husband alone who is liable.

In the areas of divorce and alimony, the Committee's recommendation would again appear to have a limited effect upon present law. Though a wife's claim to alimony may be denied if the divorce is decreed because of her "fault," it is still the general rule that in the absence of fault on her part or upon a showing of lesser fault than her husband's, she may be awarded alimony. That award is often based on other factors than those entitling a wife to be supported during the marriage. Alimony may represent a continuation of that basic support obligation, compensation for the loss of reasonably anticipated economic benefits from the marriage, an effort to prevent the wife from becoming a public charge, or— as is demonstrated by the practice of courts' granting a higher alimony award when the husband's fault has been especially reprehensible—as a means of punishing him for his marital misconduct.

In any event, to the extent that alimony awards are based on the same considerations as support obligations during marriage, the Committee's recommendation, conditioning a wife's responsibility for sharing in the family support on her having "sufficient means to do so" while not insisting that she acquire those means, would leave present law relatively unchanged.

Support obligations within the family cannot be considered in complete isolation from other legal and social phenomena. They are, for example, inextricably bound up with the matter of general employment opportunities for a married woman. These, in turn, may depend upon her age, the length of her marriage, and the number of years she has been absent from the labor market. The allocation of support obligations within the family is also profoundly influenced by the level of technological development within any country—since it may directly affect the time required to perform, and thus the monetary value of, household tasks. Still other factors that are relevant in establishing present support rights and duties between husband and wife are the biological fact that women, and not men, bear children, and the sociological presumption that young children, and therefore society as a whole, are better served if those children are cared for at home by their mothers rather than their fathers. This presumption, as we have seen,[241] is expressed in the rule that gives a divorced mother rather than a father superior rights to the custody of a child of tender years.

Except for the childbearing principle (which may not itself be immutable), all of these other factors are now in the process of rapidly accelerating change. Though the time may not be ripe for fundamental alterations in the family support laws, lawmakers should begin to pay closer attention to developments that affect this issue, with the aim of taking measures that reach beyond the restrained recommendations of the President's Commission at the earliest opportunity. True legal equality of the sexes cannot be achieved until support rights and duties between husband and wife are drastically altered. But before that is done, and in order to avoid a state of affairs in which more problems are created than solved, it is probably best to postpone fundamental changes in the rules about support until meaningful changes have occurred in most of the other areas of legal regulation considered in these pages.

MARRIED WOMEN AND THE LAW OF TORTS

Married Women and the Doctrine of Inter-Spousal Immunity

Ordinarily, in Anglo-American law, if one person causes physical injury to another, as a result of the first person's negligence or willful misconduct, the injured person is permitted to obtain legal redress from the person who caused the injury. At one time under the common law, though a married woman was theoretically liable for the injuries she inflicted in this manner, that liability was of limited significance since the law attributed her misconduct to her husband.[242]

Today, the wife's immunity from suit for tort damages and the corresponding imputed liability of the husband has almost everywhere been abrogated by statute or judicial decision.[243] The underlying philosophical premises upon which that rule was founded, however, are far from dead. They continue to be expressed with varying degrees of vigor in another rule that also originally grew out of the fiction of the unity of husband and wife. With some exceptions, that rule states that neither the husband nor the wife may bring an action for civil damages against the other for willful or negligent personal injuries caused by that other.[244]

The origins of this doctrine are directly traceable to the early common law fiction of the unity of husband and wife. Since a husband and his wife were regarded in law as one person, a suit between them would in effect have been a suit by one individual against himself—an anomaly indeed. This reason was sufficient to prevent husbands from suing their wives for negligent or willful injuries inflicted upon the former by the latter. As for wives suing husbands, in addition to being prevented from doing so by the doctrine of the unity of the spouses, they were further deterred by their common law procedural disabilities. These prohibited married women from suing anyone or being sued by anyone unless they were joined by their husbands.

Superficially, the prohibition against suits between the spouses or, as it has often been called, the doctrine of "inter-spousal immunity," appears to apply equally to husband and wife. Under that rule, wives may not sue husbands nor may husbands sue wives.

In many respects, however, the rule has had an uneven impact upon the spouses. With regard to willful torts such as assault, battery, and false imprisonment the respective social roles of husband and wife have made the husband's infliction of intentional harm upon the wife a far more likely occurrence than the reverse possibility. A greater number of wives were in practice, therefore, deprived of redress for injuries they had incurred at their husbands' hands than were husbands hurt by the willful injury-producing conduct of their wives.

But as we have seen, the common law provided that the wife's choses in action, when reduced to possession, automatically became the property of the husband.[245] To permit the wife to sue her husband for the wrongful infliction of physical harm would in the long run have resulted in a circularity of damage recovery; the damages recovered by the wife from the husband would ultimately wind up in the husband's own pocket again. Therefore, in addition to the doctrinal justification for the rule, which was based upon the fictional unity of husband and wife, the practical inutility of permitting wives to sue husbands for damage may also have contributed to the common law's denial of the right to bring such suits. As for a husband suing his wife, here too, in addition to the fictional unity of the spouses, the husband's acquisition of so much of the wife's property upon marriage may also have played a part in the law's preventing him from bringing such suits.

With the rejection of the doctrine of the spouses' legal identity, as expressed in the passage of the Married Women's Property Acts, the inter-spousal tort immunity rules were also greatly modified. The first major change was the development of a new rationale for the rule. Since husband and wife were no longer one person in the eyes of the law, the new reason for denying them the right to sue one another for personal injuries was allegedly to prevent damage to domestic tranquillity.[246] In enunciating this principle, however, actions based upon intentional and negligent torts were frequently undistinguished.

In modern times, the relaxation of the inter-spousal immunity rule has been uneven. In some states spouses may now sue one another for willful infliction of injury.[247] Where suit is based upon such intentional infliction of physical injury by one spouse upon the other, courts in these states no longer mouth the ridiculous platitude that to permit suits between husband and wife would disturb domestic harmony, which is a marked improvement over previous policy. Then, a husband could beat his wife mercilessly, causing her permanent injury, disfigurement and untold pain and suffering, but the law in its rectitude denied her the right to sue her husband because such a suit, it claimed, could destroy the peace of the home.[248] True, similar suits by husbands against wives were also prohibited. Yet statistical data hardly seems necessary to support the proposition that the incidence of husbands intentionally injuring wives far exceeded the reverse situation.

Those states which now permit suits by and between spouses for the intentional infliction of injury upon the other have, of course, discarded the doctrine of the unity of husband and wife. They have also recognized that, though in some instances suits between spouses may in fact adversely affect domestic tranquillity, where the marriage has reached a stage in which the spouses inflict intentional physical injury upon one another, not much domestic tranquillity remains to be preserved. At the same time, by continuing to deny husband and wife the right to sue one another for negligently inflicted injuries, these states presumably believe that under such circumstances, a healthy marriage relationship still subsists, and that to permit the acrimony, anger and unleashed emotions of a lawsuit between the spouses could injure that relationship.

This, at least, is the reason often assigned for the rule that still denies a wife or a husband the right to sue for personal injuries caused by the other's negligence. Rarely ever articulated but no doubt often very much in the minds of the decision-makers is the fact that many negligence suits in the modern era are based upon improper operation of an automobile, and that more often than not the operator is insured.

In view of this important fact, the successful conclusion of a wife's suit against her husband for personal injuries caused by his negligent operation of an automobile does not ordinarily result in an impairment of the husband's financial condition. Rather, the ultimate payor of any claim asserted by the wife is an institutional insurance carrier. As a result, the wife will be compensated for her injuries by someone other than the husband, and the husband, to the extent his wife is made whole by money damages, may also profit, in a sense, from his own wrong.

Thus, where husband and wife are not confronted with possible economic loss as a result of the other's lawsuit, the likelihood of upsetting domestic harmony is remote and problematical.[249] The more probable reason for preserving the inter-spousal immunity rule with regard to negligently inflicted personal injuries is not the threat to domestic harmony, but rather the possibility that the close relationship between husband and wife may lead to collusion in asserting and prosecuting claims for such injuries. The danger, which seems at least subconsciously to be feared by the decision-makers in this area, is that to permit suits between spouses for negligently inflicted injuries will result in large numbers of fraudulent claims and suits, with the husband or wife, whoever the defendant happens to be, cooperating with the plaintiff in order to assure a recovery against the affluent insurance company.[250]

Here, once again, though the law on its surface appears to apply equally to husband and wife, social factors beyond the courtroom have at times caused the rule to affect wives differently from husbands. In the early part of this century, when automobile driving was first being introduced to the American way of life, family drivers were almost exclusively husbands and fathers rather than wives and mothers. Only recently have American women begun to drive automobiles in substantial numbers. But for many years, when men were the only drivers, the effect of the inter-spousal immunity rule, which denied the right to bring suit for negligently inflicted injuries, was to cause more women than men to have no legal recourse at all to redress injuries they had incurred as a result of another's—their spouse's—negligent conduct.

The dramatic increase in the number of American women who drive automobiles has minimized the sex-discriminatory aspects of the inter-spousal immunity rule. But, as recently stated,

> [L]ess than half the jurisdictions in the United States allow an action for any personal tort between the spouses, including actions for injuries resulting from negligence. Only nineteen states have construed the Married Women's Acts to authorize an action by either spouse for a personal tort committed by the other spouse, intentional or negligent.[251]

In view of the speciousness of the expressed reasons for retention of the rule—the need to preserve domestic harmony—as illustrated above, it is clear that the real basis for the rule's preservation is the continued influence of the fictional unity of the spouses. Though the outright discriminatory results of that fiction no longer obtain because of increased participation by women in many spheres of social activity that were formerly the exclusive province of men, the philosophical foundations and unsavory history of that fiction would of themselves be sufficient reasons for its rejection in all areas of American law.

Actions for Loss of Consortium

Suppose the following two situations:

In the first, John and Mary Brown have been married for ten years. One morning, Joe Smith, an employee of Acme Brewing Company, while delivering the Company's products in one of its trucks, negligently runs down Mary Brown as she is crossing a street. As a result of that accident, Mary Brown loses her right arm and right leg and becomes permanently paralyzed.

In the second situation, it is John Brown, rather than Mary Brown who is the victim of Joe Smith's negligence. In all other respects—including the extent of his injuries—the facts are identical with those presented in the first situation.

From the foregoing, one might expect the legal consequences of these two events to be the same. To some extent, this is in fact the case. Though it has not always been true in Anglo-American legal doctrine, under present American law Mary Brown would be permitted to sue Joe Smith and his employer in her own name for the damage caused her when she was struck by the truck as a result of Smith's negligence. She now has the right in all American jurisdictions to sue for her injuries as John Brown has to sue for his and as married men have had since the early days of English law.

But when a person is physically injured, he or she may not be the only one to suffer harm as a result of those injuries. The victim who has actually been injured may have as a result endured pain and suffering, lost earnings, accumulated medical expenses and had his life expectancy substantially reduced. At the same time by causing that person to have become something less than he or she was prior to the injury, the perpetrator of the harm has also hurt other persons who had a legal right that certain attributes of the injured person remain unimpaired.

That right has been described as a "relational interest."[252] In the eyes of the law, husbands and wives have such an interest in one another. Named "consortium," the interest has been variously defined. One line of definitions would make no distinction between the economic and non-economic aspects of consortium. In *Smith v. Nicholas*,[253] for example, consortium is described as including the "exclusive rights to the services of the spouses *and* to his or her society, companionship and conjugal affection."[254] By contrast, some definitions have stressed the "services" element of consortium,[255] or have rejected entirely the non-economic aspects of consortium in deciding whether a spouse should be permitted to recover for loss of consortium as a result of injuries sustained by the other spouse.[256]

These variant definitions of consortium account in part for the common law rule which permitted a husband but not a wife to recover for an impairment or loss of the consortium of the other.[257] Thus, in the two factual situations posed at the beginning of this section, the rule at common law and in most American jurisdictions today would permit John Brown, after Mary Brown has been injured, to bring a separate suit or to join in her suit against Smith and his employer. John Brown could thus recover damages for *his* loss of his wife's consortium. This recovery would be distinct from any allowed to Mary Brown for the injuries she had directly received. Where John Brown is the one who has been injured, however, the common law rule which still persists in most jurisdictions provides that he alone can recover for the injuries sustained. As a result, Mary Brown would be denied the right to sue for the negligent invasion of her rights to consortium.

As stated by the court in *Novak v. Kansas City Transit, Inc.*[258]

Under the early common law, although a husband was permitted to recover for an impairment or loss of the consortium (including services and society) of his wife the wife could not recover for the loss of her husband's society, either because she had no such right or because she was denied any remedy for an invasion thereof.[259]

Several factors account for this rule which granted a husband but denied a wife the right to sue for loss of consortium. For one thing, earlier analogies drawn by courts to the master-servant relationship[260] seem to have led to later courts' emphasis upon the husband's proprietary right to his wife's services as a necessary precondition to the maintenance of an action for loss of consortium.[261] Since wives, unlike their husbands, were not entitled to their spouses' services, this emphasis upon the economic aspects of consortium contributed in part to the denial of the right of married women to bring an action for its loss.

The wife's general inferior social position in earlier days may also have accounted for the sex-based distinction in this area. Blackstone explained the difference in these terms:

> We may observe that in these relative injuries notice is only taken of the wrong done to the superior of the parties related, by the breach or dissolution of either the relationship itself, or at least the advantage accruing therefrom; while the loss of the inferior by such injuries is totally unregarded. One reason for which may be this; that the inferior hath no kind of property in the company, care or assistance of the superior, as the superior is held to have in those of the inferior, and therefore the inferior can suffer no loss or injury.[262]

In addition, the wife's procedural inability to sue no doubt also played an important part in her being denied the common law remedy for loss of consortium.[263]

In more recent times, still other reasons have been advanced by courts to justify the denial of the wife's right to sue for negligent invasion of her marital interests. Among them have been that the injury to the wife was too indirect or too remote;[264] that it could lead to a double recovery;[265] and that the Married Women's Acts created no new rights but merely removed existing disabilities.[266]

All of these reasons are of doubtful validity. For the most part, they can be urged with equal force against the husband's right of action for loss of consortium—but generally are not. Certainly, the "remoteness" reason would also apply to the husband's cause of action. As for the potential problem of a double recovery, where wives have been permitted to sue for loss of consortium they have generally been limited to recovering only for the loss of companionship and society. They have not been permitted to recover for the loss of support, since the latter loss may be compensated by the jury that awards a husband damages for the impairment of his earning capacity. Moreover, the possibility of a double recovery can be avoided by requiring a wife and husband to be joined as parties plaintiff where he sues for direct damages and she for loss of consortium.[267] Concededly, before the Married Women's Acts were adopted, the wife's choses in action belonged to the husband;[268] in a limited sense, therefore, double recovery for the husband's injuries may have been possible at that time. But the passage of those acts, giving to the wife complete ownership of her choses in action, has entirely eliminated that problem.

The "right to service" argument is equally baseless. Though at common law the husband had such a right to his wife's services and his wife did not have a corresponding right in his, still the husband has never been limited in his recovery to only those sums which would compensate him for the loss of those services. At all times, he has also been allowed to recover for the loss of the non-economic elements of consortium.

Though wives were generally denied the right to sue for the loss of consortium, there were some exceptions. The common law action for alienation of affections, for example, could be brought by either a husband or a wife. That action has become virtually extinct as a result of its inherent potential for abuse.[269] Nevertheless, while it prevailed, the alienation of affections action was in effect based upon a loss of consortium in all its variant meanings. Despite this apparent inconsistency, courts were able to reconcile the rule that permitted a wife to sue for loss of consortium where it was founded upon a female defendant's alienation of her husband's affections with the denial of her right to sue for a negligent invasion of consortium. In *Eschenbach v. Benjamin*,[270] the court stressed the fact that in the alienation of affection cases the injury to the wife was direct, that the husband could not recover for his own wrong, and that the problem of potential double damage recovery was therefore not present in that type of lawsuit.

A second exception to the rule denying wives the right to sue for loss of consortium was developed in the early part of this century by a few jurisdictions when the injury to the husband was caused by other types of intentional misconduct of the defendant. Examples were the defendant's unwarranted sale of liquor to the husband[271] or furnishing him with addictive drugs.[272] Even in most of these cases, however, the wife's right to recover for such injuries was denied.[273]

Despite the limited exceptions in the areas of alienation of affections and other intentional torts, the early common law rule, which denied the wife a cause of action for the negligent invasion of her rights to consortium, prevailed everywhere in the United States until 1950. In that year, the case of *Hitaffer v. Argonne Co., Inc.*[274]

was decided by the Circuit Court of Appeals of the District of Columbia.

Rejecting all arguments in opposition to granting a wife a right to sue for negligent invasion of consortium, Judge Clark, for the court, stated the underlying considerations in the following terms:

> The medieval concepts of the marriage relation to which other jurisdictions have reverted in order to reach the results which have been handed to us as evidence of the law have long since ceased to have any meaning. It can hardly be said that a wife has less of an interest in the marriage relation than does the husband or in these modern times that a husband renders services of such a different character to the family and household that they must be measured by a standard of such uncertainty that the law cannot estimate any loss thereof. The husband owes the same degree of love, affection, felicity, etc., to the wife as she to him. He also owes the material service of support, but above and beyond that he renders other services as his mate's helper in her duties, as advisor and counselor, etc. Under such circumstances it would be a judicial fiat for us to say that a wife may not have an action for loss of consortium due to negligence.[275]

Notwithstanding this persuasive abandonment of venerable law by the *Hitaffer* decision, the rule of that case was substantially rejected by most of the jurisdictions that considered the problem.[276] As of 1964, the *Hitaffer* position had been repudiated in 20 jurisdictions.[277] For the most part, these decisions have reiterated the same reasons that had been advanced before *Hitaffer* for denying the wife's right to sue for negligent invasion of consortium, or else they have suggested that the change in the rule should be made by the legislatures rather than the courts.[278] In a few jurisdictions, courts have interpreted the reforms of the Married Women's Acts as requiring the abolition of the husband's cause of action for loss of consortium rather than its extension to the wife.[279]

Despite this initial opposition of the courts, Dean Prosser has suggested that around 1958, "something of a current of support for the *Hitaffer* case set in, and since that date the trend has been definitely in the direction of approval."[280] Writing in 1964, however, he listed only 12 jurisdictions that had adopted the *Hitaffer* approach. Though some others have joined the list since then,[281] it is clear that an overwhelming majority of jurisdictions still permit a husband to sue for negligent invasion of his right to consortium as a result of his wife's injuries, but do not permit the wife to do so where her husband has been injured. There is a strong possibility, moreover, as discussed in Chapter 6 below, that the unequal consortium rule may be abrogated as a result of constitutional challenges that have been upheld by a number of courts in recent years. Significantly, such challenges, where successful, have resulted in the extension to wives of the right to sue for such loss, rather than its removal from husbands as, conceivably, might have occurred.

With regard to future prospects, the prediction has been made that "the trend will continue, and that public opinion as to the equality of the sexes will have its effect in persuading the Courts."[282] Though that prediction is probably accurate with respect to long-range developments, the acceleration of that process may depend upon the extent to which the public is informed of the existence of this sex-based discriminatory rule.

MARRIED WOMEN AND THE CRIMINAL LAW

Conspiracy

Most acts that have been made punishable by the criminal law can be committed by one person alone. The outstanding exception is found in the crime of conspiracy. Though the difficulty of precisely defining that offense has often been noted,[283] it is unanimously recognized that more than one person must act in a designated manner for a criminal conspiracy to have occurred. As stated by the court in *Commonwealth v. Donoghue,* "the broad definition or description everywhere accepted is that conspiracy is a combination between *two or more persons* to do or accomplish a criminal or unlawful act, or to do a lawful act by criminal or unlawful means."[284]

It is perhaps dramatic testimony to the tenaciousness with which the common law embraced its fictions that the theoretical identity of husband and wife led to the rule that they were incapable of conspiring together. Since two or more persons were required to act in concert for a conspiracy to be found, and since husband and wife were in the eyes of the law only one person, no great conceptual leap was required to conclude that it was impossible for them to be co-conspirators.[285]

This principle had already prevailed for several centuries in England at the time of the American Revolution. In 1889, California had the dubious distinction of becoming the first American state to hold that a husband and wife could not be convicted of criminal conspiracy.[286] And in 1933, in *People v. MacMullen*,[287] the California Supreme Court reaffirmed its prior holding. While expressing some reservations about the wisdom of the rule, the court in *MacMullen* insisted that changes in the common law rule were more appropriately made by legislative action than by judicial decision.[288]

Despite such judicial prompting, the California legislature did not take action on the rule. Partly as a result of the legislature's inaction, the California Supreme Court in the 1964 case of *People v. Pierce*,[289] overruled the earlier cases. Asserting its "responsibility for the upkeep of the common law,"[290] the court in *Pierce* held that "when a husband and wife conspire only between themselves, they cannot claim immunity from prosecution for conspiracy on the basis of their marital status."[291]

Recognizing that the historical origin of the rule lay in the fictional doctrine of unity of husband and wife, Justice Traynor, writing for a unanimous court, punned forgivably that the fiction "has been substantially vitiated by the overwhelming evidence that one plus one adds up to two, even in twogetherness."[292]

In the federal courts, the rule that a husband and wife are legally incapable of conspiring together had already been rejected by the United States Supreme Court in 1960.[293] In *United States v. Dege,* a 6-3 decision, Mr. Justice Frankfurter, writing for the majority, stated that the Court would not allow itself "to be obfuscated by medieval views regarding the legal status of women and the common law's reflection of them."[294] In his view, the former rule could proceed only on the basis of one of two assumptions: "either that responsibility of husband and wife for joint participation in a criminal enterprise would make for marital disharmony, or that a wife must be presumed to act under the coercive influence of her husband and, therefore cannot be a willing participant."[295] "[T]he former assumption," declared Justice Frankfurter, "is unnourished by sense; the latter implies a view of American womanhood offensive to the ethos of our society."[296]

Although not noted as being special admirers of legal fictions—especially those that degrade large groups of people—Mr. Chief Justice Warren and Justices Black and Whitaker dissented in the *Dege* case. At the outset, they were faced with the problem of the spouses' fictional unity which, in the early account of Serjeant Hawkins,[297] had provided the theoretical justification for the rule that husband and wife could not conspire with one another. Rather charitably, the dissenting Justices interpreted that unity as merely reflecting "an abiding belief that the communion between husband and wife is such that their actions are not always to be regarded by the criminal law as if there were no marriage."[298] Their principal fear was that a "wife, simply by virtue of the intimate life she shares with her husband, might easily perform acts that would technically be sufficient to involve her in a criminal conspiracy with him, but which might be far removed from the arm's-length agreement typical of that crime."[299] Somehow, the ancient rule was regarded as salutary, intending to preserve the "solidarity and the confidential relationship of marriage."[300] For Chief Justice Warren, it was by no means clear that "a rule accepted by so many people for so many centuries [could] be so lightly dismissed."[301] In any event, declared the Chief Justice, "the power to depose belongs to Congress, not to this Court."[302]

In addition to California, at least three other states—Colorado,[303] Illinois,[304] and Texas[305]—have repudiated the doctrine of interspousal conspiracy immunity. But apart from its rejection by the United States Supreme Court and the above mentioned states, the doctrine lives on. In England and Canada, for example, the rule persists that spouses cannot be co-conspirators.[306] In the United States the doctrine has been expressly accepted in New Jersey[307] and Pennsylvania.[308]

In many other American states the question has not come before the courts and it is therefore difficult to say what position would be taken on that matter by those states when confronted with the issue for the first time. Because of the doctrine's common law origins, however, and the fact that it is typically raised as a defense to a criminal charge, some states could decide the issue in the same manner as the California court in the early case of *People v. Mac-Mullen*,[309] and hold that changes in the common law rule should be effected by legislative rather than judicial action.

On the other hand, when those courts are faced with the issue for the first time, they may cast a glance in the direction of the Supreme Court and the states that have abrogated the common law rule by judicial decision. In recognition of the trend toward abandoning this vestigal expression of the theoretical identity of husband and wife, those courts could reject the rule at the first opportunity.

Notwithstanding Chief Justice Warren's expressed fear of possible injury to the confidential relationship of marriage as a result of judicial abandonment of the inter-spousal immunity rule,[310] it is clear that the principal reason for the rule's existence has been the fiction that husband and wife are one person in the eyes of the law. If that fiction is unrealistic, harmful, and productive of unequal legal treatment between the sexes in other spheres of activity, it should be rejected in this area as well. Moreover, as suggested by one commentator:

> An unlawful act is as objectionable when planned by husband and wife as when planned by two other parties. Since the husband and wife are in fact a plurality, their mutual encouragement, as in the case of any other combination, increases the likelihood that the substantive offense will be committed.[311]

Although, when applied to a specific factual occurrence the inter-spousal conspiracy immunity rule can result in an individual wife escaping the reach of the criminal law, acceptance of the rule, resting ultimately, as it does, upon the medieval fiction of the spouses' identity, is another instance of legal endorsement of the male superiority principle. The rule should be abrogated everywhere, either by judicial decision or by the act of the legislatures.[312]

The Doctrine of Presumed Coercion

In *O'Donnell v. State*,[313] the Oklahoma Supreme Court described the common law rule of presumed coercion as follows:

> Where a crime, with some exceptions, was committed by a married woman conjointly with or in the presence of her husband, prima facie she was not criminally liable, as it was pre-

sumed that she acted in obedience to his command and under his coercion.[314]

Writing in the eighteenth century, William Blackstone announced that this doctrine was already a thousand years old.[315] There were certain crimes to which the doctrine did not apply: treason, murder or misdemeanors[316] or offenses such as "keeping a brothel which one assumed to be 'generally conducted by the intrigues of the female sex.' "[317] Where the doctrine did apply, however, it created for wives a "powerful shield in [their] defense;"[318] that is, a presumption which "could be rebutted [only] by evidence showing clearly the absence of coercion. . . ."[319]

At first glance, this doctrine, which effectively limited the criminal capacity of married women, appears to rest upon the oft-encountered principle of the legal identity of the spouses or, more precisely, the submersion of the wife's legal personality in that of her husband.

As Professor Perkins has demonstrated,[320] however, there is good reason to believe that the original common law principle, establishing the wife's immunity from criminal prosecution for certain otherwise antisocial acts committed in her husband's presence, was not the direct product of the fictional unity of husband and wife. Rather, it seems to have resulted from an amazing complex of legal fictions which at its source, however, did in fact depend upon a sex-based discriminatory practice.

The underlying reason for the common law rule appears to have been the desire of the administrators of the English legal system to spare the lives of married women accused of certain crimes. Even as late as the beginning of the nineteenth century there were in England over 220 offenses punishable by death.[321] To soften this theoretically harsh treatment of criminal offenders, the common law resorted once again to a fiction. Early in English legal history, members of the clergy, a favored social group, were permitted to raise the fact of their religious affiliation as a defense to an accusation of a crime which could be punished by a sentence of death. This was known as the "benefit of clergy." Once such a defense was raised, the clergyman was "turned over to the ecclesiastical court, in which the procedure was such that he rarely failed to clear himself."[322]

In the beginning, benefit of clergy was available only to clerks, monks, and nuns.[323] Later, after the common law courts had gained prestige, transfer to the ecclesiastical courts no longer occurred when the benefit of clergy was pleaded. The plea was still of great value in the common law courts, however, since it limited punishment to a "brand upon the brawn of the thumb and imprisonment not to exceed a year."[324] At a still later date, in an effort to soften the rigors of the English penal system, benefit of clergy was extended to every man who could read, whether he was in fact a member of the clergy or not.[325] The art of reading was not widespread but had generally been mastered by true clerics. The courts therefore accepted this demonstration of reading skill as evidence that the accused was a clergyman, knowing all the while that he was a layman in fact. Justice was thus tempered with mercy by resort to this rather benign fiction.

There were limits of course beyond which this fictionalization process could not go. Because married women could not become nuns, the common law courts balked at extending the benefit of clergy privilege to them. The practical result was that if a husband and wife were each to commit the same crime, the life of the husband could be spared by his claiming the benefit of clergy. But because the wife could not avail herself of this defense, she would necessarily be condemned to death. It was to alleviate this harsh disparity of treatment that, Professor Perkins suggests on good authority, the doctrine of presumed coercion came into being.[326] As a result of that doctrine a wife who committed an act in the presence of her husband which was otherwise punishable by death could defend on the ground that the act was carried out upon her husband's command, and would thus not be punished at all. Since her husband could claim the benefit of clergy if he were convicted of the crime, his life at least would not be taken.

Despite this spectacle of layers of fiction one upon another, it is clear that at its base the rule that denied the benefit of clergy to married women gave rise to this elaborate doctrinal structure. Though the benefit of clergy defense is no longer of any significance and the number of offenses punishable by death are substantially fewer than in medieval England, the presumed coercion principle is far from dead.

Some courts in the United States have in recent years rejected the doctrine of presumed coercion in the light of the Married

Women's Property Acts and other developments. In California this rejection was expressed in a controlling dictum in the case of *People v. Stately.*[327] The same result was achieved more directly in the Kentucky case of *King v. City of Owensboro.*[328]

Despite such isolated instances of the rule's rejection in some jurisdictions, the claim could be made as recently as 1950 that the "majority of our courts hold the presumption still lives in a modified form."[329] Generally, the presumption is weaker and can be rebutted with a lesser showing of an absence of coercion than was true in the past. Nevertheless, the presumption is recognized in most states and, unless rebutted, prevails. In recent years, the basic presumption has been accepted or reiterated in Missouri,[330] North Carolina,[331] and Oklahoma, [332] among other states.[333]

In rejecting the common law presumption of coercion, the Appellate Department of the California Superior Court offered the following cogent reasons:

> We conclude then, that the reign of the thousand year old presumption has come to an end. In our society, where almost no bride promises to obey her husband, and where it is not accepted as the usual that a wife does what her husband wishes by way of yielding obedience to a dominant will, the basis for the presumption has disappeared. A presumption that has lost its reason must be confined to a museum; it has no place in the administration of justice.[334]

At the same time, the court in *Stately* could not reject the principle—since it was embodied in a California statute[335]— that married women lacked capacity to commit certain crimes if they acted under the actual threat or command of their husbands. All that the *Stately* case held was that a married woman could not prove that she had acted in obedience to her husband "by the mere circumstance that her husband *was present* when she offended."[336]

Thus, even in states that have rejected the presumption of coercion, a married woman is permitted to defend against criminal charges on the ground that her husband had actually "commanded" her to commit the crime.[337]

It is submitted that the same reasons that motivated the California court in *Stately* to repudiate the common law doctrine of presumed coercion require the abandonment of the husband's actual command as a limitation upon the wife's criminal capacity.[338]

Where, as in California, the preservation of that rule has been effected by statute, remedial legislation should be adopted.[339]

The "Unwritten Law" Defense

The taking of one person's life by another generally constitutes criminal homicide. This is not always the case, however. Under some circumstances, homicide is in legal contemplation deemed to be justifiable or excusable, and thus innocent in character. As a result, a person who has taken another's life "justifiably" or "excusably" is not punished by the law.

Though there are other examples of justifiable homicide, two of the most common are " (1) the killing of an enemy on the field of battle as an act of war and within the rules of war, and (2) the execution of a sentence of death pronounced by a competent tribunal."[340] Excusable homicide, on the other hand, frequently occurs when a person kills in self defense.

The defenses of justification or excuse for the taking of another's life are ordinarily available to an accused without regard to whether the accused is a man or a woman.

In one type of situation, however, some states even today permit a husband to take a person's life with impunity but do not regard a wife's comparable conduct with equal indifference. An example of the type of situation referred to is in the so-called "unwritten law" defense, set forth in a New Mexico statute as follows:

> Upon a prosecution for murder or manslaughter, in addition to other defenses which may be offered, it may be shown as a complete defense that the homicide resulted from the person's use of deadly force upon *another who was at the time of the homicide in the act of having sexual intercourse with the accused's wife.* In order for this defense to be available to the accused, the accused and his wife must have been living together as husband and wife at the time of the homicide.[341]

Similar statutes may also be found in the laws of Texas[342] and Utah,[343] among other states. By contrast, no state permits a wife to assert a correlative "unwritten law" defense if she should become so outraged by the sight of another woman engaged in an act of sexual intercourse with her husband that she takes that other woman's life.

The sex-based discriminatory aspects of such statutes are readily discernible. A rule of law that justifies a husband's killing of his wife's paramour under these circumstances, but not a wife's killing of her husband's mistress, may merely reflect an awareness of a greater resentment and a consequently lesser control over violent conduct on the part of husbands as compared with wives, when immediately confronted with the fact of a spouse's infidelity. On the other hand, by distinguishing between the sexes in this manner, such laws do more than merely reflect society's views on the matter. In a very real sense, they lend their support to those social attitudes which hold it proper, if not inevitable, for husbands to be more outraged by the adultery of their wives than wives are expected to be in the reverse situation.

To the extent that the public at large is aware of these statutes' existence, they can be understood as warning men to stay away from other men's wives. But the absence of a corresponding defense for married women means that women are not being warned to stay away from other women's husbands. Strictly speaking, a man who takes another man's wife in adultery will not be capitally punished by the state. Because of such statutes, however, he runs the risk of something very close to capital punishment. By declaring that an aggrieved husband's homicide under these circumstances will be justified in the eyes of the law, the state is in effect delegating the right of public execution to a private citizen. At the same time a correlative power is withheld from aggrieved wives. Recourse to such delegated power by a husband can be analyzed as an aggravated instance of state action, violative of the equal protection clause of the United States Constitution's Fourteenth Amendment. Admittedly, however, the question of standing to complain of such delegation is troublesome, to say the least.

Notwithstanding the ultimate resolution of such thorny problems, the availability in some states of the "unwritten law" defense to husbands, but not to wives, must be seen as another glaring expression of the American legal system's endorsement of separate standards of morality for husband and wife.

Divorce Grounds

Prior to the reign of Henry VIII, there was no question of English law discriminating between husbands and wives in granting or denying a decree of divorce. At that time, marriage was regarded by the church as a sacrament and therefore indissoluble. As a result, the ecclesiastical court in England, which had jurisdiction over marital causes, granted no absolute divorces at all. It did, however, often grant a judicial separation, called a divorce *a mensa et thoro*,[344] which merely permitted the spouses to live apart from one another without severing their marital ties.

Between the reign of Charles II and 1857, when the Matrimonial Causes Act was enacted to permit total divorces to be granted by the newly-established Court of Divorce and Matrimonial Causes, absolute divorces were frequently granted by act of Parliament.[345] From 1715 to 1800, for example, at least 134 divorces were granted in this manner.[346] In only five cases, however, were they granted on the petition of wives.[347] Professor Madden has observed that in "all of these cases there were aggravating circumstances, in addition to adultery on the part of the husband, which would make future reconciliation impossible. Thus different standards of morality were enforced between the sexes."[348]

Even with the passage of the Matrimonial Causes Act of 1857, the practice of requiring aggravating circumstances for a wife to be granted a divorce for the husband's adultery but not in the reverse situation was continued. This state of affairs persisted for another 66 years in England until, finally, under the Matrimonial Causes Act of 1923, a wife was permitted to maintain a petition for adultery alone.[349]

In the United States, absolute divorces are now granted in every state.[350] Generally, in order to procure a divorce, the plaintiff must have been a "resident" (meaning "domiciliary")[351] of the state for a designated length of time (normally one year, but in some states, such as Nevada, for as short a period as six weeks).[352] Most states require the husband or wife to be domiciled within the state as an absolute condition to the exercise of the divorce court's jurisdiction. Whether domicile is constitutionally required has never been decided by the United States Supreme Court.[353] The Court has held, however, that the domicile of one of the parties to the marriage is a sufficient constitutional basis for the exercise of a divorce court's jurisdiction, even to the extent of granting an *ex parte* divorce, *i.e.,* a divorce in which only one of the spouses participates.[354]

In most jurisdictions, there are several grounds for which an absolute divorce may be granted, with some states dissolving marriages on "easier" grounds than others. Reasons for which a marriage may be dissolved range all the way from the "easy" ground of incompatibility in New Mexico[355] to the "difficult" ground of adultery which, until recent legislative changes, was the sole ground for divorce in New York.[356]

Because of the jurisdictional aspects of divorce, it is now relatively simple for a person desiring a divorce to procure one by moving to a state in which the grounds are liberal and by establishing his or her residence there. Indeed, it may even be possible for those with sufficient financial resources and a spouse who shares in the desire to terminate the marriage relationship to procure a "quickie" divorce in Mexico.[357]

In view of the practical availability of divorce on slight or insubstantial grounds somewhere in the United States and the great mobility of our present population, there is almost an air of unreality about the enumeration of specific grounds of divorce found in the statutes of all the states. Practically speaking, the prevailing grounds of divorce are those prescribed by the states with the lowest requirements of a showing. As a result, the sex-discriminatory aspects of recognized divorce grounds in the statutes of many of our states may have a very limited practical significance. In effect, although not in stated principle, divorce in the United States may always be granted with the consent of the spouses. Often it may even be granted at the request of either husband or wife—provided that the spouse who seeks the divorce can afford to travel to the appropriate state.

Despite these possibilities for "easy" divorce, many people lack sufficient financial resources to avail themselves of a migratory divorce. For them, the divorce laws of the state in which they reside are in fact binding. Moreover, the presence of discriminatory divorce grounds in the statutes of various states, though of limited practical importance, still throws the legal system on one side or another of the social tension with regard to the status of the sexes. For these reasons, an appraisal of sex-discriminatory aspects of statutory divorce grounds is useful.

As late as 1931, it was observed by Professor Vernier that "In a dozen jurisdictions there remain discriminations of various kinds between the sexes."[358] The discriminations referred to by Professor Vernier were apparently those in which a husband, rather than a wife, received preferential treatment at the hands of the law. Now as then, however, substantially more than 12 jurisdictions permit a wife to divorce her husband upon a showing that the latter has willfully failed to fulfill his obligations of family support.[359] Only a few, however, permit a husband to divorce his wife for the same reason.[360]

To the extent that sexual misconduct of husband and wife may provide a basis for a decree of divorce the law once again has expressed, and still does express, society's double standard of morality. At least 14 of the American states have at one time or another permitted a husband, but not a wife, to be granted a divorce upon proof of the other's unchaste condition at the time of marriage.[361] And in the first quarter of the twentieth century at least three states —Texas,[362] North Carolina,[363] and Kentucky[364]—allowed a husband to be divorced from his wife if he could prove that she had committed a single act of adultery, though wives could not be granted a divorce under similar circumstances. This obviously discriminatory rule has since been abrogated in Texas and North Carolina, but persists in Kentucky.[365] The constitutional validity of such a discrimination is highly doubtful. Its existence nevertheless illustrates another area in which the might of the legal system has been enlisted in support of male dominance in sexual matters.

Though the extreme discrimination expressed in the above-mentioned Kentucky statute is, fortunately, now limited to that one state, a subtle discrimination infects a common provision that gives a husband a ground for divorce not available to the wife. The Alabama statute[366] on this subject is typical. It provides that a divorce may be granted "in favor of the husband, when the wife was pregnant at the time of marriage, without his knowledge or agency." Similar statutes may be found in many other states.[367] In no state, however, is a wife permitted a divorce if her husband, prior to marriage, had caused another woman, not his wife, to become pregnant.

Certainly, if that has in fact been the case, the economic health of the present marriage would be in jeopardy; the husband could be successfully sued in a paternity action and thereby required to provide financial support for the child of the former liaison. Only one state, Iowa, has expressly recognized the sex-discrimination in such a legal rule. However, Iowa's efforts to restore a balance are incomplete, to say the least. Under Iowa law, [368] "The husband may obtain a divorce from the wife . . . when the wife at the time of the marriage was pregnant by another than the husband, of which he had no knowledge, *unless such husband had an illegitimate child or children then living, which at the time of the marriage was unknown to the wife.*"[369] This means that the husband's premarital fathering of an illegitimate child may be offered by the wife as a defense to the husband's divorce action based upon her pregnancy by another, unknown to her husband at the time of marriage. It does not, however, constitute a separate ground for the wife's divorce.

In addition to this rather widespread discrimination in the area of divorce grounds for husband and wife, there are several miscellaneous discriminations found in a few jurisdictions. In Alabama, for example, a wife may be divorced from a husband who is addicted to drugs, but a husband may not be divorced merely because his wife suffers from the same condition.[370] This type of discrimination may stem from the same psychological factors that have produced the uneven laws for the sexes with regard to proof of freedom from venereal disease as a condition to the issuance of a marriage license.[371] Here, as there, to admit the possibility that the wife has indulged in the same vices as the husband may strike some legislatures as unthinkable.

Most states which provide that drunkenness may be a ground for a divorce make no distinction between aggrieved husbands and wives. In Kentucky, however, a sex-based discrimination appears once again. There, a wife may be granted a divorce from her husband on the ground of his drunkenness of at least one year's duration only if his condition has been "accompanied by a wasting of the husband's estate and without any suitable provision for the maintenance of the wife or children."[372] A husband, however, can be granted a divorce from his wife on the grounds of her mere drunkenness alone, without the necessity of showing any additional factors.[373] The net effect of this discrimination is that the husband can stay as drunk as he wants for as long as he wants, provided that he does not neglect his family support obligations.

The wife will have no legal cause to complain. Let her do the same, however, and this will be sufficient reason to grant the husband's petition for divorce.

These instances of sex-based discrimination in divorce grounds are, for the reasons discussed earlier, of limited practical significance. Nevertheless, they illustrate other areas wherein the law accords men and women different treatment solely because of their sex. If the principle of true legal equality of the sexes is to prevail, then these along with the other sex-based legal discriminations discussed in this essay must be terminated.

*   *   *   *   *   *   *   *   *

Though the legal regulation of women in employment has been treated rather summarily to this point, the pivotal nature of this area in the whole field of sex-based legal discrimination should be evident. Rules with regard to support obligations, alimony, domicile and other matters are fashioned to a considerable extent with the employability of women in mind. While Nature's allocation of the childbearing function has necessarily restricted their employment possibilities, women, with or without children can still be gainfully employed for long periods of time outside the home. Nor is it difficult for those of us who have grown up in an age of scientific miracle-making to believe that the present scheme of childbearing may be substantially altered if and when the scientists address themselves to the question. For these reasons and also because of the peculiar legislative history and potentially revolutionary consequences of the prohibition against sex-based employment discrimination contained in the 1964 Civil Rights Act, this subject will be explored in much greater detail in Chapters 4 and 5.

In another context, Hans Kelsen once wrote, "No social order can compensate completely for the injustice of nature."[374] Justice Charles D. Breitel has recently stated the same idea in a somewhat different form:

> Since Aristotle sought to define justice in terms of equality, the concept that at least one of the essences of justice is the treatment of equals equally and unequals unequally has infused man's thinking. Two men between whom no relevant distinction can be made must be treated alike if there is to be justice. On the other hand, to regard the child as the equal of a grown

man, again in relevant classification, would be injustice. *The rub is in the qualification of relevancy; a classification that is relevant to the goals of a society is good, while a discrimination that is irrelevant to such goals is obnoxious to it.*[375]

The jurisprudential conundrum suggested by these statements is central to any thoughtful consideration of how men and women should be treated by our legal system. To the extent that these considerations also come within the purview of the United States Constitution—an extent we suggest is substantial—this matter will also be examined in greater detail in Chapter 6, entitled, "Constitutional Aspects of Sex-Based Discrimination in American Law."

CHAPTER 4

Title VII of the 1964 Civil Rights Act and the Equal Pay Act of 1963

> "Some people have suggested to me that labor opposes 'no discrimination on account of sex' because they feel that through the years protective legislation has been built up to safeguard the health of women. Some legislation was to safeguard the health of women, but it should have safeguarded the health of men, also."
>
> Congresswoman Martha Griffiths, Cong. Rec. 2580 (1964)

THE BACKGROUND

At the beginning of the 20th century, there were in the United States 5,000,000 women workers constituting only 18 percent of the American labor force.[1] By 1966, this figure had risen to over 27,000,000 women representing 36 percent of the U.S. total.[2] At the present time, one-tenth of all family heads are women,[3] and it has been observed that "most women are no longer in the labor market to supplement their husbands' income but primarily in order to provide the necessities of life for their families."[4]

In one sense, this steady rise in the proportion of women to the total American labor force has been an encouraging development for those who seek an end to arbitrary laws that discriminate on the basis of sex. As suggested in an earlier chapter, many legal rules that distinguish between the sexes are fashioned to a considerable extent with the employability of women in mind.[5]

In another sense, however, the growth of the female labor contingent has not always been a positive force for eradicating male-female alienation and the female sense of "otherness' in American life. True, "society's prejudice against the worker-wife-mother combination appeared to soften in the expanding job market of the mid-sixties,"[6] and undoubtedly before then. Nevertheless, while the facts surrounding women's role in the labor market have sometimes accorded them a measure of economic and social independence, they have also often tended to exaggerate the sense of arbitrary and culturally determined difference between the sexes.

These negative effects of rising female employment upon the relations between the sexes have been brought about by two important economic facts. One is that women workers have received,
more often than not, considerably lower wages than men performing the same work.[7] Whether such pay differentials merely reflected
employers' honest beliefs that they are warranted by the difference
in the sex of the employees alone, or, as some have suggested, that
women, like Negroes, had become the victims of super-exploitation
by profits-at-any-price employers, the positive effects upon male-
female relations achieved by men and women working together in
industry and commerce have been largely weakened by constant
reminders of the lower economic reward for women's work than
for men's.[8]

A second factor detracting from the positive effects of increased
female employment in American life has been the general relega-
tion of women, and consequently of men also, to particular types of
jobs. Reflecting at times broad social prejudices, the desire of men
to monopolize a particular calling,[9] or the simple inertia of past
events, the practice of dividing jobs into those for men only, those
for women only, and those for both needs little documentation. A
simple glance at the workaday world will reveal which sex serves as
the clerk-typists, which as the automobile mechanics, which as the
telephone operators, which as the pilots, and which as the overwhelming majority of physicians, lawyers[10] and architects in the
United States. Though sex-based stratification of economic roles
may to some extent reflect the socially conditioned desires of men
and women themselves, there can be little doubt of past employer
resistance to the job applicant seeking employment in a position
that tradition, collective bargaining agreement,[11] or law[12] had
marked out as the exclusive preserve of the opposite sex.

Except for situations in which wage or employment opportunity
discrimination was practiced by state governments or their agencies, or required by law,[13] most discriminatory practices by employers, labor organizations, or employment agencies appeared im-
mune to attack on substantive due process or equal protection
grounds, since those constitutional safeguards are directed against
governmental rather than private interferences. Moreover, even
where state action was present, the United States Supreme Court,

among others, had on many occasions held that sex discrimination in employment was constitutionally allowable.[14] As a result, legislative treatment seemed the only way of curing this problem.

The pace of legislative enactments in this area has been uneven. In the equal pay field, despite scattered successes in the states,[15] victory at the federal level was achieved in 1963 only "after 18 years of persistent, unsuccessful efforts to get an equal pay bill to the floor of Congress. . . ."[16]

In the field of equal employment opportunities, two states—Wisconsin and Hawaii—had prohibited sex discrimination in employment by statute in 1961 and 1963, respectively. And, in 1961, the United States President's Commission on the Status of Women, established by President Kennedy's Executive Order 10980, had also been charged with reviewing progress and making recommendations in two areas: 1) private employment policies and practices, including those on wages, under federal contracts; and 2) federal government employment practices.[17] In the same Executive Order, the Commission was asked to explore, "additional affirmative steps which should be taken through legislation, executive or administrative action to assure non-discrimination on the basis of sex and to enhance constructive employment opportunities for women."[18] Significantly, except for its involvement with federal contracts, no reference to the private employment sector was contained in the Order.

In 1963, the Committee on Private Employment,[19] one of the seven created by the President's Commission on the Status of Women, recommended the issuance of an Executive Order "setting forth the federal policy of equal employment opportunity and hiring, training and promotion, and establishing a President's Committee on Merit Employment of Women [which] would place main reliance on persuasion and voluntary compliance. . . ."[20]

Despite the Committee's expansion upon its original charge by urging coverage of all employers with or without federal contracts,[21] its recommendation was restricted severely in urging no more than an Executive Order that would be backed by persuasion to comply voluntarily rather than by more stringent enforcement measures.[22] Nor did the Committee contemplate any recourse to the courts for more tangible relief from sex-based employment discrimination. It is all the more gratifying, therefore, that Title VII of the Civil Rights Act of 1964 designated as an "unlawful employment practice" sex discrimination in employment practices 'of employers, employment agencies, and labor organizations, and provided for ultimate legal redress in the courts in the form of money damages and injunctive relief for persons aggrieved by such practices—a development that will be explored later in this chapter.[23]

Regardless of their legislative origins, the federal Equal Pay Act of 1963, the prohibition against sex discrimination in employment in Title VII of the 1964 Civil Rights Act, and counterpart state laws enacted in their wake, have provided opportunities for developing a new era in male-female relationships in American society. Those opportunities must be seized, however, and possible restrictive interpretations of the two major federal statutes threaten the realization of their promise and potential. Without purporting to be a manual of practice and procedure under those statutes, the balance of this chapter and the next explores some of their important provisions and interrelations. Specifically examined are: (1) some difficult problems raised by Title VII with respect to the so-called state "protective" laws, such as the frequently encountered state hours and weight-lifting restrictions applicable only to women workers; and (2) the prevention of evasionary devices that seek to circumvent the requirements of the Equal Pay Act.

THE SEX PROVISIONS OF TITLE VII OF THE 1964 CIVIL RIGHTS ACT

The Peculiar Legislative History

Any consideration of the sex provisions of Title VII of the 1964 Civil Rights Act requires a preliminary glance at what can only be described as their peculiar legislative history. In the light of its tremendous potential for profoundly affecting the daily lives of so many Americans—both men and women—Title VII's prohibition against sex discrimination in employment had a rather inauspicious birth.

This is not to say that some species of federal legislation outlawing sex-based discrimination in employment might not have emerged eventually from a Congress in which male representatives outnumbered female representatives overwhelmingly. Agitation

for such a law, after all, had been going on for many years. Moreover, Congress had acted deliberately and responsively in enacting
the Equal Pay Act of 1963. But the prospects for the passage of
legislation prohibiting sex discrimination in hiring and promotional practices in employment were exceedingly dim in 1964. Had
the sex provisions of Title VII been presented then as a separate
bill, rather than being coupled as they were in an effusion of Congressional gimmickry with legislation aimed at curbing racial and
ethnic discrimination, their defeat in 1964 would have been virtually assured. We have no less an authority for this conclusion
than Oregon's Representative Edith Green, whose strong advocacy
of equal legal treatment for American women lends great force to
her appraisal. In her view, stated in Congress, the legislation
against sex discrimination in employment, "considered by itself,
and . . . brought to the floor with no hearings and no testimony
. . . would not [have] receive[d] one hundred votes."[24]

In fact, it was not until the last day of the bill's consideration in
Chairman Howard Smith's House Rules Committee, where it had
gone after a favorable report from the judiciary committee, that
there first appeared a motion to add "sex" discrimination to the
other types of employment discrimination that the original bill
sought to curb.[25] That motion was defeated in committee by a
vote of 8-7.[26] But after almost two weeks of passionate floor debate
in the House and just one day before the act was passed, Representative Smith, a principal opponent of the original bill, offered
an amendment to include sex as a prohibited basis for employment
discrimination.[27] Under that amendment, the previously proposed
sanctions[28] against employers, unions, hiring agencies, or their
agents, for discrimination in hiring or promotional practices
against actual or prospective employees on the basis of race, creed,
or national origin, were, with some exceptions, also to apply to
discrimination based upon the "sex" of the job applicant or employee. Offering his amendment, Representative Smith remarked,
"Now I am very serious . . . I do not think it can do any harm to
this legislation; maybe it will do some good."[29]

Despite Congressman Smith's protestations of seriousness, there
was substantial cause to doubt his motives. For four months Congress had been locked in debate over the passage of the Civil Rights
Act of 1964. Most southern representatives and a few of their

northern allies had been making every effort to block its passage. In the context of that debate and of the prevailing congressional sentiment when the amendment was offered, it is abundantly clear that a principal motive in introducing it was to prevent passage of the basic legislation being considered by Congress,[30] rather than solicitude for women's employment rights.[31]

It is not surprising, therefore, that Representative Green, expressing her hope that "the day will come when discrimination will be ended against women,"[32] also registered her opposition to the proposed amendment, stating that it "will clutter up the bill and it may later—very well—be used to help destroy this section of the bill by some of the very people who today support it."[33]

Despite these misgivings, and despite the apparent objectives of its sponsors to block passage of the entire Act, the legislation that finally emerged contained Representative Smith's amendment intact. As a result of this stroke of misfired political tactics, our federal positive law now includes a provision that had been desired for many years by those who were concerned with the economic, social and political status of American women, but which had been delayed because of the feeling that the time had not ripened for such legislation and had been specifically opposed in this instance partly because of a belief that "discrimination based on sex involves problems sufficiently different from discrimination based on . . . other factors . . . to make separate treatment preferable."[34]

What significance should be drawn from this peculiar legislative history of Title VII's prohibition against sex discrimination? It would be a most serious error to attribute to Congress as a corporate unit the apparently cynical motives of the amendment's sponsor. Though most members of Congress were intent on prohibiting employment discrimination based on race, religion and national origin, they did vote to do the same with respect to sex discrimination once the matter, regardless of its sponsor's apparent intentions, was brought to them for a vote. And when Congress adopts any legislation, especially a law with such important ramifications, one must infer a congressional intention that such legislation be effective to carry out its underlying social policy—which in this case is to eradicate every instance of sex-based employment discrimination that is not founded upon a bona fide occupational qualification.

Though the absence of Committee hearings on the sex provisions leaves the courts and the Equal Employment Opportunity Commission, the federal agency created by the Act to process complaints of employment discrimination, without specific guides for resolving difficult problems of interpretation—such as the relationship between those provisions and various state "protective" laws—Congress' general intentions are clear. Given those general intentions, the common law processes of the courts and of the EEOC in exercising its quasi-judicial function may constitute, in the end, the best vehicle for filling out, on a case by case basis, the broad command of the Act's prohibition against sex discrimination in employment. The important point is that for the first time in United States history, an authoritative national agency and the courts have been charged with the responsibility of developing viable equitable principles to govern the employment role of men and women in American society, and opposition to sex discrimination in employment has become official national policy.

The Impact of the "Sex" Provisions

Though born under such questionable circumstances, the prohibition against sex discrimination in employment has proved since 1964 to be much more than the toothless tiger one would have expected. As a matter of fact, the Equal Employment Opportunity Commission reported at the end of its first year of operations that over one-third of its processed complaints had involved charges of sex discrimination.[35] Attorneys have also been encouraged, as a result of the Act, to take cases involving sex discrimination in employment.[36] Several large cases have been settled, including one involving a back pay factor of more than $35,000,[37] and a growing number are being decided by the courts. The volume of litigation under the sex discrimination provisions of Title VII will no doubt also be increased as a result of the recent Supreme Court decision in *Newman v. Piggie Park Enterprises*,[38] holding that a person "who succeeds in obtaining an injunction under [Title II of the 1964 Civil Rights Act] should *ordinarily* recover an attorney's fee unless special circumstances would render such an award unjust."[39]

In issuing its guidelines on sex discrimination, the EEOC, whose first chairman was Franklin D. Roosevelt, Jr., and which is now chaired by Clifford L. Alexander, Jr., has begun to develop a significant body of administrative law whose potential effect upon the daily relations between the sexes will no doubt be profound.[40] Already some past patterns of sex-based job allocations show signs of cracking. Interestingly, such departures from existing employment norms have not always been in the direction of placing women in jobs previously reserved for men. The Act, after all, prohibits "sex" discrimination—and not discrimination against women. By its terms it therefore applies when men are denied a job because the one they seek has traditionally been reserved "for women only." Thus, the telephone company has already hired some males as telephone operators—to the consternation of customers who, upon hearing a male voice respond to their dialing "O," have demanded to speak to "the operator." Similar developments are occurring with regard to the employability of males as airline hosts[41]—although the right of women to be hired as pilots for the commercial airlines will undoubtedly also come up.

Aside from Title VII's specific effects upon disputes arising under it, there are a number of areas in which new legislation and other developments with respect to women's employment opportunities are directly traceable to the mood generated by the passage of Representative Smith's amendment. In 1967, for example, Presidential Executive Order 11246, which since 1965 had established a policy of non-discrimination in government employment, was amended by the addition of "sex" as a prohibited type of discrimination.[42] And still later in the same year, President Johnson signed a law permitting women to now become admirals and generals in the United States Armed Services.[43] State fair employment legislation has also been dramatically affected by the pasage of Title VII. Prior to the 1964 Civil Rights Act, only two states, Hawaii[44] and Wisconsin,[45] had prohibited sex discrimination in employment. By the beginning of 1968, however, 11 other jurisdictions had joined the ranks.[46] Though pressure for such laws undoubtedly antedated the Federal Act in some of the states it is more than a *post hoc, ergo propter hoc* fallacy to suggest that their enactment was probably hastened by the presence of the sex discrimination prohibition in the federal law.[47]

The sex provisions of Title VII have created a momentum in American society for a re-examination of some fundamental assumptions concerning women's role in the traditional family and that larger form of family called society. The ultimate effects of Title VII are still out of sight. For the moment, however, some immediate legal and social problems raised by the passage of the Act may be considered. To do so properly requires a preliminary examination of the scope and administration of the provisions prohibiting sex discrimination in employment.

Scope and Operation of Title VII's "Sex" Provisions

Title VII of the Civil Rights Act covers employers in industries affecting commerce,[48] employment agencies serving such employers,[49] and labor organizations engaged in such industries.[50] It declares that it "shall be an unlawful employment practice" for a covered employer, because of race, color, religion, sex or national origin

> (1) to fail or refuse to hire or to discharge any individual or otherwise to discriminate against any individual with respect to his compensation, terms, conditions or privileges of employment . . . or (2) to limit, segregate, or classify his employees in any way which would deprive or tend to deprive any individual of employment opportunities or otherwise adversely affect his status as an employee. . . .[51]

The Act thus protects the right of persons to obtain and hold a job without regard to these factors, as well as the right to equal treatment once the job has been obtained. In addition, Title VII makes it unlawful for employment agencies to discriminate in their classification or referral practices,[52] and for labor organizations to discriminate on the same grounds in a variety of ways.[53]

An important exception to these "unlawful employment practices" is found in the "bona fide occupational qualification" provisions of section 703(e) of the Act.[54] That section in effect permits employment discrimination based on sex, religion or national origin—but significantly not on race—"in those certain instances where religion, sex, or national origin is a bona fide occupational qualification reasonably necessary to the normal operation of that particular business or enterprise."[55]

The Commission has already held that sex is not a bona fide occupational qualification for the position of flight cabin attendant, and that males may not be denied such employment solely on the grounds of sex.[56] On the other hand, the Commission has recognized that where "it is necessary for the purpose of authenticity or genuineness, [it] will consider sex to be a bona fide occupational qualification, *e.g.*, an actor or an actress."[57] One of the knottiest problems in interpreting the bona fide occupational qualification language of the Act as applied to sex discrimination in employment, however, has been raised by the numerous state "protective" laws for women in employment.

Persons injured by the commission of an "unlawful employment practice" may ultimately procure legal redress from the federal courts.[58] Section 706(e) allows suits by the person claiming to be aggrieved[59] and authorizes the court to permit the United States Attorney General to intervene in cases of "general public importance."[60] Upon finding an intentional unlawful employment practice, the federal courts may enjoin the defendant from engaging in it, and order reinstatement or hiring of employees with or without back pay.[61] The EEOC may initiate a court proceeding on its own only to compel compliance with a previously issued order under the above provisions.[62] If there is a pattern of intentional violations, the Attorney General may also bring a civil action in a federal district court.[63]

Except for the last-named type of suit by the United States Attorney General, which need not be preceded by any EEOC investigation or previous referral to state or local agencies, the lawsuits authorized by Title VII represent the ultimate, or at least the penultimate, stage in the process of correcting the employment discriminations prohibited by the Act. The entire scheme of Title VII is designed to permit the EEOC to attempt to conciliate employment discrimination disputes.[64] No private lawsuits may therefore be brought under the Act until various waiting periods have expired, during which "the Commission has been unable to obtain voluntary compliance" with Title VII.[65] Even the Commission is prevented for prescribed periods from investigating charges on its own[66] or on an aggrieved person's initiative[67] if the alleged unfair employment practices are potentially subject to redress under state or local law.[68]

Despite attempts since the bill was first introduced in the House of Representatives to give the EEOC remedial powers if conciliation failed (that is, to conduct hearings and issue orders), the Commission's power has remained limited to investigating complaints, determining whether reasonable cause exists to believe the allegations, and attempting to conciliate the matter.[69] As a result, court proceedings following the failure of conciliation by the Commission are entirely *de novo,* and nothing "said or done during and as part of . . . [the Commission's conciliation] endeavors may be . . . used as evidence in a subsequent proceeding."[70]

Nevertheless, the Commission's investigations, findings and opinions are important, and under some circumstances attain the force of law. They may, for example, influence the Commission's decision to intervene in an aggrieved person's private suit or to refer a matter for suit by the Attorney General. In addition, good faith reliance upon and conformity with the Commission's written interpretations and opinions constitutes an absolute defense in any action or proceeding based on an alleged unlawful employment practice.[71] Such interpretive rulings have therefore been held to have legal effect,[72] and are important in developing the law of sex discrimination in employment.

Moreover, it is very likely that the Commission's powers will someday be extensively enlarged.[73] In that event, the Commission's decisions could become as authoritative in the area of sex discrimination as those of the NLRB in the field of labor-management relations.

Aside from Commission hearings and rulings and federal court suits, the process of interpreting the equal employment opportunity provisions of the 1964 Civil Rights Act can occur in a number of other procedural contexts. Since the Act makes sex discrimination "unlawful," the question whether particular conduct is covered may come up in state administrative hearings to determine, for example, whether a woman is entitled to unemployment insurance if she has been discharged because of her marriage in violation of a company rule.[74]

Similarly, provisions in collective bargaining agreements limiting job opportunities may be held to be "unlawful" by arbitrators deciding disputes under such agreements. In many cases, moreover, adherence to such union contract provisions may provide a basis for an NLRB determination that a union has committed the unfair labor practice of breaching the duty of fair representation.[75] The NLRB's actual remedy of refusing to consider a racially discriminatory collective bargaining agreement as a contract barring an election,[76] or its potential remedy of decertifying a union[77] that discriminates on the basis of race, now would appear to be available also where the offense is that of sex discrimination. The developing law on sex discrimination in employment must, as a result, be garnered from the work of all of these judicial and quasi-judicial institutions—which should explain the variety of sources relied on in the following discussion.

Title VII and State "Protective" Laws

One of the most difficult questions raised by the sex provisions of Title VII has been their effect on the so-called "protective" laws of the states. These include the widespread minimum wage and maximum hours laws applicable to women only, limitations upon women's working hours and the weight they may lift on the job, as well as other laws, apparently based upon varying legislative notions of "ladylike" and "unladylike" occupations, which occasionally prohibit women from working as bartenders or wrestlers.[78]

The potential conflict between the prohibition against sex discrimination in Title VII and state "protective" legislation for women only is rendered more than ordinarily difficult by the section of the Act which, in effect, permits sex-based employment discrimination where sex is "a bona fide occupational qualification reasonably necessary to the normal operation of [a] particular business or enterprise."[79]

In the light of this provision, the question has arisen, for example, whether an employer who, because state law limits women's working hours, insists upon hiring only men for certain jobs violates the federal Act, or whether adherence to the state hours limitation for women constitutes a "bona fide occupational qualification." Similar questions have arisen with respect to an employer's adherence to state weight-lifting restrictions for women in establishing his hiring or promotional policies, and even with respect to an employer's own weight restrictions not required by state law.

The EEOC has not ignored the likelihood of conflict between federal and state law in this area but has followed a somewhat checkered career in indicating how it would deal with it. The Commission gave its first indication of its approach on November 11, 1965, in issuing its official guidelines on sex discrimination. Significantly, the Commission divided state laws regulating women's employment into two categories: (1) laws providing benefits for female employees, such as rest periods, and (2) those barring women from employment in certain hazardous or strenuous occupations. The Commission expressed its belief that Congress had not intended to disturb laws and regulations intended to, and having "the effect of, protecting women against exploitation and hazard."[80] Consequently, the Commission stated that it would consider limitations or prohibitions imposed by such state laws or regulations as "a basis for application of the bona fide occupational qualification exception."[81]

At the same time, the Commission noted that "some state laws and regulations with respect to the employment of women, although originally for valid protective reasons, had ceased to be relevant to our technology or to the expanding role of the woman worker in our economy."[82] Thus, under its original guidelines, employers who discriminated against women would commit unlawful employment practices though they did so in accordance with the state statute, if that statute did not have the effect of protecting women from exploitation and hazard. Yet, as has been observed, "the Commission did not reveal what laws or types of laws it considered to fall within its test of protection from 'exploitation' or 'hazard'."[83]

The next step was taken on August 19, 1966, when the Commission disclaimed any authority to determine whether Title VII superseded and in effect nullified "a state law which compels an employer to deny equal employment opportunity to women," stating that in such cases it would advise the charging parties of the right to bring suit under section 706(a) of the Act to secure a judicial determination as to the validity of the state law or regulation, reserving the right to appear as *amicus curiae* and to present its views as to the proper construction of the Act.[84]

Finally, on February 21, 1968, after holding public hearings and receiving written statements on the subject from interested persons and organizations, the Commission released new guidelines on the relationship of state "protective" laws to Title VII's bona fide occupational exception to prohibited sex discrimination in employment. Those new guidelines reaffirm the distinction drawn in the first instance between discriminatory and protective state laws, while rescinding the hands-off policy of the 1966 guidelines. Henceforth, "in cases where the effect of State protective legislation appears to be discriminatory rather than protective, the Commission will proceed to decide whether that legislation is superseded by the Act."[85]

In the meantime, a number of lawsuits are pending in which the federal courts are being urged to resolve apparent conflicts between the state labor laws applying to women only and Title VII of the Civil Rights Act.[86] Although two federal district courts have upheld employers' or states' limitations on maximum weights that women may lift on a job,[87] at least one federal district court—in *Mengelkoch v. Industrial Welfare Commission of California*[88] —has adopted an abstention approach to state maximum hours legislation for women that may prove appealing to other federal courts faced with similar questions.

In *Mengelkoch,* the plaintiffs, three female employees of the defendant, North American Aviation, Inc., sued to have California's maximum hours law for women[89] declared unconstitutional as violating the 14th Amendment's equal protection clause or invalid as conflicting with Title VII of the 1964 Civil Rights Act.[90] A three-judge federal court, convened because of the plaintiff's prayer for an injunction against state enforcement of an allegedly unconstitutional state statute,[91] was first dissolved on the ground of the insubstantiality of the constitutional question in the light of settled precedents at the United States and California Supreme Court levels.[92] Then, Federal District Judge Stephens, acting alone, granted the defendants' motion to abstain from deciding the issues in the case on the grounds that "there are serious problems of interpretation and construction of the state law,"[93] that "if the state law in question is in conflict with the Civil Rights

Act of 1964, it would also conflict with . . . provisions of the
California Constitution,"[94] that "[t]he case may be disposed of
on questions of state law and federal constitutional questions
(if they exist) [and] . . . needless conflict with the administration
by the State of its own affairs may be avoided . . . ."[95] The effect
of this decision was that any relief the plaintiffs were entitled to
receive would have to come in the first instance from a state court
rather than a federal court.[96]

That the abstention approach may appeal to other federal
courts when faced with similar issues is not unlikely.[97] In many
respects, this is merely an expression on the federal court level of
the administrative abstention first announced and subsequently
abandoned by the EEOC.[98] The fact of the matter is that the reconciliation of Title VII's prohibition against sex discrimination
in employment and various state protective laws—especially those
prescribing maximum working hours or weight-lifting restrictions
for women only—is extraordinarily difficult. Moreover, as the court
in *Mengelkoch* observed, "[t]he importance of the questions which
are raised by a threat to the validity of laws affecting working wom-
en as a class from the standpoint of the orderly administration of
the law by the state is enormous."[99] It comes as no surprise, therefore, that various tribunals, whether administrative or judicial,
have tended to treat this area as a hot potato and, if the reader
will excuse the mixing of metaphors, to pass the buck.

But eventually some authoritative resolution of this problem
will no longer be avoidable. Whether it will be the state courts,
the federal courts, the EEOC with its limited authority, or even
Congress itself, some arm of government will have to spell out some
day the exact effect of the federal Act upon the state protective
laws.[100] When that is done, the choice will be narrowed to a relatively few alternatives, and it is the purpose of the balance of this
section to evaluate those alternatives with an eye toward recommending those that seem most desirable in the light of all the
circumstances.

Weight-Lifting Limitations for Women

For reasons discussed below, considerations relevant to determining the fate of state- or employer-imposed weight-lifting limits
for women employees are different from those involved in state

maximum-hour legislation, and are therefore discussed separately here.

As noted earlier, two federal district courts have upheld employers' weight-lifting restrictions on women workers in the face of a challenge based on their apparent conflict with Title VII. In *Bowe v. Colgate-Palmolive Company*,[101] the 35 pound weight limit for women was set by the employer itself rather than being required by state law. In *Weeks v. Southern Bell Telephone and Telegraph Company*,[102] it was a state rule limiting the weights that women were allowed to lift on a job to 30 pounds that was upheld.

Although both decisions relied heavily on section 604.1(3)(b) of the EEOC's own Regulations,[103] the *Bowe* case also considered at some length the standards for testing a weight-lifting limitation in the light of Title VII's prohibition against employment sex discrimination and the Act's bona fide occupational qualification provision. Relying heavily on an earlier law review study,[104] the court in *Bowe* in effect adopted the " 'test of reasonableness as developed in the many decisions interpreting the equal protection clause of the Constitution . . . [as a] standard [that] ought to afford some guidelines for business' "[105] in barring women from particular jobs on the ground that sex is "a bona fide occupational qualification reasonably necessary to the normal operation of that particular business or enterprise." As related to state protective laws, therefore, this test would appear to validate such laws that do not run afoul of the equal protection clause, and hold them invalid only if they are so unreasonable as to violate the command of that constitutional provision. But this test seems erroneous for a number of reasons. Aside from the fact that the equal protection guarantee has been interpreted begrudgingly as applied to sex discrimination and has rarely been held applicable in that area, the distinction between a constitutional and statutory provision must be borne in mind. Even if the United States Supreme Court should some day overrule its earlier decisions upholding sex discrimination in the face of a constitutional challenge, the meaning of Title VII would continue to differ from that of the 14th Amendment. What meaning should the EEOC and the courts, therefore, attribute to section 703(e) of he 1964 Civil Rights Act with respect to weight-lifting rules?

Weight-lifting restrictions for women workers, unlike limitations on women's working hours, seem presumptively valid in view of the general differences in strength between the sexes, and the fact that the lifting of heavy weights requires a sudden concentrated effort for which a minimum physical capacity or a great manipulative skill is required. Nor is it feasible in this area to adopt an approach that is suggested below[106] as one of the possibilities with respect to maximum-hour legislation, *i.e.*, extending such limitations to men as well as women. It is an unfortunate fact of economic life that many jobs do require the lifting of heavy weights and, were both men and women barred from such jobs, much of industry would come to a halt.[107] That some general limitation on the weights women may lift on a job is a reasonable restriction is therefore evident.[108]

However, even where a general limitation may be regarded as generally reasonable—50 pounds for example—many individual women may still be capable of lifting such weights, occasionally or regularly, without suffering any ill effects. Rather than being possessed of "extraordinary strength and stamina" as the court characterized such women in *Bowe*,[109] these women may have learned the skills that make it possible to lift heavy weights with relatively little strain. The important point is that for these women who are ready, willing and able to perform the tasks required on a particular job, an employer's own weight-lifting limitation or one prescribed by state law merely has the effect of keeping them from being hired or promoted to a job, in favor of male applicants for the same position—a result that seems directly opposed to the spirit as well as the letter of Title VII.

It is with regard to such women that the distinction between the statutory and constitutional commands becomes important. Whenever possible, the Act should be interpreted so as to make possible the introduction of men or women—or at least the opportunity to be so introduced—to jobs formerly reserved for the other sex only. Reconciliation of the Act, including its above mentioned exception, with a reasonable general statutory or employer-established weight-lifting restriction, could be achieved by holding that the latter merely creates a burden of proof and of persuasion in individual women applicants to show that they can perform the work in question without harmful effects, though such work requires occasional lifting of weights in excess of those permitted by the rule. That burden could be satisfied by a certificate from a family physician or some other testing procedure. While such an interpretation of the Act may create some administrative burdens for employers, the extent of those burdens should not be exaggerated.[110] One cannot overlook the fact that employers are already burdened by a multitude of governmental requirements at the state and federal levels that are deemed necessary for effectuating important social policies.

As noted earlier, the passage of Title VII's sex provisions may have a profound and salutary effect upon the entire tenor of male-female relationships in American society—one that will redound to the benefit of the total society. It is important for the courts, the EEOC, and other interested persons and groups to make the most of this opportunity by interpreting the Act's provisions to bring about those goals.

State Maximum-Hour Legislation[111]

The number of hours women may work in a day or a week is controlled by two types of statutes. One, sometimes applicable to men as well as women, provides for the payment of premium wages for hours worked in excess of a certain maximum. The effects of Title VII and the Equal Pay Act upon such laws, where they prescribe a higher minimum rate than is required under the federal Fair Labor Standards Act and apply only to women, are discussed later in this chapter. The present concern is with those laws prevailing in many states that place an absolute limitation on the number of daily or weekly working hours for women employees. Though such laws sometimes also cover children, they do not at the present time cover male adult employees.

In particular, various alternative approaches to reconciling such laws with Title VII's prohibition against sex discrimination in employment and the bona fide occupational qualification exception are examined and evaluated. Among those alternatives are: (a) to hold all maximum-hour laws for women only totally invalid as conflicting with Title VII; (b) to hold all state maximum-hour laws for women only valid as not being in conflict with Title VII and to do nothing more; (c) to hold such laws valid as not conflicting with Title VII, but to interpret Title VII as requiring the extension of state maximum-hour laws to men also; (d) to provide an ultimate solution to the problem by enacting new federal and state legislation that would make overtime work, for men as well as women, voluntary rather than compulsory.

a. To Hold All Maximum-Hour Laws for Women Only Totally Invalid as Conflicting with Title VII.

This alternative seems highly undesirable. Maximum-hour legislation for women developed only as a legislative response to early judicial indications that maximum-hour legislation for both sexes would not be permitted, a judicial attitude that has since been reversed.[112] While to strike down as conflicting with Title VII all maximum-hour laws for women only may be one way to effectuating Title VII's prohibitions against sex discrimination in employment, it is by no means the only way, and certainly is not as satisfactory as extending such protection to men also in the variety of ways suggested below. For if the concept that employers should be deterred from requiring their employees, male and female, to work longer hours reflects, as it does, enlightened social goals, then it would be a step backward in American social history for even limited expressions of those social goals to be undone.

Unfortunately, limited efforts to achieve these ends have already been undertaken at the state legislative level. Some states have repealed laws prescribing maximum hours for women workers only.[113] The net effect of such developments is that in those states neither men nor women now are protected from excessive employer demands for overtime work, and that the situation has reverted to what it was in the early years of this century when the United States Supreme Court refused to uphold New York's efforts to impose a 10-hour a day limitation on working hours for men and women.[114]

A similar approach seems to have been taken by women plaintiffs in various pending law suits seeking, as a preliminary step to their being hired or promoted to jobs that "require" the working of hours in excess of that maximum, to have state maximum-hour laws declared invalid as conflicting with Title VII or as unconstitutional under the 14th Amendment.[115] Were these plaintiffs to succeed in this effort, however, their "success," like the legislative repeal of maximum-hour laws for women, rather than representing social progress would have to be deplored.

Particularly ironic is the fact that the approach of invalidating state maximum-hour legislation may not be necessary to prevent such laws from thwarting Title VII's promise of equal job opportunity without regard to sex. For, as suggested below, Title VII can be interpreted as requiring an employer to provide equal opportunities for male and female job applicants seeking a position that he believes requires overtime work without invalidating the state maximum-hour laws for women. This could be achieved by holding that, because of Title VII, state maximum-hour laws for women only must now be extended to men also. Were this done, employers could require neither male nor female applicants to work such excess hours—thus removing this apparent justification for hiring or promoting males rather than females, though the latter, in certain cases, are senior in service, are better trained for the position, or have other equities in their favor. At the same time, by extending the maximum-hour limitation to male employees in those states having such a limitation on women's working hours, a long overdue reform in American industrial life finally will have to pass.

b.   Hold all State Maximum-Hour Laws for Women Only Valid as Not Being in Conflict with Title VII.

This, too, seems an undesirable choice, if nothing more is done. Conceivably, this result could be achieved by reasoning that state legislation prescribing maximum hours for women, but not for men, expresses the legislature's reasoned judgment that because of sex-based differences in physical strength, social roles, family responsibilities and the like, separate treatment is reasonable. In effect, this would involve the application of the equal protection test under which certain discriminatory legislation will be upheld as long as it has some reasonable basis, though the members of a reviewing court, had they been legislators rather than judges, would not have enacted such laws themselves. Once the basic legislation is validated, the next step is to hold that an employer, in following such legislation by refusing to hire or promote a woman to a job requiring hours of work in excess of those prescribed by state law, is merely applying a bona fide occupational qualification test to the job in question.[116]

One apparent obstacle to adopting this approach stems from the

1964 Civil Rights Act itself. Section 708[117] provides that "[n]othing in this title shall be deemed to exempt or relieve any person from any liability, duty, penalty or punishment provided by any present or future law of any State or political subdivision of a State, other than any such law which purports to require or permit the doing of any act which would be an unlawful practice under this title."[118]

As one commentator has suggested, however, it is possible to interpret the word "purports" in that section as excluding state statutes that retain "an underlying protective policy pertinent to the modern labor force."[119] But certainly as applied to maximum-hour laws, the effect of such an interpretation without doing anything more, would be to deny employment opportunities to masses of American women. This is by no means to suggest that the sex provisions of the Act would thereby be rendered meaningless and of little effect. There would still be significant areas in which sex discrimination in employment would be an actionable wrong, subject first to the administrative remedies of state agencies and the EEOC, and ultimately to redress in the courts. But much of the Act's potential for reshaping male-female relations in the United States would be weakened substantially were this interpretation to prevail without additional steps being taken.

Is it possible, then, to break out of this impasse? What can responsible administrative agencies, the courts, or Congress do to preserve the social gains in the employment area that have been hammered out over the years, while at the same time fulfilling Title VII's promise and potential for creating true equality of employment opportunity for men and women in the United States?

The answer is not to invalidate state protective laws for women, but rather to extend them wherever possible to men also, and if necessary to enact new laws that will preserve the protective goals of the old ones while eliminating their discriminatory impact. How this might be achieved within present constitutional and statutory limits is considered in the following section.

c. Interpret Title VII as Requiring the Extension of State Protective Laws to Men Also.

While such an approach may provoke some adverse reaction in the states—involving as it does a species of federal intrusion into a state domain, and especially abrasive where it would be effected

by the EEOC rather than the courts—it is not without precedent.
The Equal Pay Act of 1963 provides in part:

> No employer having employees subject to any provisions of this section shall discriminate within any establishment in which such employees are employed, between employees on the basis of sex by paying wages to employees in such establishment at a rate less than the rate at which he pays wages to employees of the opposite sex in such establishment for equal work on jobs the performance of which requires equal skill, effort, and responsibility, and which are performed under similar working conditions, except where such payment is made pursuant to (i) a seniority system; (ii) a merit system; (iii) a system which measures earnings by quantity or quality of production; or (iv) a differential based on any other factor other than sex. . . .[120]

This provision is part of the federal Fair Labor Standards Act which, in section 218, also provides in part:

> No provision of this chapter or of any order thereunder shall excuse noncompliance with any Federal or State law or municipal ordinance establishing a minimum wage higher than the minimum wage established under this chapter or a maximum workweek lower than the maximum workweek established under this chapter, and no provision of this chapter relating to the employment of child labor shall justify noncompliance with any Federal or State law or municipal ordinance establishing a higher standard than the standard established under this chapter.[121]

Combining the effect of these two provisions, the Department of Labor has issued interpretations which state:

> State laws providing minimum wage requirements may affect the application of the equal pay provisions of the Fair Labor Standards Act. If a higher minimum wage than that required under the Act is applicable to a particular sex pursuant to State law, and the employer pays the higher State minimum wage to male or female employees, he must also pay the higher rate to employees of the opposite sex for equal work in order to comply with the equal pay provisions of the Act.[122]

Further:

> [T]he application of the equal pay provisions of the Act may

also be affected by State legal requirements with respect to overtime pay. If as a result of a State law, female employees in an employer's establishment are paid overtime premiums for hours worked in excess of a prescribed maximum in any workday or workweek, the employer must pay male employees performing equal work in such establishment the same overtime premiums when they work such excess hours, in order to comply with the equal pay provisions of the Fair Labor Standards Act. This would be true even though both the male and the female employees performing equal work are otherwise qualified for exemption from the overtime pay requirements of section 7 of the Fair Standards Act. It would not be true, however, unless the overtime requiring the premium pay is actually being worked by the women.[123]

No cases appear to have questioned the validity of these interpretations, and in certain instances, settlements have been worked out benefiting male employees pursuant to their provisions.[124]

If such measures in the minimum wage area can be taken at the administrative level by the Department of Labor,[125] there seems to be no reason why the EEOC could not in the same manner extend to men also those state statutes limiting working hours for women only—provided, of course, that the Commission's action affects only those employers, labor organizations and employment agencies that fall within Title VII's jurisdictional ambit.[126]

How would such an extension to men of a state maximum-hour law, presently applying to women only, actually affect the question of equal job opportunities? It would simply mean that an employer could not invoke the state maximum-hour limitation for women workers as a bona fide occupational qualification permitting him to discriminate arbitrarily against a female job applicant in favor of a male applicant. He could no longer say: (1) The job requires overtime work; (2) State law forbids me to require women to work such overtime hours; (3) But it allows me to require men to do so; (4) Therefore, I will not violate Title VII by arbitrarily assigning the job to the male applicant. Since the extension of the hours limitation to men would mean that the employer could not require male employees to work overtime hours either, he simply could not use that excuse for denying female job applicants equal job opportunities.

Were the EEOC and the federal courts to interpret Title VII as requiring such extension of state maximum-hour laws to men, how are the states likely to react? Ultimately their response will be determined by the types of political pressures exerted upon their respective legislatures. Some, for example, may decide to equalize the situation by repealing present hours limitations for women workers. Though, as indicated in this chapter, such an approach is to be deplored, it is no worse than what has already been undertaken voluntarily by some legislatures or what has been specifically sought by particular women plaintiffs in pending lawsuits. A second approach may be simply to let the extension to males take effect without doing anything more. Certainly, in those states in which a state minimum wage for women has, as a result of the federal Equal Pay Act, been extended to men, no movement for the repeal of the state minimum wage for women appears to have developed. Moreover, in some states the extension of maximum-hour laws to men also may be regarded by the legislatures themselves as a highly desirable move. Though these legislative bodies would probably prefer to take such action themselves, rather than having it imposed upon them as a result of federal law, this will not always be the case; in some instances, this device may even strike the state legislatures as being preferable to their acting on their own. Finally, in some states, neither of the above two approaches will be acceptable because: (1) the repeal of a state maximum-hour law for women will strike them as a step backward; or (2) the extension of the limitation to men will strike them as creating an undue burden on employers in depriving them of the power to require any employees, male or female, to work overtime hours.[127] For them, a third approach, which in many respects is the most desirable, will also be possible. That approach is to enact laws making overtime work voluntary for both sexes. While such a law is also desirable at the federal level, state enactments will be useful to fill in the inevitable jurisdictional gaps in any future federal legislation on the subject.

The approach of extending the protection of the state maximum-hour legislation to men—which can be done initially by the EEOC and should then be ratified by the courts if challenged in individual cases—would have the double virtue of preserving past gains while fulfilling Title VII's promise of equal opportunity in employment, without regard to sex. Of all the approaches considered to this point, this seems by far the most desirable—although it, too, has its problems.[128] Until Congress and the state legislatures act on these fundamental problems, however, extension of state protective laws to men, especially those prescribing maximum hours of employment for women,[129] appears to be a satisfactory reconciliation of Title VII with those protective laws.[130]

d. Ultimate Legislative Action on Permissive Overtime Work.

That the ultimate reconciliation of the maximum hours problem with Title VII may require further congressional or state legislative action on the subject of overtime employment—for men as well as women in industries subject to their regulation—seems likely. As a point of departure in considering legislative needs here, some of the language of the three-judge federal court granting the defendants' motion to dissolve itself in *Mengelkoch* is particularly apt. In that opinion the court stated:

> It has also been pointed out that the abandonment of limitations on working hours for women would place women on an equal basis with men in the matter of overtime pay, but at the same time would also make them subject to the obligation to perform as much overtime work as required of men. This is a mixed blessing. It is not a matter of letting women earn overtime when they want to, but *an obligation to work overtime whether they want to or not on pain of being discharged.* This could result in women being squeezed out of certain industrial work rather than broadening the employment base and opportunity for women in industry. It is not so certain as plaintiffs assume that their position represents the will of many other women, even if similarly situated.[131]

Though these remarks were addressed to the *Mengelkoch* plaintiffs' efforts to invalidate California's maximum-hour law for women only, they, and especially the italicized portion of the above excerpt, are pertinent to a general consideration of the overtime problem.

It is submitted that the current state and national legislation on the subject of overtime employment is entirely inadequate to achieve the apparent aims of such laws to limit the hours of work of covered employees. Except for laws such as those in California and other states,[132] placing an absolute limit on the permissible number of hours in a day or a week that an employer may require to be worked by women only, children only, or at times women and children only,[133] overtime laws, including the wages and hours provisions of the federal Fair Labor Standard Act,[134] merely provide that workers who actually perform work in excess of a designated number of hours must be paid at premium rates, such as one and one-half times the normal rate of pay.[135] These provisions were not enacted to reward workers for their willingness to work excess hours. Rather, they were designed to deter employers from requiring their employees to work such hours. The overtime rates provided for by such laws, rather than being denominated as premium rates, are therefore probably more accurately described as penalty rates, when they are viewed from the perspective of their intended objects—employers as a class. For the idea behind such provisions was that employers, faced with the prospect of having to pay one and a half times as much for each excess hour of work as they would pay for each hour of nonovertime work, would pause before requiring their employees to work such excess hours.

But unfortunately, things have not quite worked out that way. Many employers have found that it is often more economical to pay experienced workers a premium (penalty?) rate than to engage the services of inexperienced workers at straight-time rates to complete a job at hand. When employers have done this, their employees have found that no provisions of the various wages and hours laws afforded them any job protection if they refused to comply with their employers' requests for overtime work.[136] Even under many union-management collective bargaining agreements, refusal to work overtime may be designated as a cause for discharge of an employee.[137]

The net effect is that despite widespread overtime-hours legislation at the state and federal levels, many employees (women as well as men in states not having the California-type statute for women only, and men only in states that do) frequently work 48, 58, and perhaps 68 hours in a given week—a situation not unlike that prevailing at the turn of the century when organized labor was struggling to reduce the 12-hour, 6-day week to a 10-hour, 6-day week.[138] In an era that has seen a growing awareness of the importance of parental supervision—male as well as female—of the youth of our nation, the possibility of this type of prolonged separation between parents and children, and husbands and wives, cries out for legislative correction. Not to speak of the general economic need in an era of galloping automation to distribute available work among all persons in the labor market, rather than to concentrate it in the hands of some at the expense of others.

These goals could be achieved in those states having maximum-hour laws for women only by adopting the approach proposed above,[139] the extension of those laws to men also. But not all states have such laws, and even in those that do, the inability to solicit any overtime work at all may prove a difficult burden for employers.

It is in the light of these considerations that new legislation at the federal and state levels that would represent a compromise approach may be needed. Such legislation would permit both men and women to work a designated number of hours in excess of an established norm, but would provide that no employer subject to the coverage of the law would be allowed to discharge any employee for his or her refusal to work overtime. In at least one state, Arizona, the legislature has made a tentative pass at the approach suggested herein. In 1968, Arizona excepted from its maximum-hour law female employees of employers operating in compliance with the Fair Labor Standards Act, provided that one and one-half times the regular rate is paid for hours over eight in one day, that the employer provides the employee with sufficient notice, and that *"the refusal of overtime by an employee, for just cause or reason, shall not be considered as cause for dismissal."*[140]

The shortcomings in this legislation are at least three. One is the limitation to employees covered by the Federal Act, which leaves out about 30 percent of the female work force.[141] Another is the requirement that the refusal of overtime be "for just cause or reason" in order not to be a cause for dismissal. Aside from the litigation-engendering effect of such a provision, it would seem that refusal to work more than a normal work day or work week is by definition "for just cause of reason" and that no further justification should be required. Finally, though the statute is not entirely clear on this matter, its use of the phrase "an employee" in the context of the entire statute appears to refer only to female employees, thus creating a new arbitrary distinction between the sexes, with the principle of voluntary overtime recognized for women but not for men.

The need is for new legislation by the states and the federal government, each covering the area already within its statutorily allotted jurisdiction, applying equally to employees of both sexes, and permitting hours of work in excess of 40, but in no event in excess of, say, 60. The legislation should also provide that a discharge of an employee for refusal of overtime in excess of 40 hours a week or 8 hours a day would be unlawful, entitling the discharged employee to reinstatement with back pay in a proceeding conducted by the various state and federal agencies already administering wages and hours legislation, and ultimately through court action.[142]

Were such laws to be enacted, the problem troubling the three-judge court in *Mengelkoch* would become moot. Not only would women not have "an obligation to work overtime whether they want to or not on pain of being discharged,"[143] but neither would men. In this manner, the social gains of the past would be preserved, while the opportunities afforded by Title VII will have been seized. In this area at least, the employment situation of men and women will have been equalized, with each having equality of "choice"—a concept that is central to this entire discussion of sex discrimination.

That the states can achieve such goals once they determine to do so is seen in the Arizona legislation discussed above. The feasibility of similar legislation at the federal level can also be demonstrated. For many years, the National Labor Relations Act has forbidden employers to discharge an employee for engaging in any activity protected by section 7 of the Act, such as joining a union or participating in collective action.[144] Recent federal legislation in the consumer protection field has also made it unlawful for an employer to discharge an employee because his wages have been subjected to garnishment for one indebtedness.[145] No constitutional or statutory obstacles would appear to prevent congressional and state enactment of statutes similarly prohibiting employers from discharging an employee for refusal to work overtime.

As suggested above, this may be an ultimate way of solving the problems in this area. Short of that type of solution, however, the one recommended in section (c) above, calling for EEOC or federal court extension of state protective laws for women to men also would go a long way toward creating a nation in which the promise of equal employment opportunity without regard to sex will become a reality for all. In addition to the intrinsic merits of such an extension, it may provide the necessary stimulus to state and federal action on the voluntary overtime legislation suggested herein.

Conceivably, of course, the extension to males by the EEOC and the courts of maximum-hour laws previously applying to women only could, instead of stimulating the enactment of voluntary overtime legislation, induce Congress to repeal the sex provisions of Title VII. This is not likely to happen, however. The growing resort to sex discrimination complaints and lawsuits by aggrieved female members of the work force suggests that the sex provisions of Title VII have struck a responsive chord in masses of American women. Given that response, repeal may simply become politically unthinkable. Professor Sovern has suggested, in connection with Title VII's prohibition against *racial* discrimination, that it is "an irreversible beginning: the Act will never be repealed; it will, rather, be elaborated and improved upon as the political influence of Negroes waxes and resistance to equal employment opportunity wanes."[146] The substitution of the word "women" for "Negroes" in that excerpt would not, it is believed, render that observation any less valid. In any event, this is a risk that must be run if Title VII is to represent, in the field of women's employment rights, an opportunity to forge new gains rather than a justification for undoing those that have been won in the past.

Statutes Barring Women from Specific Jobs

Many state statutes prohibit women from working in certain types of employment, such as bartending, wrestling or mining.[147] Although the United States Supreme Court has sustained such statutes in the past,[148] noting that "The Constitution does not require legislatures to reflect sociological insight, or shifting social standards,"[149] the Court, in the light of the changing jurisprudential climate surrounding this area, could invalidate such discriminations on constitutional grounds in the future. Even should the Court do this, however, the degree of discrimination required to find such a state statute unconstitutional would be higher than that required to find a violation of a statute prohibiting sex discrimination in employment.[150]

Where state statutes barring women from certain employment also regulate industries "affecting commerce," they are also vulnerable to attack under the Title VII—provided, of course, that the jobs from which they bar women are not deemed properly reserved for men only under the "bona fide occupational qualification" provision. It should also be noted—as the converse of the proposition stated in the last paragraph—that although the EEOC and the courts, in construing Title VII, determine that an employer violates the Act by refusing to employ a woman in a job barred to her by a state statute, the statute would not necessarily be deemed unconstitutional in either an intrastate or an interstate factual context.

The EEOC has already indicated how it would deal with some of these laws in a general counsel's opinion letter released on August 23, 1966[151] antedating the Commission's latest pronouncement that it would no longer avoid determining whether state "protective" laws are invalidated by the Act.[152] In the August 23 letter the Commission ruled that a section of a union contract which excludes female employees from working as bartenders violates Title VII "unless a state statute or local ordinance prohibits females from tending bar."[153] Having taken this position with respect to a provision of a union contract, the Commission, unless it subsequently overrules its earlier determination, will be hard pressed to avoid a ruling when it considers the question that state statutes barring women from such jobs also violate the Act. It must be emphasized that the Commission's task is to interpret the statute and not the Constitution. If females cannot, pursuant to the statute, be kept out of bartending by private agreement when a state statute forbids such employment, neither can they be barred by the state statute itself or a local ordinance.

By contrast, the Commission does not appear yet to have had an occasion to state its position on state laws that do not permit women to wrestle or to be licensed to wrestle.[154] No reason appears, however, why this area should be treated any differently than bartending. A recent opinion of the New York Supreme Court, Appellate Division, in *Calzadilla v. Dooley*,[155] has sustained a discriminatory wrestling rule against an equal protection attack, noting that "it is *of interest* that petitioner does not cite section 291 of the [New York] Executive Law which provides that one has a civil right not to be discriminated against because of sex."[156] Petitioner's failure to cite the New York law in *Calzadilla* is not only "of interest," but is also rather inexplicable. While the New York law, like Title VII, deals in terms only with the employment relationship as such, it would also appear to have a spill-over effect in criminal prosecutions or administrative proceedings purporting to enforce statutes that run counter to the policy expressed in the later acts.[157]

Notwithstanding what has been stated in the preceding paragraph, one obvious difference separates bartending from wrestling. While both pursuits run counter to traditional notions of women's social role, wrestling requires a measure of physical arduousness not always present in bartending. The same is true with respect to the occupation of mining which, under the laws of many states, is also barred to women.[158] But this factor should not, of itself, permit the EEOC to rule that such laws survive Title VII. While actual or supposed differences in the physical capacity of men and women to engage in certain jobs may deter many women from applying for such work, they should not be denied this opportunity if they choose it. If, in individual cases, women's greater physical weakness turns out to be actual rather than supposed and if it interferes with their proper performance of a job, this would be a justifiable reason for their not being retained. Employer expense could be avoided, moreover, were applicants for various jobs, male or female, required to take reasonable physical examinations, testing their ability to meet the physical requirements of the job, or to provide a physician's certificate as previously suggested with regard to state weight-lifting restrictions for women workers.[159]

For what must be stressed here, as in this entire area, is the fundamental goal of making choice available to men and women alike. That some women choose a wrestling career is evidenced by the cases upholding statutes or other rules forbidding them this choice and by the actual conduct of wrestling matches between women in other states. The experience during World War II, when the economy was marked by a shortage of industrial manpower, also demonstrated that womanpower was in many cases capable of performing such physically exacting jobs as operating lift trucks in the warehouse and longshore industries, and driving long distance trucks in the transportation industry. The frequency with which women cab drivers and bus drivers are now encountered in many American cities also contrasts sharply with the situation that existed only 25 years ago, when such sights were rare or even non-existent.

To these considerations may be added those suggested in 1968 by the Task Force on Labor Standards of the Citizens' Advisory Council on the Status of Women. Recommending the total repeal of existing laws that prohibit the employment of adult women in certain occupations, the Task Force noted that:

> The justification for these laws is generally premised on the concept that such occupations are considered hazardous or injurious to health and safety. Hazards associated with such work can be eliminated or at least controlled by adequate health and safety regulations applicable to all workers without resorting to absolute occupational prohibitions applicable to women only.[160]

Again, while such laws may still survive attacks on constitutional grounds, the enactment of Title VII's sex provisions provides the EEOC and the courts with an opportunity to strike such laws down where they affect employees covered by the Act.

CHAPTER 5

The Relationship Between The Equal Pay Act of 1963 and Title VII

> "I do not believe sufficient attention may have been paid to possible conflicts between the wholesale insertion of the word 'sex' [in Title VII] and in the Equal Pay Act. The purpose of my amendment is to provide that in the event of conflicts, the provisions of the Equal Pay Act shall not be *nullified.*" Senator Bennett (R. Utah) U.S.E.E.O.C., *Legislative History of Titles VII and XI of Civil Rights Act of 1964* p. 3233 (1969). (Emphasis supplied.)

THE Federal Equal Pay Act was enacted in 1963, one year before passage of the 1964 Civil Rights Act. In contrast to Title VII's prohibition against sex discrimination in employment opportunities, the Equal Pay Act was supported by an extensive legislative history, including elaborate committee hearings demonstrating widespread wage discrimination against women.[1]

The heart of the Equal Pay Act is found in Section 3, adding a new subsection (d) to Section 6 of the Fair Labor Standards Act of 1938 (FLSA), which provides in part that:

> No employer having employees subject to any provisions of this section shall discriminate, within any establishment in which such employees are employed, between employees on the basis of sex by paying wages to employees in such establishment at a rate less than the rate at which he pays wages to employees of the opposite sex in such establishment for equal work on jobs the performance of which requires equal skill, effort, and responsibility, and which are performed under similar working conditions, except where such payment is made pursuant to (i) a seniority system; (ii) a merit system; (iii) a system which measures earnings by quantity or quality of production; or (iv) a differential based on any other factor other than sex: Provided, That an employer who is paying a wage rate differential in violation of this subsection shall not,

in order to comply with the provisions of this subsection, reduce the wage rate of any employee.[2]

The Act also states that labor organizations or their agents shall
not "cause or attempt to cause" covered employers to discriminate
against an employee in violation of the above subsection.[3] Though
the Equal Pay Act became generally effective one year after its date
of enactment, an exception was made in the case of employees
covered by a bona fide collective bargaining agreement in effect
at least 30 days prior to the enactment of the Act. For them the
equal pay amendments were to take effect two years after the date
of enactment or upon the termination of the collective bargaining contract, whichever occurred first.[4] This was presumably designed to allow an opportunity for the adjustment of existing contracts calling for sex-based wage differentials.

As part of the FLSA, the equal pay provisions are subject to
the Act's administrative and enforcement procedures. In addition,
under the FLSA there is a two-year limitation period on actions
for unpaid wages,[5] which, in the case of willful violations, is extended to three years.[6] The FLSA also allows injunction suits to
be brought by the Secretary of Labor[7] and provides criminal penalties for willful violators.[8] It is clear that the remedies for equal
pay violations under the FLSA are more effective than those established under Title VII, the latter being limited to the investigative
and conciliation efforts of the EEOC, with eventual legal action,
where feasible, by the complainant.

Though Title VII of the 1964 Civil Rights Act also applies to
sex-based wage discrimination,[9] it does not replace the earlier Act.
In fact, § 703(h) of Title VII provides in part that it is not an unlawful employment practice under Title VII "for any employer
to differentiate upon the basis of sex in determining the amount
of the wages or compensation paid or to be paid to employees of
such employer if such differentiation is authorized by the provisions of section 6(d) of the Fair Labor Standards Act of 1938, as
amended 29 U.S.C. 206 (d)."[10] The EEOC also has interpreted
Title VII as requiring "that its provisions be harmonized with the
Equal Pay Act . . . in order to avoid conflicting interpretations
or requirements with respect to situations to which both statutes
are applicable,"[11] and has accordingly decided to apply "to equal
pay complaints filed under Title VII the relevant interpretations

of the Administrator, Wage and Hour Division, Department of Labor."[12] Elsewhere, the Commission has stated that section 703(h) "merely incorporates by reference into Title VII the enumerated defenses set forth in the Fair Labor Standards Act (which were added to that Act by the Equal Pay Act of 1963), together with such interpretive rulings thereon as the Wage-Hour Administration has made or may make."[13] The potential dangers to the purpose of Title VII's sex provisions inherent in an undifferentiated adherence to this approach toward the relationship between the two Acts are discussed below.[14] Finally, it should be noted that the Department of Labor, in amending its regulations under the Equal Pay Act, has also taken cognizance of the subsequent enactment of Title VII's sex provisions, and indicated that they are relevant to its own functions.[15]

In many respects, the goal of eliminating sex-based wage discrimination is central to both the Equal Pay Act and Title VII's sex discrimination provisions. While Title VII's scope is in one sense much broader than that of the Equal Pay Act, dealing as it does with equal employment opportunity as well as wage discrimination, much of its thrust with respect to employment opportunity also affects the question of wage discrimination. Thus, a female employee denied an opportunity to be promoted to a higher paying job because state law limits her working hours and her job requires hours of work in excess of that limit, will ordinarily be more disturbed by the loss of the higher pay than by the loss of the opportunity to do the work of the higher paying job.

Although the Equal Pay Act preceded Title VII, some of its provisions, as well as interpretations under it, are relevant to a consideration of the relationship between state "protective" legislation, applicable only to women workers, and Title VII of the 1964 Civil Rights Act. These are considered in this chapter, and the suggestion is made that past interpretations of the Equal Pay Act by the Wage-Hour Administrator of the Department of Labor may need to be revised to harmonize them with the later Title VII, and that such an approach will better serve the ultimate goals of eliminating sex-based discrimination in wages and employment opportunity than any slavish adherence by the EEOC to the earlier interpretations under the Equal Pay Act. Before dealing with that question, however, this chapter will consider some other problems raised by the Equal Pay Act, such as (1) the responsibility of trade unions for wage discrimination; (2) the "establishment" coverage of the Equal Pay Act; and (3) efforts to circumvent the Act by assigning male workers additional duties to justify sex-based wage differentials.

The Responsibility of Trade Unions for Wage Discrimination

Since it is the employer who pays his employees their wages, it is only natural that any statute aimed at eliminating wage discrimination in employment will provide penalties of a civil and criminal nature, as does the Equal Pay Act, for employers who violate its provisions. But as noted earlier, the Act also provides that unions shall not "cause or attempt to cause" an employer to commit a violation.[16]

That numerous collective bargaining agreements contain provisions contravening the principle of equal pay for equal work was recognized by Congress in postponing the effective date of the Act for employees covered by such agreements to permit adjustment of those agreements.[17] But the phrase "cause or attempt to cause" as any student of the law of torts would quickly recognize, is rife with interpretative problems.

The Department of Labor has dealt with part of these problems in its Interpretive Bulletin on the Equal Pay Act, stating that covered labor organizations and their agents

> must refrain from strike or picketing activities aimed at inducing an employer to institute or maintain a prohibited wage differential, and must not demand any terms or any interpretation of terms in a collective bargaining agreement with such an employer which would require the latter to discriminate in the payment of wages contrary to the provisions of section 6(d)(1). Section 6(d)(2), together with the special provision in section 4 of the Equal Pay Act of 1963 allowing a deferred effective date for application of the equal pay provisions to employees covered by specified existing collective bargaining agreements (see § 800.101), are indicative of the legislative intent that in situations where wage rates are governed by collective bargaining agreements, unions representing the employees shall share with the employer the responsibility for ensuring that the wage rates required by such

agreements will not cause the employer to make payments that are not in compliance with the equal pay provisions. . . .[18]

It would thus appear that to avoid running afoul of the Act a labor organization must not make contract demands that violate the principle of equal pay for equal work or engage in collective action to achieve such ends. Where existing contracts provide for sex-based wage discrimination, it would also appear that unions would be well advised at least to communicate publicly to co-contracting employers their understanding that the law now requires the elimination of such discrimination by raising the wages of the lower paid sex to that of the higher paid sex where they are performing "equal work," and that the union is agreeable to this move.

That something more than its silence may be required to find that a labor union has not violated the Act appears in a decision of the Wisconsin Industrial Commission,[19] applying its own state fair employment practices act.[20] Although the latter contains no "cause or attempt to cause" language, it does prohibit labor organizations from discriminating on the basis of sex. Nevertheless, the Wisconsin Commission, though finding that a union discriminated against the female complainants by signing a contract that "established different wage rates on account of sex," held that it "need not be jointly liable for back pay because the record shows it made a valid attempt to eliminate the discriminatory practice of wage differentials."[21] The valid attempt apparently consisted of union proposals, during new contract negotiations, that the same rate be paid to both sexes engaged in similar work—a proposal that had been rejected by the employer.[22]

THE "ESTABLISHMENT" COVERAGE OF THE EQUAL PAY ACT

The Equal Pay Act, in adding subsection (d)(1) to section 6 of the FLSA prohibits sex-based wage discrimination by employers against employees subject to the section, "within any establishment in which such employees are employed . . ."[23] Interpreting this provision, the Department of Labor has stated that

it is clear from the language of the Act that in each distinct physical place of business where the employees of an employer work (including but not limited to, the employer's own establishments), the obligation of the employer to comply with the equal pay requirements must be determined *separately with reference to those of his employees who are employed in that particular establishment.*[24]

The literal terms of the "establishment" provisions and of its interpretation by the Department of Labor would therefore appear to permit an employer to establish a new facility across the street from his present one, place the women employees in the new facility and continue sex-based wage differentials with impunity. For as long as he did not discriminate within the particular establishment, he would presumably not violate the Act.

Indeed, the suggestion has been made that

> application of the law could be avoided where a single establishment is involved by assigning all males to certain operations and all females to other, different operations [and that when] multiple establishments are involved, the same thing could be accomplished by limiting the personnel of particular establishments to one sex.[25]

But the possibility of this type of lawful wage discrimination within a single establishment has been impliedly repudiated by the Department of Labor in one of its regulations, taking cognizance of the passage of Title VII. The Department of Labor has noted that "wage classification systems which designate certain jobs as 'male jobs' and other jobs as 'female jobs' " may contravene Title VII of the Civil Rights Act of 1964 "except where sex is a bona fide occupational qualification."[26]

While not dispositive of the multi-establishment possibility, this regulation does indicate the Department of Labor's understanding that the Equal Pay Act may need to be harmonized with Title VII. Given that understanding, employers would be well advised not to attempt to circumvent the Equal Pay requirements of either Act by the separate establishment device. For though section 703 (h) of Title VII also permits employers to apply different standards of compensation "to employees who work in different locations,"[27] this is qualified by a proviso that such differences must not be "the result of an intention to discriminate" on any of the prohibited grounds.[28] Thus, an employer who sets up a new establishment, or moves his employees around to separate existing establishments so that the same type of work was performed in one by males and in another by females, and maintains a wage differential between establishments, would violate both Title VII and the Equal Pay Act, if his purpose in making these moves was to discriminate because of sex.

Moreover, it would seem, that if under these circumstances the wage discrimination complaint were lodged with the Department of Labor rather than with the EEOC, the Department would be entirely competent in its determining whether the Equal Pay Act had been violated, to first decide whether the provisions of Title VII had been contravened. This would not be a usurpation of the EEOC's jurisdiction nor a violation of congressional intent in devising remedies for Title VII infractions. The Department of Labor would merely be applying the standards of Title VII (and/or interpretations of Title VII by the EEOC and the courts) to the enforcement of the Equal Pay Act, a task entrusted to it when Congress made the equal pay provisions part of the FLSA. This technique has been employed by arbitrators in determining the legality of an employment discrimination clause in a collective bargaining agreement,[29] and by state administrative agencies in trying to decide whether the discharge of a female employee for having married in contravention of a company rule disqualified her from receiving unemployment compensation.[30] No reason appears why such a procedure cannot be equally employed by the Department of Labor in administering the Equal Pay provisions of the Fair Labor Standards Act.

OTHER WAYS IN WHICH THE USE OF TITLE VII CAN CLOSE POTENTIAL LOOPHOLES IN THE EQUAL PAY ACT

Since the setting up of separate establishments may be difficult for most employers, that type of attempted avoidance of the Equal Pay Act—which was shown in the previous section to be preventable by harmonizing the Equal Pay Act with Title VII—is not nearly as serious a possibility for circumventing the Act as the requirement in section 6(d)(1) that the work, for which equal compensation must be paid, be "on jobs the performance of which requires equal skill, effort, and responsibility and which are performed under similar working conditions . . ."[31] The Act's allowance of wage discrimination based on a "system which measures earnings by quantity or quality of production"[32] is also susceptible of abuse unless, in interpreting it, the goals of eliminating employment discrimination expressed in both Acts are constantly kept in mind.

One thing is beginning to emerge very clearly from the regulations of the Department of Labor and some of the federal court opinions in sex-based wage discrimination cases. No longer will an employer be allowed to pay employees of one sex (which in the cases have usually been males) a higher wage rate than employees of the other sex, if the extra job effort, skill or responsibility of the former is only slight or occasional or insubstantial.[33]

Where such differences are substantial, however, a number of federal court cases have recognized them as a basis for sex-based wage discrimination presumably permitted by the Equal Pay Act. Thus in *Wirtz v. Dennison Mfg. Co.*,[34] male machine operators on the third shift were permitted to be paid at a higher base rate than female machine operators on the first and second shifts, on the ground that 10 percent of the time worked on the third shift required additional duties over those required of women on the first two shifts. Similarly in *Kilpatrick v. Sweet*,[35] a higher wage rate for a male employee was upheld on the basis of "substantial differences in terms of skills and responsibility between the jobs performed by" the male employee and the female plaintiff.[36]

The problem with these cases is that they give very little attention to the circumstances under which these jobs were assigned to the male or female employees in the first place. Widespread employment opportunity and wage discrimination had obviously existed in American life prior to the enactment of the two Acts under consideration here. How many American women now work at jobs requiring little skill or responsibility,[37] not because they are incapable of acquiring the skill or assuming the responsibility of higher paying jobs, but because, in the past, they have been denied the opportunity to do so by the discriminatory practices of employers, labor organizations and employment agencies? For the Act to permit wage discrimination on the basis of differences in skills or responsibility without allowing an examination of the reasons for those differences may have the effect of destroying much of its effectiveness.

To avoid that result, the harmonization of the Equal Pay Act with Title VII is once again crucial. Section 703(h) of Title VII permits wage discrimination based on "quantity and quality of production" but this exception is subject to the qualification that it not be "the result of an intention to discriminate because of" the prohibited grounds, including sex.[38] It would appear that the limitation periods for actions under both Acts can be observed by the agencies and the courts by restricting recoveries to the period allowed (since the wage discrimination would have occurred within that limitation period) but by looking as far back as necessary to determine whether the present wage discrimination occurring within the limitation periods of either or both Acts is the result of past discriminatory conduct with respect to employment opportunity.[39]

This suggested approach will, of course, have to overcome the inevitable claim that Title VII's provisions can in no sense be applied retroactively. Conflicting views on this question have already been expressed. For example, the Supreme Court's decision in *Hamm v. City of Rock Hill*,[40] that Title VII of the 1964 Civil Rights Act abated convictions of civil rights workers for engaging in lunch counter sit-ins has been characterized as giving "a certain retroactive effect to the Civil Rights Act."[41] By contrast, a recent federal district court opinion in *United States v. Local 36, Sheet Metal Workers International Association*,[42] has held in an Attorney General's "pattern or practice" suit that "discriminatory actions and conduct which occurred prior to the [effective date of the Civil Rights Act, July 12, 1965] cannot constitute a violation of the Act.[43] In so holding, the court stressed the Interpretative Memorandum on Title VII by Senators Clark and Case, which stated that the effect of the title was "prospective and not retrospective."[44] However, this observation was made by the senators only with reference to seniority rights between employees themselves and solely as those rights affected the question of layoffs or firing. Threfore, an employer who had been discriminating in the past "would not be obliged—or indeed, permitted—to fire whites in order to hire Negroes, or to prefer Negroes, or, once Negroes are hired, to give them special seniority rights *at the expense of the white workers hired earlier.*"[45] Presumably, the senators would have also included the word "males" along with "whites" and the word "females" along with "Negroes" had they been addressing themselves, at the time they prepared their memorandum, to the subject of sex-based discrimination. But this would not dispose of the question as to whether an employee who had been the victim of *wage* discrimination ultimately stemming from a prior employment opportunity discrimination would now be entitled to have the wage discrimination corrected, bearing in mind that the correction would not require—nor would it be permitted under the Equal Pay Act—the reduction of the male employees' wage scale. In effect, the employer, whose past conduct had created the situation, would bear the entire financial cost of correcting it. (Employers would also have new incentives for promoting women to higher paying job classifications, since under the above proposal, women who could prove that they had been previously discriminated against with respect to job opportunities would be entitled to the pay rates of the higher job classification, though they continued to work in the lower job classification).

Among other ways, this could be achieved by resorting to the time-honored device (which, in this case, is probably more fact than fiction) of the continuing wrong, *i.e.,* that the initial discrimination is, in effect, repeated every day and moment of the employees' relationship with the employer. Restricting the recovery of wages to the limitations period following the effective date of Title VII would, moreover, preserve the prospective thrust of that legislation, though the initial employment opportunity discrimination producing the wage discrimination might have occurred prior to its enactment.

Moreover, it is not even absolutely necessary, in order to achieve these goals, for the Department of Labor to refer to the provisions of Title VII. For the Equal Pay Act generally allows wage discrimination "based on any other factor than sex."[46] Interpreting this provision, the Department of Labor has held that the requirements for exceptions to the equal pay standard "are not met unless the factor of sex *provides no part of the basis* for the wage differential."[47] Although this provision and its interpretation appear to collide head-on with the Act's exceptions based on skill, responsibility, etc., they can be reconciled by a holding that higher rates for men (or women) on jobs requiring higher skills, responsibility, etc., are permissible, unless the lower paid employee can show that, at any time, she or he was denied an opportunity, on grounds of sex alone, to be employed on that job.[48]

The Meaning of "Effort"

The Act's exception for differences in effort required on the job, though sharing some of the same attributes as the exceptions based on skill, responsibility and working conditions, is sufficiently dissimilar to warrant separate treatment. As has been suggested earlier in this essay,[49] the *general* differences in the physical stamina of the sexes, subject to exceptions in individual cases, must be conceded. Thus, on many jobs in which men are being paid higher wages than women because greater physical effort is apparently required,[50] most women have not wanted or sought an opportunity to be so employed.[51] Where, in individual cases, a woman has sought and been denied the opportunity to be employed in such a job, however, this fact could serve as a basis for a wage discrimination finding.

Recognizing these physical facts, the EEOC has held that an employer might, without violating Title VII, adopt physical standards (not sex standards) reasonably related to a job "even though the standards might operate to exclude a disproportionate number of one sex."[52]

But whether additional physical effort justifies additional pay will not always be a simple matter to determine. Discussing the exception of differences in working conditions, for example, the Department of Labor's Interpretive Bulletin suggests that account must be taken of whether they are the kind customarily taken into consideration in setting wage levels.[53] The same test would appear properly to apply to wage differentials based on differences in physical effort. But aside from the need to ascertain that custom itself has not been the product of sex discrimination,[54] much evidence suggests that industry has not always rewarded greater physical effort with higher pay. Indeed, physical effort has frequently been less highly rewarded than the factors of skill or responsibility in employment. Before particular instances of wage discrimination are therefore permitted on the basis of greater physical effort, custom in the industry and enterprise must be closely scrutinized.

There is still another possible interpretation of the phrase "effort" in the Equal Pay Act that may limit its potential for circumventing the principle of equal pay for equal work. If there are general differences in the physical strength of men and women, the amount of effort required by males generally to lift, let us say, 60 pounds may be no greater than the amount of effort expended by females generally in lifting 25 pounds. The important question is the relative effort expended by each worker. Were this interpretation to prevail, wage differences between the sexes would be permitted only on the basis of extreme differences in physical effort, provided that such effort were customarily rewarded in the particular enterprise or industry with higher pay rates than those received by either women or men who were not required to exert such efforts on their own job.

This suggested interpretation of the word "effort," moreover, would not have the result of requiring the same wage rates for the sexes though they were in work requiring a different degree of mental exertion. For, as suggested in an earlier footnote, the discussion here has been confined to the matter of physical effort, as opposed to mental effort.[55] The two are further distinguishable in that, although mental capacity may vary tremendously between individuals of the same sex, there is a general difference in physical capacity between men as a group and women as a group. Nor would this interpretation of the word "effort" as applied to physical exertion be prevented by the provision of the Equal Pay Act permitting a system of compensation "which measures earnings by quantity or quality of production,"[56] since the interpretation of that phrase could incorporate the interpretation of "effort" suggested above.

What must be stressed is that the words "skill, effort, responsibility, and similar working conditions" should not be interpreted to weaken the Act's stated purpose of eliminating sex-based wage discrimination. The interpretation of these phrases suggested herein may be one way to prevent that from happening.

THE EQUAL PAY ACT AND STATE "PROTECTIVE" LAWS

The difficulties in reconciling so-called state protective laws for women only with the bona fide occupational qualification of Title VII of the 1964 Civil Rights Act have been explored in Chapter 4. The present inquiry seeks to determine whether the legislative history or the text of the Equal Pay Act or administrative interpretations and court decisions under it shed any light on that problem. That the two Acts are related is evident from the reference in section 703 (h) of Title VII to the earlier Equal Pay Act,[57] the EEOC's administrative deference to the Equal Pay interpretations of the Wage-Hour Administrator of the Department of Labor,[58] and the reference in at least one of those interpretations to the sex provisions of Title VII.[59]

The interpretations will be considered first. Section 800.183 of the Department of Labor's Interpretive Bulletin provides:

> In making a determination as to the application of the equal pay provisions of the Fair Labor Standards Act, legal restrictions in State or other laws upon the employment of individuals of a specified sex, with respect to such matters as hours of work, weight-lifting, rest periods, or other conditions of such employment, will not be deemed to make otherwise equal work unequal or be considered per se as justification for an otherwise prohibited differential in wage rates. For example, under the Act, the fact that a State law limits the weights which women are permitted to lift would not justify a wage differential in favor of all men regardless of job content. The Act would not prohibit a wage differential paid to male employees whose weight-lifting activities required by the job involve so significant a degree of extra effort as to warrant a finding that their jobs and those of female employees doing similar work do not involve equal work within the meaning of the Act. However, the fact that there is an upper limit set by State law on the weights that may be lifted by women would not justify a wage differential to male employees who are not regularly required to lift substantially greater weights or expend the extra effort necessary to make the jobs unequal. The requirement of equal pay in such situations depends on whether the employees involved are actually performing "equal work" as defined in the Act, rather than on legal restrictions which may vary from State to State.[60]

While at first blush, this passage appears to reject wage differentials based upon restrictions under state "protective" laws, a close reading reveals that it does not do this at all. This interpretive regulation merely holds that state protective laws will not be recognized as a justification for a sex-based wage differential where men and women are performing similar work. Where the work is dissimilar, however, (as where men do lift substantially greater weights than women), the differential is allowable. But on the crucial question as to whether males may be paid a differential for lifting greater weights than women, if the reason for this state of facts is the state restriction on weight-lifting for women, the regulation is ambiguous. Though it does not explicitly concede that it would be permissible under these circumstances, the entire context of this regulation strongly implies that it would. Some support for the proposition that state maximum-hours legislation for women may have been intended to serve as a permissible basis for sex-based wage differentials where there was, because of such laws, a difference in the actual hours worked, also appears from an isolated and questionable item of legislative history of the Equal Pay Act.[61]

The thrust of this interpretive regulation and this item of legislative history would therefore be to approve generally the principle of state protective laws, and to allow sex-based differentials where work is divided between male and female employees on the basis of what is allowable under these laws. If, therefore, the command of section 703 (h) to permit wage differentials that are allowed under the Equal Pay Act is interpreted, as it has been, to require the EEOC to accept the interpretations of the Wage-Hour Administrator in determining whether sex-based discrimination has occurred under Title VII, all state protective laws for women would survive Title VII's prohibition against sex discrimination in employment —certainly in the area of wage discrimination and, logically, also in the realm of employment opportunity discrimination. But as will be demonstrated below, compelling reasons militate against such a mechanical interpretation of section 703 (h) and the Department of Labor's interpretations.

There is still another item of legislative history behind the Equal Pay Act of 1963 that may have some bearing on the continued viability of state "protective" laws. The Senate Report on the Equal Pay Bill[62] suggests that there was no intention to invalidate wage-rate differentials based on hazardous or objectionable work even though there incidentally might be a division on sex lines. This may have been the source of the later guidelines by the EEOC stating that state laws protecting women against exploitation and hazard would be honored.[63] But it is one thing to say that a wage differential may be paid for hazardous work actually performed, and it is quite a different thing to hold that state laws denying women the opportunity to work on such jobs should they choose to do so, and provided that they can perform the duties, are also valid—unless such laws are validated by the previous item of legislative history and the Wage-Hour Administrator's interpretation discussed above.[64]

It is submitted that this isolated bit of legislative history, and the Administrator's interpretation of the relationship between state-protective legislation and the Equal Pay Act, should, in the light of specific language in the Act itself and other interpretations by the Administrator, not be followed. The specific language of the Act referred to is that provision of section 6(d)(1) permitting wage differentials "based on any other factor than sex."[65] The Administrator of the Department of Labor has interpreted this provision stringently, stating that the requirements for an exception to the Act's prohibition of sex-based wage discrimination "are not met *unless the factor of sex provides no part of the basis for the wage differentials.*"[66] Elsewhere, the EEOC has noted that the "principle of non-discrimination in employment requires that applicants be considered on the basis of individual capacities and not on characteristics generally attributed to a group."[67]

Taking these provisions together, it is very doubtful that a state law restricting women's working hours or weights to be lifted on a job, without taking into account the individual capacities of particular women, can be said to be a law in which the factor of sex plays no part. If, then, sex-based differences in actual work performed, which are in turn based upon restrictions in such laws, produce differences in pay, it would appear that the Wage-Hour Administrator, as well as the EEOC, would be required to hold such pay differences unlawful under either Act. For the Department of Labor this would mean repudiating any implication in its regulation, section 800.163, that such state laws were all necessarily valid, regardless of the individual ability of particular job applicants. This repudiation would flow from the terms of the Equal Pay Act itself prohibiting wage discrimination based upon sex, and the Administrator's own interpretation of that prohibition.[68] Above all, it would require the harmonization of the Equal Pay

Act with the later sex provisions of Title VII in the manner suggested in the preceding pages.[69]

For the EEOC, the reconciliation of state protective laws with Title VII requires, among other things, resisting a mechanical application of section 703(h), since, to apply that provision uncritically could result in blanket approval of all state protective legislation regardless of its impact on equal employment opportunity for male and female workers. To avoid such a result, the EEOC's position should be that section 703(h) requires it, as well as the Labor Department, to allow wage differentials where they are truly based on differences in skill, effort, responsibility, working conditions, and the like—provided that placement in such jobs was not the result of a past denial of equal employment opportunity, regardless of when that might have occurred.

Both agencies can also follow the same path they have taken with respect to state minimum wage laws, and hold as applicable to men many of the state protective laws presently worded to apply to women only. Where, as in the area of weight-lifting restrictions for women only, they might not choose to do this, they can at least interpret such state laws in the light of their respective Acts as requiring that individual women be permitted to demonstrate that they can lift heavier weights than those permitted by the respective state statutes, without harmful effects. Finally, on the question of maximum-hour legislation, each can begin to engage in lobbying activities addressed to Congress and the states for the enactment of laws making overtime work for both sexes voluntary rather than compulsory.

Conclusion

The sex provisions of the 1964 Civil Rights Act came into being in a most unusual way. Individual members of Congress may have had different reasons for voting them into law. Some may have hoped that it would cause the collapse of the whole gamut of federal equal employment legislation, others may have sincerely wished to extend the Act's guarantees to women as well as to racial, religious and ethnic groups. Some may have been convinced of the need to do this by the testimony adduced in connection with the Equal Pay Act of 1963, others may have sensed that in the light of increasing agitation for corrective legislation by women's groups and their male allies, political expediency required an affirmative vote. Some may have thought about the effects of the Act on state "protective" laws, others—probably most—did not think about this problem at all. But when all is said and done, Title VII is with us and is here to stay.

As for the Equal Pay Act, though its legislative enactment proceeded more deliberately than Title VII's sex provisions, the sheer number of exceptions and qualifications in the Act have created the danger of evasion by those covered by it.

These last two chapters have attempted to show some ways in which the promise of these two important pieces of legislation can be realized without sacrificing the important social gains that have been achieved over the years, or creating a situation in which meaningful individual differences can no longer be separately rewarded in American industry. The ways of doing this suggested herein may not be the only ones. The important point is that the enactment of these two federal laws marks an important stage in the development of healthful relations between the sexes in the United States. Not only must every effort be exerted to guarantee that this legislation will not be undone, but it must be assured that the maximum gains for the principle of equal treatment be achieved under these existing laws. Once set in motion, the principle of sexual equality may not this time, as it did after the adoption of the 19th Amendment to the United States Constitution, become only a memory for a few. Instead, it may become a goal towards which all Americans, male and female, will strive for the greater good of the nation and the peace of the world.

CHAPTER 6

Constitutional Aspects of Sex-Based Discrimination in American Law

> "Our cases hold that people who stand in the same relationship to their government cannot be treated differently by that government. To do so . . . would be to treat them as if they were, somehow, less than people." Mr. Justice Fortas, dissenting in *Avery v. Midland County, Texas*—U.S.—.88 S. Ct. 1114, 1127, n. 2 (1968).

> "The Constitution does not require things which are different in fact or opinion to be treated in law as though they were the same." Mr. Justice Frankfurter in *Tigner v. Texas*, 310 U.S. 141, 147 (1940).

Eᴀʀʟɪᴇʀ ᴄʜᴀᴘᴛᴇʀꜱ in this book have demonstrated that American law, whether in the shape of legislation, court decisions or administrative action, continues in many instances to accord men and women different treatment solely because of sex.[1] Such differences in treatment have often been challenged in the courts as alleged violations of state or federal constitutional provisions. But for the most part, these constitutional attacks have met with failure, leading to, among other things, persistent pressure for a federal constitutional amendment that would specifically prohibit legal discrimination based on sex (the so-called "equal rights" amendment).

In recent years—no doubt partly due to a general rekindling of interest in the status of women in society and the emergence of positive corrective legislation in the field—constitutional challenges of laws that discriminate on grounds of sex have increased. There are many indications in fact that reliance upon existing constitutional provisions as a basis for attacking many expressions of sex-based legal discrimination is no longer as fruitless an approach as it may have been in the past.

The purposes of the present chapter are, therefore, three: (1)

To describe and analyze leading decisions that have disposed of constitutional attacks upon laws that discriminate on the basis of sex; (2) To discern the current developments in this area, including a forecast of the shape of things to come; and (3) To consider the desirability *vel non* of the proposed equal rights amendment.

OLD AND NEW CASES

In reviewing judicial decisions dealing with constitutional attacks upon sex-discriminatory laws, separate consideration of cases decided before and after 1963 seems advisable. For in that year, the Committee on Civil and Political Rights of the President's Commission on the Status of Women published its report which included the following recommendation:

> . . . Notwithstanding doubts generated by some earlier decisions, the Committee believes [the] principle of equality [of rights under the law for all persons, male or female,] is implicit in the 5th and 14th amendments to the United States Constitution which guarantee to all persons due process and equal protection of the laws without arbitrary discrimination. It is confident, in the light of recent developments, that they will be interpreted by the courts today to give full recognition to this principle.
>
> The Committee . . . urges interested groups to give high priority to uncovering and challenging by court action [existing] discriminatory laws and practices. . . .[2]

Since 1963, the increasing resort to constitutional challenge of a variety of sex-based discriminatory laws, many not having been challenged on constitutional grounds before, suggests that the committee's exhortation may have been heeded by interested groups and persons. The enactment of 1963 of the federal Equal Pay Act and in 1964 of a prohibition against sex discrimination in employment in Title VII of the 1964 Civil Rights Act may also have stimulated attorneys and clients to consider constitutional attacks on a broad range of sex-based discriminatory laws. Finally, unlike the situation in prior years, a growing number of post-1963 decisions have either sustained such constitutional challenges or have included vigorous dissenting opinions urging that they should be sustained.

THE PRE-1963 CASES

Looking first, then, at the cases decided before 1963, we find that as a general rule differences in legal treatment of the sexes had for many years survived a variety of challenges,[3] invoking the privileges and immunities clause,[4] the equal protection clause[5] and the due process clause[6] of the United States Constitution.

Thus, it had been held that a statute requiring a husband to consent to a wife's will depriving him of more than two-thirds of her estate did not violate the equal protection guarantee though the husband could make such disposition without the wife's consent;[7] that a law providing that only resident voters could protest the annexation of their property by a municipality was consistent with the equal protection guarantee though women, not privileged to vote at the time, could not protest such annexation;[8] that, prior to the adoption of the Nineteenth Amendment, since the right of suffrage was not one of the privileges of United States citizenship, a state could deny women the right to vote;[9] and that the states could constitutionally prevent women from selling intoxicating beverages[10] or from serving as jurors.[11] Even a state constitutional provision guaranteeing to "both male and female citizens" the equal enjoyment of "all civil, political and religious rights and privileges"[12] has been held not to prohibit a road poll tax imposed on men only, since sex-based classification had "always been made, and, unless prohibited in express terms in the Constitution . . . is a natural and proper one to make."[13] Nor has a state constitutional command that "No person shall, on account of sex, be disqualified from entering upon or pursuing any lawful business, vocation, or profession" been sufficient to prevent the state from barring a woman from "mixing" drinks in an establishment where she is neither the on-sale licensee nor his wife.[14]

The underlying social and legal attitudes of the courts in these cases are perhaps best illustrated by the concurring opinion of Mr. Justice Bradley in *Bradwell v. the State*,[15] a United States Supreme Court case holding that women could constitutionally be denied a license to practice law on the mere grounds of their sex. In Justice Bradley's view,

> Man is, or should be, woman's protector and defender. The natural and proper timidity and delicacy which belongs to the

female sex evidently unfits it for many of the occupations of civil life. The constitution of the family organization, which is founded in the divine ordinance, as well as in the nature of things, indicates the domestic sphere as that which properly belongs to the domain and functions of womanhood. The harmony, not to say identity, of interests and views, which belong, or should belong, to the family institution is repugnant to the idea of a woman adopting a distinct and independent career from that of her husband.

* * *

The paramount destiny and mission of woman are to fulfill the noble and benign offices of wife and mother. This is the law of the Creator. And the rules of civil society must be adapted to the general constitution of things, and cannot be based upon exceptional cases.[16]

Such candid expressions of belief in a divinely ordained order of things in which, when all is said and done, a woman's place was in the home, were rare, however, in constitutional litigation. But unfortunately for the later history of sex-based discriminatory laws, the 1908 decision of the United States Supreme Court in *Muller v. Oregon,*[17] and particularly some language in that case that was unnecessary to the decision, has often been invoked by the courts in upholding a wide variety of such laws.

The *Muller* case, perhaps known best for the introduction of the "Brandeis brief," concerned the validity of Oregon's law limiting the hours of work for female factory employees to 10 a day. That law was challenged, by an employer who had been convicted of violating it, as contravening the due process and equal protection guarantee of the Fourteenth Amendment. In response to that attack, the Supreme Court first approved its earlier decision in *Lochner v. New York*[18] invalidating a New York law—which had provided that no worker, male or female, could be required or permitted to work in bakeries more than sixty hours in a week or ten in a day—on the ground that the law was not, "as to men, a legitimate exercise of the police power of the state, but an unreasonable, unnecessary, and arbitrary interference with the right and liberty of the individual to contract in relation to his labor, and as such was in conflict with, and void under, the Federal Constitution."[19]

In *Muller,* however, the Oregon statute, which was similar to the New York law in most respects except that it applied to female workers only, was upheld because of the discerned differences between the sexes. In the court's words:

The two sexes differ in structure of body, in the functions to be performed by each, in the amount of physical strength, in the capacity for long-continued labor, particularly when done standing, the influence of vigorous health upon the future well-being of the race, the self-reliance which enables one to assert full rights, and in the capacity to maintain the struggle for subsistence. *This difference justifies a difference in legislation,* and upholds that which is designed to compensate for some of the burdens which rest upon her.[20]

As suggested elsewhere in this chapter, there is a serious question whether the *Muller* case would be decided today in the same way. New constitutional standards that have since been evolved to test, for equal protection and/or due process purposes, a statutory abridgment of "basic" civil rights would perhaps require, for a *Muller*-type statute to survive today, a greater justification for the interference with the "basic" right to work than the Court found sufficient in that case. Indeed, it is possible that where they apply to women only such statutes may in the future be required to be extended to men either by the Supreme Court itself, under the principles discussed on pages 182 to 188 in this chapter, or by the Equal Employment Opportunity Commission, where Title VII of the 1964 Civil Rights Act applies.

But for the time being at least, *Muller* represents "good law." Aside from its holding, however, the case is of special importance for some language it contains. The Court in *Muller* simply could not resist giving expression to some old-fashioned male supremacist notions. While rising to a greater level of sophistication than Mr. Justice Bradley's observations in the *Bradwell* case, the words of Mr. Justice Brewer in *Muller v. Oregon* have continued to plague later constitutional litigation over a broad range of sex-based discriminatory laws. As he saw it,

[H]istory discloses the fact that woman has always been dependent upon man. He established his control at the outset by superior physical strength, and this control in various forms, with diminishing intensity, has continued to the present. As minors, though not to the same extent, she has been looked upon in the courts as needing especial care that her rights may be preserved. . . . Though limitations upon personal and contractual rights may be removed by legislation, there is that in her disposition and habits of life which will operate against a full assertion of those rights. . . . *Differentiated by these matters from the other sex, she is properly placed in a class by herself, and legislation designed for her protection may be sustained, even when like legislation is not necessary for men, and could not be sustained.* It is impossible to close one's eyes to the fact that she still looks to her brother and depends upon him. Even though all restrictions on political, personal, and contractual rights were taken away, and she stood, so far as statutes are concerned, upon an absolutely equal plane with him, it would still be true that she is so constituted that she will rest upon and look to him for protection. . . .[21]

From this language has been extracted the principle that "sex is a valid basis for classification," a principle that is often repeated mechanically without regard to the purposes of the statute in question or the reasonableness of the relationship between that purpose and the sex-based classification. The subsequent reliance in judicial decisions upon the *Muller* language is a classic example of the misuse of precedent, of later courts being mesmerized by what an earlier court had *said* rather than what it had *done*. For though *Muller* was concerned only with a protective labor statute which took account of the general physical differences between the sexes, it has been cited, as Murray and Eastwood point out, in cases "upholding the exclusion of women from juries, differential treatment in licensing various occupations and the exclusion of women from state supported colleges."[22]

SOME ANALYTICAL APPROACHES

The problem with the formulation, "sex is an allowable basis for classification," is simply that it is too broad in its sweep. Granted that general physical differences between the sexes can be demonstrated, these should not automatically justify laws that distinguish between the sexes on the basis of non-physical differences, or those based upon physical differences that do not take into account the many technological developments that have substantially minimized or eliminated the practical significance of those differences, or those that do not make provision for the many individual men or women whose physical limitations and strengths do not conform to the general pattern.

The logical infirmities of the doctrine of "classification by sex" have been pointed out in a seminal article by Murray and East-wood.[23] Suggesting that the doctrine has "implications comparable to those of the now discredited doctrine of 'separate but equal' " and should therefore also be declared unconstitutional, they have urged the substitution of a functional analysis as the proper test for determining whether laws treating the sexes differently are valid under the Fifth and Fourteenth Amendments. They have also noted that

> If laws classifying persons by sex were prohibited by the Constitution, and if it were made clear that laws recognizing functions, *if performed,* are not based on sex per se, much of the confusion as to the legal status of women would be eliminated.[24]

Thus, under the functional analysis, courts would no longer be able to uphold laws that distinguish between the sexes merely by repeating the *Muller* shibboleth that the general differences between the sexes "justifies a difference in legislation," since to do so would violate the Fifth and Fourteenth Amendments, as the President's Commission on the Status of Women has urged the United States Supreme Court to reinterpret the application of those amendments to laws that classify on the basis of sex.[25] Nor would there be any need to adopt the proposed equal rights amendment, which provides that "equality of rights under the law shall not be denied or abridged by the United States or by any State on account of sex,"[26] since the same, perhaps better, results could be achieved by reinterpreting the Fifth and Fourteenth Amendments.

The functional analysis proposed by Murray and Eastwood appears to be a necessary first step for the development of tests to determine the constitutional validity of laws that, directly or indirectly, accord men and women different treatment in what appear to be highly similar circumstances. This analytical starting point not only rejects the shop-worn legal slogan, "sex is a reasonable basis for classification," that has produced so much judicial misunderstanding in the past, but also requires lawmakers (courts as well as legislatures) to carefully examine the differences between male and female characteristics as related to particular legislative goals.

At the same time, it is unclear whether the suggested functional approach requires the recasting of present statutes and judge-made rules of law to eliminate any reference to sex, or whether such references to sex would not per se invalidate the rule or statute, with the functional inquiry being invoked merely to test their ultimate constitutionality. For example, would state statutes prescribing maximum working hours for women, but not for men, be *ipso facto* unconstitutional? Or would they be valid if, instead of referring to women as such, they declared that any person for whom more than eight hours of work in a day or 48 hours in a week would be harmful could not be required to work such excess hours, and perhaps created a presumption of harmfulness if that person were a woman? Or could the reference to sex remain in such statutes, with their constitutionality determined by the reasonableness of their application, via the functional analysis, to particular persons in specific circumstances?

The proposed test does not purport to be either the only or a complete approach to the constitutional analysis of sex-based discriminatory legislation. For one thing, there are many situations in which the general attributes of one sex or the other may themselves be the functions needing to be considered. For example, there can be very little argument with the proposition that, as a general rule, males are physically stronger than females. Legislation taking account of those differences will therefore continue to be constitutionally valid, provided that such legislation is not founded upon an exaggerated notion of the extent of those physical differences. Utah's 15-pound limitation upon the weights that women are permitted to carry on a job[27] may be so unreasonable an appraisal of women's general physical capacity as to violate the equal protection guarantee if, as is the case, a similar restriction does not also apply to men. By contrast, the 50-pound limitation in California[28] may be constitutionally valid, though individual women will have little difficulty or suffer no harmful effects in lifting weights in excess of such limits.[29]

Moreover, because the right to work may be properly characterized as "basic," a state abridgment should be upheld only if it goes no further than is absolutely necessary to achieve the legislative purpose. For example, statutory weight-lifting restrictions, to survive constitutional challenges, may have to be worded or interpreted as establishing merely a presumption of women's inability to lift weights in excess of the limit without harmful effects, while providing them with the right to rebut that presumption. Nor is it inconceivable that in this era of great technological development where employers can, without too much effort or expense, furnish their employees with mechanical devices to assist them in lifting heavy weights, the failure of an employer to provide his employees with such devices may have to be taken into consideration in determining the constitutionality of a state weight-lifting restriction for women as applied to individual situations. Stated differently, the equal protection clause may be violated by a state statute that limits weights women may lift on a job (thus depriving them of equal opportunity for employment which because of Title VII's jurisdictional limitations cannot always be corrected by that statute) without at the same time requiring employers to furnish their employees, wherever feasible, with the tools that will assist them to lift what would otherwise be unmanageable weights.

Related to this last point and of crucial importance in the development of standards for testing the constitutionality of laws that appear to discriminate between the sexes is the *quantum* of justification that will be required to uphold sex-based discriminatory laws. Especially in the application of the Fourteenth Amendment's equal protection clause, there appear to have developed two distinct standards for testing legislative or court-made classifications, depending upon whether the classification merely circumscribes some general, institutional, economic activity or whether it restricts what—so far imprecisely—has come to be regarded as a "basic" civil right.

Closely analogous to the proposed distinction between "preferred" and "unpreferred" constitutional freedoms,[30] the developing differences in the constitutional law approach to "basic" civil rights and those which, for want of a better term, can perhaps be described as "non-basic" may have profound implications for the fate of sex-based discriminatory laws in the future.

Where a right, privilege, activity, etc. is properly characterized as being "non-basic," a rule of law that classifies people so as to restrict its exercise by one group while permitting it to be exercised by another will ordinarily be upheld under established constitutional principles, if there is *some* reasonable basis for the classification. But where a civil right that has been infringed by a rule is properly characterized as "basic" the "any rational basis" test for upholding it against an equal protection or due process challenge will not suffice. Under such circumstances the state will be required to sustain a much greater burden of justification to support the classification. Thus, in *Skinner v. Oklahoma*,[31] a state law requiring the sterilization of certain types of habitual criminals was subjected to "strict scrutiny"[32] in determining the reasonableness of the classification, since the right to bear children is "one of the basic civil rights of man."[33] Similarly, in *Loving v. Virginia*,[34] describing the right to be married as another basic civil right,[35] the Supreme Court rejected the contention that a miscegenation statute "should be upheld if there is any possible basis for concluding that [it serves] a rational purpose"[36] and instead, subjecting the racial classification of such a statute to the "most rigid scrutiny,"[37] held that it violated both the equal protection and due process clauses of the Fourteenth Amendment.

Admittedly, the *Loving* case is somewhat ambiguous as to whether its primary distinction for testing a classification against an equal protection attack is founded upon a racial as opposed to a non-racial classification or whether it proceeds from the "basic" civil right versus "non-basic" civil right dichotomy—although both tests may be appropriate depending upon whether an equal protection or due process challenge has been invoked. In either respect, however, the consequences for laws that discriminate on account of sex may be far-reaching. For if the distinction is in fact founded upon the racial classification, then it is difficult to oppose the observation made by the federal district court in *United States v. York*[38] that no reason exists "why adult women, as one of the specific groups that compose humanity, should have a lesser measure of protection than a racial group."[39] On the other hand, if the differences in the tests for equal protection purposes are between general economic regulations and statutes directly impinging on fundamental rights or personal liberties, as contended by Judge Hoffman of the Pennsylvania Superior Court, dissenting in *Com-*

monwealth v. Daniels,[40] and suggested by Mr. Justice Douglas in
Levy v. Louisiana[41] an overriding statutory purpose or compelling
state interest would be required to justify laws having the latter
effect, including many of those that subject males and females to
different treatment in otherwise comparable situations.

Of course, the problem with a "basic" versus a "non-basic" distinction in determining the different burdens of justification that
will support the imposition of a disability on one sex but not the
other or according one sex a benefit withheld from the other is that,
like the elaboration of the extent to which the Fourteenth Amendment's due process clause makes the Bill of Rights applicable to
the States,[42] the result will inevitably depend upon a court's
visceral rather than its cerebral behavior. One person's "basic"
will frequently be another person's "non-basic." Be that as it may,
this developing distinction appears to be one way of cracking the
solid wall of Supreme Court decisions upholding a wide variety
of laws that distinguish, often with some justification but without
compelling reasons, between the sexes. Indeed, as Mr. Justice
Douglas has observed in *Levy v. Louisiana,* the Court has "been
extremely sensitive when it comes to basic civil rights . . . and
[has] not hesitated to strike down an invidious classification *even
though it had history and tradition on its side."*[43]

The *Levy* case, which held that denying illegitimate children
the right to recover for their mother's wrongful death violated the
Equal Protection Clause, has other important implications for the
future of sex-based discriminatory laws. One potential danger in
any constitutional challenge to a law that confers a benefit on one
sex but withholds it from the other has been that, if the challenge
succeeded, the benefit might be withdrawn. Under the authority of
the *Levy* case, however, it would appear to be consistent with the
Supreme Court's role as final interpreter of the Equal Protection
Clause for it to *confer* the same benefit upon the sex from which
it had been previously withheld. This is of particular importance
in the field of protective labor legislation where, as previously suggested,[44] litigants have sought to eliminate rather than to extend
the discriminatory benefit.

Given these developing analytical approaches to the constitutionality of legal rules that by their terms or effects distinguish between the sexes, it would appear that each type of law would have

to be separately examined to determine its individual fate. One important point should be borne in mind in this connection—and that is that though a particular sex-discriminatory rule of law may survive a constitutional challenge, this will not preclude a legislature or court from altering a statute or judicial precedent, respectively, on the grounds of policy. But returning to the question of the constitutionality of such legal rules, the significant new fact is that many formerly sacred cows are standing on the brink of constitutional invalidation, and with only a slight amount of pressure, seem bound to topple. Without purporting to be an exhaustive exploration of the ability of all types of sex-discriminatory laws to satisfy emerging constitutional standards in this area, the following sections examine some of those types and attempt to forecast their ultimate fate if challenged on constitutional grounds.

Actions for Loss of Consortium

Actions for loss of consortium have been described in an earlier chapter[45] as a variety of the rights of action allowed to persons who suffer indirect loss resulting from direct injuries inflicted upon persons to whom they bear a particular relationship. Though some jurisdictions permit suits for loss of consortium by wives as well as husbands where the opposite spouse has been negligently injured, the majority adhere to the common law rule allowing such causes of action to husbands but not to wives.

Former attacks—successful as well as unsuccessful—upon this sex-based discriminatory rule have almost always claimed that the particular version of the Married Woman's Property Act in the jurisdiction required the husband's right of action to be extended to the wife in a comparable situation. But in recent years, litigants have increasingly invoked constitutional arguments in challenging this type of discrimination.

In *Owen v. Illinois Baking Corporation*[46] a federal district court in Michigan invalidated the discriminatory consortium rule on constitutional grounds without extensive discussion. Noting that "to grant a husband the right to sue on this right while denying the wife access to the courts in the assertion of this same right is too clearly a violation of Fourteenth Amendment equal protection guarantees to require citation of authority,"[47] the court, sitting in a diversity suit, rejected the forum state's substantive law which denied the right to sue for loss of consortium. Although its decision is laudable, the *Owen* case's unquestioned acceptance of the equal protection argument without analysis or consideration of opposing arguments is rather surprising in view of the long history of separate treatment of the sexes in this area.

And basing its decision on only a slightly more extensive examination of the constitutional question, an Ohio Court of Common Pleas in *Clem v. Brown*[48] has also held that a state's rule permitting husbands but not wives to recover for loss of consortium deprives a wife of "equal protection of the law."[49]

The results in *Owen* and *Clem* were apparently approved in 1967 by the Wisconsin Supreme Court in *Moran v. Quality Aluminum Casting Co.*[50] In that case the court indicated that the right to recover for loss of consortium should be extended to wives in the interest of logic and "justice,"[51] but based its actual decision to do this on a re-reading of Wisconsin's unique "equal rights" statute.[52]

By contrast, at least three courts have come to an opposite conclusion. The Supreme Court of West Virginia, in what appears to be the earliest reported case challenging the one-way consortium rule on equal protection grounds, sustained such discrimination in 1962 on the ground that it had existed at common law and that the State Constitution preserved the common law[53]—a rather questionable holding since even state constitutional provisions may be invalid if they violate provisions of the United States Constitution.[54] And in 1966, the Supreme Court of Tennessee expressly rejected the result in *Owen* and *Clem v. Brown,* holding that the Tennessee rule allowing a husband but not a wife recovery for loss of consortium "does not work a 'discrimination' [and is] no more than a practical and logical classification."[55]

Similarly, the United States Court of Appeals for the Seventh Circuit, applying Indiana law in a diversity action in 1968 rejected the equal protection argument in this area, emphasizing the danger of double recovery for loss of the husband's earnings in his own suit and in the wife's consortium suit if the latter were allowed.[56] Impliedly recognizing that a husband could also recover for loss of the wife's earnings in his own consortium suit, the court nevertheless upheld this discrimination against an equal protection challenge on the grounds that "Since 87.8% of married men are employed and only 34.4% of wives are employed . . . Indiana could infer that more often in a wife's suit than a husband's, the jury would award her duplicating damages for some of the same elements of injury."[57]

This is indeed strange reasoning. For one thing it overlooks the ease with which Indiana could require both causes of action to be joined in one suit, as has been done by other jurisdictions,[58] thus avoiding any possibility of double recovery. Indeed, a reasonable argument can be made that the equal protection principle requires a state to establish such a procedural requirement if its purported justification for discriminating between the sexes would thereby be eliminated[59]—much as employers may be required to provide labor-saving machinery to their employees to avoid discriminating between the sexes on the basis of their general physical differences.[60] But even if this argument were rejected, the quantitative difference between employed husbands and wives is not great enough to justify, constitutionally, such difference in treatment. If the danger to be avoided is that of double recovery, then qualitatively the risk is just as serious if it can occur in 34.4 percent of the cases as it would be in 87.8 percent of the cases—unless we are to grant the possibility that being "slightly" pregnant is somehow fundamentally different from being "very" pregnant, as far as the fact of pregnancy is concerned. Finally, nowhere in its opinion does the court consider the possibility that the disparity in husbands' and wives' employment rates may be the result of past discriminatory practices which, because not previously prohibited by law, can be regarded as law-approved. To the extent this is a factor, the court's approach once more justifies a present discrimination by relying on a past practice without discerning the discriminatory features of the latter—a common analytical failing where sex-based legal discrimination is in question.

Even where the constitutional attack has not been directly successful, it seems to have stimulated at least one state supreme court, Maryland's, to develop a new theory permitting a wife to recover for the loss of her husband's consortium where such recovery had not been allowed before. In *Deems v. Western Maryland Railway Co.*,[61] that court found it "unnecessary to decide whether the Equal Protection Clause compels a holding that the wife shall have a separate cause of action for loss of her husband's consortium due to injuries sustained by him because of the negligence of a third party,"[62] by holding that in the future when *"either* husband or wife claims loss of consortium by reason of physical injuries sustained by the other as a result of the alleged negligence of the defendant, that claim can only be asserted in a joint action for injury to the marital relationship."[63] Avowedly skirting "a possible conflict between the present law and the federal constitution,"[64] the *Deems* result, which will affect suits seeking recovery for husbands' as well as wives' loss of consortium, proceeds upon a "legal entity" theory of the marriage relationship.

Though having the effect of equalizing the spouses' positions with respect to rights of action for loss of consortium, the result in *Deems* would have been more satisfactory had it been squarely based upon the equal protection argument. For the "legal entity" theory is too reminiscent of, and in fact derived from, the discredited medieval concept of the legal unity of husband and wife.[65]

A similar process seems to have also occurred in New York. Noting that in that state "it is rare, if not unknown, to try a husband's action separately from his wife's negligence action" and that if this should occur, "motions to consolidate would quickly resolve that difficulty," the New York Court of Appeals, in *Millington v. Southeastern Elevator Co.*[66] has "on the basis of policy and fairness"[67] overruled prior law by extending to wives the right to sue for loss of consortium. The equal protection attack on the prior sex-based discriminatory rule that had also been made in that case was thereby avoided although the court intimated that had it not altered the rule on policy grounds, it would have been persuaded on the constitutional point by the decision of the United States Supreme Court in *Levy v. Louisiana.*[68]

As noted earlier, the *Levy* case held that if a state allows a woman's "legitimate" children to recover for her wrongful death and conscious pain and suffering it could not deny this remedy to her "illegitimate" children. In *Millington,* while not deciding the point, the New York Court of Appeals noted that such "reasoning would seem applicable here since it is concluded that there is no basis for the existing discrimination."[69]

Though the *Millington* decision did not rule on the equal protection argument, the extent to which the *Levy* case will influence future cases in this field is of some moment. The meaning of *Mill-*

ington's reference to *Levy* is somewhat unclear. For one thing, if, as the court had already decided, there was "no basis for the existing discrimination," this would have been a sufficient reason for invalidating such a rule (denying to wives but permitting husbands the right to sue for loss of consortium) on either policy or constitutional grounds. Perhaps the only significance to the reference to the *Levy* case in *Millington* is to point out that on *Levy's* authority, invalidation on constitutional grounds would have been appropriate, but that in line with the established policy of avoiding constitutional decisions whenever possible, this was being done in *Millington*. On the other hand, the reference to *Levy* may have been made to dispel any doubts that the granting or withholding of causes of action could be subject to equal protection restrictions.

One difficulty attorneys will have to overcome if they attempt to rely upon *Levy* in seeking to invalidate the discriminatory consortium rule on equal protection grounds is the Supreme Court's observation in that case that "He [the illegitimate child] is subject to all the responsibilities of a citizen, including the payment of taxes *and conscription under the Selective Service Act.* How under our constitutional regime can he be denied correlative rights which other citizens enjoy?"[70] Since women are not presently subject to military conscription,[71] the question arises whether this would distinguish the sex-based discriminatory consortium rule from the invalidated distinction between the rights of legitimate and illegitimate children to sue for wrongful death.

Neither in the Supreme Court decision itself nor in any of the lower court decisions in *Levy*[72] does the sex of the five illegitimate children, on whose behalf the suit was brought, appear. However, even if all five were male, it would seem that the conscription point would not render the *Levy* case inapposite to the consortium issue. Aside from the fact that use of the word "He" in reference to illegitimate children in general is a grammatical and legalistic conceit probably intended to embrace members of both sexes (a tradition that is not without its own sex-discriminatory implications), the allusion to military conscription can be interpreted as containing the implied qualification, "unless otherwise reasonably exempted from such a requirement."

Whether the total exemption of women from the obligation of military service is reasonable may be the subject of considerable debate. If the functional analysis is employed, then, recognizing the general physical differences between the sexes and the physically exacting demands of many military tasks, much of the present exemption can be seen as not being based on sex (despite the reference in the law to males as such) but rather to the functions that must be performed. But many tasks within the military are not of such a nature and often merely duplicate civilian jobs—such as typist, clerk, automobile driver—which can be performed by women as well as men. To the extent, therefore, that *Levy's* reference to military conscription is crucial, reliance upon that case to successfully attack the unequal consortium rule on equal protection grounds may be inappropriate as long as the present scheme of military conscription law remains unaltered.

Significantly, the handful of cases that have dealt with the equal protection attack on the rule denying wives but allowing husbands the right to sue for loss of consortium have, regardless of their outcome, tended to dispose of the equal protection question in summary fashion. Either they have held that a prohibited discrimination was so patent that citation of authority was not even needed[73] or they have indicated with equally little discussion that the constitutional challenge was without merit.[74]

Having said all that, how should the discriminatory consortium rule fare when challenged, as it inevitably will be, in the United States Supreme Court? It is submitted that the Court should invalidate this sex-based discriminatory rule on equal protection grounds by extending the right of action to married women where it presently is accorded only to married men, rather than by removing such right from the latter.[75] But the manner in which the Court does this, or more precisely its rationale for such a decision, will be of crucial importance for the future of other sex-based discriminatory legal rules.

In line with developing equal protection standards the Court will first have to decide whether the right to sue for loss of consortium is a "basic" or "non-basic" right—since, if it is properly classified as "basic," the burden of justifying the distinction between the sexes will be much greater than otherwise.[76] In this connection the fact that the sex-based classification with respect to the right to sue for loss of consortium has "history and tradition on its side"[77] will not prevent the Court from either categorizing such

right as "basic" or from striking the classification down if it is invidious.[78] It is submitted that the right to sue for loss of consortium
is no less basic than the right to sue for wrongful death in the
Levy case—though in both cases, the right either has not always
or does not now exist in all American jurisdictions. Indeed, this
may be the ultimate significance of the reference to *Levy* in the
Millington case.[79]

Should the right to recover for loss of consortium come to be
regarded, therefore, as "basic"—thus subjecting the classification to
"rigid scrutiny"[80]—the burden upon any party seeking to sustain
the sex-based classification in this area would be great. A reasonable argument can be made moreover that, to satisfy this burden,
it is insufficient merely to show that existing differences between
the situation of the sexes are extensive—as, for instance, that the
likelihood of double recovery is greater when wives sue for loss of
consortium than when such actions are brought by husbands.[81]
For to the extent that it lies within the power of the state, by legislation or court decision, to mitigate the effects of such differences,
its failure to do so should be taken into account in passing upon the
constitutionality of the unequal consortium rule. Were such a
principle adopted in this area, the claim that double recovery is a
more serious danger when wives, as opposed to husbands, are allowed to sue for loss of consortium would not be a constitutional
justification for the discrimination—since the states that make such
a distinction could, and in a basic sense would have to, restructure
their procedural rules to require husband-wife joinder when either
seeks to recover for negligent invasion of consortium.

As the number of constitutional challenges to the sex-based
discriminatory consortium rule multiply, the likelihood that the
United States Supreme Court, the final arbiter of federal constitutional disputes, will agree to review lower state or federal court
decisions in this area will also increase. When that is done, it is
hoped that the court will once and for all declare this inequality
violative of both the equal protection and due process clauses of
the U.S. Constitution's Fourteenth Amendment, and that it will
do so along the lines suggested herein. For if the Court were to do
this, not only would it in one fell swoop invalidate on constitutional grounds most, if not all, the unequal consortium rules in
every American jurisdiction, but it would also broaden the con-

ceptual foundation for successful constitutional challenges of a great variety of other sex-based discriminatory laws and official practices.

Statutory Sex-Based Differences in Sentencing for the Same Crime

In *Commonwealth v. Daniels,*[82] the Pennsylvania Superior Court was confronted with an equal protection challenge to the sentencing provisions of the state's Muncy Act[83] which, like statutes in some other states,[84] requires women to be sentenced differently (and generally more severely) than men upon conviction of the same crime. Specifically, the Muncy Act provides that any *female* pleading guilty to or being convicted for a crime punishable by imprisonment for more than a year must be sentenced to confinement in the State Industrial Home for Women and that the sentence "shall be merely a general one . . . and shall not fix or limit the duration thereof."[85]

In *Daniels* the trial court had first sentenced the woman defendant, who had been convicted of robbery, to a one-to-four-year term in the Philadelphia County Prison. Thirty-one days later the Court vacated the original sentence on the grounds that the Muncy Act provided the exclusive basis for sentencing women under these circumstances. Pursuant to the terms of the Act the court then re-sentenced the defendant to the State Industrial Home for Women without fixing a maximum or minimum term of imprisonment. One effect of this indeterminate sentence was that the defendant could now be required to serve the maximum term for the crime of robbery, ten years, as opposed to her original maximum four year sentence. In addition, under the demonstrated parole practices of the Muncy authorities, defendant would have to serve a minimum of three years at that institution, whereas, had her original sentence—one that could have been imposed on a male convicted of the same crime—been valid, she would have been eligible for parole in one year.

In a divided opinion in *Daniels,* the Pennsylvania Superior Court held the Muncy Act did not violate the equal protection clause because of a discerned reasonable connection between the classification by sex and the purposes of the legislation. In the court's opinion

[T]he legislature reasonably could have concluded that indeterminate sentences should be imposed on women as a class, allowing the time of incarceration to be matched to the necessary treatment in order to provide more effective rehabilitation. Such a conclusion could be based on the physiological and psychological makeup of women, the type of crime committed by women, their relation to the criminal world, their roles in society, their unique vocational skills and pursuits, and their reaction as a class to imprisonment, as well as the number and type of women who are sentenced to imprisonment rather than given suspended sentences. Such facts could have led the legislature to conclude that a different manner of punishment and rehabilitation was necessary for women sentenced to confinement.[86]

In addition, the Superior Court in *Daniels,* one judge dissenting, suggested that the legal-factual premises of defendant's equal protection argument were also in error. That is, her assumption that a man would have been sentenced to a maximum term of four years as opposed to her maximum of ten years was "invalid . . . [since the court could not] speculate as to what the sentence would have been had the person robbing the bar in question been a male."[87]

The weakness of the court's reasoning in this last point was underscored by Judge Hoffman's dissent, which in effect emphasized that the sex-based discrimination rested not on what *would,* but rather upon what *could,* occur in the sentencing process. For under the terms of the Muncy Act, all "women sentenced for offenses punishable by imprisonment for more than one year *must* be sentenced to the maximum permissible term. Men, on the other hand, *may* be sentenced to lesser terms."[88] The Act, in Judge Hoffman's view, therefore constituted "an arbitrary and invidious discrimination against women offenders as a class."[89] Because personal liberties or fundamental rights were involved here, the "any rational basis" formula for testing the Muncy Act against the equal protection challenge would not do. Instead, to sustain the Act, the state "must show a subordinate interest that is compelling."[90] Therefore,

To justify such discriminatory treatment, the Commonwealth must demonstrate more than the fragmentary and tenuous theories presented to us. Absent any *compelling* psychological, statistical, or scientific data, we cannot, nor should we, sanction a legislative scheme which is patently arbitrary and manifestly unfair.[91]

It is perhaps to the credit of the majority opinion in *Daniels*— despite its tendency to repeat the oft-encountered error of justifying rank discriminations on the mere difference of sex alone— that it did not resort to the homilies of the past that confinement in a State Industrial Home for Women or a comparable institution partakes more of the nature of treatment than of punishment.[92] That approach would appear to have been put to a lasting rest by the U.S. Supreme Court's decision in *In re Gault*[93] suggesting that confinement by any other name is still confinement. But the problem with the Superior Court's view is that in the name of the legislature's general and undifferentiated right to classify on the basis of sex, women could be subjected to the severest kind of disadvantage—not in the areas of employment opportunities, property rights, divorce grounds, but in the fundamental right to personal liberty. If any area cries out for judicial redress on the basis of the Fourteenth Amendment command, this is one.

Indeed, shortly after the above was written, the Pennsylvania Supreme Court reversed the lower court in the *Daniels* case.[94]

Apparently[95] not adopting Judge Hoffman's detailed analysis of the constitutional aspects of the question, the Pennsylvania Supreme Court simply held in *Daniels* that "an arbitrary and invidious discrimination exists in the sentencing of men to prison and women to Muncy, with resulting injury to women,"[96] and that no "reasonable and justifiable difference or deterrent [is discernible] between men and women which would justify a man being eligible for a shorter maximum prison sentence than a woman for the commission of the same crime, especially if there is no material difference in their records and the relevant circumstances."[97]

Significantly, however, the Pennsylvania Supreme Court did not reject the fundamental allowability of classification by sex, as in the employment area, since "there are undoubtedly significant biological, natural and practical differences between men and women [justifying such classification] under some circumstances. . . ."[98]

Additional movement in the same direction came in early 1968 in a federal district court decision in *United States ex rel. Robinson v. York*[99] striking down as violative of the equal protection guarantee a Connecticut statute[100] allowing "women to be sentenced for longer terms than it or any other statute permits for men found guilty of committing identical offenses. . . ."[101] In *Robinson* the state had argued that the statute in question, unlike statutes dealing with incarceration in penal institutions, was an expression of the state's attempt to provide for "women and juveniles a special protection and every reformative and rehabilitative opportunity,"[102] and that a longer term of imprisonment for women in such an institution was therefore justified. Relying upon the remarks of Mr. Justice Fortas in the *Gault* case, however, the court in *Robinson* rejected this euphemistic distinction between penal and reformatory institutions, noting that in Connecticut, "the predominant criterion for judgment imposed on those convicted of violating its criminal laws continues to be punishment,"[103] and holding that the statute as applied to the sentences of the female petitioner in the case "constituted an invidious discrimination against her which is repugnant to the equal protection of the laws guaranteed by the fourteenth amendment."[104]

More important than the result in *Robinson*, however, is the method by which the court reached it. Significantly, great reliance was placed upon the Supreme Court's decision in *Loving v. Virginia*.[105] While noting that in *Loving* the strict standards the Supreme Court had enunciated for upholding a classification against an equal protection challenge had been directed toward a *racial* classification, the court nevertheless applied the same standards in *Robinson* because it could see no reason "why adult women, as one of the specific groups that compose humanity, should have a lesser measure of protection than a racial group."[106] As a result, the statute "which singles out adult women convicted of misdemeanors for imposition of punishment for longer terms than may be imposed on men, must be supported by a *full measure of justification* to overcome the equal protection which is guaranteed to them by the fourteenth amendment."[107]

It is important to note also that the opinion in *Robinson,* as well as that of the Pennsylvania Supreme Court in *Daniels,* did not criticize or reject earlier Supreme Court decisions in which sex-based classifications had been upheld. In particular, approving reference was made in *Robinson* to *Muller v. Oregon*[108] upholding an Oregon statute limiting women's working hours to 10 a day, *Goesart v. Cleary*[109] upholding Michigan's rule preventing most women from becoming licensed bartenders, and *Hoyt v. Florida*[110] sustaining Florida's exclusion of women from jury duty unless they affirmatively volunteer to serve. In *Robinson* the court noted that those earlier Supreme Court decisions had each determined that the classifications drawn in the respective statutes were reasonable in the light of their purposes.

> Thus, in *Muller* the Court took account of the differences in physical structure, strength and endurance of women, as well as the importance of their health to the future well being of the race, in sustaining the work hour limitation. . . . It noted a woman's family and home responsibilities in upholding the jury duty exemption in *Hoyt* . . . and acknowledged in *Goesart* that the Michigan legislature might legitimately be avoiding the "moral and social problems" which it believed could be produced by females tending bar in saloons. . . .[111]

As for the sex-based distinction inherent in the Connecticut statute, however, the *Robinson* opinion observed that nothing "in the different nature of men and women noted by the Supreme Court in the *Muller, Goesart,* and *Hoyt* cases suggests any reasonable or just relation between the misdemeanors involved here and the inequality in potential punishments permitted by § 17-360."[112]

In sum, the *Robinson* decision reiterated the classic test for determining whether a statutory classification can withstand an equal protection attack, that the classification and the purpose of the statute must be reasonably related, but held that the burden of showing such a reasonable connection was heavier on the state where the classification was of women as a group and resulted in a deprivation of personal liberty than it might have been perhaps in the area of economic regulation and the classification was not based upon one's condition at birth. The state not having satisfied this burden in *Robinson,* the immediate release of the petitioner was ordered.[113] While *Robinson* seemed to approve of the Supreme Court decisions in *Hoyt, Goesart* and *Muller,* such approval was by no means necessary to its decision. It is possible to read the *Robinson* court's reference to those earlier cases as saying merely that, even if they were still "good law," they did not require the sentencing classification to be upheld, where the absence of any reasonable relation between the purposes of the statute and the classification was so clear. For, as discussed elsewhere in this volume, though the earlier Supreme Court decisions may still be "good law" in that the Supreme Court has not overruled them, the Court may have ample reason for doing so, at least in respect to the *Hoyt* and *Goesart* situations, if not in regard to the economic regulation involved in the *Muller* case. Indeed, notwithstanding the *Robinson* court's apparent approval of those earlier decisions, its analysis of the discriminatory legislation involved in the Connecticut statute may also be pertinent to a reconsideration of those earlier Supreme Court cases upholding a variety of sex-based discriminatory laws.

The various opinions in the *Daniels* and *Robinson* cases are of extreme importance for a number of reasons. For one thing, they undermine earlier cases in other jurisdictions upholding sex-based discrimination in sentencing rules and practices.[114] They also represent a significant breakthrough, as does *White v. Crook,*[115] in the realm of jury service, and some of the consortium cases discussed in the last section,[116] in the undifferentiated "sex is a reasonable basis for classification" approach that has held sway for so long in this area. What is more important is that their analytical approach— emphasizing the greater burden of justification to sustain an unequal deprivation of a "basic" civil right or analogizing a female group to a racial group—creates the possibility of successfully attacking, on constitutional grounds, a variety of other sex-based discriminatory rules and practices. In their own way, this handful of decisions may be the early heralds of a new day in the general treatment of men and women in American law and life.

Constitutional Attack Upon Sex-Based Variations in the Age of Majority and Related Concepts

The sex-based disparities in minimum age requirements for marriage and for achieving adult status described in Chapter 2 are subject to constitutional attack in a variety of contexts.[117] The United States Supreme Court has indicated in separate cases, for example, that: 1) marriage is one of the "basic civil rights of man";[118] and 2) the condition of being a juvenile does not deprive a person of certain constitutional protections.[119] The time may therefore come when a male, who under state law may not marry without parental consent before the age of 21 though females in that state may do so at 18, will challenge that type of rule—perhaps successfully—as a violation of the equal protection and due process guarantees of the United States Constitution.[120]

The rights to contract, to convey property, or generally to deal with one's business affairs, while perhaps not rising to the level of a "basic civil right," are nevertheless fundamental in modern American society. Although distinctions drawn between young and older persons may be permissible, the constitutional validity of sex-based discrimination between young persons themselves is more questionable. Thus we may also see in the near future constitutional challenges by males of state statutes prescribing an eighteen-year general age of majority for females and a twenty-one-year age for males.[121]

For a lower age of majority for one sex as compared with the other may be either a benefit or a burden, depending upon the circumstances. It is a benefit, in a very real sense, in permitting a young person to engage in unfettered buying and selling and other facets of commercial life. Where males are prevented by law from engaging in such activities for longer periods than females, an equal protection attack, based upon the irrationality of the classification, may be available—especially when one recalls the general reverse age differential in sexual matters.[122]

That a lower age of majority can also be a burden is illustrated by the 1964 Illinois case of *Jacobson v. Lenhart*.[123] In Illinois, as indicated earlier, the statutory age of majority for most purposes is twenty-one for all males and eighteen for all females.[124] An extension of that rule distinguishes between the sexes in defining the disability of minority during which a general statute of limitations will be tolled. Specifically, Section 21 of the Illinois Limitations Act provides with respect to personal actions:

> If the person entitled to bring an action . . . is, at the time of the cause of action accrued, within the age of twenty-one

years, or if a female, within the age of eighteen years, or insane, or mentally ill, or imprisoned on a criminal charge, he or
she may bring the action within two years after the disability
is removed.[125]

Thus, a 17 year old male injured as a result of another's negligence, for example, will not be barred from suing for such injury
until he has reached the age of 23. By contrast, a female must sue
before reaching the age of 20, unless the limitation period is tolled
by another type of disability, such as insanity, mental illness or imprisonment on a criminal charge.

In the *Jacobson* case, the female plaintiff had been injured,
allegedly as a result of defendant's negligence, when she had just
turned 18. She brought suit at age 22. Suit by a male under the
same circumstances would not have been barred, but in her case,
as a result of the statute, it was. To her contention that the sex-
based age differential for tolling the limitation period was unconstitutionally "arbitrary, discriminatory and without relation
to the apparent purpose of the statute,"[126] the court first stated
the traditional formula for testing alleged violations of the equal
protection guarantee: "A classification of a group of persons is not
arbitrary if there is a sound basis in reason and principle for regarding one class of individuals as a separate and distinct class for
the purposes of the particular classification."[127] Then repeating
a century old comment upon the general differentiation in the ages
of majority of males and females that "in the opinion of the legislature, females at the age of eighteen possess as much discretion as
males at the age of twenty-one, and are then fitted to attain their
majority . . . ,"[128] the Court concluded that "legislative and
judicial recognition that females mature physically, emotionally
and mentally before male persons, [is] . . . a reasonable basis for
the classification," and therefore that any change in the rule should
be made by the legislature rather than the courts.

The problem with the court's reasoning in *Jacobson* is its acceptance as an undifferentiated fact that females acquire "discretion"
earlier than males. For "discretion" is not fungible. In each case it
is important to ask, "discretion for what?" Certainly, if the reference is to "discretion" with regard to one's business affairs—which,
after all, is what is involved in not permitting one's cause of action
to be barred by a statute of limitations—the mores and practices of

a society that has traditionally encouraged males and discouraged females from actively participating in this area cannot be ignored. Against that social background, a legislative determination that females achieve "discretion" earlier than males as applied to this specific area of conduct is not merely a matter about which reasonable people may differ, but stands out as an arbitrary and unreasonable classification prohibited by the equal protection clause of the U.S. Constitution.

To the extent that contracts entered into during minority can be disaffirmed by a minor, state laws prescribing different ages of majority for males and females also appear vulnerable to constitutional attack—notwithstanding the specific result in the *Jacobson* case. For the right to disaffirm is clearly a benefit. When it is conferred on one sex and arbitrarily withheld from another, though the latter is similarly situated, it would appear to violate fundamental constitutional rights. As *Levy v. Louisiana* demonstrates, moreover, correction of this inequity can take the form of conferring the benefit upon the sex from which it has been withheld rather than removing it from the other.

In sum, whether achieving the age of majority be regarded as a benefit or a burden, unequal rules for males and females in this area, wherever they exist, appear to be vulnerable at this date to due process and equal protection attacks. Equalization of treatment in this area, as in others discussed in this volume, should go a long way toward eliminating unfair social, as well as other legal, disparities between the sexes in American life.

Obscene or Vulgar Language in the Presence of Women

In one area in which legal consequences differ if women rather than men are in the factual setting, the First Amendment guarantees of free speech and expression, in addition to the previously discussed constitutional provisions, may be implicated. This is the area of permissible utterances in the presence of women.

Arizona Criminal Code § 13-377 is typical of many statutes on the subject. It provides, in part, that a person who "in the presence of or hearing of any woman or child, or in a public place, uses vulgar, abusive or obscene language, is guilty of a misdemeanor. . . ."[129]

The interpretative problems raised by the words "vulgar, abusive or obscene language" are not unlike those that have bedeviled the courts in the pornography cases,[130] and are beyond the scope of the present work. Nevertheless, one can't help noting that arriving at objective standards for ascertaining whether particular words are "vulgar, abusive, or obscene," even in a geographically limited community, may be extraordinarily difficult.

Important for present purposes, however, are the expressed and implied classifications of situations in which the utterance of the same words may or may not violate the statute. Thus, if they are spoken "in a public place" (a formulation that is not itself free of interpretive difficulty) the statute is violated regardless of the sex or age of the hearers. (That someone must have heard the words is implied by the statute, since a finding that the words had in fact been spoken could not otherwise be made.) By contrast, consequences will differ with the age or sex of the hearer if the objectionable words are uttered in a non-public place.

Thus, provided that the statute survives constitutional attacks on the grounds of vagueness or uncertainty in the meaning of "vulgar, abusive or obscene," the speaking of particular words in the presence or hearing of children will constitute a misdemeanor. The same will be true if they are uttered in the presence or hearing of women. But, applying the maxim of *expressio unius, exclusio alterius,* it is clear that no matter how "vulgar, abusive or obscene" particular words may be, their utterance in the presence of men in a non-public place will not *per se* subject the speaker to any criminal penalties.

Several features of this statute are noteworthy in the present context. First, the utterance of such words in the hearing of women, though not in their presence is punishable. Though this formulation may have been designed to cover the situation in the *Gault* case itself—in which a telephone is used to communicate the offensive words—its literal terms appear to permit prosecution of a person who uses such words without knowledge that they are being overheard by members of the female sex.

Second, the juxtaposition of women and children as the persons to be spared the ordeal of hearing obscene, vulgar or abusive words is reminiscent of the common law's time-honored practice of treating women like infants or, at times, idiots.[131] Designating children to be insulated from certain kinds of speech or literature may be a reasonable classification in exercising the police power.[132] The same cannot be said of adult women, however, unless, that is, one first accedes to Justice Frankfurter's comments in *Goesart v. Cleary*,[133] a case involving only the power of the state to prohibit women from selling alcoholic beverages, that the states may draw "a sharp line between the sexes,"[134] and that "the Constitution does not require legislatures to reflect sociological insight, or shifting social standards, any more than it requires them to keep abreast of the latest scientific standards,"[135] and then extends those comments to an area involving the preferred freedoms of speech and expression. Similarly, while the U.S. Supreme Court has, on the basis of its view that women are "still regarded as the center of home and family life,"[136] decided that a state may let women, and not men, choose whether to serve on a jury, such a role within the family and home bears no reasonable relationship to a statute penalizing speakers of vulgar or obscene words in the presence or hearing of women but not of men.

The only possible explanation of such statutes is that once more they express social attitudes that women are essentially of a different species than men, that they are brittle objects to be spared the reality of everyday living, and that they are in a fundamental sense second-class citizens—all of which raise serious questions concerning the ability of such laws to withstand attacks on due process and equal protection grounds.

For what must be emphasized here is that these words are not regarded in the statute as inherently evil, wicked or punishable—as evidenced by the failure to make a criminal offense their utterance in the private presence of men. The statute simply reflects a legislative determination that women, because of notions about their brittleness, their delicacy, in a word, their "otherness"— are to be sheltered from this aspect of speech and expression. Here, as in other areas, women as well as men may ultimately have become the "victims" of such protection—so inextricably is it linked to numerous social and legal rules keeping the sexes from relating to one another primarily as people.

All this is not to suggest of course that the gates of social living be opened to a flood of four-letter words in daily speech—although it may be observed that much of our emotional responses to these words is entirely irrational.[137] The point is that, objectionable or not, it is wrong, unreasonable, and probably unconstitutional, to punish those who would utter them in the hearing of women but not of men.[138]

Somewhat instructive of legislative and judicial attitudes in this regard is the language of Justice Jones of the Mississippi Supreme Court in *State v. Hall*,[139] rejecting for Mississippi the decision of *White v. Crook*[140] in which a three-judge federal court had held that Alabama's exclusion of women from jury service violated the equal protection clause. In the *Hall* case, Justice Jones offered the following reason, among others, for sustaining Mississippi's jury exclusion rule for women:

> The legislature has the right to exclude women so they may continue their service as mothers, wives, and homemakers, and also to protect them (in some areas they are still upon a pedestal) from the filth, obscenity, and noxious atmosphere that so often pervades a courtroom during a jury trial.[141]

To "protect" women from "filth, obscenity" and the like, however, is also to protect them from certain aspects of the reality of everyday life, to perpetuate as a matter of law, ancient chivalric notions which have often served as a mask for men's economic and sexual exploitation of women. The point that must be emphasized here is that any constitutional doubts that might attend such obscenity statutes if they were applied without regard to the sex of the hearers are intensified when they apply to women hearers only. It is submitted that such statutes can be invalidated as violating both the free speech guarantees of the First Amendment and the equal protection clause of the Fourteenth Amendment, and that when the courts have an occasion to invalidate them for these reasons, the respect that men and women bear toward one another as fellow human beings will be enhanced rather than diminished.

Women in Employment

In Chapter 4 it was seen that recent federal and state legislation, where applicable, requires women to be paid equally as well as men for performing equal work and prohibits the withholding of employment opportunities—with respect to hiring, promotion and other working conditions—on the basis of sex.[142] Also examined therein were potential loopholes in these laws and ways of closing them, as well as their effect upon various state "protective" laws applying to women only—particularly those prescribing maximum working hours and maximum weight-lifting restrictions or barring women from certain kinds of employment. That it would be consistent with the past practices of the Equal Employment Opportunity Commission in administering Title VII of the 1964 Civil Rights Act and of the U.S. Department of Labor in administering the Equal Pay Act of 1963 for those agencies and the courts to reconcile those Acts with various state "protective" laws by requiring that, whenever feasible, the latter be applied to men as well as to women was also suggested. For in this manner, the congressional goal of furthering equality of the sexes could be implemented without sacrificing important past social gains in the employment sphere.

But, as mentioned in that chapter,[143] the inequality of employment opportunity created by state "protective" laws for women has also been the subject of attack on equal protection grounds. The rejection of such an attack, on the basis of "settled precedents," in *Mengelkoch v. Industrial Welfare Commission of California*,[144] has in fact precipitated an effort to procure review of the constitutional arguments in the United States Supreme Court.[145] There are also many situations to which the jurisdictional reach of Title VII and the Equal Pay Act do not extend.[146] In those instances a constitutional challenge would appear to be the principal if not the exclusive way of seeking to end the discriminatory effects of such legislation. For these reasons, an examination of the constitutional law aspects of such legislation is appropriate here.

Statutes Imposing Weight-Lifting Restrictions on Women or Barring Them from Certain Types of Employment

In discussing the possibilities of attacking on constitutional grounds various statutes and official practices according men and women different treatment in the employment sphere, one must take as a starting point the decision of the United States Supreme Court in *Goesart v. Cleary*.[147] As the reader will recall from Chapter 2, that decision held that it was not a violation of the Fourteenth Amendment's Equal Protection Clause for the state of Michigan to prohibit women, who were not the wives or daughters of male owners of liquor establishments, to act therein as bartenders.

More important than the result in *Goesart*, however, was the court's rationale in reaching it. In effect, the court in *Goesart* applied the "any rational basis" test for equal protection purposes. Indeed, this was intimated in Justice Frankfurter's remark that "Since the line [the legislators] have drawn *is not without a basis in reason,* we cannot give ear to the suggestion that the real impulse behind this legislation was an unchivalrous desire of male bartenders to monopolize the calling."[148]

But, as noted earlier, there has developed in equal protection and due process litigation *two* tests whose application to a particular case will depend upon whether the statute or official practice abridges a right that is properly characterized as "basic" or "nonbasic."[149] In *Goesart,* however, the Court did not even begin to explore the possibility that the right involved in that case—the right to procure a job—might be properly placed in a "basic" category, thus subjecting the state statute to the "most rigid scrutiny" and in effect placing a greater burden of justification on the party seeking to have the validity of the statute upheld than would ordinarily exist.

It is submitted that the right of Americans to procure employment is fundamental, and is to be distinguished from general business activities which can constitutionally be regulated on an "any rational basis" showing.[150] Certainly the right to procure a job—or more precisely the right to have government not impede the opportunity to freely negotiate a job with an employer, unless in furtherance of some absolutely *overriding* state policies—would appear to be just as fundamental as the right to marry, characterized as basic in *Loving v. Virginia*.[151] Indeed, a reasonable argument can be made that the right to be free of unwarranted governmental interference with the opportunity to work is more basic than the right to marry, since personal decisions to marry or not will often be affected by the financial circumstances of the prospective groom or bride. Were this view adopted, it would not be sufficient for equal protection standards that a legislature had some reasonable basis for barring women from the occupation of bartending, wrestling or mining—especially when one recalls that in individual cases the actual impact of such legislation is to impose a condition of perpetual unemployment on particular women. If the impact of various state "protective" statutes upon the "right to work" is seen in this light, then it is entirely possible that legislatures now have an obligation to do precisely what, in *Goesart v. Cleary*, Justice Frankfurter declared was beyond their responsibility, namely, "to reflect sociological insight, or shifting social standards."[152] This approach is implicit in the Court's recent utterance in the *Levy* case that the fact that history and tradition was on its side would not per se validate discriminatory legislation.[153]

That the right to work is basic in our society has in fact been recognized by the Supreme Court itself. In *Truax v. Raich*,[153a] the Court struck down as an equal protection violation an Arizona statute prohibiting employers from employing more than 20 percent of their work force from among aliens. In a statement that is relevant herein for a number of reasons, the Court noted that

> It is sought to justify this act as an exercise of the power of the State to make reasonable classifications in legislating to promote the health, safety, morals and welfare of those within its jurisdiction. But this admitted authority, with the broad range of legislative discretion that it implies, does not go so far as to make it possible for the State to deny to lawful inhabitants, because of their race or nationality, the ordinary means of earning a livelihood. It requires no argument to show that the right to work for a living in the common occupations of the community is of the very essence of the personal freedom and opportunity that it was the purpose of the Amendment to secure.[153b]

In sum, the Court would be properly performing its role as final interpreter of the U.S. Constitution were it to overrule the *Goesart* case and to invalidate, as equal protection violations, any state statutes categorically denying women the opportunity to earn their living in any calling they choose to pursue, without regard to their individual capacities, needs and talents.

In effect, the suggestions made earlier as to the role and responsibility of the Equal Employment Opportunity Commission in invalidating such laws under the command of Title VII of the 1964 Civil Rights Act whenever they come within its jurisdictional reach would be equally applicable to the courts when faced with constitutional challenges to such statutes. At the very least, to withstand equal protection challenges, such statutes would have to be modified so as merely to create presumptions of women's inability to perform particular jobs, while according them reasonable opportunity, by physical examinations, physician's certificates of fitness or otherwise, to overcome such presumptions. The same principles would apply to the various weight-lifting limitations in state statutes, as suggested in Chapter 6's discussion of the effects of Title VII upon such laws or regulations.

Hours Limitations

Recognizing the effect the state hours limitations for women have upon their employment opportunities and that their official denial or infringement constitutes the violation of a "basic civil right" is central to any attempt to deal with the constitutional aspects of such limitations. With this background, it is possible that the appeal in the *Mengelkoch*[154] case, unless refused by the U.S. Supreme Court on the grounds of insubstantiality of the federal questions presented therein,[154a] could very well be decided by the Court holding that such limitations violate the equal protection clause in that they cannot withstand the "rigid scrutiny" and the great burden of justifications required for state interferences with *basic* civil rights.

To hold such laws to be invalid, however, without doing anything more would confront the Court with the same type of agonizing dilemma that has faced the EEOC; that is, in the name of achieving equality of treatment for men and women in this area, it could find itself abrogating a useful piece of social legislation which, though incomplete, had represented a step in the direction of social progress. It is submitted, however, that, once again like the EEOC, the Supreme Court has available to it the means of preserving equality without sacrificing progress, and that specifically, it can do this by extending on the basis of existing constitutional principles the protection of such laws to men where they presently apply to women only.

At the outset it should be recognized that the constitutional-extension approach recommended with respect to hours limitations has been deliberately not recommended in the previous discussion of statutes imposing weight-lifting limitations or absolutely barring women from certain occupations. By contrast, the "extension" approach is also urged with respect to state minimum wages for women only, discussed in the next section.

The principal reason for advocating such an approach in the hours limitations and minimum wages areas, but not to weight-lifting limitations and statutory employment bars, is that if it were adopted in the latter two situations, large sections of industry would simply come to a grinding halt. For example, if the Court were to decide (assuming it has the constitutional authority to do so) that the way to remove the inequality inhering in a rule that bars only women from the occupation of mining would be to extend the bar to men, it would simply mean that mining would not be carried on in the states with such laws—hardly a tolerable result. Similarly, if it should hold that a state's 50-pound weight-lifting limitation were to be extended to men, it would simply mean that certain objects would not get lifted in the course of that state's industrial life—hardly more tolerable than the last result.

Perhaps, these effects on industry merely demonstrate that with respect to such statutes or regulations the states would be able to satisfy the greater burden of justification in abridging the basic civil right of employment in this manner—although, rather than completely validating such legislation, the Court could require that the laws be recast to permit individual women to establish that they can perform the work without harmful effects. In addition, as suggested earlier, constitutional considerations may require the states to supplement such statutes with others requiring employers to install labor saving machines, where they are available, to minimize the physical strain attendant upon lifting excessively heavy objects.

But when it comes to hours limitations or minimum wages, extension of the protection to male employees, where it presently applies to women only, would not have such drastic consequences. Industry would go on. It would simply mean that the cost to employers might be increased, an interference that has been constitutionally allowed when effected by either state or federal action. The question remains whether it is within the constitutional authority of the United States Supreme Court, if it holds that the present hours limitations violate the equal protection clause because they apply to women workers only, to decree that henceforth these laws, where they exist, must also be applied to men.

The suggestion that the Supreme Court should do this might strike some readers as advocating the nakedest kind of federal judicial interference with the state's legislative processes. In their eyes, it is "bad" enough for the Court to hold, as it has frequently done, that a particular law enacted by a state is unconstitutional and therefore must cease to exist. But it would be altogether a different process for the Court to hold, as has been suggested herein, that the law as it stands is invalid, but that rather than being abrogated, it would remain in force with the additional feature that, despite its specific limitation to women, it would now be allowed to apply also to men—a group that the legislature had not intended to benefit in enacting the legislation in question. In fact, the argument would run, had the members of these legislatures realized that such laws would be declared unconstitutional for applying only to women, they might have preferred no protective laws at all to having them apply equally to members of both sexes.

But, it is submitted, that this result is not as unthinkable as might first appear, and that, indeed it is consistent with what the Court has done, properly, in a number of other situations. Moreover, the manner of construing such statutes may mitigate what, at first blush, would appear to be legislative usurpation by the Supreme Court should it devise a solution similar to the one recommended herein.

For one thing, as suggested earlier in this book,[155] the 1905 decision in *Lochner v. New York,* invalidating hours limitation for both sexes and the 1908 decision in *Muller v. Oregon,* sustaining similar legislation for women only had much to do with influencing the states to enact such laws only for women, on the principle that half a loaf was better than none. In effect, it was the past conduct of the U.S. Supreme Court itself which largely, if not entirely, accounted for the proliferation of state protective laws applying to women only. But as demonstrated earlier, the Supreme Court, in *United States v. Darby,*[156] rejected in 1940 the thinking that had led it to invalidate the New York protective hours law in the *Lochner* case. Indeed, there can be little doubt that the Court, were it faced today with the same set of facts confronting it in the *Lochner* case, would uphold such a statute. Unfortunately, because of inertia or other reasons having nothing to do with the merits, the states did not react to the *Darby* case by enacting new laws extending the previous women-only protections to men. Part of the explanation for this inaction probably involves a lack of sensitivity to the effects such one-sided laws had on women's employment opportunities. It is also possible that these effects had not been forcefully brought to their attention by citizen participants in the states' political processes.

In sum, therefore, since the Supreme Court itself can be regarded as being largely responsible for the fact that states had enacted many protective laws in the labor sphere for women only, it should be regarded as an act of atonement for the Court itself to hold, as suggested, that such laws are invalid as they presently stand and that the remedy—unless the states should act to repeal such laws *in toto*—would be to "extend" them to men only.[157]

This result could be facilitated, moreover, were the Supreme Court to construe such laws, as it can logically do in the light of their historical background, as not simply according the protection to women only, but rather as signifying that the protection is accorded to all persons, except males. Rather than being a semantic manipulation, this construction would be consistent with what probably was the intention of many state legislatures when they enacted such laws, though by their terms, they applied only to women. Having been informed by the Supreme Court in the *Lochner* and *Muller* cases that despite their desire to provide such protection to both sexes, they could constitutionally do so only with regard to women, it is not unreasonable to read their subsequently enacted laws in the manner suggested above.

Were the statutes providing maximum hours protection for women only interpreted as suggested, that is, that in fact they provide such protection to all persons except men, a determination by the Court that such statutes violate equal protection standards for the reasons suggested earlier, and that the appropriate remedy would be to invalidate the exclusion of men would be entirely consistent with what the Court has previously done. In effect, the Court would be telling the states, "Whether you enact maximum hours legislation or not is entirely up to you. But if you do, then you must do so impartially without regard to sex."

Is this not in essence what the Court did in *Brown v. Board of Education*[158] and its progeny? Didn't the Court in those cases tell the states, in effect, "Whether you have a system of public education is up to you. But if you do, you must administer it without regard to race."

Perhaps an even closer analogy can be found in the Court's recent decision in *Levy v. Louisiana*.[159] As mentioned earlier, that decision held that a denial to illegitimate children of a right to recover for wrongful death of their mother, where her legitimate children could recover for the same wrong, violated the equal protection guarantee. But the Court's remedy for such a violation was not to remove from the legitimate children the right to recover for their mother's wrongful death, but rather to extend this right to her illegitimate children. Is this not a direct analogue to what has been urged above with respect to maximum hours legislation (and minimum wage legislation below)? That it is within the Court's power and consistent with precedent for it to hold that the invalidity of such legislation being applied to women only must be cured by extending its coverage to men also, rather than by removing it from women. Couldn't the state have urged in *Levy* that "were we aware that we would be required to extend this protection (the right to sue for a mother's wrongful death) to a group that we had originally excluded—illegitimate children—we would rather not have accorded such protection to any children, legitimate or otherwise."

To be sure, one might argue that the Louisiana statute in *Levy*, at least as interpreted by that state's supreme court, clearly excludes illegitimates, whereas the state maximum hours laws confers benefits on women only. But it is no accident that the maxim, *expressio unius, exclusio alterius,* has become a commonplace in American statutory construction. Nor does the fact that the U.S. Supreme Court in *Levy* overruled a state court's interpretation of a statute distinguish *Levy* from the maximum hours legislation considered herein. For the Supreme Court in *Levy* did not reverse the state court simply because it disagreed with the latter's interpretation of the statute—a course that would have been beyond the Court's own constitutional authority. Rather, it held that it is unconstitutional for the state supreme court to so interpret the statute. The result would have not been different had the Louisiana legislature been explicit on this point when it enacted the statute, thus removing the need for state court interpretation of its meaning.

Even some state courts, exercising their power to entertain federal constitutional challenges to state laws, have achieved similar results. Thus, in *Clem v. Brown,* an Ohio Court of Common Pleas, holding that the state's rule permitting husbands but not wives to recover for loss of consortium deprives a wife of "equal protection of the law"[160] remedied this inequality by extending the right to wives rather than by removing it from husbands. Similarly, the decision of a federal district court in Michigan in *Owen v. Illinois Baking Corporation*[161] was one more example of a federal district court curing what it regarded as a constitutionally infirm one-way consortium rule by extending the right to sue to married women.

As long ago as 1871, the United States Supreme Court held that a state could not limit the right to sue on a cause of action created under state law so as to deprive the federal courts of the power to entertain such suits if jurisdiction was otherwise present.[161a] Commenting upon this case in 1961, the Court of Appeals of the 4th Circuit noted that "Wisconsin sought to limit her wrongful death action, *which she could have repealed entirely,* to her own courts. The limitation was held not to be binding upon federal courts sitting in Wisconsin, which, when adjudicating a cause of action arising under the Wisconsin statute, should ignore the limitation."[161b] Though the result in the earlier case was dictated by the requirements of Article III of the U.S. Constitution, conferring the Judicial Power upon the United States, rather than by the equal protection clause of the 14th Amendment, it is another illustration of the Court's past practice of implementing constitutional provisions by extending a state-created benefit beyond the limits intended by the state, while recognizing that the state could, if it wanted, remove the benefit from all.

In short, there would appear to be ample precedent for the United States Supreme Court, when confronted with a constitutional challenge to state hours limitations (or minimum wage requirements) for women only, to require such protections to apply to men as well. If, in response to such a Supreme Court ruling, some states decide to repeal various protective laws altogether, that would be a course of conduct entirely within their competence—although their decision to do so or not would be obviously subject to a variety of political pressures within their own borders. Certainly, that would be no worse than a determination by the Court that such existing laws for women only must, in effect, be repealed, by holding them invalid without doing anything more.

But the importance of a Supreme Court ruling along the lines suggested above is that it would relieve the states of exerting any new initiative to extend the previous protection to men also. It would in fact impose upon them the burden of repealing such laws, should they decide to pursue that course. Since that would also require state initiative, since state initiative in any sphere may be often more difficult to develop than tolerance of the status quo, and since many forces within the states would oppose such initiatives, the likelihood that significant numbers of states would respond to such Supreme Court rulings by repealing existing protective legislation is not too great.[161c]

But the most important consideration of all is that were the Supreme Court to follow the course of conduct suggested herein, it would not only undo the harmful effects of some of its prior decisions permitting various types of sex discrimination, but would do so in a manner that would preserve important social gains of the past. Were this to occur, the fears of many who have opposed the "equal rights" amendment because of what they saw as its threat to existing legislation that, though only partial in not applying to men, was nevertheless needed, would be allayed. For the course of action urged herein would achieve as much or more than what could be achieved under the equal rights amendment, without undoing much that was worthy of preservation.

Minimum Wage Laws Applicable to Women Only

Although in a few states[162] and under the federal Fair Labor Standards Act,[163] minimum wage laws apply to all employees regardless of sex, in the majority of states such laws apply only to women or to women and minors, but not to adult males.[164] The tendency of this sex-based disparity in minimum wage coverage to foster inequality of employment opportunity or in actual wages is probably not as great as in some other unequal laws in the employment sphere. For one thing, wage minima prescribed by these laws are often unrealistically low and do not achieve the level of going wage rates dictated by the principle of supply and demand. In most cases, moreover, male employees command real wages in the labor market far in excess of the state minima, so that males have not been aware, and have therefore not complained, of being the objects of discrimination.

But as demonstrated in Chapter 4, males are occasionally paid less than the minimum wage rates prescribed for women in their states.[165] Where the enterprise or individual employee is subject to the jurisdictional reach of Title VII of the 1964 Civil Rights Act or the Equal Pay Act of 1963, this disparity can be corrected by requiring the state minimum wage law to be extended to men also. This has been required by both the Department of Labor and the EEOC,[166] and in effect represents an incorporation of the state statute by reference into the federal law, with their equal pay and equal opportunity principles then causing the extension.

In situations which are not affected by Title VII and the Equal Pay Act, however, males will occasionally be the victims of discrimination when, as a result of state law, they receive lower wages than women employed on the same or similar work. And—also occasionally—women may find in such situations, that employers are provided with an incentive for hiring only males since presumably lower wages could be paid.

The question that must then be faced is whether either or both situations, where they occur beyond the reach of the federal legislation, can be corrected on the basis of constitutional principles. Specifically, is there constitutional warrant, or more precisely any constitutional prohibition against, the United States Supreme Court requiring states that presently prescribe minimum wages for women to extend their laws to men? It is submitted that, as in the case of state hours legislation for women only, state laws prescribing minimum wages for women only should be declared by the Supreme Court to be in violation of the equal protection clause of the United States Constitution's Fourteenth Amendment. Furthermore, it would be consistent with the Supreme Court's previous actions in a number of areas to remedy such unconstitutionality by holding that such laws, until and unless repealed, also apply to men, rather than merely that they are invalid and can be ignored by employers.

Minimum wage laws applying to women only have been the subject of considerable constitutional litigation in the state and federal courts.[167] While the state courts originally upheld such laws against a variety of constitutional attacks[168] the United States Supreme Court in 1923 held in *Adkins v. Children's Hospital*[169] that a state law prescribing minimum wages for women violated the Fifth Amendment's prohibition against the taking of liberty or property without due process of law. In effect, the Court in *Adkins* distinguished the *Muller* case by emphasizing the connection between the hours limitation for women workers upheld there and the general physical differences between the sexes.[170] More important, however, was the Court's recognition that the adoption of the Nineteenth Amendment and the general emancipatory trend for women in the law prevented her being "given special protection or be[ing] subject to special restraint in her contractual relationships."[171] In the Court's eyes, because of its view of the principle of freedom of contract, minimum wage legislation for women tended to be regarded as a special restraint rather than a special protection.

But fourteen years later, the *Adkins* case was overruled by the United States Supreme Court in *West Coast Hotel Co. v. Parrish*.[172] Upholding a Washington statute that resembled in its essential respects the one invalidated in *Adkins*, the *Parrish* decision rejected the earlier case's view that liberty of contract was, as a result of the due process clauses of the Fifth and Fourteenth Amendments, constitutionally inviolable. In *Parrish*, the Court recognized that "regulation which is reasonable in relation to its subject and is adopted in the interests of the community is due process."[173] Relying on earlier cases[174] that had been ignored in *Adkins* the Court noted that it had been previously recognized that the employment relationship could be regulated by the state in the exercise of the police power. It is important to note that the cases relied on by the Court in *Parrish* were all cases that made no distinction between the sexes insofar as the constitutionality of the states' regulation of the employment relationship was concerned.[175]

There was no reason why the result in *Parrish* could not have rested on the above grounds alone. Indeed, a few years later, the Supreme Court, in *United States v. Darby* sustained the federal Fair Labor Standards Act which prescribed minimum wages for both men and women. Significantly, the Court in *Darby* noted that

Since our decision in *West Coast Hotel Co. v. Parrish*, 300 U.S. 379, it is no longer open to question that the fixing of *a minimum wage* is within the legislative power and that the bare fact of its exercise is not a denial of due process under the Fifth more than under the Fourteenth Amendment.[176]

Thus the Court in *Darby* believed that what had been significant in *Parrish* was the upholding of a minimum wage and not a minimum wage for women. If one looks at what the Court did in *Parrish* rather than what it said, it will be seen at once that this is in fact what occurred.

But the *Parrish* case appears to stand in the way of any argument urging the unconstitutionality, as violating the equal protection clause, of a minimum wage law applicable only to women. For one thing, though *Parrish* in fact overruled *Adkins* simply on the basis of a revised view of due process requirements as related to the "liberty to contract" concept, the Court in *Parrish* somehow felt impelled to emphasize that this was a statute applying only to women and that the state had an interest in their "health . . . and their protection from unscrupulous and overreaching employers."[177] It is submitted that, in the light of what it had previously said and done in that case, this discussion was entirely unnecessary to the result in *Parrish*. For another thing, the Court noted,[178] in response to one of Justice Sutherland's dissenting observations[179] that

> The argument that the legislation in question constitutes an arbitrary discrimination, because it does not extend to men, is unavailing. This Court has frequently held that the legislative authority, acting within its proper field, is not bound to extend its regulation to all cases which it might possibly reach. The 'legislature is free to recognize degrees of harm and it may confine its restrictions to those classes of cases where the need is deemed to be clearest.'[180]

The problem with the Court's reasoning here was that it took no account whatsoever of the positive harm done by this particular legislation in placing some women at a disadvantage to men insofar as employment opportunity was concerned or with respect to the harm occasionally suffered by male employees who might be impelled to bid for jobs at lower wage rates in order to compete successfully against women for available jobs.[181]

That the Court ignored these possible effects of such legislation is probably explained by its implied assumption that it was faced with an "either-or" situation. Either it would sustain the legislation as applied to women only or else it would have to invalidate the law. That it could constitutionally exercise its power by sus-

taining the law as not being in violation of the due process clause
of the Fourteenth Amendment while at the same time, in order to
make it conform to the equal protection clause of that amendment, requiring it to apply to men also, did not—and in the light
of constitutional precedents of the period probably could not—
occur to the Court. But as demonstrated in the preceding section
dealing with state hours limitations, it would be consistent with
what the Court has done in the last twenty-five years were it to
take this position today. Certainly were the attack on such laws,
because of their impact on employment opportunities, based on
equal protection grounds, the Court could determine that they
cannot stand as presently applied because, infringing a basic civil
right—the right to work—they cannot sustain the great burden of
justification required to support such laws. But, as suggested
earlier, the cure for such invalidity would not be to abrogate the
laws but to interpret them as also applying to men. Among other
ways to such a result would be for the Court to hold, as it has
often done in the past, that if a law can be construed as being either
constitutional or unconstitutional, the former construction will
prevail.[182]

THE "EQUAL RIGHTS" AMENDMENT?

The preceding pages in this chapter have demonstrated that,
despite a period of relative desuetude in this area, existing provisions of the U.S. Constitution, and principally the equal protection
and due process guarantees expressed or implied in the Fifth and
Fourteenth Amendments, have been increasingly invoked in the
state courts and the lower federal courts to successfully challenge
a wide variety of laws and official practices that continue to work
an arbitrary discrimination between the sexes.[183] As some of these
cases make their way to the Supreme Court, the Court, influenced
by the reasoning of the opinions below and perhaps more responsive to the present sociological climate surrounding the question
of women's legal status than it has been in the past, may drastically
revise its prior approach to determining the kind and extent of
official sex discrimination that is allowable. In a fundamental
sense, the 1963 prophecy of the U.S. President's Commission on
the Status of Women appears to be in the process of fulfilling
itself.

As will be recalled, it was a belief in the eventual revision of the Supreme Court's approach to the question of sex discrimination in the law that led the President's Commission to withhold any recommendation with respect to the proposed "equal rights" amendment.[184] That amendment has for many years attracted a substantial number of proponents, however, and there are undoubtedly many persons who, even today, believe that its adoption is a necessary step toward achieving full legal equality between the sexes. Whether such a belief is warranted is the subject of the present section.

The crucial language of the proposed equal rights amendment to the United States Constitution states that "Equality of rights under the law shall not be denied or abridged by the United States or by any State on account of sex." Proposals of this sort have been introduced in each Congress since 1923,[185] and are currently before the 90th Congress.[186]

In 1950 and 1953 the Senate approved the proposed amendment, but with the "Hayden rider" added on the floor.[187] That "rider" provided that the amendment "shall not be construed to impair any rights, benefits, or exemptions now or hereafter conferred by law, upon persons of female sex."

In evaluating the amendment and rider, therefore, there are three possible results. One is to recommend adoption of the amendment alone, another is to recommend adoption of the amendment together with the rider, and the third is to recommend, if not the rejection of the amendment and/or rider, at least an abatement of any efforts to secure their adoption.

For reasons to be explained below, it is this final alternative that is urged herein.

Given the premises and outlook that have been expressed throughout this volume, it is abundantly clear that the amendment with the rider attached can, in no event, be acceptable. To qualify the amendment's requirement of equality with the command that certain special legal privileges enjoyed by women "now or hereafter" shall not be impaired is not to require equality at all. It is of course one thing to say that *some* of these existing legal privileges and benefits may continue to be held valid under the various evolving standards for testing differences in treatment of various identifiable social and human groups. It is quite another thing to say that any privilege previously conferred or to be conferred in the future upon women only is to be automatically validated. Rather than expressing the principle of equality, the amendment with the rider would in effect create a situation in which women would be "more equal" than men. Indeed, if as has been suggested in this chapter, certain existing legal benefits and privileges accorded to women only may, unless extended to men also, violate existing constitutional provisions, then the adoption of the amendment with the rider would raise a serious question as to its validity in the light of the existing Fifth and Fourteenth Amendments to the United States Constitution.[188]

If the principal villain in this area is, as has been suggested, the status of "otherness" that a male dominated society has imposed on women, the adoption of the amendment with the rider would constitute the granting of a blank check to the legislatures to perpetuate if not aggravate existing inequalities.

Of course, the comments that have just been made have been addressed to the potential effects of the amendment with the rider, and are by no means intended to impugn the motives of its sponsor or of those senators who have supported the rider. In all likelihood, support of the rider has been motivated principally by a fear that the adoption of the amendment without the rider would lead to the abrogation of useful social legislaion, such as the minimum wage and maximum hours laws for women only.[189] But, as has been demonstrated in this chapter, the principle of equality of treament without regard to sex can be implemented without sacrificing these important social gains of the past. This can be done by the device of extending, wherever feasible, such laws to men also. As has been shown, the court can do this alone—although legislatures, provided they wanted to take the initiative to do so, could subsequently repeal such laws, a not too likely event in the light of our social and political history.

What, then, of the amendment alone, that is, without the rider? At first blush there is a certain beguiling panacea-like quality about the amendment for those who are dedicated to the quest for equal dignity between the sexes. It would seem that, were the amendment adopted, it would be capable of achieving this goal in one fell swoop. Indeed, there occasionally have been intimations in some judicial opinions that sex discrimination in the law could not be constitutionally invalidated "unless prohibited in express terms in the Constitution. . . ."[190]

But it is submitted that were the amendment adopted, it would have little or no effect upon existing constitutional doctrine in the area of sex discrimination. Then, as now, the crucial factor will continue to be the responsiveness of the judiciary to the social impulse toward equality of treatment without regard to sex. For example, pursuant to a functional analysis, a court could hold, even after the adoption of the proposed amendment, that a law exempting women from strenuous military service is not one that denies or abridges any right (of men) on account of sex, but is rather one that is reasonably based upon the general physical (functional) differences between the sexes. Similar results could also be obtained in many other areas in which men and women are presently accorded different legal treatment.

Many proponents of the amendment appear to be motivated by a belief that the United States Supreme Court and lower state and federal courts have in the past held existing provisions of the United States Constitution, in particular the Fifth and Fourteenth Amendments, inapplicable to women. The fact is, however, that the courts have not done this at all. Instead, they have generally held that the existing constitutional provisions do apply to women, but that within the limits of those provisions, women in many situations constitute a class that can reasonably be subjected to separate treatment. It is submitted that the adoption of the equal rights amendment would not fundamentally change the picture. While the proposed amendment states that equality of rights shall not be abridged on account of sex, sex classifications could continue if it can be demonstrated that though they are expressed in terms of sex, they are in reality based upon function. On the other hand, under existing constitutional provisions, particular classifications of men and women that cannot be shown to be based upon function, are vulnerable to attack—as has already been demonstrated in some lower state and federal courts with respect to discriminatory laws in the realm of jury service, differences in punishment for identical crimes, right to sue for loss of consortium, and the like.

Of course, the presence of the amendment in the Constitution would not be entirely without special effects. In order to achieve the results suggested in the preceding paragraphs, the judiciary would have to overcome the specific language of the amendment. But the point that must be stressed is not only that this would not be impossible of achievement, but that judges could in fact do this very easily, adopting the analytical approach (functional analysis) mentioned earlier.

If adoption of the equal rights amendment would have little impact upon existing constitutional law doctrine in the area of sex discrimination, proponents of equality of legal treatment for men and women will find that, as a tactical matter, their energies will be better spent in other activities directed toward this goal. Every day spent in working for the amendment is a day that is taken away from informing the American public of the continued areas of unequal treatment, or from participating in the presently growing number of challenges to such treatment based on existing constitutional provisions.

Given the recent developments in the area of sex discrimination, there is every indication that great changes are in the offing, and that, in the tradition of the common law, such changes will take place with respect to specific, discrete situations, rather than with a potentially destructive and self-defeating blunderbuss approach. The need is for greater numbers of people of both sexes, lawyers and non-lawyers alike, to begin turning their attention to the legal problems in this area and toward devising new approaches, only a few of which have been suggested herein, to the solution of those problems.

CHAPTER 7

Summary and Conclusions

> "What seems to me the most significant common traits in these *peaceful societies* are that they all . . . make very little distinction between the ideal characters of men and women, particularly that they have no ideal of brave, aggressive masculinity." Geoffrey Gorer, "Man Has No 'Killer' Instinct," *New York Times Magazine*, November 27, 1966, at p. 107. (Emphasis supplied.)

THE LEGAL STATUS of American women has risen to the point that it is not now far below that of American men. For the most part, the common law disabilities of married women—contractual incapacity, loss of rights to manage, control and receive the income from real property owned prior to marriage, the complete transference to the husband of all premarital personal property—have been abrogated by statute. Though legislative reforms in these areas were initially resisted by many courts, the trend of judicial decisions in recent years has been toward implementation of their spirit as well as their letter.

Similarly, unmarried women, whose legal situation has at all times during Anglo-American legal history been immeasurably better than their married sisters', have also made substantial progress in closing the gap between their own legal status and that of American men. Legal obstructions to women's right to vote having been swept aside by the Nineteenth Amendment, the denial of the right, duty, or privilege—depending upon one's point of view—to serve on juries having been for the time being at least denounced as an unconstitutional practice, the enactment into federal law of the principle of equal pay for equal work regardless of sex, and of a prohibition, supported by penal-type sanctions for violators, against sex-based discrimination in employers' and unions' hiring practices—have all elevated the status of women regardless of their marital situation. Not only have these measures helped provide the means whereby American women can share in and contribute to the life and work of American society; they have also paved the way toward an eventual emancipation that will be complete in every detail.

Nor should the parallels drawn in an earlier portion of this essay between the past and present condition of American women and American Negroes obscure the fundamental differences in their respective situations. Despite the persistence of much legal and social discrimination based upon sex, women continue to live in the closest daily intimacy with men. By contrast, Negroes have yet to achieve anything even resembling close physical contact with white persons in the ordinary business of daily living—notwithstanding the recent dramatic strides in the employment area where most people do spend a good part of their waking hours. But the most important differences between a white-male-dominated society's treatment of women and of Negroes is that, though high emotions exist in both instances, the utter social and sexual dependence of the male upon the female has necessarily tempered the manner in which the female is treated.

Many persons will no doubt protest the characterization of American society as male-dominated. At every turn, they believe, they can point to examples in the daily lives of married couples, at least among those who can be described as belonging to the "middle class," in which it is the wife rather than the husband who directly or indirectly makes the crucial decisions for the family. But it is by no means the aim of this essay to urge the substitution of the tyranny of women for that of men. In the face of laws and social mores that relegate them to an inferior condition, many women have undoubtedly developed compensating personality and character traits designed to assist them in combating their second-class status in law and society. By indirection, guile, subterfuge, manipulation, and other even less worthy techniques, some women find a means of asserting their will in what strikes them with substantial justification—although no doubt with less justification today than in the past—as being essentially a man's world. Such has always been the response of those who have been the objects of discrimination.

Discrimination, whether social or legal or both, not only stunts the personal development of its objects, causing them to become less socially productive; it also often nurtures the development of many traits and characteristics that on any objective scale would be deemed undesirable and unworthy. Confronted by a threat to his survival, man adapts his character to the exigencies of the situation, the result at times being the loss of integrity and a part of his humanity. Thus has it often been with women who, to some people, appear to hold an upper hand in the male-female relationship despite legal and social restrictions. In many cases, they have achieved such a position at the expense of sacrificing essential components of their character.

But if there are some who would doubt the proposition that despite past progress in the campaign to emancipate women under the law their legal position is still essentially inferior to that of men, let them be referred to the preceding pages in this essay. In one area of legal regulation after another, they will find women continuing to be treated either differently from men or less favorably, and judges and legislators continuing to emphasize distinctions between the sexes which, though they are the results of prior unequal treatment, are often presented as justifications for such unequal treatment in the future. Though a principal aim of the Married Women's Acts was no doubt the burial of the common law fiction of the unity of husband and wife, that fiction still plays an important direct or indirect role in numerous areas of law. Even in the field of married women's contract and property rights in which the most dramatic improvement of the married women's inferior common law position has occurred, significant pockets of rules and decisions continue to preserve the effects, if not the rationale, of the old common law rule. And in the rules of law that govern such questions as a married woman's domicile, her name, and her right to sue for loss of consortium, the past looms large. Even such a vaunted area as the community property system falls short of being a paradise on earth for married women, since the husband's supremacy is still being maintained in many ways. Nevertheless, the philosophical foundations of that system probably lend themselves much more readily to the eventual development of truly equal property relations between the sexes than those underlying the common law marital property regimes.

We have also seen that paradise is still beyond reach for most single women—or those we have termed women without regard to marital status. Though jury service is regarded by many people as an oppressive burden, it need not remain such; indeed, it will not be so regarded once adequate financial compensation schemes for jury service are developed. Meanwhile, the present state of the law encourages women to follow the line of least resistance and thereby deny themselves the opportunity of playing a limited role in an important area of public life. As for laws that prescribe different minimum ages for males and females for various types of activities, the picture is somewhat more complex. In most instances, and especially in the field of contractual capacity, no logical reasons appear to justify separate minimum ages for males and females. The troublesome question—and it is by no means suggested that a complete answer has been offered in these pages—is in the prescription of minimum ages for marriage. The difficulty lies not so much in acceptance of the principle that a uniform age should apply to both sexes, as in the determination of what that uniform age should be, in view of the infinite variety of factual situations that can arise.

Not unexpectedly, the most important area in which the American legal system continues to discriminate in a direct sense is in the regulation of sexual conduct. Former statutes that in effect permitted a husband, but not the wife, to engage in an occasional act of adultery have largely disappeared, now being found only in the laws of Kentucky.[1] Similarly, the rule exempting a female marriage applicant from the duty of furnishing proof of freedom from venereal disease now also appears to be limited to one state—Washington.[2] But almost everywhere the special crimes of statutory rape, seduction and enticement impose different standards of behavior upon females than they do upon males; the criminal abortion laws, while not in legal contemplation a "cause" of women's fatalities, contribute significantly to the production of those deaths, without having that effect upon males; the definition of prostitution and the enforcement of laws prohibiting prostitution and related crimes express law's partisanship with regard to the conflicting views of the appropriate modes of sexual conduct for males and females; and the "unwritten law" defense for married men, but not for married women, also leaves no doubt where "law" stands on such matters.

Nor are these the only types of discriminatory legal regulations of sexual conduct. No attempt has been made herein to present an exhaustive survey of the laws that discriminate on the basis of sex. In the field of legal regulation of sexual conduct alone may be added such other instances of discrimination as the New York law that permits a finding that a female is a "person in need of super-vision" at a higher age than for a male;[3] the unequal administration by colleges and universities of their legal role *in loco parentis,* expressed by separate rules of conduct for male and female students;[4] and the pervasive "man-in-the-house rule" found in the social welfare laws of most states, under which a woman receiving assistance under the Aid to Needy Children program may have that aid discontinued, and the support responsibility foisted upon any man, husband or not, who is found to be living in her house, while no such curbs are imposed upon the sexual conduct of male recipients of federal or state social welfare assistance.[5]

In sexual matters, the law, as does society at large, often appears ambivalent, vacillating between a view of woman as an object to be protected—Ibsen's doll in a doll's house—and an object of scorn, distrust and aversion. Premarital chastity of women is to be pre-served at all costs, while that of men may be lost without severe legal consequences. Admittedly, society at large is not in complete agreement that the double moral standard of the past should be abandoned, and there is room for debate on this question as in all others raised in these pages. The important point, however, is that no one should doubt the position assumed by the American legal system with regard to these questions. Given law's profound influ-ence upon social attitudes, those who believe that separate sexual and moral standards for men and women are hypocritical and im-moral will find that they have to wage a battle against some specific legal rules as well as social attitudes in general if their views on these questions are to prevail.

Many legal expressions of discriminatory attitudes based on sex can and will be corrected by lawmakers themselves, solely because of their revised appraisal of the policy considerations underlying such rules in the first place. Their willingness to make such changes will of course be influenced by the extent to which they are sub-jected to the normal political pressures urging them to do so. The development of such pressures will in turn depend upon the extent to which the public is informed of the existence of these sex-based inequities in the law—which has been one of the primary goals of this book.

But as demonstrated in Chapter 6, it is highly possible that in many areas of the law, the goals of equal treatment without regard to sex may be achieved by force of constitutional principles, and regardless of the views that state and federal lawmakers may themselves hold as to the policy considerations behind the rules that presently discriminate on the grounds of sex. The possibility of achieving such results represents a continuing challenge to the ingenuity of attorneys who are sensitive to the need to ensure equal dignity between the sexes—at least to the extent that legal rules can achieve such ends.

In the employment area, which is in many respects the most crucial, the possibility of significant breakthroughs is clearly upon us as a result of Title VII and the Equal Pay Act. But here too, attorneys who are sympathetic to the underlying goals of this recent legislation will have to remain alert to ensure that these statutes are not circumvented as a result of apparent "loopholes" in their provisions. In Chapters 4 and 5 some approaches to preventing such circumvention were suggested—although they were by no means the only ones that can be taken to that problem.

Much can be read and heard these days about the traumatic effects the social and legal emancipation of women have had upon the psychological condition of both sexes. The major culprit is said to be the phenomenon of "role reversal." In the old days a man was a man and he did man's things; a woman was a woman and she did woman's things. Now all that is changed, and as a result neither men nor women, or so the argument runs, know what they are and what they should do. This is said to have led to dramatic increases in the divorce rate, criminality, and mass psychoneurosis.

The ultimate word on that question will of course have to be given by psychologists, psychiatrists and their professional brethren. But here, several comments may be offered. The first is that as these pages have demonstrated, women's legal and social emancipation is far from complete. If the partial emancipation of women to date has had an unsettling effect upon the psychological stability of both men and women, a certain amount of this may be inevitable; change and instability are in many respects synonymous. On the other hand, the psychological problems presumably resulting from such changes may merely reflect the very incompleteness of women's legal emancipation and the fact that it is still an ongoing process. When women will have achieved true and complete legal and social equality with men, the problem of men or women knowing who or what they are is likely to disappear. For at that time, both men and women will be able to recognize themselves for what they have always been—people. The psychological well-being of our total population may therefore be the most important single reason for getting on with the job of erasing all remaining pockets of legal and social inequality between the sexes.

Finally, a word on the future of sex-based discrimination in American law. Despite the suggestion made in an earlier part of this volume that Americans in general, and American women in particular, are unconcerned with the problem of sex-based legal discrimination, there are many indications that the situation is changing rapidly. The very existence of the United Nations Commission on the Status of Women, the United States President's Commission on the Status of Women, and the Governors' Commission on the Status of Women in 50 states are clear signs that interest in this subject is on the increase—most significantly among those who have had no previous professional concern with the status of women. The recent enactment of the Equal Pay Act and the Equal Employment Opportunity provisions of the Civil Rights Act of 1964 also suggests that public officials are prepared to respond positively to expressions of concern over the disparity in the legal treatment of men and women in the United States.

Nor can we overlook the increasing frequency with which sex-discriminatory legal rules are now being challenged on the basis of constitutional principles—both by individuals and by such groups as the newly formed National Organization for Women (N.O.W.).

Hopefully this essay may play a small part in stimulating further interest in this long neglected field of human rights.

APPENDICES

Title VII of the Civil Rights Act of 1964[*]

SEC. 701. DEFINITIONS

For the purposes of this title—

(a) The term "person" includes one or more individuals, labor unions, partnerships, associations, corporations, legal representatives, mutual companies, joint-stock companies, trusts, unincorporated organizations, trustees in bankruptcy, or receivers.

(b) The term "employer" means a person engaged in an industry affecting commerce who has twenty-five or more employees for each working day in each of twenty or more calendar weeks in the current or preceding calendar year, and any agent of such a person, but such term does not include (1) the United States, a corporation wholly owned by the Government of the United States, an Indian tribe, or a State or political subdivision thereof, (2) a bona fide private membership club (other than a labor organization) which is exempt from taxation under section 501(c) of the Internal Revenue Code of 1954: *Provided*, That during the first year after the effective date prescribed in subsection (a) of section 716, persons having fewer than one hundred employees (and their agents) shall not be considered employers, and, during the second year after such date, persons having fewer than seventy-five employees (and their agents) shall not be considered employers, and, during the third year after such date, persons having fewer than fifty employees (and their agents) shall not be considered employers: *Provided further,* That it shall be the policy of the United States to insure equal employment opportunities for Federal employees without discrimination because of race, color, religion, sex or national origin and the President shall utilize his existing authority to effectuate this policy.

(c) The term "employment agency" means any person regularly undertaking with or without compensation to procure employees for an employer or to procure for employees opportunities to work for an employer and includes an agent of such a person; but shall not include an agency of the United States, or an agency of a State or political subdivision of a State, except that such terms shall include the United States Employment Service and the system of State and local employment services receiving Federal assistance.

(d) The term "labor organization" means a labor organization engaged in an industry affecting commerce, and any agent of such an organization, and includes any organization of any kind, any agency, or employee repre-

[*] 78 Stat. 253, 42 U.S.C. § 2000e et seq. (1964).

sentation committee, group, association, or plan so engaged in which employees participate and which exists for the purpose, in whole or in part, of dealing with employers concerning grievances, labor disputes, wages, rates of pay, hours, or other terms or conditions of employment, and any conference, general committee, joint or system board, or joint council so engaged which is subordinate to a national or international labor organization.

(e) A labor organization shall be deemed to be engaged in an industry affecting commerce if (1) it maintains or operates a hiring hall or hiring office which procures employees for an employer or procures for employees opportunities to work for an employer, or (2) the number of its members (or, where it is a labor organization composed of other labor organizations or their representatives, if the aggregate number of the members of such other labor organization) is (A) one hundred or more during the first year after the effective date prescribed in subsection (a) of section 716, (B) seventy-five or more during the second year after such date or fifty or more during the third year, or (C) twenty-five or more thereafter, and such labor organization—

(1) is the certified representative of employees under the provisions of the National Labor Relations Act, as amended, or the Railway Labor Act, as amended;

(2) although not certified, is a national or international labor organization or a local labor organization recognized or acting as the representative of employees of an employer or employers engaged in an industry affecting commerce; or

(3) has chartered a local labor organization or subsidiary body which is representing or actively seeking to represent employees of employers within the meaning of paragraph (1) or (2); or

(4) has been chartered by a labor organization representing or actively seeking to represent employees within the meaning of paragraph (1) or (2) as the local or subordinate body through which such employees may enjoy membership or become affiliated with such labor organization; or

(5) is a conference, general committee, joint or system board, or joint council subordinate to a national or international labor organization, which includes a labor organization engaged in an industry affecting commerce within the meaning of any of the preceding paragraphs of this subsection.

(f) The term "employee" means an individual employed by an employer.

(g) The term "commerce" means trade, traffic, commerce, transportation, transmission, or communication among the several States; or between a State and any place outside thereof; or within the District of Columbia, or a possession of the United States; or between points in the same State but through a point outside thereof.

(h) The term "industry affecting commerce" means any activity, business, or industry in commerce or in which a labor dispute would hinder or obstruct commerce or the free flow of commerce and includes any activity or industry "affecting commerce" within the meaning of the Labor-Management Reporting and Disclosure Act of 1959.

(i) The term "state" includes a State of the United States, the District of Columbia, Puerto Rico, the Virgin Islands, American Samoa, Guam, Wake Island, the Canal Zone, and Outer Continental Shelf lands defined in the Outer Continental Shelf Lands Act.

SEC. 702. EXEMPTION

This title shall not apply to an employer with respect to the employment of aliens outside any State, or to a religious corporation, association, or society with respect to the employment of individuals of a particular religion to perform work connected with the carrying on by such corporation, association, or society of its religious activities or to an educational institution with respect to the employment of individuals to perform work connected wth the educational activities of such institution.

SEC. 703. DISCRIMINATION BECAUSE OF RACE, COLOR, RELIGION, SEX, OR NATIONAL ORIGIN

(a) It shall be an unlawful employment practice for an employer—

(1) to fail or refuse to hire or to discharge any individual, or otherwise to discriminate against any individual with respect to his compensation, terms, conditions, or privileges of employment, because of such individual's race, color, religion, sex, or national origin; or

(2) to limit, segregate, or classify his employees in any way which would deprive or tend to deprive any individual of employment opportunities or otherwise adversely affect his status as an employee, because of such individual's race, color, religion, sex, or national origin.

(b) It shall be an unlawful employment practice for an employment agency to fail or refuse to refer for employment, or otherwise to discriminate against, any individual because of his race, color, religion, sex, or national origin, or to classify or refer for employment any individual on the basis of his race, color, religion, sex, or national origin.

(c) It shall be an unlawful employment practice for a labor organization—

(1) to exclude or to expel from its membership, or otherwise to discriminate against, any individual because of his race, color, religion, sex, or national origin;

(2) to limit, segregate, or classify its membership, or to classify or fail or refuse to refer for employment any individual, in any way which would deprive or tend to deprive any individual of employment opportunities, or would limit such employment opportunities or otherwise adversely affect his status as an employee or as an applicant for employment, because of such individual's race, color, religion, sex, or national origin; or

(3) to cause or attempt to cause an employer to discriminate against an individual in violation of this section.

(d) It shall be an unlawful employment practice for any employer, labor organization, or joint labor-management committee controlling apprenticeship or other training or retraining, including on-the-job training programs to discriminate against any individual because of his race, color, religion, sex, or national origin in admission to, or employment in, any program established to provide apprenticeship or other training.

(e) Notwithstanding any other provision of this title, (1) it shall not be an unlawful employment practice for an employer to hire and employ employees, for an employment agency to classify, or refer for employment any individual, for a labor organization to classify its membership or to classify or refer for employment any individual, or for an employer, labor organization, or joint labor-management committee controlling apprenticeship or other training or retraining programs to admit or employ any individual in any such program, on the basis of his religion, sex, or national origin in those certain instances where religion, sex, or national origin is a bona fide occupational qualification reasonably necessary to the normal operation of that particular business or enterprise, and (2) it shall not be an unlawful employment practice for a school, college, university, or other educational institution or institution of learning to hire and employ employees of a particular religion if such school, college, university, or other educational institution or institution of learning is, in whole or in substantial part, owned, supported, controlled, or managed by a particular religion or by a particular religious corporation, association, or society, or if the curriculum of such school, college, university, or other educational institution or institution of learning is directed toward the propagation of a particular religion.

(f) As used in this title, the phrase "unlawful employment practice" shall not be deemed to include any action or measure taken by an employer, labor organization, joint labor-management committee, or employment agency with respect to an individual who is a member of the Communist Party of the United States or of any other organization required to register as a Communist-action or Communist-front organization by final order of the Subversive Activities Control Board pursuant to the Subversive Activities Control Act of 1950.

(g) Notwithstanding any other provision of this title, it shall not be an unlawful employment practice for an employer to fail or refuse to hire and employ any individual for any position, for an employer to discharge any individual from any position, or for an employment agency to fail or refuse to refer any individual for employment in any position, or for a labor organization to fail or refuse to refer any individual for employment in any position, if—

(1) the occupancy of such position, or access to the premises in or upon which any part of the duties of such position is performed or is to be performed, is subject to any requirement imposed in the interest of the national security of the United States under any security program in effect pursuant to or administered under any statute of the United States or any Executive order of the President; and

(2) such individual has not fulfilled or has ceased to fulfill that requirement.

(h) Notwithstanding any other provision of this title, it shall not be an unlawful employment practice for an employer to apply different standards of compensation, or different terms, conditions, or privileges of employment pursuant to a bona fide seniority or merit system, or a system which measures earnings by quantity or quality of production or to employees who work in different locations, provided that such differences are not the result of an intention to discriminate because of race, color, religion, sex, or national origin, nor shall it be an unlawful employment practice for an employer to give and to act upon the results of any professionally developed ability test provided that such test, its administration or action upon the results is not designed, intended or used to discriminate because of race, color, religion, sex or national origin. It shall not be an unlawful employment practice under this title for any employer to differentiate upon the basis of sex in determining the amount of the wages or compensation paid or to be paid to employees of such employer if such differentiation is authorized by the provisions of section 6(d) of the Fair Labor Standards Act of 1938 as amended (29 U.S.C. 206(d)).

(i) Nothing contained in this title shall apply to any business or enterprise on or near an Indian reservation with respect to any publicly announced employment practice of such business or enterprise under which a preferential treatment is given to any individual because he is an Indian living on or near a reservation.

(j) Nothing contained in this title shall be interpreted to require any employer, employment agency, labor organization, or joint labor-management committee subject to this title to grant preferential treatment to any individual or to any group because of the race, color, religion, sex, or national origin of such individual or group on account of an imbalance which may exist with respect to the total number or percentage of persons of any race, color, religion, sex, or national origin employed by any employer, referred or classified for employment by any employment agency or labor organization, admitted to membership or classified by any labor organization, or admitted to, or employed in, any apprenticeship or other training program, in comparison with the total number or percentage of persons of such race, color, religion, sex, or national origin in any community, State, section, or other area, or in the available work force in any community, State, section, or other area.

SEC. 704. OTHER UNLAWFUL EMPLOYMENT PRACTICES

(a) It shall be an unlawful employment practice for an employer to discriminate against any of his employees or applicants for employment, for an employment agency to discriminate against any individual, or for a labor organization to discriminate against any member thereof or applicant for membership, because he has opposed any practice made an unlawful employment practice by this title, or because he has made a charge, testified, assisted, or participated in any manner in an investigation, proceeding, or hearing under this title.

(b) It shall be an unlawful employment practice for an employer, labor organization, or employment agency to print or publish or cause to be printed or published any notice or advertisement relating to employment by such an employer or membership in or any classification or referral for employment by such a labor organization, or relating to any classification or referral for employment by such an employment agency, indicating any preference, limitation, specification, or discrimination, based on race, color, religion, sex, or national origin, except that such a notice or advertisement may indicate a preference, limitation, specification, or discrimination based on religion, sex, or national origin when religion, sex, or national origin is a bona fide occupational qualification for employment.

SEC. 705. EQUAL EMPLOYMENT OPPORTUNITY COMMISSION

(a) There is hereby created a Commission to be known as the Equal Employment Opportunity Commission, which shall be composed of five members, not more than three of whom shall be members of the same political party, who shall be appointed by the President by and with the advice and consent of the Senate. One of the original members shall be appointed for a term of one year, one for a term of two years, one for a term of three years, one for a term of four years, and one for a term of five years, beginning from the date of enactment of this title, but their successors shall be appointed for terms of five years each, except that any individual chosen to fill a vacancy shall be appointed only for the unexpired term of the member whom he shall succeed. The President shall designate one member to serve as Chairman of the Commission, and one member to serve as Vice Chairman. The Chairman shall be responsible on behalf of the Commission for the administrative operations of the Commission, and shall appoint, in accordance with the civil service laws, such officers, agents, attorneys, and employees as it deems necessary to assist it in the performance of its functions and to fix their compensation in accordance with the Classification Act of 1949, as amended. The Vice Chairman shall act as Chairman in the absence or disability of the Chairman or in the event of a vacancy in that office.

(b) A vacancy in the Commission shall not impair the right of the remaining members to exercise all the powers of the Commission and three members thereof shall constitute a quorum.

(c) The Commission shall have an official seal which shall be judicially noticed.

(d) The Commission shall at the close of each fiscal year report to the Congress and to the President concerning the action it has taken; the names, salaries, and duties of all individuals in its employ and the moneys it has disbursed; and shall make such further reports on the cause of and means of eliminating discrimination and such recommendations for further legislation as may appear desirable.

(e) The Federal Executive Pay Act of 1956, as amended (5 U.S.C. 2201–2209), is further amended—

(1) by adding to section 105 thereof (5 U.S.C. 2204) the following clause:
"(32) Chairman, Equal Employment Opportunity Commission"; and

(2) by adding to clause (45) of section 106(a) thereof (5 U.S.C. 2205(a)) the following: "Equal Employment Opportunity Commission (4)."

(f) The principal office of the Commission shall be in or near the District of Columbia, but it may meet or exercise any or all its powers at any other place. The Commission may establish such regional or State offices as it deems necessary to accomplish the purpose of this title.

(g) The Commission shall have power—

(1) to cooperate with and, with their consent, utilize regional, State, local, and other agencies, both public and private, and individuals;

(2) to pay to witnesses whose depositions are taken or who are summoned before the Commission or any of its agents the same witness and mileage fees as are paid to witnesses in the courts of the United States;

(3) to furnish to persons subject to this title such technical assistance as they may request to further their compliance with this title or an order issued thereunder;

(4) upon the request of (i) any employer, whose employees or some of them, or (ii) any labor organization, whose members or some of them, refuse or threaten to refuse to cooperate in effectuating the provisions of this title, to assist in such effectuation by conciliation or such other remedial action as is provided by this title;

(5) to make such technical studies as are appropriate to effectuate the purposes and policies of this title and to make the results of such studies available to the public;

(6) to refer matters to the Attorney General with recommendations for intervention in a civil action brought by an aggrieved party under section 706, or for the institution of a civil action by the Attorney General under section 707, and to advise, consult, and assist the Attorney General on such matters.

(h) Attorneys appointed under this section may, at the direction of the Commission, appear for and represent the Commission in any case in court.

(i) The Commission shall, in any of its educational or promotional activities, cooperate with other departments and agencies in the performance of such educational and promotional activities.

(j) All officers, agents, attorneys, and employees of the Commission shall be subject to the provisions of section 9 of the Act of August 2, 1939, as amended (the Hatch Act), notwithstanding any exemption contained in such section.

SEC. 706. PREVENTION OF UNLAWFUL EMPLOYMENT PRACTICES

(a) Whenever it is charged in writing under oath by a person claiming to be aggrieved, or a written charge has been filed by a member of the Commission where he has reasonable cause to believe a violation of this title has occurred (and such charge sets forth the facts upon which it is based) that an employer, employment agency, or labor organization has engaged in an unlawful employment practice, the Commission shall furnish such employer, employment agency, or labor organization (hereinafter referred to as the "respondent") with a copy of such charge and shall make an investigation of such charge, provided that such charge shall not be made public by the Commission. If the Commission shall determine, after such investigation, that there is reasonable cause to believe that the charge is true, the Commission shall endeavor to eliminate any such alleged unlawful employment practice by informal methods of conference, conciliation, and persuasion. Nothing said or done during and as a part of such endeavors may be made public by the Commission without the written consent of the parties, or used as evidence in a subsequent proceeding. Any officer or employee of the Commission, who shall make public in any manner whatever any information in violation of this subsection shall be deemed guilty of a misdemeanor and upon conviction thereof shall be fined not more than $1,000 or imprisoned not more than one year.

(b) In the case of an alleged unlawful employment practice occurring in a State, or political subdivision of a State, which has a State or local law prohibiting the unlawful employment practice alleged and establishing or authorizing a State or local authority to grant or seek relief from such practice or to institute criminal proceedings with respect thereto upon receiving notice thereof, no charge may be filed under subsection (a) by the person aggrieved before the expiration of sixty days after proceedings have been commenced under the State or local law, unless such proceedings have been earlier terminated, provided that such sixty-day period shall be extended to one hundred and twenty days during the first year after the effective date of such State or local law. If any requirement for the commencement of such proceedings is imposed by a State or local authority other than a requirement of the filing of a written and signed statement of the facts upon which the proceeding is based, the proceeding shall be deemed to have been commenced for the purposes of this subsection at the time such statement is sent by registered mail to the appropriate State or local authority.

(c) In the case of any charge filed by a member of the Commission alleging an unlawful employment practice occurring in a State or political subdivision of a State, which has a State or local law prohibiting the practice alleged and establishing or authorizing a State or local authority to grant or seek relief from such practice or to institute criminal proceedings with respect thereto upon receiving notice thereof, the Commission shall, before taking any action with respect to such charge, notify the appropriate State or local officials and, upon request, afford them a reasonable time, but not less than sixty days (provided that such sixty-day period shall be extended to one hundred and twenty days during the first year after the effective day of such State or local law), unless a shorter period is requested, to act under such State or local law to remedy the practice alleged.

(d) A charge under subsection (a) shall be filed within ninety days after the alleged unlawful employment practice occurred, except that in the case of an unlawful employment practice with respect to which the person aggrieved has followed the procedure set out in subsection (b), such charge shall be filed by the person aggrieved within two hundred and ten days after the alleged unlawful employment practice occurred, or within thirty days after receiving notice that the State or local agency has terminated the proceedings under the State or local law, whichever is earlier, and a copy of such charge shall be filed by the Commission with the State or local agency.

(e) If within thirty days after a charge is filed with the Commission or within thirty days after expiration of any period of reference under subsection (c) (except that in either case such period may be extended to not more than sixty days upon a determination by the Commission that further efforts to secure voluntary compliance are warranted), the Commission has been unable to obtain voluntary compliance with this title, the Commission shall so notify the person aggrieved and a civil action may, within thirty days thereafter, be brought against the respondent named in the charge (1) by the person claiming to be aggrieved, or (2) if such charge was filed by a member of the Commission, by any person whom the charge alleges was aggrieved by the alleged unlawful employment practice. Upon application by the complainant and in such circumstances as the court may deem just, the court may appoint an attorney for such complainant and may authorize the commencement of the action without the payment of fees, costs, or security. Upon timely application, the court may, in its discretion, permit the Attorney General to intervene in such civil action if he certifies that the case is of general public importance. Upon request, the court may, in its discretion, stay further proceedings for not more than sixty days pending the termination of State or local proceedings described in subsection (b) or the efforts of the Commission to obtain voluntary compliance.

(f) Each United States district court and each United States court of a place subject to the jurisdiction of the United States shall have jurisdiction of actions brought under this title. Such an action may be brought in any judicial district in the State in which the unlawful employment practice is alleged to have been committed, in the judicial district in which the employment records relevant to such practice are maintained and administered, or in the judicial district in which the plaintiff would have worked but for the alleged unlawful employment practice, but if the respondent is not found within any such district, such an action may be brought within the judicial district in which the respondent has his principal office. For purposes of sections 1404 and 1406 of title 28 of the United States Code, the judicial district in which the respondent has his principal office shall in all cases be considered a district in which the action might have been brought.

(g) If the court finds that the respondent has intentionally engaged in or is intentionally engaging in an unlawful employment practice charged in the complaint, the court may enjoin the respondent from engaging in such unlawful employment practice, and order such affirmative action as may be appropriate, which may include reinstatement or hiring of employees, with or without back pay (payable by the employer, employment agency, or labor organization, as the case may be, responsible for the unlawful employment practice). Interim earnings or amounts earnable with reasonable diligence by the person or persons discriminated against shall operate to reduce the back pay otherwise allowable. No order of the court shall require the admission or reinstatement of an individual as a member of a union or the hiring, reinstatement, or promotion of an individual as an employee, or the payment to him of any back pay, if such individual was refused admission, suspended, or expelled or was refused employment or advancement or was suspended or discharged for any reason other than discrimination on account of race, color, religion, sex or national origin or in violation of section 704(a).

(h) The provisions of the Act entitled "An Act to amend the Judicial Code and to define and limit the jurisdiction of courts sitting in equity, and for other purposes," approved March 23, 1932 (29 U.S.C. 101-115), shall not apply with respect to civil actions brought under this section.

(i) In any case in which an employer, employment agency, or labor organization fails to comply with an order of a court issued in a civil action brought under subsection (e), the Commission may commence proceedings to compel compliance with such order.

(j) Any civil action brought under subsection (e) and any proceedings brought under subsection (i) shall be subject to appeal as provided in sections 1291 and 1292, title 28, United States Code.

(k) In any action or proceeding under this title the court, in its discretion, may allow the prevailing party, other than the Commission or the United States, a reasonable attorney's fee as part of the costs, and the Commission and the United States shall be liable for costs the same as a private person.

SEC. 707

(a) Whenever the Attorney General has reasonable cause to believe that any person or group of persons is engaged in a pattern or practice of resistance to the full enjoyment of any of the rights secured by this title, and that the pattern or practice is of such a nature and is intended to deny the full exercise of the rights herein described, the Attorney General may bring a civil action in the appropriate district court of the United States by filing with it a complaint (1) signed by him (or in his absence the Acting Attorney General), (2) setting forth facts pertaining to such pattern or practice, and (3) requesting such relief, including an application for a permanent or temporary injunction, restraining order or other order against the peson or persons responsible for such pattern or practice, as he deems necessary to insure the full enjoyment of the rights herein described.

(b) The district courts of the United States shall have and shall exercise jurisdiction of proceedings instituted pursuant to this section, and in any such proceeding the Attorney General may file with the clerk of such court a request that a court of three judges be convened to hear and determine the case. Such request by the Attorney General shall be accompanied by a certificate that, in his opinion, the case is of general public importance. A copy of the certificate and request for a three-judge court shall be immediately furnished by such clerk to the chief judge of the circuit (or in his absence, the presiding circuit judge of the circuit) in which the case is pending. Upon receipt of such request it shall be the duty of the chief judge of the circuit or the presiding circuit judge, as the case may be, to designate immediately three judges in such circuit, of whom at least one shall be a circuit judge and another of whom shall be a district judge of the court in which the proceeding was instituted, to hear and determine such case, and it shall be the duty of the judges so designated to assign the case for hearing at the earliest practicable date, to participate in the hearing and determination thereof, and to cause the case to be in every way expedited. An appeal from the final judgment of such court will lie to the Supreme Court.

In the event the Attorney General fails to file such a request in any such proceeding, it shall be the duty of the chief judge of the district (or in his absence, the acting chief judge) in which the case is pending immediately to designate a judge in such district to hear and determine the case. In the event that no judge in the district is available to hear and determine the case, the chief judge of the district, or the acting judge, as the case may be, shall certify this fact to the chief judge of the circuit (or in his absence, the acting chief judge) who shall then designate a district or circuit judge of the circuit to hear and determine the case.

It shall be the duty of the judge designated pursuant to this section to assign the case for hearing at the earliest practicable date and to cause the case to be in every way expedited.

SEC. 708. EFFECT ON STATE LAWS

Nothing in this title shall be deemed to exempt or relieve any person from any liability, duty, penalty, or punishment provided by any present or future law of any State or political subdivision of a State, other than any such law which purports to require or permit the doing of any act which would be an unlawful employment practice under this title.

SEC. 709. INVESTIGATIONS, INSPECTIONS, RECORDS, STATE AGENCIES

(a) In connection with any investigation of a charge filed under section 706, the Commission or its designated representative shall at all reasonable times have access to, for the purposes of examination, and the right to copy any evidence of any person being investigated or proceeded against that relates to unlawful employment practices covered by this title and is relevant to the charge under investigation.

(b) The Commission may cooperate with State and local agencies charged with the administration of State fair employment practices laws and, with the consent of such agencies, may for the purpose of carrying out its functions and duties under this title and within the limitation of funds appropriated specifically for such purpose, utilize the services of such agencies and their employees and, notwithstanding any other provision of law, may reimburse such agencies and their employees for services rendered to assist the Commission in carrying out this title. In furtherance of such cooperative efforts, the Commission may enter into written agreements with such State or local agencies and such agreements may include provisions under which the Commission shall refrain from processing a charge in any cases or class of cases specified in such agreements and under which no person may bring a civil action under section 706 in any cases or class of cases so specified, or under which the Commission shall relieve any person or class of persons in such State or locality from requirements imposed under this section. The Commission shall rescind any such agreement whenever it determines that the agreement no longer serves the interest of effective enforcement of this title.

(c) Except as provided in subsection (d), every employer, employment agency, and labor organization subject to this title shall (1) make and keep such records relevant to the determinations of whether unlawful employment practices have been or are being committed, (2) preserve such records for such periods, and (3) make such reports therefrom, as the Commission shall prescribe by regulation or order, after public hearing, as reasonable, necessary, or appropriate for the enforcement of this title or the regulations or orders thereunder. The Commission shall, by regulation, require each employer, labor organization, and joint labor-management committee subject to this title which controls an apprenticeship or other training program to maintain such records as are reasonably necessary to carry out the purpose of this title, including, but not limited to, a list of applicants who wish to participate in such program, including the chronological order in which such applications were received, and shall furnish to the Commission, upon request, a detailed description of the manner in which persons are selected to participate in the apprenticeship or other training program. Any employer, employment agency, labor organization, or joint labor-management committee which believes that the application to it of any regulation or order issued under this section would result in undue hardship may (1) apply to the Commission for an exemption from the application of such regulation or order, or (2) bring a civil action in the United States district court for the district where such records are kept. If the Commission or the court, as the case may be, finds that the application of the regulation or order to the employer, employment agency, or labor organization in question would impose an undue hardship, the Commission or the court, as the case may be, may grant appropriate relief.

(d) The provision of subsection (c) shall not apply to any employer, employment agency, labor organization, or joint labor-management committee with respect to matters occurring in any State or political subdivision thereof which has a fair employment practice law during any period in which such employer, employment agency, labor organization, or joint labor-management committee is subject to such law, except that the Commission may require such notations on records which such employer, employment agency, labor organization, or joint labor-management committee keeps or is required to keep as are necessary because of differences in coverage or methods of enforcement between the State or local law and the provisions of this title. Where an employer is required by Executive Order 10925, issued March 6, 1961, or by any other Executive order prescribing fair employment practices for Government contractors and subcontractors, or by rules or regulations issued thereunder, to file reports relating to his employment practices with any Federal agency or committee, and he is substantially in compliance with such requirements, the Commission shall not require him to file additional reports pursuant to subsection (c) of this section.

(e) It shall be unlawful for any officer or employee of the Commission to make public in any manner whatever any information obtained by the Commission pursuant to its authority under this section prior to the institution of any proceeding under this title involving such information. Any officer or employee of the Commission who shall make public in any manner whatever any information in violation of this subsection shall be guilty of a misdemeanor and upon conviction thereof, shall be fined not more than $1,000, or imprisoned not more than one year.

SEC. 710. INVESTIGATORY POWERS

(a) For the purpose of any investigation of a charge filed under the authority contained in section 706, the Commission shall have authority to examine witnesses under oath and to require the production of documentary evidence relevant or material to the charge under investigation.

(b) If the respondent named in a charge filed under section 706 fails or refuses to comply with a demand of the Commission for permission to examine or to copy evidence in conformity with the provisions of section 709(a), or if any person required to comply with the provisions of section 709(c) or (d) fails or refuses to do so, or if any person fails or refuses to comply with a demand by the Commission to give testimony under oath, the United States district court for the district in which such person is found, resides, or transacts business, shall, upon application of the Commission, have jurisdiction to issue to such person an order requiring him to comply with the provisions of section 709(c) or (d) or to comply with the demand of the Commission, but the attendance of a witness may not be required outside the State where he is found, resides, or transacts business and the production of evidence may not be required outside the State where such evidence is kept.

(c) Within twenty days after the service upon any person charged under section 706 of a demand by the Commission for the production of documentary evidence or for permission to examine or to copy evidence in conformity with the provisions of section 709(a), such person may file in the district court of the United States for the judicial district in which he resides, is found, or transacts business, and serve upon the Commission a petition for an order of such court modifying or setting aside such demand. The time allowed for compliance with the demand in whole or in part as deemed proper and ordered by the court shall not run during the pendency of such petition in the court.

Such petition shall specify each ground upon which the petitioner relies in seeking such relief, and may be based upon any failure of such demand to comply with the provisions of this title or with the limitations generally applicable to compulsory process or upon any constitutional or other legal right or privilege of such person. No objection which is not raised by such a petition may be urged in the defense to a proceeding initiated by the Commission under subsection (b) for enforcement of such a demand unless such proceeding is commenced by the Commission prior to the expiration of the twenty-day period, or unless the court determines that the defendant could not reasonably have been aware of the availability of such ground of objection.

(d) In any proceeding brought by the Commission under subsection (b), except as provided in subsection (c) of this section, the defendant may petition the court for an order modifying or setting aside the demand of the Commission.

Sec. 711. Notices to be Posted

(a) Every employer, employment agency, and labor organization, as the case may be, shall post and keep posted in conspicuous places upon its premises where notices to employees, applicants for employment, and members are customarily posted a notice to be prepared or approved by the Commission setting forth excerpts from or, summaries of, the pertinent provisions of this title and information pertinent to the filing of a complaint.

(b) A willful violation of this section shall be punishable by a fine of not more than $100 for each separate offense.

Sec. 712. Veterans' Preference

Nothing contained in this title shall be construed to repeal or modify any Federal, State, territorial, or local law creating special rights or preference for veterans.

Sec. 713. Rules and Regulations

(a) The Commission shall have authority from time to time to issue, amend, or rescind suitable procedural regulations to carry out the provisions of this title. Regulations issued under this section shall be in conformity with the standards and limitations of the Administrative Procedure Act.

(b) In any action or proceeding based on any alleged unlawful employment practice, no person shall be subject to any liability or punishment for or on account of (1) the commission by such person of an unlawful employment practice if he pleads and proves that the act or omission complained of was in good faith, in conformity with, and in reliance on any written interpretation or opinion of the Commission, or (2) the failure of such person to publish and file any information required by any provision of this title if he pleads and proves that he failed to publish and file such information in good faith, in conformity with the instructions of the Commission issued under this title regarding the filing of such information. Such a defense, if established, shall be a bar to the action or proceeding, notwithstanding that (A) after such act or omission, such interpretation or opinion is modified or rescinded or is determined by judicial authority to be invalid or of no legal effect, or (B) after publishing or filing the description and annual reports, such publication or filing is determined by judicial authority not to be in conformity with the requirements of this title.

SEC. 714. FORCIBLY RESISTING THE COMMISSION OR ITS REPRESENTATIVES

The provisions of section 111, title 18, United States Code, shall apply to officers, agents, and employees of the Commission in the performance of their official duties.

SEC. 715. SPECIAL STUDY BY THE SECRETARY OF LABOR

The Secretary of Labor shall make a full and complete study of the factors which might tend to result in discrimination in employment because of age and of the consequences of such discrimination on the economy and individuals affected. The Secretary of Labor shall make a report to the Congress not later than June 30, 1965, containing the results of such study and shall include in such report such recommendations for legislation to prevent arbitrary discrimination in employment because of age as he determines advisable.

SEC. 716. EFFECTIVE DATE

(a) This title shall become effective one year after the date of its enactment.

(b) Nothwithstanding subsection (a), sections of this title other than sections 703, 704, 706, and 707 shall become effective immediately.

(c) The President shall, as soon as feasible after the enactment of this title, convene one or more conferences for the purpose of enabling the leaders of groups whose members will be affected by this title to become familiar with the rights afforded and obligations imposed by its provisions, and for the purpose of making plans which will result in the fair and effective administration of this title when all of its provisions become effective. The President shall invite the participation in such conference or conferences of (1) the members of the President's Committee on Equal Employment Opportunity, (2) the members of the Commission on Civil Rights, (3) representatives of State and local agencies engaged in furthering equal employment opportunity, (4) representatives of private agencies engaged in furthering equal employment opportunity, and (5) representatives of employers, labor organizations, and employment agencies who will be subject to this title.

Executive Order 11246—Equal Employment Opportunity

PART I. NON-DISCRIMINATION IN GOVERNMENT EMPLOYMENT

Sec. 101. It is the policy of the Government of the United States to provide equal opportunity in Federal employment for all qualified persons, to prohibit discrimination in employment because of race, color, religion, sex or national origin, and to promote the full realization of equal employment opportunity through a positive, continuing program in each executive department and agency. The policy of equal opportunity applies to every aspect of Federal employment policy and practice.

Sec. 102. The head of each executive department and agency shall establish and maintain a positive program of equal employment opportunity for all civilian employees and applicants for employment within his jurisdiction in accordance with the policy set forth in Section 101.

Sec. 103. The Civil Service Commission shall supervise and provide leadership and guidance in the conduct of equal employment opportunity programs for the civilian employees of and applications for employment within the executive departments and agencies and shall review agency program accomplishments periodically. In order to facilitate the achievement of a model program for equal employment opportunity in the Federal service, the Commission may consult from time to time with such individuals, groups, or organizations as may be of assistance in improving the Federal program and realizing the objectives of this Part.

Sec. 104. The Civil Service Commission shall provide for the prompt, fair, and impartial consideration of all complaints of discrimination in Federal employment on the basis of race, color, religion, sex or national origin. Procedures for the consideration of complaints shall include at least one impartial review within the executive department or agency and shall provide for appeal to the Civil Service Commission.

Sec. 105. The Civil Service Commission shall issue such regulations, orders, and instructions as it deems necessary and appropriate to carry out its responsibilities under this Part, and the head of each executive department and agency shall comply with the regulations, orders, and instructions issued by the Commission under this Part.

PART II. NON-DISCRIMINATION IN EMPLOYMENT BY
GOVERNMENT CONTRACTORS AND SUBCONTRACTORS

Subpart A. Duties of the Secretary of Labor

Sec. 201. The Secretary of Labor shall be responsible for the administration of Parts II and III of this Order and shall adopt such rules and regulations and issue such orders as he deems necessary and appropriate to achieve the purposes thereof.

Subpart B. Contractor's Agreements

Sec. 202. Except in contracts exempted in accordance with Section 204 of this Order, all Government contracting agencies shall include in every Government contract hereafter entered into the following provisions:

"During the performance of this contract, the contractor agrees as follows:

"(1) The contractor will not discriminate against any employee or applicant for employment because of race, color, religion, sex or national origin. The contractor will take affirmative action to ensure that applicants are employed, and that employees are treated during employment, without regard to their race, color, religion, sex or national origin. Such action shall include, but not be limited to the following: employment, upgrading, demotion, or transfer; recruitment or recruitment advertising; layoff or termination; rates of pay or other forms of compensation; and selection for training, including apprenticeship. The contractor agrees to post in conspicuous places, available to employees and applicants for employment, notices to be provided by the contracting officer setting forth the provisions of this nondiscrimination clause.

"(2) The contractor will, in all solicitations or advertisements for employees placed by or on behalf of the contractor, state that all qualified applicants will receive consideration for employment without regard to race, color, religion, sex or national origin.

"(3) The contractor will send to each labor union or representative of workers with which he has a collective bargaining agreement or other contract or understanding, a notice, to be provided by the agency contracting officer, advising the labor union or workers' representative of the contractor's commitments under Section 202 of Executive Order No. 11246 of September 24, 1965, and shall post copies of the notice in conspicuous places available to employees and applicants for employment.

"(4) The contractor will comply with all provisions of Executive Order No. 11246 of Sept. 24, 1965, and of the rules, regulations, and relevant orders of the Secretary of Labor.

"(5) The contractor will furnish all information and reports required by Executive Order No. 11246 of September 24, 1965, and by the rules, regulations, and orders of the Secretary of Labor, or pursuant thereto, and will permit access to his books, records, and accounts by the contracting agency and the Secretary of Labor for purposes of investigation to ascertain compliance with such rules, regulations, and orders.

"(6) In the event of the contractor's noncompliance with the nondiscrimination clauses of this contract or with any of such rules, regulations, or orders, this contract may be cancelled, terminated or suspended in whole or in part and the contractor may be declared ineligible for further Government contracts in accordance with procedures authorized in Executive Order No. 11246 of Sept. 24, 1965, and such other sanctions may be imposed and remedies invoked as provided in Executive Order No. 11246 of September 24, 1965, or by rule, regulation, or order of the Secretary of Labor, or as otherwise provided by law.

"(7) The contractor will include the provisions of Paragraphs (1) through (7) in every subcontract or purchase order unless exempted by rules, regulations or orders of the Secretary of Labor issued pursuant to Section 204 of Executive Order No. 11246 of Sept. 24, 1965, so that such provisions will be binding upon each subcontractor or vendor. The contractor will take such action with respect to any subcontract or purchase order as the contracting agency may direct as a means of enforcing such provisions including sanctions for noncompliance: *Provided, however,* That in the event the contractor becomes involved in, or is threatened with, litigation with a subcontractor or vendor as a result of such direction by the contracting agency, the contractor may request the United States to enter into such litigation to protect the interests of the United States."

Sec. 203. (a) Each contractor having a contract containing the provisions prescribed in Section 203 shall file, and shall cause each of his subcontractors to file, Compliance Reports with the contracting agency or the Secretary of Labor as may be directed. Compliance Reports shall be filed within such times and shall contain such information as to the practices, policies, programs, and employment policies, programs, and employment statistics of the contractor and each subcontractor, and shall be in such form, as the Secretary of Labor may prescribe.

(b) Bidders or prospective contractors or subcontractors may be required to state whether they have participated in any previous contract subject to the provisions of this Order, or any preceding similar Executive order, and in that event to submit, on behalf of themselves and their proposed subcontractors, Compliance Reports prior to or as an initial part of their bid or negotiation of a contract.

(c) Whenever the contractor or subcontractor has a collective bargaining agreement or other contract or understanding with a labor union or an agency referring workers or providing or supervising apprenticeship or training for such workers, the Compliance Report shall include such information as to such labor union's or agency's practices and policies affecting compliance as the Secretary of Labor may prescribe: *Provided,* That to the extent such information is within the exclusive possession of a labor union or an agency referring workers or providing or supervising apprenticeship or training and such labor union or agency shall refuse to furnish such information to the contractor, the contractor shall so certify to the contracting agency as part of its Compliance Report and shall set forth what efforts he has made to obtain such information.

(d) The contracting agency or the Secretary of Labor may direct that any bidder or prospective contractor or subcontractor shall submit, as part of his Compliance Report, a statement in writing, signed by an authorized officer or agent on behalf of any labor union or any agency referring workers or providing or supervising apprenticeship or other training, with which the bidder or prospective contractor deals, with supporting information, to the effect that the signer's practices and policies do not discriminate on the grounds of race, color, religion, sex or national origin, and that the signer either will affirmatively cooperate in the implementation of the policy and provisions of this Order or that it consents and agrees that recruitment, employment, and the terms and conditions of employment under the proposed contract shall be in accordance with the purposes and provisions of the Order. In the event that the union, or the agency shall refuse to execute such a statement, the Compliance Report shall so certify and set forth what efforts have been made to secure such a statement and such additional factual material as the contracting agency or the Secretary of Labor may require.

Sec. 204. The Secretary of Labor may, when he deems that special circumstances in the national interest so require, exempt a contracting agency from the requirement of including any or all of the provisions of Section 202 of this Order in any specific contract, subcontract, or purchase order. The Secretary of Labor may, by rule or regulation, also exempt certain classes of contracts, subcontracts, or purchase orders (1) whenever work is to be or has been performed outside the United States and no recruitment of workers within the limits of the United States is involved; (2) for standard commercial supplies or raw materials; (3) involving less than specified amounts of money or specified numbers of workers; or (4) to the extent that they involve subcontracts below a specified tier. The Secretary of Labor may also provide, by rule, regulation, or order, for the exemption of facilities of a contractor which are in all respects separate and distinct from activities of the contractor related to the performance of the contract: *Provided,* That such an exemption will not interfere with or impede the effectuation of the purposes of this Order: *And provided further,* That in the absence of such an exemption all facilities shall be covered by the provisions of this Order.

Subpart C. Powers and Duties of the Secretary of Labor and the Contracting Agencies

Sec. 205. Each contracting agency shall be primarily responsible for obtaining compliance with the rules, regulations, and orders of the Secretary of Labor with respect to contracts entered into by such agency or its contractors. All contracting agencies shall comply with the rules of the Secretary of Labor in discharging their primary responsibility for securing compliance with the provisions of contracts and otherwise with the terms of this Order and of the rules, regulations, and orders of the Secretary of Labor issued pursuant to this Order. They are directed to cooperate with the Secretary of Labor and to furnish the Secretary of Labor such information and assistance as he may require in the performance of his functions under this Order. They are further directed to appoint or designate, from among the agency's personnel, compliance officers. It shall be the duty of such officers to seek compliance with the objectives of this Order by conference, conciliation, mediation, or persuasion.

Sec. 206. (a) The Secretary of Labor may investigate the employment practices of any Government contractor or subcontractor, or initiate such investigation by the appropriate contracting agency, to determine whether or not the contractual provisions specified in Section 202 of this Order have been violated. Such investigation shall be conducted in accordance with the procedures established by the Secretary of Labor and the investigating agency shall report to the Secretary of Labor any action taken or recommended.

(b) The Secretary of Labor may receive and investigate or cause to be investigated complaints by employees or prospective employees of a Government contractor or subcontractor which allege discrimination contrary to the contractual provisions specified in Section 202 of this Order. If this investigation is conducted for the Secretary of Labor by a contracting agency, that agency shall report to the Secretary what action has been taken or is recommended with regard to such complaints.

Sec. 207. The Secretary of Labor shall use his best efforts, directly and through contracting agencies, other interested Federal, State, and local agencies, contractors, and all other available instrumentalities to cause any labor union engaged in work under Government contracts or any agency referring workers or providing or supervising apprenticeship or training for or in the course of such work to cooperate in the implementation of the purposes of this Order. The Secretary of Labor shall, in appropriate cases, notify the Equal Employment Opportunity Commission, the Department of Justice, or other appropriate Federal agencies whenever it has reason to believe that the practices of any such labor organization or agency violate Title VI or Title VII of the Civil Rights Act of 1964 or other provision of Federal law.

Sec. 208. (a) The Secretary of Labor, or any agency, officer, or employee in the executive branch of the Government designated by rule, regulation, or order of the Secretary, may hold such hearings, public or private, as the Secretary may deem advisable for compliance, enforcement, or educational purposes.

(b) The Secretary of Labor may hold, or cause to be held, hearings in accordance with Subsection (a) of this Section prior to imposing, ordering, or recommending the imposition of penalties and sanctions under this Order. No order for debarment of any contractor from further Government contracts under Section 209(a) (6) shall be made without affording the contractor an opportunity for a hearing.

Subpart D. Sanctions and Penalties

Sec. 209. (a) In accordance with such rules, regulations, or orders as the Secretary of Labor may issue or adopt, the Secretary or the appropriate contracting agency may:

(1) Publish, or cause to be published, the names of contractors or unions which it has concluded have complied or have failed to comply with the provisions of this Order or of the rules, regulations, and orders of the Secretary of Labor.

(2) Recommend to the Department of Justice that, in cases in which there is substantial or material violation or the threat of substantial or material violation of the contractual provisions set forth in Section 202 of this Order, appropriate proceedings be brought to enforce those provisions, including the enjoining, within the limitations of applicable law, of organizations, individuals, or groups who prevent directly or indirectly, or seek to prevent directly or indirectly, compliance with the provisions of this Order.

(3) Recommend to the Equal Employment Opportunity Commission or the Department of Justice that appropriate proceedings be instituted under Title VII of the Civil Rights Act of 1964.

(4) Recommend to the Department of Justice that criminal proceedings be brought for the furnishing of false information to any contracting agency or to the Secretary of Labor as the case may be.

(5) Cancel, terminate, suspend, or cause to be cancelled, terminated, or suspended, any contract, or any portion or portions thereof, for failure of the contractor or subcontractor to comply with the nondiscrimination provisions of the contract. Contracts may be cancelled, terminated, or suspended absolutely or continuance of contracts may be conditioned upon a program for future compliance approved by the contracting agency.

(6) Provide that any contracting agency shall refrain from entering into further contracts, or extensions or other modifications of existing contracts, with any noncomplying contractor, until such contractor has satisfied the Secretary of Labor that such contractor has established and will carry out personnel and employment policies in compliance with the provisions of this Order.

(b) Under rules and regulations prescribed by the Secretary of Labor, each contracting agency shall make reasonable efforts within a reasonable time limitation to secure compliance with the contract provisions of this Order by methods of conference, conciliation, mediation, and persuasion before proceedings shall be instituted under Subsection (a) (2) of this Section, or before a contract shall be cancelled or terminated in whole or in part under Subsection (a) (5) of this Section for failure of a contractor or subcontractor to comply with the contract provisions of this Order.

Sec. 210. Any contracting agency taking any action authorized by this Subpart, whether on its own motion, or as directed by the Secretary of Labor, or under the rules and regulations of the Secretary, shall promptly notify the Secretary of such action. Whenever the Secretary of Labor makes a determination under this Section, he shall promptly notify the appropriate contracting agency of the action recommended. The agency shall take such action and shall report the results thereof to the Secretary of Labor within such time as the Secretary shall specify.

Sec. 211. If the Secretary shall so direct, contracting agencies shall not enter into contracts with any bidder or prospective contractor unless the bidder or prospective contractor has satisfactorily complied with the provisions of this Order or submits a program for compliance acceptable to the Secretary of Labor or, if the Secretary so authorizes, to the contracting agency.

Sec. 212. Whenever a contracting agency cancels or terminates a contract, or whenever a contractor has been debarred from further Government contracts, under Section 209(a) (6) because of noncompliance with the contract provisions with regard to nondiscrimination, the Secretary of Labor, or the contracting agency involved, shall promptly notify the Comptroller General of the United States. Any such debarment may be rescinded by the Secretary of Labor or by the contracting agency which imposed the sanction.

Subpart E. Certificates of Merit

Sec. 213. The Secretary of Labor may provide for issuance of a United States Government Certificate of Merit to employers or labor unions, or other agencies which are or may hereafter be engaged in work under Government contracts, if the Secretary is satisfied that the personnel and employment practices of the employer, or that the personnel, training, apprenticeship, membership, grievance and representation, upgrading, and other practices and policies of the labor union or other agency conform to the purposes and provisions of this Order.

Sec. 214. Any Certificate of Merit may at any time be suspended or revoked by the Secretary of Labor if the holder thereof, in the judgment of the Secretary, has failed to comply with the provisions of this Order.

Sec. 215. The Secretary of Labor may provide for the exemption of any employer, labor union, or other agency from any reporting requirements imposed under or pursuant to this Order if such employer, labor union, or other agency has been awarded a Certificate of Merit which has not been suspended or revoked.

PART III. NON-DISCRIMINATION PROVISIONS IN FEDERALLY ASSISTED CONSTRUCTION CONTRACTS

Sec. 301. Each executive department and agency which administers a program involving Federal financial assistance shall require as a condition for the approval of any grant, contract, loan, insurance, or guarantee thereunder, which may involve a construction contract, that the applicant for Federal assistance undertake and agree to incorporate, or cause to be incorporated, into all construction contracts paid for in whole or in part with funds obtained from the Federal Government or borrowed on the credit of the Federal Government pursuant to such grant, contract, loan, insurance, or guarantee, or undertaken pursuant to any Federal program involving such grant, contract, loan, insurance, or guarantee, the provisions prescribed for Government contracts by Section 203 of this Order or such modification thereof, preserving in substance the contractor's obligations thereunder, as may be approved by the Secretary of Labor, together with such additional provisions as the Secretary deems appropriate to establish and protect the interest of the United States in the enforcement of those obligations. Each such applicant shall also undertake and agree (1) to assist and cooperate actively with the administering department or agency and the Secretary of Labor in obtaining the compliance of contractors and subcontractors with those contract provisions and with the rules, regulations, and relevant orders of the Secretary, (2) to obtain and to furnish to the administering department or agency and to the Secretary of Labor such information as they may require for the supervision of such compliance, (3) to carry out sanctions and penalties for violation of such obligations imposed upon contractors and subcontractors by the Secretary of Labor or the administering department or agency pursuant to Part II, Subpart D, of this Order, and (4) to refrain from entering into any contract to this Order, or extension or other modification of such a contract with a contractor debarred from Government contracts under Part II, Subpart D, of this Order.

Sec. 302. (a) "Construction contract" as used in this Order means any contract for the construction, rehabilitation, alteration, conversion, extension, or repair of buildings, highways, or other improvements to real property.

(b) The provisions of Part II of this Order shall apply to such construction contracts, and for purposes of such application the administering department or agency shall be considered the contracting agency referred to therein.

(c) The term "applicant" as used in this Order means an applicant for Federal assistance or, as determined by agency regulation, other program participant, with respect to whom an application for any grant, contract, loan, insurance, or guarantee is not finally acted upon prior to the effective date of this Part, and it includes such an applicant after he becomes a recipient of such Federal assistance.

Sec. 303. (a) Each administering department and agency shall be responsible for obtaining the compliance of such applicants with their undertakings under this Order. Each administering department and agency is directed to cooperate with the Secretary of Labor, and to furnish the Secretary such information and assistance as he may require in the performance of his functions under this Order.

(b) In the event an applicant fails and refuses to comply with his undertakings, the administering department or agency may take any or all of the following actions: (1) cancel, terminate, or suspend in whole or in part the agreement, contract, or other arrangement with such applicant with respect to which the failure and refusal occurred; (2) refrain from extending any further assistance to the applicant under the program with respect to which the failure or refusal occurred until satisfactory assurance of future compliance has been received from such applicant; and (3) refer the case to the Department of Justice for appropriate legal proceedings.

(c) Any action with respect to an applicant pursuant to Subsection (b) shall be taken in conformity with Section 602 of the Civil Rights Act of 1964 (and the regulations of the administering department or agency issued thereunder), to the extent applicable. In no case shall action be taken with respect to an applicant pursuant to Clause (1) or (2) of Subsection (b) without notice and opportunity for hearing before the administering department or agency.

Sec. 304. Any executive department or agency which imposes by rule, regulation, or order requirements of nondiscrimination in employment, other than requirements imposed pursuant to this Order, may delegate to the Secretary of Labor by agreement such responsibilities with respect to compliance standards, reports, and procedures as would tend to bring the administration of such requirements into conformity with the administration of requirements imposed under this Order: *Provided,* That actions to effect compliance by recipients of Federal financial assistance with requirements imposed pursuant to Title VI of the Civil Rights Act of 1964 shall be taken in conformity with the procedures and limitations prescribed in Section 602 thereof and the regulations of the administering department or agency issued thereunder.

PART IV. MISCELLANEOUS

Sec. 401. The Secretary of Labor may delegate to any officer, agency, or employee in the Executive branch of the Government, any function or duty of the Secretary under Parts II and III of this Order, except authority to promulgate rules and regulations of a general nature.

Sec. 402. The Secretary of Labor shall provide administrative support for the execution of the program known as the "Plans for Progress."

Sec. 403. (a) Executive Orders Nos. 10590 (January 19, 1955), 10722 (August 5, 1957), 10925 (March 6, 1961), 11114 (June 22, 1963), and 11162 (July 28, 1964), are hereby superseded and the President's Committee on Equal Employment Opportunity established by Executive Order No. 10925 is hereby abolished. All records and property in the custody of the Committee shall be transferred to the Civil Service Commission and the Secretary of Labor, as appropriate.

(b) Nothing in this Order shall be deemed to relieve any person of any obligation assumed or imposed under or pursuant to any Executive Order superseded by this Order. All rules, regulations, orders, instructions, designations, and other directives issued by the President's Committee on Equal Employment Opportunity and those issued by the heads of various departments or agencies under or pursuant to any of the Executive orders superseded by this Order, shall, to the extent that they are not inconsistent with this Order, remain in full force and effect unless and until revoked or superseded by appropriate authority. References in such directives to provisions of the superseded orders shall be deemed to be references to the comparable provisions of this Order.

Sec. 404. The General Services Administration shall take appropriate action to revise the standard Government contract forms to accord with the provisions of this Order and of the rules and regulations of the Secretary of Labor.

Sec. 405. This Order shall become effective thirty days after the date of this Order.

Gardenia WHITE et al., Plaintiffs,
United States of America, by Nicholas
deB. Katzenbach, Attorney General of
the United States, Plaintiff-Intervenor,

v.

Bruce CROOK et al., Defendants.
Civ. A. No. 2263-N
United States District Court
M. D. Alabama, N. D.
Feb. 7, 1966.
251 F. Supp. 401 (1966).

Before RIVES, Circuit Judge, and ALLGOOD and JOHNSON, District Judges.

PER CURIAM.

This action was instituted as a class action by male and female residents of Lowndes County, Alabama, against the individual members of the jury commission of Lowndes County, Alabama. Subsequently, the plaintiffs amended by adding as defendants other officials of Lowndes County and the State of Alabama, who, according to the amended complaint, performed certain functions in connection with the jury selection and jury use in Lowndes County, Alabama. By the complaint as amended, plaintiffs alleged that the defendants have systematically excluded Negro male citizens and female citizens of both races from jury service in Lowndes County, Alabama. Because of the challenge to the Alabama statute which totally excludes women from jury service, a three-judge district court was designated and convened, pursuant to 28 U.S.C. §§ 2281, 2284, to try this case. Subsequently, the United States moved for leave to intervene pursuant to § 902 of the Civil Rights Act of 1964; this motion was based upon a complaint in intervention and a certification by the Attorney General of the United States that, in his judgment, this case was of general importance.

This case was submitted on the issues made up by the pleadings and proof, and, upon consideration of the evidence, consisting of the oral testimony of several witnesses, together with the exhibits thereto, this Court now proceeds to make and enter in this memorandum opinion, as authorized by Rule 52, Federal Rules of Civil Procedure, the appropriate findings of fact and conclusions of law.

The plaintiffs, male and female Negro citizens and residents of Lowndes County, Alabama, seek the defendants, through this Court, as provided under the Constitution and laws of the United States, injunctive
relief to remedy alleged conduct of the defendants (including the denial
to the plaintiffs of the equal protection of the laws on account of race or
color) in violation of the Fourteenth Amendment to the Constitution and
42 U.S.C. § 1981. The plaintiffs bring this action in their own behalf and
on behalf of others similarly situated, pursuant to Rule 23(a) (3) of the
Federal Rules of Civil Procedure. The plaintiff-intervenor is the United
States of America; its standing to intervene is established by 42 U.S.C.
§ 2000h-2 and by Rule 24(b) of the Federal Rules of Civil Procedure. The
defendants are the members and clerk of the jury commission of Lowndes
County, Alabama; the judge for the Second Judicial Circuit of Alabama,
which includes Lowndes County; the probate judge and the sheriff of
Lowndes County; the solicitor and the clerk of the Second Judicial Circuit
of Alabama, which includes Lowndes County; the foreman of the grand
jury of Lowndes County; and the solicitor of Lowndes County.

By leave of this Court, upon an appropriate petition, the Alabama Circuit Judges Association filed its brief as amicus curiae. The brief filed on
behalf of the Alabama Circuit Judges Association concerns itself with the
relief sought by the plaintiffs and the plaintiff-intervenor against the defendant circuit judge; the Association emphasizes in its brief that it does
not oppose any relief sought other than that sought against the circuit
judge for the Second Judicial Circuit of Alabama, which includes
Lowndes County.

The procedure for the selection of jurors in Alabama is controlled by
statute.[1] Each county in Alabama has a jury commission composed of
three members appointed by the Governor.[2] These commissioners, in
order to be qualified, must be electors of the county, reputed for their
fairness, impartiality, integrity and good judgment; the commissioners so
appointed serve for the tenure of the Governor who appoints them.[3] The
jury commissioners are required to place on the jury roll "the names of all
male citizens of the county who are generally reputed to be honest and
intelligent men and are esteemed in the community for their integrity,
good character and sound judgment."[4] The clerk of the jury commission
is required by law to "obtain the name of every male citizen of the county
over twenty-one and under sixty-five years of age and their occupation,
place of residence and place of business * * *."[5] The jury commission
is required to maintain a jury roll containing the name of "every male

---

[1] These statutes are codified in the Code of Alabama, Recompiled 1958, Title
30. All statutory references to the qualifications of and to the procedure for the
selection of jurors in Alabama as set forth in this opinion will be to Title 30,
Code of Alabama, Recompiled 1958.

[2] With some exceptions provided by local Acts or Acts of local application.

[3] Sections 8, 9 and 10.

[4] Section 21.

[5] Section 18.

citizen living in the county who possessed the qualifications herein prescribed and who is not exempted by law from serving on juries."[6] As a part of the procedural requirements the names of the persons on the jury roll must also be printed on separate cards, which are placed in a jury box. It is the duty of the commission to see that the name of each person possessing the qualifications to serve as a juror and not exempted by law from jury duty "is placed on the jury roll and in the jury box."[7] The Alabama law further requires the jury commission and its clerk to scan the registration lists, the list returned to the tax assessor, any city directories and telephone directories, and any and every other source of information, and to visit every precinct in the county at least once a year.[8]

When jurors are required for a court session, the presiding judge draws from the jury box the names of the individuals to serve as jurors during the term in question. These jurors may be either petit jurors or grand jurors as the situation requires. The names so drawn are sent to the clerk of the court, and the clerk prepares a venire; the venire containing these names is sent to the sheriff who summons the persons listed to appear and serve.[9] The presiding judge has the authority to pass upon claims for exemptions, excuses and qualifications of those individuals who have been summoned to appear and serve as jurors.[10] Either party in civil and criminal cases has a right to examine jurors as to their qualifications, interests, or any bias that would affect the trial of the case. In civil actions each party has a certain number of preemptory challenges, and in criminal cases the struck jury method is the exclusive means of selecting juries.

The 1960 census reflects that the total population of Lowndes County was 15,417 and that Negroes comprised 80.7% of the total county population and 72.0% of the adult male population. The white males between the ages of 21 to 65 totaled 738, and the nonwhite males between the ages of 21 to 65 totaled 1,798. The white females between the ages of 21 to 65 totaled 789, and the nonwhite females between the ages of 21 to 65 totaled 2,278.[11] The evidence in this case reflects that before each term of court the presiding judge of the Second Judicial Circuit would draw at random from the jury box a sufficient number of cards (usually 110) to provide jurors for the next term of court to be conducted in Lowndes County. When the number of cards in the jury box became depleted to the extent that the judge could not make a complete draw, he notified the clerk of the jury commission, who informed the commissioners that the box required refilling. At times the jury commissioners refilled the

[6] Section 20. To the extent that this section uses the word "every" it is a permissive as opposed to a mandatory requirement. Fikes v. State, 263 Ala. 89, 81 So. 2d 303.

[7] Section 24.

[8] Section 24.

[9] Section 30.

[10] Sections 4 and 5.

[11] United States Bureau of Census. United States Census of Population: 1960. General Population Characteristics, Alabama.

box or added names on their own initiative; when they filled the jury box, they would put approximately 250 names in it. The testimony reflected that the judge found it necessary to suggest that the jury box be refilled "probably once a year." The Lowndes County jury commissioners, in selecting persons they considered to be qualified for jury service, used as their primary source the Lowndes County voting lists on which no Negroes were named. The other source (personal knowledge) accounted for the names of seven Negroes listed on the Lowndes County jury roll in the twelve-year period from 1953 until this action was commenced. From 1953 to the time this suit was instituted, Negroes comprised little more than 1% of the persons selected by the commissioners as eligible and qualified for jury service in Lowndes County, Alabama. There was no conflict in the evidence to the effect that there were a substantial number of Negro citizens residing in Lowndes County who were qualified for jury services under Alabama law. As a matter of fact, it was stipulated between counsel that there were qualified Negroes in Lowndes County whose names had not been placed on the jury rolls or in the jury box by the jury commission. The actual procedure followed by the jury commission of Lowndes County, Alabama, in replenishing the jury box was for the commission to borrow the qualified voter list from the county probate judge, to meet, and during the course of the meeting have one of the commissioners read the names of all males on the qualified voter list, most of whom were known to one or more of the commissioners. As the list was read, the persons whose names appeared thereon were either summarily approved or rejected as prospective jurors. Discussion of the qualifications was generally unnecessary. It is especially significant that there were no Negroes registered to vote in Lowndes County prior to March 1, 1965. Literacy was not considered by the commissioners as an absolute prerequisite in order for a person to be deemed by them qualified for jury service. As a matter of fact, the jury commissioners have not used any method for testing a person's ability to read and write. As the names were read from the qualified voter list, those approved by the commissioners were recorded on jury cards. The cards were placed in the jury box for use by the presiding judge. The extent to which the qualified voter lists were used by the commissioners is revealed by comparing the contemporaneous voting lists with the venire lists from 1953 to the time this case was tried. This analysis reflects that 98.0% of the names on the venires of prospective jurors appeared on the contemporaneous voting lists. It is especially significant that there were no Negroes registered to vote in Lowndes County prior to March 1, 1965; the voting lists for Lowndes County, Alabama, during this time included the names of approximately 1200 white male citizens. Thus, no Negroes' names appeared on the jury commissioners' primary source for finding and selecting prospective jurors. The evidence further reflected that the commissioners made some efforts to secure the names of persons considered qualified as potential jurors whose names were not on the qualified voter lists. These efforts resulted in the names of seven Negroes being placed in the jury box from 1953 until August 25, 1965, the date this action was commenced. During this period—approximately twelve years—these seven Negroes were drawn for jury service a total of nineteen times. After the complaint in this action was filed, the jury commission met to replenish the jury box and at that time the names of 19 Negroes were placed in the box. The evidence reflected that the jury commissioners considered this to be a sufficient number to satisfy the requirements of the law. No Negro has ever served on a civil or criminal petit jury in Lowndes County, Alabama.

In addition to the above procedure, which resulted, in the opinion of this Court, in an extremely aggravated case of systematic exclusion by reason of race, the commissioners followed a procedure which restricted the number of qualified white persons whose names were placed in the jury box. An analysis of the jury records as offered and received in evidence in this case reflects that a very limited number of persons has constituted the core of the county jury system in Lowndes County, Alabama, and that the names of this extremely limited group have been repeatedly circulated through the jury box. As a matter of fact, the names of only 670 persons have been on cards in the box since 1953. Of these 670 individuals, 211 have had their names in the box six or more times, and some as many as fifteen or sixteen times. These 211 persons collectively account for 66.5% of the total of 2,748 names, including repeats that have appeared on the venire lists in Lowndes County, Alabama, from 1953 to the present time. Fifty-seven of these persons were called for jury service three successive terms. Seven of them were called for jury service four successive terms.

The procedures as outlined above, adopted and followed by the jury commissioners in Lowndes County, Alabama, since 1953, have resulted in jury service in that county being limited to a small number of adult, white male citizens, with Negro male citizens and female citizens of both races being systematically excluded either by practice or, in the case of the women, by statute.

[The court's discussion of the systematic exclusion of Negroes by race has been omitted.]

II. Statutory Exclusion of Women From Jury Service in Alabama

As stated earlier in this opinion, jury service on the part of the citizens of the United States is considered under our law in this country as one of the basic rights and obligations of citizenship. The women plaintiffs on behalf of themselves and other women similarly situated contend very forcefully that the Alabama statute that bars their exercise of this basic right is unconstitutional.[14] This attack on Alabama's complete

[14] Title 30, § 21, Code of Alabama, Recompiled 1958, is the Alabama statute that restricts jury service to male citizens. That statute in pertinent part states as follows: "§ 21. *Qualifications of persons on jury roll.*—The jury commission

exclusion of women from jury service is based on the Equal Protection Clause of the Fourteenth Amendment. The argument that the Fourteenth Amendment was not historically intended to require the states to make women eligible for jury service reflects a misconception of the function of the Constitution and this Court's obligation in interpreting it. The Constitution of the United States must be read as embodying general principles meant to govern society and the institutions of government as they evolve through time. It is therefore this Court's function to apply the Constitution as a living document to the legal cases and controversies of contemporary society. When such an application to the facts in this case is made, the conclusion is inescapable that the complete exclusion of women from jury service in Alabama is arbitrary.

Jury service is a form of participation in the processes of government, a responsibility and a right that should be shared by all citizens, regardless of sex. The Alabama statute that denies women the right to serve on juries in the State of Alabama therefore violates that provision of the Fourteenth Amendment to the Constitution of the United States that forbids any state to "deny to any person within its jurisdiction the equal protection of the laws." The plain effect of this constitutional provision is to prohibit prejudicial disparities before the law. This means prejudicial disparities for all citizens—including women. See Fay v. People of State of New York, 332 U.S. 261, 67 S.Ct. 1613, 91 L.Ed. 2043; Hoyt v. State of Florida, 368 U.S. 57, 82 S.Ct. 159, 7 L.Ed.2d 118; see also Hernandez v. State of Texas, supra.

The courts have not heretofore been called on to decide a case presenting the constitutional validity of a state's complete exclusion of women from service as jurors. Hoyt v. State of Florida, supra, and Fay v. People of State of New York, supra, were concerned with systems of jury selection under which service by women was voluntary. Significantly, in Hoyt v. State of Florida, supra, the Supreme Court's opinion concluded as follows:

> "Finding no substantial evidence whatever in this record that Florida has arbitrarily undertaken to exclude women from jury service, a showing which it was incumbent on appellant to make * * *, we must sustain the judgment of the Supreme Court of Florida. * * *" 368 U.S. 57, 69, 82 S.Ct. 159, 166.

Further, the Chief Justice and Justices Black and Douglas assigned as their sole reason for concurring that, "We cannot say from this record

shall place on the jury roll and in the jury box the names of all male citizens of the county * * *." Only three states—Alabama, Mississippi and South Carolina—totally bar women from jury service. All others either treat women and men on the same basis or provide some form of voluntary service for women. The prohibition against women serving on juries in Alabama does not apply to federal juries by reason of the Civil Rights Act of 1957, 28 U.S.C. § 1861—that Act deleting that portion of the law that disqualified persons for service on federal juries who are incompetent to serve on a grand or petit jury by the law of the state in which the federal district court is held.

that Florida is not making a good faith effort to have women perform jury duty without discrimination on the ground of sex." 368 U.S. at 69, 82 S.Ct. at 167. Moreover, the *Hoyt* and *Fay* cases presented challenges from a viewpoint entirely different from the present case. In those cases the parties defendant challenged the composition of the juries because of the systematic exclusion of women. In this case it is the women themselves who assert their right to serve as jurors, or, more accurately, their right not to be excluded from jury service solely because of their sex.

Women are allowed to serve on juries in the federal courts and in the courts of forty-seven states. Only in three—Alabama, Mississippi and South Carolina—are women completely excluded from jury service. The time must come when a state's complete exclusion of women from jury service is recognized as so arbitrary and unreasonable as to be unconstitutional. As to Alabama, we can see no reason for not recognizing that fact at the present time.

Even though this Court finds and holds that the exclusion of women from jury service in Alabama by a statutory provision is arbitrary in view of modern political, social and economic conditions, this Court is fully aware that the Alabama statute has been regarded and relied upon as constitutional by all alike. This Court believes public policy is best served by holding that that part of the decision in this case to the effect that Alabama's prohibition of jury service for women is unconstitutional should be prospective in its application, and, for that reason, should have no retroactive effect. See generally, Linkletter v. Walker, 381 U.S. 618, 85 S.Ct. 1731, 14 L.Ed.2d 601, and Tehan, Sheriff, etc. v. United States ex rel. Shott, January 19, 1966, 86 S.Ct. 459. However, to eliminate any possible misunderstanding, this Court specifically declares that, for the future, commencing not later than a time designated, women have a right not to be excluded as a class from jury service in Alabama courts.

UNITED STATES ex rel.
Carrie ROBINSON
v.
Janet YORK, Superintendent, Connecticut
State Farm for Women.
Civ. No. 12376.
United States District Court
D. Connecticut.
Feb. 28, 1968.
281 F. Supp. 8 (1968).

MEMORANDUM OF DECISION ON PETITION FOR A WRIT OF
HABEAS CORPUS

BLUMENFELD, District Judge.

The petitioner, Carrie Robinson, age thirty-eight, by this petition for
a writ of habeas corpus challenges the constitutionality of Conn.Gen.Stats.
§ 17-360, under the provisions of which she was sentenced to the Connecticut State Farm for Women, Niantic, for an indefinite term not to exceed
three years. That statute provides:

"Women over sixteen years of age belonging to any of the following
classes may be committed by any court of criminal jurisdiction to said
institution: First, persons convicted of, or who plead guilty to, the
commission of felonies; second, persons convicted of, or who plead
guilty to, the commission of misdemeanors, including prostitution,
intoxication, drug-using and disorderly conduct; third, unmarried
girls between the ages of sixteen and twenty-one years who are in
manifest danger of falling into habits of vice or who are leading vi-
cious lives, and who are convicted thereof in accordance with the provisions of section 17-379; fourth, women sentenced to jails. Only such
offenders may be committed to said institution as in the opinion of
the trial court will be benefited physically, mentally or morally by
such commitment, and, immediately upon commitment, a careful
physical and mental examination, by a competent physician, shall be
made of each person committed. The court imposing a sentence on
offenders of any class shall not fix the term of such commitment.
Commitment to said institution shall be made within one week after
sentence is imposed, but no offender shall be committed to said institution without being accompanied by a woman in addition to the

officer. The trial court shall cause a record of the case to be sent with the commitment papers on blanks furnished by the institution. The duration of such commitment, including the time spent on parole, shall not exceed three years, except when the maximum term specified by law for the crime for which the offender was sentenced exceeds that period, in which event such maximum term shall be the limit of detention under the provisions of this chapter, and, in such cases, the trial court shall specify the maximum term for which the offender may be held under such commitment."[1]

Petitioner contends that § 17-360 violates the equal protection clause of the fourteenth amendment to the Constitution of the United States by permitting adult women to be imprisoned for periods in excess of the maximums applicable to men guilty of the same substantive crimes.[2]

On November 18, 1966, before the Ninth Circuit Court in Middletown, Mrs. Robinson pleaded guilty to one count of breach of the peace and one of resisting arrest, misdemeanors carrying maximum sentences respectively of one year and six months.[3] Conn. Gen. Stats. §§ 53-174, 53-165. Seven months later, on June 23, 1967, petitioner was released on parole from the State Farm. On October 11, 1967, again in the Ninth Circuit Court, she entered guilty pleas to charges of being found intoxicated and willful destruction of property. The sentences entered on these counts were suspended and petitioner was returned as a parole violator to the State Farm under her original sentence.

* * *

Denial of Equal Protection

Starting with the undisputed reading of § 17-360 to permit women to be sentenced for longer terms than it or any other statute permits for men found guilty of committing identical offenses, the question presented is whether the sentence of the petitioner to an indefinite term of imprisonment not to exceed three years because she is a woman over the age of sixteen denied to her equal protection of the laws guaranteed by the fourteenth amendment.[4]

---

[1] This is the version of § 17-360 contained in the 1965 supplement to the General Statutes in effect at the time Mrs. Robinson was sentenced in November 1966. Two subsequent substitutions for the section (in practical effect amendments) were approved in May and June of 1967, apparently without reference to each other. Public Act 152 § 20, May 25, 1967; Public Act 555 § 74, June 21, 1967. While these changes leave some confusion as to the present wording of the section in some particulars, they have no bearing on the determinations reached in this action.

[2] No provision comparable to § 17-360 exists for adult males.

[3] These were separate counts in a single information charging the commission of both offenses on the same date.

[4] Amendment XIV, Sec. 1:
"No State shall make or enforce any law which shall abridge the privileges or immunities of citizens of the United States; nor shall any State deprive any person of life, liberty, or property, without due process of law; nor deny to any person within its jurisdiction the equal protection of the laws."

Legislative Discretion

It must be recognized that wide discretion is allowed to the state's legislature to establish reasonable classifications in promoting the safety and welfare of those within its jurisdiction. As the Supreme Court noted in Skinner v. Oklahoma, 316 U.S. 535, 541, 62 S.Ct. 1110, 86 L.Ed. 1655 (1942), a "large deference" must be paid to the state in passing on the validity of a classification effected by its criminal statutes.

> "[A] State is not constrained in the exercise of its police power to ignore experience which marks a class of offenders or a family of offenses for special treatment. Nor is it prevented by the equal protection clause from confining 'its restrictions to those classes of cases where the need is deemed to be clearest.' * * * 'the law does all that is needed when it does all that it can, indicates a policy, applies it to all within the lines, and seeks to bring within the lines all similarly situated so far and so fast as its means allow.' " (316 U.S. at 540, 62 S.Ct. at 1113).

Basis of the Classification

This deference to legislative classifications can extend to classifications based on sex. For example, the Supreme Court has upheld an Oregon statute forbidding women to work more than ten hours a day, Muller v. Oregon, 208 U.S. 412, 28 S.Ct. 324, 52 L.Ed. 551 (1908); a Michigan rule preventing most females from becoming licensed bartenders, Goesaert v. Cleary, 335 U.S. 464, 69 S.Ct. 198, 93 L.Ed. 163 (1948); and a Florida enactment excluding women from jury duty unless they affirmatively volunteer to serve, Hoyt v. Florida, 368 U.S. 57, 82 S.Ct. 159, 7 L.Ed.2d 118 (1961). In each of these cases the Court found that the classification rested on "some difference which [bore] a reasonable and just relation to the act in respect to which the classification [was] proposed;" that it was not "made arbitrarily, and without any such basis." Gulf, C. & S. F. Ry. v. Ellis, 165 U.S. 150, 155, 17 S.Ct. 255, 257, 41 L.Ed. 666 (1897). Cf. Baxstrom v. Herold, 383 U.S. 107, 86 S.Ct. 760, 15 L.Ed.2d 620 (1966).

Thus, in *Muller* the Court took account of the differences in physical structure, strength and endurance of women, as well as the importance of their health to the future well being of the race, in sustaining the work hour limitation, 208 U.S. at 422, 28 S.Ct. 327, 52 L.Ed. 556. It noted a woman's family and home responsibilities in upholding the jury duty exemption in *Hoyt*, 368 U.S. at 62, 82 S.Ct. 163, 7 L.Ed.2d 122, and acknowledged in *Goesaert* that the Michigan legislature might legitimately be avoiding the "moral and social problems" which it believed could be produced by females tending bar in saloons, 335 U.S. at 466, 69 S.Ct. 199, 93 L.Ed. 165.

Purpose of Classification

While it would be difficult to find a more distinctive basis for classification of adults than the natural difference between a man and a woman, that does not end judicial inquiry. Although the law in question is applicable alike to all adult women, "[j]udicial injury under the Equal Protection Clause * * * does not end with a showing of equal application among the members of the class defined by the legislation. The courts must reach and determine the question whether the classification[s] drawn in the statute are reasonable in light of its purpose * * *"—in this case whether greater punishment for women is an arbitrary or invidious discrimination between adult men and adult women who commit a breach of the peace or resist arrest. McLaughlin v. Florida, 379 U.S. 184, 191, 85 S.Ct. 283, 13 L.Ed.2d 222 (1964); Skinner v. Oklahoma, 316 U.S. 535, 62 S.Ct. 1110, 86 L.Ed. 1655; Muller v. Oregon, 208 U.S. 412, 28 S.Ct. 324, 52 L.Ed. 551. Since legislative discretion is limited to exercise for reasonable purposes, the court must determine whether the classification in § 17-360 "bears a * * * just relation to the act in respect of which the classification is proposed * * *." Gulf, C. & S. F. Ry. v. Ellis, 165 U.S. at 155, 17 S.Ct. at 257; McLaughlin v. Florida, 379 U.S. at 191, 85 S.Ct. 288, 13 L.Ed.2d 228; Carrington v. Rash, 380 U.S. 89, 93, 85 S.Ct. 775, 13 L.Ed. 2d 675 (1965).

The Relation Between Punishment and Sex of the Offender

This statute, which singles out adult women convicted of misdemeanors for imposition of punishment by imprisonment for longer terms than may be imposed on men, must be supported by a full measure of justification to overcome the equal protection which is guaranteed to them by the fourteenth amendment. In Loving v. Virginia, 388 U.S. 1, 87 S.Ct. 1817, 18 L.Ed.2d 1010 (1967), where penalties were imposed on the basis of racial classification, the Supreme Court enunciated a strict standard for testing equal protection:

> "At the very least, the Equal Protection Clause demands that racial classifications, especially suspect in criminal statutes, be subjected to the 'most rigid scrutiny.' Korematsu v. United States, 323 U.S. 214, 216 [65 S.Ct. 193, 194, 89 L.Ed. 194] (1944), and, if they are ever to be upheld, they must be shown to be necessary to the accomplishment of some permissible state objective * * *." (388 U.S. at 11, 87 S.Ct. at 1823).

While the Supreme Court has not explicitly determined whether equal protection rights of women should be tested by this rigid standard, it is difficult to find any reason why adult women, as one of the specific groups that compose humanity, should have a lesser measure of protection than a racial group. The same sort of "strict scrutiny" has been applied for the protection of habitual criminals who were held to have been invidiously discriminated against in violation of equal protection by Oklahoma's sterilization law. Skinner v. Oklahoma, 316 U.S. 535, 62 S.Ct. 1110, 86 L.Ed. 1655. The Supreme Court stated:

> "We are dealing here with legislation which involves one of the basic civil rights of man [referring to the right to have offspring]. * * *

We mention these matters not to reëxamine the scope of the police power of the States. We advert to them merely in emphasis of our view that *strict scrutiny* of the classification which a State makes in a sterilization law is essential, lest unwittingly or otherwise invidious discriminations are made against groups or types of individuals in violation of the constitutional guaranty of just and equal laws." (Emphasis added) (316 U.S. at 541, 62 S.Ct. at 1113).

Cf. Baxstrom v. Herold, 383 U.S. 107, 86 S.Ct. 760, 15 L.Ed.2d 620; Truax v. Raich, 239 U.S. 33, 36 S.Ct. 7, 60 L.Ed. 131 (1915).

Turning now to the statute attacked by this action. The state seeks to justify § 17-360 by noting that it is one among a number of provisions in that title of the General Statutes dealing with "Humane And Reformatory Agencies And Institutions" as distinguished from the "Penal Institutions" authorized in Title 18, and that it is, therefore, "part of the integral whole which constitutes the State's attempt to provide for women and juveniles a special protection and every reformative and rehabilitative opportunity."[5] Respondent's Brief at 18. This purports to be a way of concealing the abrasive nature of imprisonment under the charming image of an educational institution. But this should not blind one to the fact that the institution is still a place of imprisonment.

There are a number of things that could well be said in defense of separate institutions for women, but merely calling the State Farm for Women a reformatory, and, therefore, distinguishable from the penal system does not make it so. What Mr. Justice Fortas noted in the recent case of In re Gault, 387 U.S. 1, 87 S.Ct. 1428, 18 L.Ed.2d 527 (1967), with regard to juvenile institutions is equally applicable here:

> "It is of no constitutional consequence—and of limited practical meaning—that the institution to which he is committed is called an Industrial School. The fact of the matter is that, however euphemistic the title, a 'receiving home' or an 'industrial school' for juveniles is an institution of confinement in which the child is incarcerated for a greater or lesser time. His world becomes 'a building with whitewashed walls, regimented routine and institutional hours * * *.' * * * His world is peopled by guards, custodians, state employees, and 'delinquents' confined with him for anything from waywardness to rape and homicide." (387 U.S. at 27, 87 S.Ct. at 1443).

[5] What scant legislative history there is does reveal a belief by those who supported it at a hearing before the Joint Standing Committee on Humane Institutions in February 1917 that the new institution would provide a reformative opportunity not available to women in the prison and jails. That hope was based mostly on features of the proposed farm which are today present in the prison as well or are of little substance, e.g., farm work, a rural location, a name with less stigma attached to it, a woman superintendent. Hearings on S.B. 12 and S.B. 126 Before the Joint Standing Committee on Humane Institutions at 73-86 (February 21, 1917).

Moreover, none of the special features which might justify distinguishing the state's treatment of juveniles[6] from that it accords adults exist in the case of commitment of adult women to the State Farm. E. g., Conn.Gen. Stats. § 17-72 (adjudication of juvenile court that a child is delinquent is not a criminal conviction); Conn.Gen.Stats. § 17-73 (delinquency proceedings inadmissible as evidence in some criminal prosecutions); Conn.Gen. Stats. § 17-67 (juvenile court hearings held in private); Conn. Gen.Stats. § 17-66 (pre-hearing investigations).

Even assuming, as the state alleges, that there is a difference in the quality of treatment and conditions of incarceration at the Farm, those facts are not enough to justify a longer period of imprisonment for adult women as opposed to adult men. Of course, imprisonment need not be all of one kind. There are ample reasons for separate institutions, and the state may permissibly introduce priorities and coordination between them; but if it matters what kind of facilities are provided, it matters even more that there shall be no invidious discrimination with respect to the length of imprisonment.

In Connecticut the predominant criterion for judgment imposed on those convicted of violating its criminal laws continues to be punishment. When it came to a discussion of values in a system of penology some forty years after § 17-360 had been enacted, the Governor's Prison Study Committee's proposal for the establishment of the Sentence Review Board,[7] rather tartly remarked:

> "We do not accept the simplistic view that the only purpose of sentencing is the rehabilitation of the individual offender. Deterrence of others through punishment and prevention through restraint are also important goals of the criminal law. This complex of objectives, including rehabilitation, seems best suited to an initial adjustment by judicial action in the sentencing process."[8]

This may be regarded as a fair statement of penological principles to guide Connecticut's judiciary at the time of sentencing: Informed by what the convicted defendant had done, the court should determine what his future should be; there are two matters which should particularly concern the court, deterrence of others and punishment of the offender. Both touch the liberty of the defendant.

Insofar as the future protection of society is concerned, the state has failed to carry its burden in support of the proposition that a greater period of imprisonment is necessary for the deterrence of women than for men. And it is hardly an open question that women, as such, do not de-

---

[6] It should be noted that such features were not enough to justify what was held to be a denial of due process of law in *Gault*.

[7] Conn.Gen.Stats. §§ 51-194, 51-197 (1958).

[8] Governor's Prison Study Committee, A Procedure for Reviewing Sentences, at 6-7 (Mimeo No. 19, 1956), cited in R. Donnelly. J. Goldstein, & R. Schwartz, Criminal Law, at 28 (1962).

serve greater punishment than men. In our society any discrimination in the treatment of women is benignly in their favor.

Nor is there any support for the claim that women require a longer time to become rehabilitated as useful members of society. Indeed, where rehabilitation under supervision without physical restraint is deemed suitable, any person found guilty of a crime may be placed on probation, without regard to sex. Conn.Gen.Stats. § 54-111. While it might not be impossible to conjure up special circumstances where less onerous conditions of restraint could be argued by some to compensate for a lengthier imprisonment, such an argument would be as applicable to men as to women. Recognizing that in interpreting the Constitution the establishment of relationships between remote concepts can be dangerously misleading, Mr. Justice Frankfurter pointed out: "* * * the Constitution is 'intended to preserve practical and substantial rights, not to maintain theories.' Davis v. Mills, 194 U.S. 451, 457, [24 S.Ct. 692, 48 L.Ed. 1067]." Rochin v. California, 342 U.S. 165, 174, 72 S.Ct. 205, 210, 96 L.Ed. 183 (1952). Among the rights protected by the Constitution, next to life itself, none is more basic than liberty. However narrowly "liberty" may be defined, this statute restrains it. No punishment which a state may impose weighs more heavily on an individual than imprisonment in an institution.

Connecticut recognizes no distinction based on the sex of the individual regarding protection of person or property. It accords no higher position to men in such matters than to women. Neither should it, in the name of serving their own good or otherwise, justify a longer period of deprivation of personal liberty for women. Nor has it offered any proof, or even suggested, that it was necessary for the protection of society to forestall women convicted of breach of peace or resisting an officer from again committing those crimes to imprison them for a longer time than men convicted of those same offences. It may be granted that a broad discretion should be given to the courts in order that the punishment imposed should bear a proper relation to the enormity of the offense. But the circumstances which may affect the sentences must be circumstances connected with the crime. That there are differences between women and men cannot be denied, but that these differences justify a longer imprisonment of women cannot be sustained. There is no connection whatsoever between a breach of peace or resistance to arrest and being a woman. Those misdemeanors may be committed by persons of either sex.

Nothing in the different nature of men and women noted by the Supreme Court in the *Muller, Goesaert,* and *Hoyt* cases suggests any reasonable or just relation between the misdemeanors involved here and the inequality in potential punishments permitted by § 17-360. Yet, such a relation would have to be found if the classification at issue is to be upheld. Most of the state courts which have faced similar questions have found no reason to justify longer imprisonment for women than for men. State v. Beddow, 32 N.E.2d 34 (Ct.App.Ohio 1939) (statute providing for incarceration of women on a state farm for indeterminate periods upheld where men and women faced same maximum limits); Ex parte Brady, 116 Ohio St. 512, 157 N.E. 69 (Sup.Ct.1927) (habeas denied where statute provided for same maximum as men faced, the court concluding that "so long as both the man and the woman may not be imprisoned for a longer or lesser period than that fixed by the statute there is no discrimination in classification." (at 72), Ex parte Fenwick, 110 Ohio St. 350, 144 N.E. 269 (Sup.Ct.Ohio 1924), appeal denied sub nom., Fenwick v. Myers, 275 U.S. 485, 48 S.Ct. 27, 72 L.Ed. 386 (1927) (habeas denied where woman sentenced to a definite term under a statute like § 17-360 since she "[was] not restrained of her liberty for a longer period than permitted by the assault and battery statute, the same as any person convicted thereunder * * *." (144 N.E. at 271) (dicta)); Morgan v. State, 179 Ind. 300, 101 N.E. 6 (1913) (statute permitting commitment of males found not guilty of murder by reason of insanity to Indiana colony for the criminally insane without an insanity inquest held unconstitutional); contra, Ex parte Gosselin, 141 Me. 412, 44 A.2d 882 (1945) (statute fixing maximum indeterminate sentence for women at 3 years upheld despite fact that the maximum faced by men was 2 years, the court concluding simply that the legislative classification was reasonable for the accomplishment of rehabilitation).

This much is clear enough—the application of the provisions of § 17-360 to the sentences of the petitioner in this case constituted an invidious discrimination against her which is repugnant to the equal protection of the laws guaranteed by the fourteenth amendment.

* * *

Since the petitioner has concurrently served more than six months of a sentence for the offense of resisting arrest and more than one year of the sentence for breach of the peace, the maximums which might be constitutionally imposed, law and justice require that an order for the petitioner's immediate release should be entered.

This opinion constitutes the court's findings of fact and conclusions of law.

It is ordered that the respondent shall release and absolutely discharge the petitioner from custody as promptly as possible consistent with the administrative regulations at the State Farm for Women.

If an appeal from the following order is desired, this will constitute a certificate of probable cause under 28 U.S.C. § 2253.

---

[9] [sic] There is no room for a contention that the petitioner is not serving both of the sentences she is attacking. See Rowe v. Peyton, 383 F.2d 709, 716-18 (4th Cir. 1967). [This note appeared in the original opinion, but there was no text reference to it.]

NOTES

Chapter 1.   Introduction

1. 78 Stat. 255 (1964), 42 U.S.C. §§ 2000e-2(a)-(j) (1964). The prohibition against sex discrimination was inserted in the law as half-joke, half-tactical maneuver, at the urging of congressmen who were attempting to block passage of the Civil Rights Act of 1964. See remarks of Representative Edith Green of Oregon, a staunch advocate of women's rights, 110 CONG. REC. 2581 (daily ed. Feb. 8, 1964):

> [I]f I correctly understand the mood of the House, those gentlemen of the House who are most strong in their support of women's rights this afternoon, probably gave us the most opposition when we considered the bill which would grant equal pay for equal work just a very few months ago. . . . As much as I hope the day will come when discrimination will be ended against women, I really and sincerely hope that this amendment will not be added to this bill. It will clutter up the bill and it may later—very well—be used to help destroy this section of the bill by some of the very people who today support it. And I hope that no other amendment will be added to this bill on sex or age or anything else, that would jeopardize our primary purpose in any way.

For further discussion of the prohibition against employment sex discrimination in the Civil Rights Act of 1964, see chaps. 4 and 5 *infra*.

2. UNITED NATIONS DEPARTMENT OF ECONOMIC AND SOCIAL AFFAIRS, CIVIL AND POLITICAL EDUCATION OF WOMEN 60 (1964). In some other countries, though women have the right to vote, that right is subjected to conditions and limitations not imposed on men. *Id.* at 59.

3. The revision of the French Civil Code in this area went into effect on February 1, 1966. As a result of the new law, "a wife, without asking the permission of her husband, can take a job or open a checking account. The husband can no longer simply choose housing without consulting his wife, nor make all the decisions about the children's education." *N.Y. Times*, February 2, 1966, p. 3, col. 1. Loi n° 65-570 du 13 juillet 1965, [1965] J.O. 6044(1); Recueil Dalloz Sirey, 31 août 1965, p. 233.

4. *See* Warren, *Husband's Right to Wife's Services*, 38 HARV. L. REV. 421, 423. (1925); reprinted in ASSOCIATION OF AMERICAN LAW SCHOOLS, SELECTED ESSAYS ON FAMILY LAW 460, 461 (1950) [hereinafter cited as ESSAYS ON FAMILY LAW]: "The interpretation of [Married Woman's Acts] frequently fell into the hands of judges who as young lawyers had been educated in the legal supremacy of the husband."

5. *See, e.g.,* Justice Black's dissent in United States v. Yazell, 382 U.S. 341 (1966) wherein, commenting upon the Court's acceptance of a Texas rule of coverture since abolished, he states: "It seems at least unique to me that this Court in 1966 should exalt this archaic remnant of a primitive caste system to an honored place among the laws of the United States."

6. *See* FLEXNER, CENTURY OF STRUGGLE (1959).

7. The legal and social situation of American women has frequently been compared with that of the American Negro. *See, e.g.,* DE BEAUVOIR, THE SECOND SEX xxiii (Bantam ed. 1961); Crozier, *Constitutionality of Discrimination Based on Sex,* 15 B.U.L. REV. 723, 727-28 (1935). The similarities are indeed striking: Both groups are easily identifiable; both are objects of a discrimination largely influenced by sexual factors; both have been victims of an extraordinary economic exploitation; both have at times been denied fundamental political rights (*e.g.,* jury service and the vote); and both have responded to social and legal injustice with widespread protest movements and civil disobedience leading, with varying degrees of success, to modifications of legal norms and a consequent restructuring of social attitudes.

8. *But cf.* item in *N.Y. Times,* Wednesday, October 13, 1965, p. 32, col. 3, headlined "Protest Proposed on Women's Jobs," reporting that "subtle opposition to the new law ordering equal employment opportunity for women may require them to march on Washington to obtain their rights, a woman Professor of Law at Yale University said yesterday;" *see also* report of the planned picketing of the 1968 Miss America Pageant in Atlantic City, N.J. by a group of "feminine activists" describing themselves as part of a "growing women's underground, a women's liberation movement." In the group's eyes, the beauty queen is a "degrading, mindless girlie symbol forced daily to compete for male approval, enslaved by ludicrous beauty standards we ourselves are conditioned to take seriously." *Albuquerque Tribune,* September 5, 1968, p. 1, col. 2.

9. DE BEAUVOIR, *op. cit. supra* note 7, this chap.

10. FRIEDAN, THE FEMININE MYSTIQUE (1963).

11. MCGINLEY, SIXPENCE IN HER SHOE (1964).

12. The Woman's Party has concentrated its efforts on seeking the adoption of an "Equal Rights" Amendment to the United States Constitution, which states in part: "Equality of rights under the law shall not be denied or abridged by the United States or by any State on account of sex." *See* S.J. Rep. 43, 88th Cong. First introduced in 1923, the Amendment has often been reported favorably by the Senate Judiciary Committee. On several occasions it has passed the Senate with the "Hayden rider," which provides that the Amendment "shall not be construed to impair any rights, benefits, or exemptions now or hereafter conferred by law, upon persons of female sex." 96 CONG. REC., 873, 81st Cong. 2d sess. (1950); 99 CONG. REC. 8974, 83d Cong., 1st sess. (1953). The felt need for such an Amendment has arisen from narrow interpretations of the applicability of the Fourteenth Amendment's equal protection clause to classifications based on sex. *See* REPORT OF THE COMMITTEE ON CIVIL AND POLITICAL RIGHTS TO THE PRESIDENT'S COMMISSION ON THE STATUS OF WOMEN 32, n.38 (1963) [hereinafter cited as CCPR REPORT]. Opposition to the Amendment has often come from those who seek equality between the sexes but fear that the adoption of the Amendment, with the rider, could perpetuate existing inequalities. The Committee on Civil and Political Status of the President's Commission on the Status of Women has therefore not taken a position on the proposed amendment. Instead it has suggested that the Fifth and Fourteenth Amendments may not be dead letters in this area, and has urged interested groups to bring selective litigation aimed at applying those Amendments to problems of sex-based inequality. *Id.* The constitutional aspects of sex-based legal discrimination are dealt with in greater detail in chap. 6.

13. Established by Exec. Order No. 10980, 26 Fed. Reg. 12059 (1961), the Commission submitted its report, AMERICAN WOMEN, to the President in October 1963.

14. *See* U.S. WOMEN'S BUREAU, DEPARTMENT OF LABOR, THE LEGAL STATUS OF WOMEN IN THE UNITED STATES OF AMERICA: UNITED STATES SUMMARY AS OF JANUARY 1, 1953, Women's Bureau Bull. 157 (Rev. 1956); *see also* reports for individual states.

15. *See* U.N. COMMISSION ON THE STATUS OF WOMEN, LEGAL STATUS OF MARRIED WOMEN (1958).

16. *See* notes 13-15 *supra*, this chap.

17. DE BEAUVOIR, *op. cit. supra* note 7, this chap.

18. *See, e.g.*, CAL. LAB. CODE § 1251: "No female employee shall be requested or be permitted to lift any object weighing 50 pounds or over."

19. *See* Bosley v. McLaughlin, 236 U.S. 385 (1915); Muller v. Oregon, 208 U.S. 412 (1908).

20. *See, e.g.*, CAL. CIV. CODE § 138(2), which provides in part: "As between parents claiming the custody, neither parent is entitled to it as of right; but other things being equal, if the child is of tender years, custody should be given to the mother. . . ."

21. *See, e.g.*, MO. REV. STAT. § 452.120 (1949), which declares that the rights of parents to custody shall be equal in a divorce proceeding. Decisions have held nevertheless that all other things being equal, custody of a child or children of tender years should be awarded to the mother; *See* Long v. Long, 280 S.W.2d 690 (Mo. 1955).

22. Though child custody decisions usually speak of the "best interests of the child" test (*see* Sayre, *Awarding Custody of Children*, 160 ANNALS 66 (1932), reprinted in ESSAYS ON FAMILY LAW 588)), it has been recognized that parents may have a species of property interest in the child when they are engaged in a custody dispute. *See* May v. Anderson, 345 U.S. 528 (1953), discussed in Hazard, *May v. Anderson: Preamble to Family Law Chaos*, 45 VA. L. REV. 379 (1959).

23. 62 Stat. 605, 50 U.S.C. App. § 453 (1951).

24. *See generally* Paulsen, *Support Rights and Duties Between Husband and Wife*, 9 VAND. L. REV. 709 (1956).

25. *See, e.g.*, Bradway, *Why Pay Alimony?*, 32 ILL. L. REV. 295 (1937), reprinted in ESSAYS ON FAMILY LAW 1040.

26. Child support is normally sought at the same time as custody, though in some states it may be the subject of a separate action where a parent who has custody has not received a support award. *See, e.g.*, Oravec v. Superior Court, 115 Cal. App. 2d 581, 252 P.2d 364 (1953).

27. *See, e.g.*, Daggett, *Division of Property Upon Dissolution of Marriage*, 6 LAW & CONTEMP. PROB. 225 (1939), reprinted in ESSAYS ON FAMILY LAW 1053.

28. But contrast the designation of a woman, Mme. Indira Gandhi, to head the world's second most populous nation, India, with the gimmickry of the election of Mrs. Lurleen Wallace as the governor of Alabama.

29. WEBSTER'S THIRD NEW INTERNATIONAL DICTIONARY OF THE ENGLISH LANGUAGE UNABRIDGED 648 (1965).

30. *Id.*

31. *See* Skolnick, *The Sociology of Law in America: Overview and Trends*, LAW AND SOCIETY 4, 14 (Summer 1965): "The sociology of William Graham Sumner is typically cited as the source of the view that law cannot contribute significantly to social change in this area [race relations]. A recent article by Ball, Simpson and Ikeda . . . [revises] . . . the Sumnerian hypothesis approximately as follows: laws cannot change feelings immediately, but men can perform acts prescribed by law. In addition, alterations in conduct are the most effective inducers of change in thought and feeling;" *see also* Olmstead v.

United States, 277 U.S. 438, 485 (1928). Justice Brandeis' description of "government" in *Olmstead* as "the potent, omnipresent teacher . . . [which] for good or for ill . . . teaches the whole people by its example" can be applied with equal validity to Law itself.

32. Viewed from the opposite end of the law-society spectrum, it is very possible that in the area of male-female relationships, the social attitudes of important sections of the American population have been somewhat ahead of the law for some time. See *e.g.*, text following note 111, chap. 3, *infra*, discussing the present inutility of the married woman's domicile rule. In some limited respects, therefore, there may be less sex-based discrimination than the law would have us believe. If true, this may also account in part for the absence of militancy with regard to "women's rights." The major need in those areas, therefore, would be for the law to catch up with the dominant attitudes among American opinion leaders.

33. *See* pp. 10-13 *infra*.

34. *See* pp. 28-31 *infra*.

35. *See* text following note 242 in chap. 3 *infra*.

36. *See* pp. 25-27 *infra*.

37. This is not to say that men have entirely rid themselves of ideas of natural male supremacy. Very few men, however, are today prepared to publicly justify sex-based discrimination on that ground.

38. Traynor, *Is This Conflict Really Necessary?*, 37 TEXAS L. REV. 655, 672 (1959): "The reverse of the coin is that it [New Hampshire's policy of preventing various obligations to attach to a married woman] foists protection upon all married women who come into New Hampshire even though they may have long since ceased to be the victims of protection in their own states, which are most concerned with their welfare."

39. *But cf.* MONTAGU, THE NATURAL SUPERIORITY OF WOMEN (1953), presenting psychological and biological data that establish women's greater adaptability to certain kinds of stress and consequently their greater fitness for survival as compared with men; see also the summary of the report on the effects of smoking on the health of women smokers, prepared by Statistician E. Cuyler Hammond of the American Cancer Society.

> Despite the fact that his statistics show that heavy-smoking women have higher disease and early-death rates, Dr. Hammond finds that most of them still do not fare as badly as men. Their increased risk of heart-artery disease (almost twice as much as nonsmokers) and of lung cancer is only about half as great as the smoking man's increased risk. *The truth is, women seem to have an inherent biological superiority and survival capacity over men.* The difference in overall number of deaths among the Cancer Society volunteers is striking: there were more than half as many again among the men, although there were many fewer men in the study. Even if enough women smoked heavily enough and long enough to incur the same added risk of early death as male smokers, says Dr. Hammond, the actual death rates among women would still be lower *because of that innate superiority.* TIME, March 4, 1966, p. 34, col. 3. (Emphasis supplied.)

40. DE BEAUVOIR, *op. cit. supra* note 7, this chap., at xiii; *see also* MONTAGU, MAN'S MOST DANGEROUS MYTH: THE FALLACY OF RACE 16 (4th ed. 1964), in which myths of female as well as of racial inferiority are compared in that both "deny a particular group equality of opportunity and then assert that because that group has not achieved as much as the group enjoying complete freedom of opportunity it is obviously inferior and can never do as well."

41. See text following note 114 in chap. 3 *infra*.

42. *See* FLEXNER, *op. cit. supra* note 6, this chap. at 23-40.

43. *See* p. 28 *infra*; *see also* chap. 6 *infra passim*.

Chapter 2.   Law and the Single Girl

1. Many, but not all, of the rules of law examined in this section often affect married as well as single women. For the most part, however, it is because they are *women* and not because they are *married*. For this reason, "Law and the Single Girl" has been deemed an appropriate title for this section. There is of course a large area of law (mainly in the spheres of contract and property relations), in which a woman's marriage has caused, and often still does, dramatic changes in her legal rights and liabilities. The legal status of married women *per se* will be examined in chap. 3 *infra*.

2. Anonymous, 1 Salk 44, 91 Eng. Rep. 44, (K.B. 1704); Anderson v. Peterson, 36 Minn. 547, 32 N.W. 861 (1887).

3. *See, e.g.*, COL. REV. STAT. ANN. § 135-1-2 (14) (1963); MISS. CODE ANN. § 648 Repl. (1956).

4. ILL. ANN. STAT. ch. 3, § 131 (Smith-Hurd Repl. 1961).

5. *See, e.g.*, MINN. STAT. ANN. § 525.80 (1945) which now provides that "The word 'minor' means a person under the age of 21 years." Prior to the amendment by Minn. Laws, 1937, ch. 435, § 24, this section provided that the word "minor" meant a male person under the age of twenty-one years or a female person under the age of eighteen years. In Missouri, between 1865 and 1921, females were adults at eighteen; males did not attain majority until they were twenty-one. Now, males and females both attain majority at age twenty-one. MO. REV. STAT. § 457.010 (1959).

6. *See* ALA. CODE, tit. 34, § 76 (1) (1940); CAL. CIV. CODE § 25; MINN. STAT. ANN. § 525-80 (1945).

7. *See* text following note 1 in chap. 3 *infra*.

8. *See* p. 10 *infra*.

9. *See* pp. 18-25 *infra*.

10. Loving v. Virginia, 388 U.S. 1 (1967); *cf.* McLaughlin v. Florida, 379 U.S. 184 (1965); Perez v. Lippold, 32 Cal.2d 711, 198 P.2d 17 (1948).

11. *See, e.g.*, Drinan, *The Loving Decision and the Freedom to Marry*, 29 OHIO ST. L. J. 358 (1968).

12. CONN. GEN. STAT. ANN. § 46-5 (d) (Repl. 1959) [minors]; FLA. STAT. ANN. § 741.04 (Repl. 1963) [21 years]; HAWAII REV. LAWS §§ 323-2, 9, 10 (1955) [20 years]; IDAHO CODE ANN. § 32-202 (Repl. 1963) [18 years]; KY. REV. STAT. § 402-210 (Supp. 1965) [lowered in 1964 to 18 years in any county except the county of residence]; LA. CIV. CODE ANN. arts. 20, 97 (West 1952) [minors]; MISS. CODE ANN. § 461 (Repl. 1956) [21 years]; PA. STAT. tit. 48 § 1-5 (c) (Repl. 1965) [21 years]; S.C. CODE ANN. §§ 20-24 to 24-2 (1962) [18 years]; W. VA. CODE ANN. § 4686 (1961) [21 years].

13. CONN. GEN. STAT. REV. § 46-5 (d) (Repl. 1959) [16 years]; ME. REV. STAT. ANN. tit. 166, § 5 (1954) [16 years]; MO. REV. STAT. § 451.090 (1949) [16 years]; TENN. CODE ANN. § 36-408 (1956) [16 years].

14. JACOBS & GOEBEL, DOMESTIC RELATIONS: CASES AND MATERIALS 133 (4th ed. 1961).

15. *Id.; see also generally* Kingsley, *The Law of Infants' Marriages,* 9 Vand. L. Rev. 593 (1956).

16. *See* Swindlehurst, *Some Phases of the Law of Marriage,* 30 Harv. L. Rev. 124, 137 (1916).

17. Harris, Ch. J., dissenting in State v. Graves, 228 Ark. 378, 307 S.W.2d 545, 550 (1957).

18. The Committee on Civil and Political Rights of the President's Commission on the Status of Women has acknowledged the differences in minimum age requirements for marriages for males and females. It has recommended, however, that "The Women's Bureau of the Department of Labor or some other appropriate agency be directed to study further and make appropriate proposals for reform with respect to" that area and several others. CCPR Report 27.

19. Occasionally, local school boards have taken the position that the marriage of public school students constitutes a ground for expulsion, McLeod v. State ex rel. Colmer, 154 Miss. 468, 122 So. 737, 63 A.L.R. 1161 (1929); or their being barred from "co-curricular activities," Cochrane v. Mesick, 360 Mich. R. 390, 103 N.W.2d 569 (1960); or their being denied admission to a new school, Nutt v. Board of Educ., 128 Kan. 507, 276 Pac. 1065 (1929). As seen in the cases cited, such efforts have generally failed when attacked in the courts.

20. *See* Flexner, Century of Struggle 23 (1959), describing the early steps toward equal education for American women.

21. When parents consent, the minimum age problems for marriage are considerably different from situations where such consent is not required. Some arguments for and against retention of a lower age for girls than boys where parental consent is given are: *For:* 1) Parents, wiser and more emotionally secure than their infant offspring, are best equipped to assess the merits and disadvantages of early marriage; 2) in special situations such as premarital pregnancy (other factors for successful marriage being present), early marriage for girls may do more good than harm. *Against:* 1) Parents, conditioned by their own backgrounds to scorn women's efforts away from home and hearth, may not exercise the best judgment in granting or withholding consent.

22. *See* note 12, this chap. *supra.*

23. *See* Jacobs & Goebel, Statutory Supplement to Domestic Relations: Cases and Materials 16-17, col. 5 (4th ed. 1961) [hereinafter cited as Jacobs & Goebel, Statutory Supplement].

24. Wash. Rev. Code § 26.04.210 (Supp. 1965).

25. Peterson v. Widule, 157 Wis. 641, 147 N.W. 966 (1914), discussed in 27 Harv. L. Rev. 573 (1914); 28 Harv. L. Rev. 112 (1914); 13 Mich. L. Rev. 39 (1914).

26. Wisc. Stat. § 2339 m (1) (1913); Wisc. Sess. Laws, 1913, 1060-1062.

27. 157 Wis. at 648, 147 N.W. at 968. (Emphasis supplied.)

28. *See, e.g.,* Vondal v. Vondal, 175 Mass. 383, 56 N.E. 586, 78 Am. St. Rep. 502 (1900).

29. Laws of Md. 1939, ch. 558, at 1132.

30. Md. Ann. Code art. 16, § 38 (1924 ed.). (Emphasis supplied.)

31. *See* U.S. Women's Bureau, Legal Status of Women: Analysis of Sex Distinctions 5 (mimeo Jan. 1, 1944), "Fourteen states, under varying conditions, may grant divorce for the wife's unchaste character (usually before marriage), without a corresponding remedy for the wife: Alabama, Arizona,

Georgia, Iowa, Kansas, Kentucky, Mississippi, Missouri, New Mexico, North Carolina, Oklahoma, Tennessee, Virginia, Wyoming." According to that same report, West Virginia allowed the husband an annulment for the wife's premarital unchastity, but no similar remedy was allowed to the wife against the husband. *Id.*

32. McAllister v. McAllister, 71 Tex. 695, 10 S.W. 294 (1888).

33. *Id.* at 696, 10 S.W. at 295.

34. TIME, December 10, 1965, p. 35.

35. *See* Willcox, *Legislation in Iowa Compared with the Law Proposed for the Suppression of Vice in Illinois,* 36 J. CRIM. L. 926 (1913), examining a law "pertaining to the social evil . . . proposed for Illinois by the Vigilance Association"; see also THE SOCIAL EVIL (Seligman ed. 1912).

36. George, *Legal, Medical and Psychiatric Considerations in the Control of Prostitution,* 60 MICH. L. REV. 717 (1962).

37. *Id.*

38. PERKINS, CRIMINAL LAW 335 (1957); see also HOME OFFICE SCOTTISH HOME DEPARTMENT REPORT OF THE COMMITTEE ON HOMOSEXUAL OFFENSES AND PROSTITUTION 79 (1957) [hereinafter cited as WOLFENDEN REPORT]:

Prostitution in itself is not, in this country, an offense against criminal law. Some of the activities of prostitutes are, and so are the activities of some others who are concerned in the activities of prostitutes. But it is not illegal for a woman to 'offer her body to indiscriminate lewdness for hire' provided that she does not, in the course of doing so, commit any one of the specific acts which would bring her within the ambit of the law.

39. Ferguson v. Superior Court, 26 Cal. App. 554, 558, 147 Pac. 603, 605 (1915).

40. LA. REV. STAT. § 14.82 (1950).

41. City of Saint Louis v. Green, 190 S.W.2d 634 (Mo. App. 1945).

42. *E.g.,* women prostitutes to accommodate non-prostitute women who wish to engage in homosexual relations. KINSEY, POMEROY & MARTIN, SEXUAL BEHAVIOR IN THE HUMAN MALE 596 (1948).

43. State v. Gardner, 174 Iowa 748, 156 N.W. 747 (1916).

44. *E.g.,* ILL. ANN. STAT. ch. 38, §§ 11-18 (Smith-Hurd 1961); WIS. STAT. ANN. § 944.31 (1958); *but cf.* Ellis v. State, 65 Tex. Crim. 480, 145 S.W. 339 (1912), suggesting that a single act of intercourse does not violate TEX. PEN. CODE ANN. art. 607 (14) (1952), which provides criminal penalties for "all male persons who habitually associate with prostitutes."

45. *E.g.,* OHIO REV. CODE § 2905.27 (Anderson Supp. 1965); HAWAII REV. LAWS §§ 309-30 (1955); GA. CODE ANN. § 26-6204 (1953); MISS. CODE ANN. § 2333 (1956).

46. State v. Davis, 165 N.E.2d 504 (Cincinnati, Ohio, Munic. Ct. 1959).

47. 18 U.S.C. § 2421 (1958).

48. Caminetti v. United States, 242 U.S. 470 (1917).

49. Whitt v. United States, 261 F.2d 907 (6th Cir. 1959).

50. *See* MUELLER, LEGAL REGULATION OF SEXUAL CONDUCT (1961).

51. State v. Gardner, 174 Iowa 748, 156 N.W. 747 (1916).

52. State v. Oge, 227 Iowa 1094, 290 N.W. 1 (1940).

53. Warner v. State, 202 Ind. 479, 175 N.E. 661 (1931); see also Annot., "Isolated Acts of Sexual Intercourse as Constituting Criminal Offense of Adultery or Fornication or Illicit Cohabitation," 74 A.L.R. 1361 (1931).

54. George, *supra* note 36, this chap. at 759.

55. *Id.* at 730.

56. A girl in a house of prostitution can entertain between 30 and 100 men in a 20-hour period. Williams, *The Suppression of Commercialized Prostitution in the City of Vancouver*, 27 J. Soc. Hyg. 364, 371 (1941).

57. *Cf.* Ex Parte Carey, 57 Cal. App. 297, 207 P. 271 (1922).

58. *See* Carter, Sin and Science (1945).

59. *Id.* at 56-57.

60. *See* Flexner, Prostitution in Europe 107 (1914): "[A]s a matter of history, no proposition aiming at punishment [of prostitution] has ever involved both participants. The harlot has been branded as an outcast and flung to the wolves: she alone,—never the man, her equal partner in responsibility."

61. *Id.* at 108.

62. *Id.*

63. To be entirely accurate, one must add, with the Pinafore's captain, "Well, hardly ever!" A handful of states do in fact penalize females, in terms of statutory rape or similar criminal concepts, for certain types of sexual misconduct with underage males. *See, e.g.,* Col. Rev. Stat. § 40-2-25 (k) (1963); W. Va. Code § 61-2-15 (1966). These statutes are rare exceptions that prove the rule, however. They also illustrate one legislative approach to correcting the present general sex-based inequality of treatment in this realm.

64. *See, e.g.,* Miller v. State, 16 Ala. App. 534, 535, 70 So. 314, 315 (1918).

65. People v. Hernandez, 39 Cal. Rptr. 361, 393 P.2d 673 (1961); *cf.* N.M. Stat. Ann. § 40A-9-3 (1964) which provides that a "reasonable belief on the part of the male at the time of the alleged crime that the female was sixteen years of age or older is a defense to criminal liability for statutory rape."

66. *See, e.g.,* People v. Gibson, 232 N.Y. 458, 459, 134 N.E. 531, 532 (1922), where it is stated:

> The intention of the law is to protect unmarried girls from carnal copulation, such intercourse being fraught with peril to the morals of the community and to the well-being of the individual. With the age of consent fixed at eighteen years, it may not confidently be stated that all girls under that age do not comprehend what they are doing when they consent to intercourse. The law, however, deals with all, and not with individuals. *In law, the act of intercourse, or the attempt to have intercourse, is without their consent, and against their will. The state says that they do not consent, or that their apparent consent shall be disregarded. It offers resistance for them. It deals with the case as rape; not as a mere statutory offense.* (Emphasis supplied.)

67. *But see* pp. 23-24 *infra* for the probable underlying reasons for the rule.

68. Mass. Gen. Laws Ann. ch. 272, § 4 (Repl. 1956). (Emphasis supplied.)

69. Mass. Gen. Laws Ann. ch. 272, § 3 (Repl. 1956).

70. *See, e.g.,* Cal. Pen. Code § 272.

71. *Id.*

72. In a personal interview with a California prosecuting attorney, I was told that a district attorney would "feel silly" if he were to prosecute a 22 year old girl under the contributing to the delinquency statute for having sexual relations with a 17 year old boy. No such compunction would arise, however, in prosecuting a 22 year old male for statutory rape because he had engaged in sexual intercourse with a 17 year old girl. Though one prosecutor doth not an entire judicial system make, one may safely assume that his views are shared by most, if not all, other prosecuting attorneys.

73. D.C. Code Ann. § 22-3001 (1961).

74. FLA. STAT. § 794.05 (1961).
75. MASS. GEN LAWS ANN. ch. 272, § 4 (Repl. 1956).
76. MISS. CODE ANN. § 2359 (1942) (Repl. 1956).
77. MISS. CODE ANN. § 2360 (Repl. 1956). (Emphasis supplied.)
78. ILL. ANN. STAT. ch. 38, § 409 (Smith-Hurd 1961).
79. CONN. GEN. STAT. ANN. § 53-224 (1960).
80. IND. ANN. STATS. § 10-4201 (Repl. 1956).
81. IOWA CODE ANN. § 698.1 (1946).
82. MD. ANN. CODE art. 27, § 462 (1957).
83. MO. REV. STAT. § 559.260 (1959).
84. *See* note 68, this chap., *supra*.
85. *See, e.g.*, MINN. STAT. ANN. § 617.07 (1963).
86. People v. Gibbs, 70 Mich. 425, 38 N.W. 257 (1888).
87. *See, e.g.*, IOWA CODE ANN. § 700.1 (1946): "any unmarried woman of previously chaste character"; see also MINN. STAT. ANN. § 617.07 (1963); but *cf.* CONN. GEN. STAT. ANN. § 53-224 (1960): "minor female"; D.C. CODE § 22.301 (1961): "any female of previous chaste character between the ages of sixteen and twenty-one years . . ."; MO. REV. STAT. § 599.310 (1959): requiring that the female victim be below age 21.
88. *See, e.g.*, MICH. STAT. ANN. § 28.8001 (Repl. 1954).
89. IOWA CODE ANN. § 700.2 (1946); see also MINN. STAT. ANN. § 617.07 (1963) which also provides a special two year limitation period for prosecution.
90. MO. REV. STAT. § 559.260 (1959).
91. *See, e.g.*, MD. ANN. CODE art. 72A, § 3 (1957), which gives the parent a cause of action "for loss of the wages or services of their minor child when such loss is occasioned by the seduction of the child, or by an injury wrongfully or negligently inflicted upon it." Though, grammatically, this provision seems to apply where the minor child is a male as well as a female, the seduction part of the cause of action, in the light of the historical meaning of the word "seduction," is probably intended to refer to female children only. § 17 of the Bankruptcy Act, 11 U.S.C.A. § 35, setting forth certain debts *not* affected by a discharge, include "liabilities for . . . seduction of an unmarried female, or for breach of promise of marriage accompanied by seduction . . . ." Thus, revulsion at such conduct has influenced national policy. Though a bankrupt may be relieved of the financial liability he incurs as a result of his negligent taking of another's life, he will not be so relieved for civil liabilities caused by his act of seduction.
92. *See, e.g.*, FLA. STAT. § 795.01 (1961); MASS. GEN. LAWS ANN. ch. 272, § 1 (Repl. 1956).
93. *But cf.* MISS. CODE ANN. § 2051 (Repl. 1956), a statute on enticement of children below the age of 14, which does not by its terms distinguish between male and female children. This contrasts with the Mississippi statute on "seduction," MISS. CODE ANN. § 2054 (Repl. 1956) which specifically refers to "female" victims under the age of 18. As in the case of the Maryland statute (see note 91, *supra*, this chap.), however, the historical meaning of the word "enticement" would probably limit the statute's application to situations involving female victims and male defendants. However, if one were to rely upon the express wording of the Mississippi statute, it could be made to apply to a female defendant who entices a young boy away from his parents' home for purposes of entering into a clandestine marriage.
94. *See* GA. CODE ANN. § 26-1303 (Repl. 1953); ME. REV. STAT. ANN. tit. 17, § 3151 (1964).

95. Mass. Gen. Laws Ann. ch. 265, § 23 (Repl. 1956); Ind. Ann. Stat. § 10-4201 (Repl. 1956).

96. Fla. Stat. § 794.05 (1961); Minn. Stat. Ann. § 617.02 (1963); Cal. Pen. Code § 26.

97. Tenn. Code Ann. § 39-3706 (1955).

98. Note, *Statutory Rape: A Defense,* 38 So. Cal. L. Rev. 131 (1965).

99. *See* Miss. Code Ann. § 2359 (Repl. 1956) under which the crime may be committed by "any male person" if the victim is "any unmarried female person of previously chaste character *younger than himself.*" (Emphasis supplied.)

100. D.C. Code § 22-3002 (1961).

101. *See* note 99, this chap. *supra.*

102. Md. Ann. Code, art. 27, § 462 (1957).

103. Iowa Code Ann. § 698.1 (1946).

104. Kans. Gen. Stat. Ann. § 21-909 (Repl. 1963).

105. Such statutes also appear to concede law's limitations in controlling sexual experimentation between young lovers. *See* Morris Ploscowe, Sex And The Law 169 (rev. ed. 1962).

106. Not to speak of direct injustice to males. *See, e.g.,* State v. Snow, 293 Mo. 143, 252 S.W. 629 (1923), in which, despite the fact that the female victim was a young prostitute, the male defendants who were "callow youths of otherwise blameless lives" were convicted of statutory rape.

107. *See* pp. 7-9 *supra.*

108. *See, e.g.,* Ill. Ann. Stat. ch. 3, § 131 (Smith-Hurd 1961).

109. People v. Ratz, 115 Cal. 132, 46 Pac. 915 (1896).

110. Cal. Pen. Code § 274.

111. *See* Leavy and Charles, *California's New Therapeutic Abortion Act: An Analysis and Guide to Medical and Legal Procedure,* 15 U.C.L.A. L. Rev. 1 (1967).

112. Leavy & Kummer, *Criminal Abortion: A Failure of Law,* 50 A.B.A.J. 52 n.2 (1964).

113. Harper, *Abortion Laws in the United States,* in Calderone, Abortion In The United States (1958).

114. Packer & Gampell, *Theraupetic Abortion: A Problem in Law and Medicine,* 11 Stan. L. Rev. 417 (1959).

115. Leavy & Kummer, *Criminal Abortion: Human Hardship and Unyielding Laws,* 35 So. Cal. L. Rev. 123 (1962).

116. Leavy & Kummer, note 112, *supra,* this chap.

117. Gebhard, Pomeroy, Martin & Christenson, Pregnancy, Birth And Abortion 213 (1958).

118. Cal. Pen. Code § 275, which is also typical of statutes in other states, makes it a felony for any woman to solicit any abortifacient of another or to submit to an operation "or to the use of any means whatever, with intent thereby to procure a miscarriage, unless the same is necessary to preserve her life. . . ." In many states, however, the woman abortee is considered a victim rather than an accomplice to the offense of abortion. See Annot., 139 A.L.R. 933 (1942).

119. *See* note 118, this chap., *supra.*

120. *See* Flexner, Century Of Struggle (1959), for a stirring historical account of the Women's Rights Movement in the United States.

121. The brewing and distilling industry financed much of the organized opposition to women's suffrage because they feared women's prohibition senti-

ments. *Id.* at 296-98. Other business and corporate interests, disturbed by the acceleration of "communistic" developments as the Federal Income Tax, the Federal Reserve System, and anti-trust legislation, looked with apprehension upon "the addition of a large body of new voters, control of which appeared uncertain and . . . whose leaders were vocal in the cause of further reform." *Id.* at 302.

122. Technically the Nineteenth Amendment did not by itself confer the right of suffrage on women; it merely prohibited discrimination on the basis of sex "in legislation prescribing the qualification of suffrage." State v. Mittle, 120 S.C. 526, 531, 113 S.E. 335, 337 (1922). It has been pointed out that "this somewhat formalistic distinction is essential to a thorough appreciation of the generally limited application of the nineteenth amendment," insofar as its effects on women's rights to serve on juries or to hold appointive office are concerned. Note, *Classification on the Basis of Sex and the 1964 Civil Rights Act,* 50 IOWA L. REV. 778, 780-81 (1965).

123. White v. Crook, 251 F. Supp. 401 (N.D. Ala. 1966).

124. In an 1879 dictum the Supreme Court declared that a state may constitutionally "confine" jury duty to "males." Strauder v. West Virginia, 100 U.S. 303, 310 (1879). As recently as 1961 the Court avoided a re-examination of the validity of that dictum. Hoyt v. Florida, 368 U.S. 57, 60 (1961). The effect upon the Strauder dictum of Ballard v. United States, 329 U.S. 187 (1946), is also uncertain. In Ballard, a 5-4 decision reversing defendants' convictions for mail fraud, Justice Douglas and three other Justices held that notwithstanding California's practice of not calling women for jury service, failure of a federal court sitting in that state to do so required reversal of defendants' convictions in the exercise of the Court's supervisory powers over the federal judicial system. Since women in California were eligible for jury service, CAL. CIV. PROC. CODE § 198 (1954), they were therefore also qualified in the federal courts which sat in that state, according to federal law in force at that time. Judicial Code § 275, 28 U.S.C. § 411 [now 28 U.S.C. § 1861 (1946)]. But "whether the method of *selecting a jury* in the federal court from those qualified is or is not proper is a question of *federal* law." (Emphasis supplied.) 329 U.S. at 192. Justice Douglas, having thus distinguished the question of the method of selection from that of qualification, proceeded to characterize federal law as requiring women not to be systematically excluded from juries, finding in prior opinions a policy "to make the jury 'a cross-section of the community' and truly representative of it." 329 U.S. at 191. Justice Jackson concurred on other grounds. Four of the Justices dissented. Justice Burton wrote a separate dissenting opinion in which he stated, *inter alia,* that the general advance of women toward equal status with males "emphasizes the lack of reason for making a point of the presence or absence of either sex, as such, on either grand or petit juries." 329 U.S. at 205. Read in the context of the particular issues in *Ballard,* however, the effect of Justice Burton's position was to say that because women are approaching full legal equality with men, it is proper intentionally to exclude them from juries. Strange reasoning indeed!

125. Juries of matrons were impanelled: 1) when a widow claimed to be pregnant and a question of inheritance arose; and 2) when a woman under sentence of death pleaded for a stay of execution until her child was born. Note, *Courts—Women Jurors—Automatic Exemption,* 36 TUL. L. REV. 858 (1962), citing 3 BLACKSTONE, COMMENTARIES *363 and 4 BLACKSTONE, COMMENTARIES *394 respectively; see also BARRETT-LENNARD, THE POSITION IN LAW OF WOMEN 4 (1883).

126. Utah Code Ann. 78-45-10 (1953); *see* Note, *Courts—Women Jurors—Automatic Exemption,* 36 Tul. L. Rev. 858 (1962).

127. 28 U.S.C. § 1861 (1946).

128. But federal jury clerks apparently may still follow a custom of recognizing state exemptions in excusing persons from federal jury service if those exemptions are asserted by those called for a qualification interview, and they do not result in a denial to defendants of any of their rights in selection of a jury. United States v. Van Allen, 208 F. Supp. 331 (S.D.N.Y. 1962).

129. *See* CCPR Report 11; *see also* 26 F.R.D. 409, 431 (1960); *N.Y. Times,* March 2, 1966, story headlined "Women in Congress Score Jury Sex Bias," reporting that eight women "congressmen" in a letter to the Attorney General urged a ban on sex discrimination in the selection of juries in both Federal and state courts, and also pointed out "that many Federal district courts had failed to give full effect to the purpose of the Civil Rights Act of 1957, which made women eligible to serve on Federal juries."

130. *E.g.,* H.R. Rep. No. 3284, 88th Cong., 1st sess. (1963).

131. *See* CCPR Report 11; since the text accompanying this note was written, Congress enacted the Jury Selection and Service Act of 1968, P.L. 90-274, 82 Stat. 53, amending 28 U.S.C. §§ 1861-1869. Significant features of the new Act are the plan for random jury selection, 28 U.S.C. § 1863, and the increase in jurors' fees from $10.00 to $20.00 per day, 28 U.S.C. § 1871. The latter reform is consistent with what is urged herein as a necessary step to alleviate the economic loss presently suffered by both men and women when called to serve on federal or state court juries. *See* p. 31 *infra.*

132. *See* CCPR Report 13, Table 1.

133. *Id.*

134. *Id.*

135. *Id.*

136. *Id.*

137. 368 U.S. 57 (1961).

138. Fla. Stat. Ann. § 40.01 (1) (1961).

139. Chief Justice Warren and Justices Douglas and Black concurred only because they could not say from the record that Florida was "not making a good faith effort to have women perform jury duty without discrimination on the ground of sex." 368 U.S. at 69.

140. *Id.* at 61-62. (Emphasis supplied.)

141. *Id.* at 64.

142. *Id.* at 65.

143. *See, e.g.,* Cal. Lab. Code § 1251.

144. *See, e.g.,* Del. Code Ann. Tit. 19, § 302 (c) (1953), repealed, 50 Del. Laws, ch. 65 § 1 (1955); Md. Ann. Code, art. 100 § 52 (1957).

145. *See, e.g.,* N.M. Stat. § 59-5-1 (Repl. 1960).

146. *See* pp. 33-34 *infra.*

147. 77 Stat. 56 (1963), 29 U.S.C. § 206 (d) (1964).

148. 77 Stat. 56 (1963), 29 U.S.C. § 206 (d) (1964) provides in part: "No employer having employees subject to any provisions of this section shall discriminate, within any establishment in which such employees are employed, between employees on the basis of sex by paying wages to employees in such establishment at a rate less than the rate at which he pays wages to employees of the opposite sex in such establishment for equal work on jobs the performance of which requires equal skill, effort, and responsibility, and which are performed under similar working conditions, except where such payment is made pursuant

to (i) a seniority system; (ii) a merit system; (iii) a system which measures earnings by quantity or quality of production; or (iv) a differential based on any other factor other than sex . . . ."

149. *See* REPORT OF THE COMMITTEE ON PROTECTIVE LABOR LEGISLATION TO THE PRESIDENT'S COMMISSION ON THE STATUS OF WOMEN 7 (1963) [hereinafter cited as CPLL REPORT].

150. 78 Stat. 255, 42 U.S.C. §§ 2000e-2 (a)- (j) (1964).

151. *See* Murray & Eastwood, *Jane Crow and the Law: Sex Discrimination and Title VII*, 34 GEO. WASH. L. REV. 232, 233 (1965).

152. *See, e.g.*, State v. Hunter, 208. Ore. 282, 300 P.2d 455 (1956).

153. *See, e.g.*, Fitzpatrick v. Liquor Control Commission, 316 Mich. 83, 25 N.W.2d 118 (1946); *but cf.* Brown v. Foley, 158 Fla. 734, 29 So. 2d 870 (1947).

154. 335 U.S. 464 (1948).

155. *Id.* at 466.

156. The Court in *Goesart* stated, however, "we cannot give ear to the suggestion that the real impulse behind this legislation was an unchivalrous desire of male bartenders to try to monopolize the calling." 335 U.S. at 467. *Cf.* Wilson v. Hacker et al., 101 N.Y.S. 2d 461 (1950), granting an injunction at the behest of a restaurant and tavern owner against picketing by a union, the Bartender's League of America, to secure a union shop agreement, where the union refused to accept women members and would therefore require three women employees of plaintiff to be discharged if the agreement were entered into.

157. 335 U.S. at 466. (Emphasis supplied.)

158. 78 Stat. 255, 42 U.S.C. § 2000e-2 (1964).

159. 78 Stat. 255, 42 U.S.C. § 2000e-2 (e) (1) (1964).

160. Even so, the blanket exclusion of women would still be of doubtful validity. As one sage of the People has observed, "Though the Good Lord may not have made all men equal, He made an awful lot of 'equalizers.' "

161. *See* chaps. 4 and 5 *infra*.

Chapter 3.   Law and the Married Woman

1. Under the rule of primogeniture, "the eldest son, and only the eldest son, succeeded. The other children had no share in the inheritance." RADIN, HANDBOOK OF ANGLO-AMERICAN LEGAL HISTORY (1936). Obviously, this rule also required the disinheritance of all of a man's daughters if he left surviving him at least one son. The rule of primogeniture has of course disappeared in modern times. *Id.* at 408. So has a related rule, the general postponement of women in matters of inheritance, under which, "if a man died leaving daughters, they would not inherit if there were male kinsmen, i.e., brothers, uncles or cousins, within the terms of the original feoffment." *Id.* at 409.

2. Some women's rights in the public sphere were also lost as a result of marriage. After women had been given a limited right to vote in certain English municipal elections, Municipal Corporations Act, 1869, 32 & 33 Vict. c. 55, they lost this right under the doctrine of coverture as soon as they were married. *See* The Queen v. Harrald, [1872] 7 Q.B. 361, holding that the Act was intended to remove a woman's disability from voting only where that disability arose from her being a female—and that married women still had no right to vote;

discussed in Barrett-Lennard, The Position in Law of Married Women (1883).

3. Blackstone, Commentaries* 433.

4. United States v. Yazell, 382 U.S. 341, 361 (1966) (Black, J. dissenting).

5. Radin, *The Common Law of the Family*, VI National Law Library, Legal Relations 79 (1939) [hereinafter cited as Radin]; *see also* Madden, Handbook of the Law of Persons and Domestic Relations 91-92 (1931), [hereinafter cited as Madden].

6. Radin 175.

7. *Id. See also* Madden 83.

8. Black's Law Dictionary 305 (1951) defines "chose in action" variously as: "A personal right not reduced into possession, but recoverable by a suit at law. . . . A right to personal things of which the owner has not the possession, but merely a right of action for their possession. . . . A right to receive or recover a debt, demand, or damages on a cause of action *ex contractu* or for a tort or omission of a duty."

9. Radin 175, Madden 85.

10. Madden 94.

11. *E.g.*, where her husband had been banished, had abjured the realm, was a nonresident alien, or had been transported, Madden 96, or with reference to her separate equitable estate, see pp. 38-40 *infra*.

12. Madden 96.

13. *See* Williams, *The Legal Unity of Husband and Wife*, 10 Modern L. Rev. 16, 20 (1947); *cf.* United States v. Dege, 364 U.S. 51 (1960); People v. Pierce, 40 Cal. Rptr. 845, 395 P.2d 893 (1964).

14. *See* Williams, *supra* note 13, this chap., at 24.

15. *Cf.* People v. Stately, 91 Cal. App. 2d Supp. 943, 206 P.2d 76 (1949).

16. Radin 175; Madden 156.

17. 1 Blackstone, Commentaries* 443.

18. *Cf.* Williams, *supra* note 13, this chap., at 19.

19. Madden 21-22.

20. The husband, on the other hand, acquired a comparable interest (curtesy) in his wife's real property. In his case not only did he have to survive his wife to inherit his share of her property, but unlike his wife, his taking was contingent upon the birth of issue during the marriage.

21. Radin 172; Madden 179.

22. *See* Paulsen, *Support Rights and Duties Between Husband and Wife*, 9 Vand. L. Rev. 709 (1956).

23. Since the wife could not contract during marriage, the husband was not liable for contracts she purportedly made at that time. Exceptions to this rule, however, were based upon the husband's duty to support his wife, which led to the husband's liability to reimburse third persons for "necessaries" they furnished to her if he failed to provide them himself. The husband was also liable for contracts made by his wife while acting as his agent.

24. Radin 176; Madden 205-206.

25. *Id.*

26. Radin 176-177.

27. Radin 177.

28. Radin, Handbook of Anglo-American Legal History 524 (1936).

29. 3 Pomeroy, Equity Jurisprudence 1101 (5th ed. 1941).

30. Madden 101.

31. *Id.*

32. *Id.* at 102.

33. Hulme v. Tenant, 1 Bro. C.C. 16, 28 Eng. Rep. 958 (Ch. 1778) and authorities cited therein.

34. MADDEN 104.

35. *See, e.g.,* Fettiplace v. Gorges, 1 Ves. Jr. 46, 30 Eng. Rep. 223 (1789); Rich v. Cockell, 9 Ves. Jr. 369, 32 Eng. Rep. 644 (1804). Some American courts have held that a wife does not have the power to dispose of her separate equitable estate unless it has been expressly conferred. See *e.g.,* Holliday v. Hively, 198 Pa. 335, 47 A. 988 (1901); Bressler v. Kent, 6 Ill. 426, 14 Am. Rep. 67 (1871).

36. MADDEN 105.

37. *Id.*

38. *Id.* at 108.

39. *Id.* at 103.

40. *Id.*

41. *See, e.g.,* Warren, *Husband's Rights to Wife's Services,* 38 HARV. L. REV. 421 (1925); reprinted in ESSAYS ON FAMILY LAW 460.

42. "There came, therefore, to be not in theory but in fact one law for the rich and another for the poor. The daughters of the rich enjoyed, for the most part, the considerate protection of equity, the daughters of the poor suffered under the severity and injustice of the common law." DICEY, LAW AND PUBLIC OPINION IN ENGLAND 383 (2d ed. 1914).

43. "The first Married Woman's Act was passed in Mississippi in 1839, and other states followed by about 1850." CLARK, CASES AND PROBLEMS ON DOMESTIC RELATIONS 322 (1965).

44. *See* BARRETT-LENNARD, THE POSITION IN LAW OF WOMEN 159 (1883).

45. *See, e.g.,* WOLLSTONECRAFT, A VINDICATION OF THE RIGHTS OF WOMAN (3rd ed. 1796); MILL, THE SUBJECTION OF WOMEN (1869).

46. *See* Chapter III, *The Beginnings of Organization Among Women,* in FLEXNER, CENTURY OF STRUGGLE 41 (1959), and Chapter V, *The Seneca Falls Convention, 1848,* at p. 71 of the same book.

47. "The interpretation of [Married Women's Acts] frequently fell into the hands of judges who as young lawyers had been educated in the legal supremacy of the husband." Warren, *Husband's Rights to Wife's Services,* 38 HARV. L. REV. 421, 423 (1925); reprinted in ESSAYS ON FAMILY LAW 460, 461.

48. "Today the more obvious legal disabilities of married women have been eliminated, notwithstanding a determined rear-guard action by the Courts, who demonstrated a real hostility to the Married Women's Acts. Some strongholds of disability remain unconquered, however. . . ." CLARK, CASES AND PROBLEMS ON DOMESTIC RELATIONS 322 (1965).

49. *See* note 4, this chap., *supra.*

50. On a recent visit to Denmark, I lived in an apartment owned by a married couple, each of whom bore different surnames.

51. *See, e.g.,* Wilty v. Jefferson Parish Democratic Executive Comm., 245 La. 145, 157 So.2d 718, 727 (1963 Sanders, J., concurring), "The common law fiction of merger between husband and wife, from which a change of the wife's legal name arises, has never obtained in Louisiana. Rather, this state has followed the civil law doctrine. After marriage, the legal name of a married woman continues to be her maiden name, or patronym. The surname of the husband is used only as a matter of custom to indicate the marital status of the wife. See . . . Planiol, Traité Elémentaire de Droit Civil (An English Translation by the Louisiana State Law Institute) No. 390." *Cf. also* Paragraph 7, section 1 of the new Family Code of the German Democratic Republic (East Germany),

effective April 1, 1966, which provides that "the married partners bear a common family name. They may choose the name of the husband or the name of the wife. The children are given the common family name." It has been noted that "this arrangement does not exclude the use, in individual cases warranted by special interests, of a double-barrelled name formed by adding to the common family name the name borne before marriage." Beyer, *On Some Aspects of the New Family Code,* 1 LAW AND LEGIS. IN THE G.D.R. 45, 46 (1966).

52. Chapman v. Phoenix National Bank of the City of New York, 85 N.Y. 437 (1881).

53. *Id.* at 449. (Emphasis supplied.)

54. People ex. rel. Rago v. Lipsky et al, 327 Ill. App. 63, 63 N.E.2d 642 (1945).

55. ILL. ANN. STAT. 1943, ch. 46 § 6-54 (1965).

56. People v. Lipsky, 327 Ill. App. at 70, 63 N.E.2d at 647.

57. Bacon v. Boston Electric Railway Co., 256 Mass. 30, 31, 152 N.E. 35, 36, 47 A.L.R. 1100 (1926).

58. 256 Mass. at 32, 152 N.E. at 36.

59. In re Kayaloff, 9 F. Supp. 176 (D.C. 1934).

60. *See, e.g.,* Emery v. Kipp, 154 Cal. 83, 97 Pac. 17 (1908); Ray v. American Photo Player Co., 46 Cal. App. 311, 189 Pac. 130 (1920).

61. In Emery v. Kipp, *supra* note 60, this chap., it was held that a married woman's interest in real property was properly determined in a quiet title action, though she had been served by publication under her maiden name. The woman had acquired title prior to marriage and record title was still in her maiden name. But the decision does not stand for the rule that a married woman may use her maiden name after marriage over her husband's objection. It rests rather on the inconvenience that complainants in quiet title actions would be faced with if they were required to search beyond the record title of real property to discover whether the names of unmarried women owners had been changed by marriage. For this reason the *Emery* opinion suggests that even a male record title owner could be sued in a quiet title action under the name that appears on the record, though his name had been changed in a legal proceeding outside of the state, or in some other manner. *Id.* at 89.

62. People v. Darcy, 59 C.A.2d 342, 350, 139 P.2d 118 (1943).

63. *See, e.g.,* Galanter v. Galanter, 133 N.Y.S.2d 266 (1954); *cf.* Mark v. Kahn, 333 Mass. 517, 131 N.E.2d 758 (1956) in which the father's right to seek an injunction was recognized, but the case was remanded for a further hearing to determine whether the best interests of the child would be served by retaining the father's name.

64. IOWA CODE ANN. § 674.1 (1947). (Emphasis supplied.)

65. IOWA CODE ANN. § 674.10 (1946). (Emphasis supplied.)

66. KY. REV. STAT. § 401.010 (1964). (Emphasis supplied.)

67. COL. REV. STAT. ANN. § 20-1-1 (1963).

68. *See, e.g.,* MINN. STAT. ANN. § 518.27 (1945) which states ". . . in all actions for a divorce *brought by a woman,* if a divorce is granted, the court may change the name of such woman, who shall thereafter be known by such name as the court designates in its decree" (emphasis supplied); *see also* MO. STAT. ANN. § 452.100 (1949): "When the *wife* shall obtain a divorce . . . the court, upon her request, shall make an order changing her name to that of any former husband, or to her maiden name, as she may elect." (Emphasis supplied.)

69. MICH. STAT. ANN. § 25.181 (1966).

70. *Id.*

71. *But cf.* 2 VERNIER, AMERICAN FAMILY LAWS 184 (1932) [hereinafter cited

as VERNIER], citing So. Dakota Law, Comp. L. 1929, §§ 143a, 143b, which permits a change of name to be made whenever a divorce is granted, at the discretion of the court or upon the application of either party, but which does not apply when custody of a minor child, issue of the marriage, is given to the mother.

72. *But cf.* Reinken v. Reinken, 35 Ill. 409, 184 N.E. 639 (1933) which held that pursuant to the common law rule that an individual may lawfully change his name without resort to legal proceedings, a wife, after a decree of divorce, may resume her maiden name regardless of whether permission to do so is given in the decree; and that the statute in relation to names, permitting an individual to apply to the court for an order changing his name, does not abrogate the common law rule. This decision, however, involved the rights of a divorced, rather than a married woman, to change her name informally. The court stated at 184 N.E. 640: "[W]e fail to see how by dropping the name 'Reinken' she has inflicted any fraud, inconvenience, or possible loss on her *divorced* husband." (Emphasis supplied). Nor were there any reasons in the Reinken case why the wife could not have been granted the right to change her name by court decree. The decree had granted her that right in fact, the issue being whether she could accept the benefits of the decree and then contest it, the court holding that the decree gave her no more than she would have without it —insofar as her right to resume her maiden name was concerned. But where statutes provide exceptions to the right to have a formal name change, it is likely that they would serve as a basis for enjoining an informal name change that violated the policy of the statute.

73. MICH. STAT. ANN. § 27-3178 (561) (Repl. 1962).

74. *Id.*

75. RESTATEMENT, CONFLICT OF LAWS § 9 (1934).

76. In re Schultz' Estate, 316 Ill. App. 540, 45 N.E.2d 577, 582 (1942), *rev'd on other grounds* 384 Ill. 148, 51 N.E.2d 140 (1943).

77. Wells v. People, 44 Ill. 40 (1867).

78. Peirce v. Peirce, 379 Ill. 185, 39 N.E.2d 990 (1942).

79. *Id.*

80. *See* Williams v. North Carolina, 317 U.S. 287 (1942).

81. *See, e.g.,* Ives v. Salisbury's Heirs, 56 Vt. 565 (1884); Tripp v. Tripp, 240 S.C. 334, 126 S.E.2d 9 (1962).

82. *See, e.g.,* RESTATEMENT, CONFLICT OF LAWS § 149 (1934), "The status of a guardian and ward is created and terminated by the state of the domicil of the ward."; *but cf.* Paulsen & Best, *Appointment of a Guardian in the Conflict of Laws,* 45 IOWA L. REV. 212, 215 (1960), "The case law has generally rejected the *Restatement* principle."

83. The word "residence" is sometimes intended to convey the meaning of "domicile." In federal court actions, the jurisdictional basis of which is solely the diverse citizenship of the parties, proper venue is in the district of either the plaintiff's or the defendant's residence. 28 U.S.C. § 1391 (a) (1948). For most other federal court cases, the only district in which the action may be brought is the one in which "all defendants reside." 28 U.S.C. § 1391 (b) (1948).

84. *See, e.g.,* Brown v. Hows, 163 Tenn. 178, 42 S.W.2d 210 (1931); Berry v. Wilcox, 44 Neb. 82, 62 N.W. 249 (1895).

85. *See, e.g.,* Bigney v. Secretary of Commonwealth, 301 Mass. 107, 16 N.E.2d 573 (1938).

86. *See, e.g.,* Georgia v. Waterville, 107 Vt. 347, 178 Atl. 893 (1935). Some courts have recently divided over whether state residency requirements for welfare recipients violate constitutional provisions, including the equal protec-

tion guarantee. Compare B. — v. S. —, *reported at* 8 WEL. L. BULL. 11 (May, 1967). Should the U.S. Supreme Court hold such requirements to be unconstitutional, *see* Shapiro v. Thompson, *prob. juris. noted*, 389 U.S. 1032 (1968), other areas in which domicile or residency now play an important role may also be affected.

87. *See* 55 AM. JUR. *Universities and Colleges* § 16 (1946).

88. *See* State v. Wimby, 119 La. 139, 43 So. 984 (1907).

89. *See* Commonwealth v. Kernochan, 129 Va. 405, 106 S.E. 367 (1921).

90. *See* GOODRICH, CONFLICT OF LAWS 40 (4th ed. Scoles 1964).

91. *Id.*

92. New York Trust Co. v. Riley, 24 Del. Ch. 354, 16 A.2d 772 (1940), affirmed 315 U.S. 343 (1941). Though "domicile" and "nationality" are distinct concepts, they are not entirely unrelated. Under the laws of many countries a woman loses her nationality automatically upon marriage to an alien or if she acquires her husband's nationality by the marriage. U.N. DEPT. OF ECONOMIC AND SOCIAL AFFAIRS, NATIONALITY OF MARRIED WOMEN *passim* (1963). In this connection, a *Convention on the Nationality of Married Women* has been proposed by the United Nations and signed by a number of countries. See UNITED NATIONS COMMISSION ON THE STATUS OF WOMEN, LEGAL STATUS OF MARRIED WOMEN 100-103 (1958). The Convention generally eliminates the automatic loss of citizenship for a woman who marries an alien. In the United States, prior to September 22, 1933, American women lost their citizenship by marrying an alien, although American men who married aliens did not lose theirs. U.S. INTER-AMERICAN COMMISSION OF WOMEN, A COMPARISON OF THE POLITICAL RIGHTS OF MEN AND WOMEN IN THE UNITED STATES (74th Congress, 2d session, Senate Document No. 270) Washington, 1936 [hereinafter cited as COMPARISON]. Under present American law, marriage of a United States national to an alien does not affect nationality, whether the national be a man or a woman, unless he or she makes a formal renunciation of nationality before a court. *Id.*

93. In re Paullin, 92 N.J. Eq. 419, 113 Atl. 240 (1921).

94. Hoffhines v. Hoffhines, 146 Md. 350, 126 Atl. 112 (1924).

95. CCPR 20. The statistical summary of state laws governing married women's domicile is derived from Table 2, CCPR 21, which, in turn, was prepared by the Women's Bureau, Department of Labor. The figures reflect the situation as of March 6, 1963.

96. *Id.*

97. *See* Burns v. Burns, 145 Neb. 213, 15 N.W.2d 753 (1944); Smith v. Smith, 205 Ore. 650, 289 P.2d 1086 (1955); *but cf.* Galvin v. Dailey, 109 Iowa 332, 80 N.W. 420 (1899); and Harrison v. Harrison, 20 Ala. 629 (1852).

98. CCPR 20.

99. *Id.*

100. Williamson v. Osenton, 232 U.S. 619 (1913).

101. CCPR 20.

102. *Id.*

103. CCPR 20-21: "The traditional rule that the domicile of a married woman automatically follows that of her husband is inconsistent with the partnership principle of marriage and contrary to the universal trend toward legal equality of men and women. For example, the law governing domicile for purposes such as voting, holding public office, jury service, taxation, and probate should be the same for married women as it is for married men. We note that the potential impact of domiciliary rules on the family is extremely complex, particularly in a Federal system, and therefore urge that further study of

this aspect of domicile be made, with a view to liberalizing the existing rules governing domicile of married women."

104. *Id.*

105. *See, e.g.,* Younger v. Gianotti, 176 Tenn. 139, 138 S.W.2d 448 (1940), Estate of Wickes, 128 Cal. 270, 60 Pac. 867 (1900).

106. Estate of Wickes, 128 Cal. 270, 278, 60 Pac. at 870. (Emphasis supplied.)

107. 176 Tenn. at 140; 138 S.W.2d at 449.

108. 75 Ariz. 308, 256 P.2d 249 (1953).

109. 75 Ariz. at 309; 256 P.2d at 250. (Emphasis supplied.)

110. *See* pp. 93-94 *infra.*

111. *See* pp. 94-95 *infra.*

112. *But see* Kenkel, *Observational Studies of Husband-Wife Interaction in Family Decision-Making* in SUSSMAN, SOURCEBOOK, IN MARRIAGE AND THE FAMILY 144 (2d ed. 1963).

113. *See* pp. 73-75 *infra.*

114. 382 U.S. 341 (1966).

115. For comments on the Circuit Court decision, *see* 1965 DUKE L.J. 386 (1965); 50 VA. L. REV. 1236 (1964); 67 W. VA. L. REV. 161 (1965); 16 BAYLOR L. REV. 412 (1964). For comments on the Supreme Court decision, *see* 45 NEB. L. REV. (1966); 18 S.C.L.Q. 328 (1966); 40 ST. JOHN'S L. REV. 292 (1966).

116. *See* pp. 61-69 *infra.*

117. TEX. REV. CIV. STAT. ANN. art. 4626 (Repl. 1960).

118. Texas Acts 1963, 58th Leg. p. 1188, ch. 472, § 6.

119. *See, e.g.,* Clearfield Trust Co. v. United States, 318 U.S. 363 (1943); D'Oench, Duhme & Co. v. Federal Deposit Ins. Corp., 315 U.S. 447 (1942).

120. United States v. Yazell, 382 U.S. 341, 352-53 (1965).

121. *See* text at note 120, this chap., *supra.*

122. United States v. Yazell, 382 U.S. 341, 343 (1965).

123. *Id.* at 349.

124. *Id.* at 350.

125. United States v. Yazell, 334 F.2d 454, 456 (5th Cir. 1964) (dissent).

126. *Id.*

127. United States v. Yazell, 382 U.S. 341, 361 (1965) (dissent).

128. *Id.*

129. *See* note 118, this chap., *supra.*

130. *See* Brief for the United States, p. 15, n. 10, cited in United States v. Yazell, 382 U.S. 341, 351 (1965).

131. MICH. STAT. ANN. § 26.181 (Repl. 1957).

132. *See* MICH STAT. ANN. §§ 26.181, 26.183 (Repl. 1957).

133. KY. REV. STAT. § 404.010 (2) (1963).

134. *Id.*

135. GA. CODE ANN. § 53.503 (Repl. 1961). (Emphasis supplied.)

136. *Id.*

137. ALA. CODE tit. 34, § 74 (1958).

138. Huntsville Bank, etc. Co. v. Thompson, 212 Ala. 511, 103 So. 477 (1925).

139. *See, e.g.,* FLA. STAT. ANN. § 708.08 (1965); KY. REV. STAT. § 404.020 (1963); IND. ANN. STAT. § 38.102 (Smith-Hurd 1963).

140. *See* p. 68 *infra.*

141. UTAH CODE ANN. § 75-4-3 (1953).

142. MD. ANN. CODE art. 45, § 15 (1957).

143. CAL. CODE CIV. PROC. §§ 1811-1821.

144. FLA. STAT. ANN. §§ 62.38-62.46 (1941).

145. NEV. REV. STAT. §§ 124.010-124.050 (1957).
146. PA. STAT. ANN. tit. 48, §§ 41-48 (Repl. 1965).
147. TEX. REV. CIV. STAT. ANN. art. 4626 (Repl. 1960).
148. FLA. STAT. ANN. § 62.41 (1941).
149. FLA. STAT. ANN. § 62.43 (1941).
150. *Id.*
151. In some of the community property states that prohibit a husband from making a gift of community property without the wife's consent in writing, some limitation may be found in the husband's power to act as a guarantor or surety. This is substantially different, however, from regarding a husband as a person who has no capacity to act as such.
152. Currie, *Married Women's Contracts: A Study in Conflict-of-Laws Method*, 25 U. CHI. L. REV. 227 (1958). For evidence of retrogression in this field, *see* the Official Comments to UCC § 3-305. That section sets forth the defenses of a party to an instrument as against a holder in due course. Official comment (7) to that modern code section provides, in part, that the "test of the defense here stated is that of excusable ignorance of the contents of the writing signed. The party must not only have been in ignorance, but must also have had no reasonable opportunity to obtain knowledge. In determining what is a reasonable opportunity all relevant factors are to be taken into account, including the age *and sex* of the party. . . ." (Emphasis supplied.)
153. MINN. STAT. ANN. § 519.02 (1947).
154. For a discussion of the property rights of married women in the 8 community property states, *see* pp. 61-69 *infra.*
155. Those states are Alabama, Florida, Indiana, North Carolina, and Texas. CCPR 16.
156. Childs v. Charles, 46 Ga. App. 648, 168 S.E. 914 (1933).
157. *See* pp. 52-59 *supra.*
158. *See* pp. 61-69 *infra.*
159. *See* pp. 67-69 *infra.*
160. *See* p. 65 *infra.*
161. *Id.*
162. *Cf.* note 153, this chap., *supra.*
163. CCPR 18.
164. *See* Daggett, *The Civil Law Concept of the Wife's Position in the Family*, 15 ORE. L. REV. 291, 293 (1936).
165. *See* Wilty v. Jefferson Parish Democratic Executive Comm., 245 La. 145, 156, 157 So.2d 718, 727 (1963) (Sanders, J. concurring): "The common law fiction of merger between husband and wife . . . has never obtained in Louisiana. Rather, this state has followed the civil law doctrine."
166. *See* Fernandez v. Wiener, 326 U.S. 340, 365 (1945) (Douglas, J. dissenting): "Much may be said for the community property theory that the accumulations of property during marriage are as much the product of the activities of the wife as those of the titular breadwinner."
167. *See, e.g.,* CAL. CIV. CODE §§ 162, 163.
168. *See, e.g.,* CAL. CIV. CODE § 164.
169. *See* Poe v. Seaborn, 282 U.S. 101 (1930); United States v. Malcolm, 282 U.S. 792 (1931).
170. Okla. Laws 1939, ch. 62, art. 2, p. 356; Ore. Laws 1943, ch. 440, p. 656.
171. Commissioner v. Harmon, 323 U.S. 44, 48 (1944).
172. Now INT. REV. CODE OF 1956, § 6013.
173. Depending upon the language of the repealing statutes and other facts,

some community property may still exist in the states that once enacted such statutes. *See* Cudlip, *Repeal of Michigan Community Property Act,* 27 MICH. STATE BAR J. 13 (July, 1948); Moshofsky, *Repeal of the Community Property Law,* 28 ORE. L. REV. 311 (1949).

174. DE FUNIAK, PRINCIPLES OF COMMUNITY PROPERTY §§ 22, 24 (1943); 2 AMERICAN LAW OF PROPERTY § 7.2 (Casner ed. 1952); MCKAY, COMMUNITY PROPERTY § 9.43 (2d ed. 1925).

175. Terr. Laws of Idaho 1866-67, ch. 9, p. 65; Laws of Wash. Terr. 1869, p. 318.

176. *See* Lay, *Community Property: Its Origins and Importance to the Common Law Attorney,* 5 J. FAM. LAW 51 (1965).

177. *Id.* at 52-53.

178. Though separate statutory and judicial development has caused many differences to arise between the eight community property systems within the United States, their basic structures remain similar. For this reason, a discussion of California community property law will serve to illustrate the essentially common features of the system as practiced in all eight states.

179. ARMSTRONG, 1 CALIFORNIA FAMILY LAW 431 (1953).

180. *Id.*

181. In 1850, California adopted the "common law of England" as its official rule of decision "in all the courts of this State." Cal. Stats. 1850, c. 95, p. 219 [now CAL. CIV. CODE § 22.1].

182. *See, e.g.,* Van Maren v. Johnson, 15 Cal. 308 (1860); Spreckels v. Spreckels, 116 Cal. 339, 48 Pac. 228 (1897).

183. *Id. See also* Packard v. Arellanes, 17 Cal. 525 (1861): "The title to [community] property rests in the husband and for all practical purposes he is regarded by law as the sole owner. It is true, the wife is a member of the community and entitled to an equal share of the acquets and gains, but so long as the community exists, her interest is a mere expectancy and possesses none of the attributes of an estate, either at law or in equity."

184. The husband's powers of management and control did not extend to the wife's *separate* property. The separate property of either husband or wife consists essentially of all property acquired before marriage, some property acquired during marriage (by gift, devise or descent), and the rents and issues of separate property. CAL. CIV. CODE §§ 162 and 163.

185. The philosophical basis for entrusting management and control powers exclusively in the husband may be gleaned from the following statement by a delegate to the state's constitutional convention. "Sir, the God of Nature made woman frail, lovely, and dependant. . . ." BROWN, DEBATES IN THE CONVENTION OF CALIFORNIA 259 (1850).

186. CAL. CIV. CODE §§ 172 and 172a.

187. CAL. CIV. CODE § 156.

188. *Id. See* discussion of married women's domicile, pp. 46-52 *supra.*

189. Cal. Stats. 1891, ch. 220, p. 425, § 1 (now CAL. CIV. CODE § 172).

190. Cal. Stats. 1901, ch. 190, p. 598, § 1 (now CAL. CIV. CODE § 172).

191. Cal. Stats. 1917, ch. 583, p. 829, § 2 (now CAL. CIV. CODE § 172a).

192. Cal. Stats. 1927, ch. 265, p. 484, § 1 (now CAL. CIV. CODE § 161a).

193. Cal. Stats. 1923, ch. 18, p. 29, § 1 (now CAL. PROB. CODE § 201). In New Mexico, even at this late date, the husband, but not the wife, has the power of testamentary disposition over one-half of the community property. N.M. STAT. ANN. §§ 29-1-8, 29-1-9 (1953).

194. Cal. Stats. 1951, ch. 1102, p. 2860, § 1 (now CAL. CIV. CODE § 171c).

195. CAL. CIV. CODE § 171c also gave the wife the power to manage and control "community property money damages received by her for personal injuries suffered by her." This provision has been rendered moot by the adoption in 1957 of CAL. CIV. CODE § 163.5, making all damages awarded a married person in a civil action for personal injuries his or her *separate* property. Unlike the granting to the wife of management and control powers over her community property earnings, § 163.5 was added not to increase the wife's interest in marital property, but rather to counteract a formalistic rule which had barred her recovery in a personal injury action if her husband's negligence had been a contributory cause of her injuries. *See* Kesler v. Pabst, 43 Cal.2d 254, 273 P.2d 257 (1954); Zaragosa v. Craven, 33 Cal.2d 315, 202 P.2d 73 (1949). Because of new problems created by the 1957 legislation, however, California in 1968 reverted to classifying most personal injury damage awards received by a married person as community property. CAL. CIV. CODE § 163.5.

196. The important deficiencies in the community property system, however, are in my view somewhat different from those noted in Professor Powell's conclusion that the common law system excels in important respects, wherein he states: "the community property system [is] lacking as a system of marital property. Its complexity is such as not to be offset by those values claimed for it by its most ardent protagonists. It injects useless uncertainty and unjustifiable barriers into transactions between the spouses as a unity and third persons. It submerges the individual husband or wife in a purely imaginary third entity—the family, in a fashion promoting the ultimate welfare of no one. . . . The writer realizes that many may be shocked at his disregard of the alleged protection of helpless wives implicit in this system. Somehow he cannot bring himself to believe that the husbands of California and of Washington are more ruthless, less loving, than the husbands of Pennsylvania and New York. The wives of those two old states have not found themselves suffering under the closest approach to the individualistic standard yet existent in any of these United States. The vaunted protection of married women is an intellectual hang-over from the time when woman was a salable chattel and ill consorts with the modernity and wisdom otherwise so characteristic of the West Coast." Powell, *Community Property—A Critique of the Regulation of Intra-Family Relations*, 11 WASH. L. REV. 12, 38 (1936), reprinted in ESSAYS ON FAMILY LAW, 525, 549-50.

197. *See* Addison v. Addison, 62 Cal. App.2d 584, 43 Cal. Rptr. 97, 399 P.2d 897 (1965).

198. Boyd v. Oser, 23 Cal.2d 613, 145 P.2d 312 (1944).

199. *See* CAL. CIV. CODE § 158.

200. CAL. CODE CIV. PROC. § 370.

201. *See* Sanderson v. Nieman, 17 Cal.2d 563, 110 P.2d 1025 (1941).

202. Yearout v. American Pipe & Steel Corp., 74 Cal. App.2d 139, 143, 168 P.2d 174, 176 (1946); *see also* Secondo v. Superior Court, 105 Cal. App. 179, 286 P. 1089 (1930).

203. *See* Martin & Miller, *Estate Planning and Equal Rights*, 36 CAL. S. BAR J. 613, 615 (1961).

204. *See* CAL. REV. & TAX. CODE §§ 13551, 13694.

205. CAL. PROB. CODE § 202.

206. CAL. CIV. CODE § 146 (a).

207. *See* Bulpitt v. Bulpitt, 107 Cal. App.2d 550, 237 P.2d 539 (1951).

208. CAL. CIV. CODE § 146 (b). Since most California divorces are granted on grounds of extreme cruelty, an unequal division of community property is the rule rather than the exception.

209. Not all community property states require equal division of community property when divorce is granted on specified grounds. Thus, for example, under the Arizona statute, ARIZ. REV. STAT. § 25-318 (1956), the court is given a broad discretion and may award the greater portion of community property to either party. *See* Matlow v. Matlow, 89 Ariz. 293, 361 P.2d 648 (1961).

210. *See* FOOTE, LEVY & SANDER, CASES AND MATERIALS ON FAMILY LAW 913 (Temporary edition 1966): "Many states have statutory provisions . . . giving the divorce court discretion to make an equitable division of the individually owned property of the spouses. But frequently neither the enabling statute nor the awarding decree differentiates clearly between property division and support payments. In some states the wife's separate property is included in the pool of divisible property only to the extent that it was derived from the husband. *See, e.g.,* Wis. Stat. Ann. § 247.26 (Supp. 1965). Even where there is no explicit statutory authority for property divisions, some courts have asserted an inherent equitable power. *See, e.g.,* Johnson v. Johnson, 137 Mont. 11, 349 P.2d 310, 21 MONT. L. REV. 230 (1960)."

211. It is clear that in a common law joint tenancy, the wife's right to manage and control the jointly owned property is coequal to that of her joint tenant husband's.

212. CAL. CIV. CODE § 173.

213. CAL. PROB. CODE § 201.

214. *Id.*

215. Plager, *The Spouse's Nonbarrable Share: A Solution in Search of a Problem,* 33 U. CHI. L. REV. 681 (1966).

216. MARSH, MARITAL PROPERTY IN CONFLICT OF LAWS 45 (1952).

217. Sayre, *A Reconsideration of Husband's Duty to Support and Wife's Duty to Render Services,* 29 VA. L. REV. 857, 859 (1943).

218. *See* Paulsen, *Support Rights and Duties Between Husband and Wife,* 9 VAND. L. REV. 709 (1956).

219. 3 VERNIER, AMERICAN FAMILY LAWS 109 (1935). In 1935, Professor Vernier had found such legislation in 17 jurisdictions. *Id.* Professor Paulsen has grouped those statutes into 3 types: "(1) Those that provide that husband and wife contract toward each other—obligations of mutual respect, fidelity and support; (2) those which provide that the wife shall support her husband if he is unable because of infirmity to do so; and (3) those which require a wife to support a husband who is likely to become a public charge." Paulsen, *Support Rights and Duties Between Husband and Wife,* 9 VAND. L. REV. 712 (1956). Since "statutes of the first type set forth a moral duty only," *Id.,* one may heartily endorse Professor Paulsen's observation that "the creation of a duty in the wife only when disaster strikes the husband falls a good deal short of treating the sexes equally."

220. *See* VERNIER, *supra* note 219, this chap., at 111: "[U]nder the statutes . . . the wife is under duty to support the husband only if he is poor. The fact that the wife may be financially independent does not, however, lighten the husband's duty to support her if he is able."

221. *See* pp. 70-71 *infra.*

222. *See* Brown, *The Duty of the Husband to Support the Wife,* 18 VA. L. REV. 823 (1932): "No part of the law has been more completely transformed in the past century than that relating to husband and wife. . . . But certain phases of even this branch of law remain substantially unchanged, and of these one of the most conspicuous examples is that relating to the duty of the husband to support the wife. It is entirely clear that the married women's acts in the var-

ious states have not substantially affected the binding force of this obligation." *See also* Sayre, *A Reconsideration of Husband's Duty to Support and Wife's Duty to Render Services*, 29 VA. L. REV. 857 (1943) in which the husband and wife's respective common law duties of support and to render services are described as "fantastically unchanged, through succeeding generations when the nature of the family and the other rights and duties of husbands and wives apart from their families have clearly changed." *See also* Paulsen, *supra* note 218, this chap., at 710: "It is startling that the great nineteenth century movement toward the legal equality of the marriage partners has left the duty of the husband to support his wife so little changed."

223. *See* text at note 120, this chap., *supra*.

224. *See* pp. 66-67 *supra*.

225. *See* Paulsen, *supra* note 218, this chap., at 739.

226. *Id.* at 740.

227. *See* p. 51 *supra*.

228. *See* p. 96 *infra*.

229. *See* Paulsen, *supra* note 218, this chap., at 735.

230. *Id. passim*.

231. Crozier, *Marital Support*, 15 B.U.L. REV. 28 (1915).

232. *But cf.* Lippman, *The Breakdown of Consortium*, 30 COLUM. L. REV. 651, 658 (1930), in which the husband's common law cause of action for criminal conversation is described as resting upon "the *proprietary* interest of the husband in the *body* and services of the wife." (Emphasis supplied.)

233. *See* Crozier, *supra* note 231, this chap., at 40.

234. *Id.*

235. *See* Paulsen, *supra* note 218, this chap., at 709.

236. G. MURDOCK, *Social Structure* (1949), in HOWARD & SUMMERS, LAW: ITS NATURE, FUNCTIONS AND LIMITS 179-180 (1965). (Emphasis supplied.)

237. *See* chaps. 4 and 5 *infra*.

238. CCPR 23, note 26.

239. *Id.* at 22-23.

240. *E.g.*, IOWA CODE §597.14 (1954); MINN. STAT. ANN. §519.05 (1947).

241. *See* p. 3 *supra*.

242. PROSSER, TORTS 891 (3d ed. 1964).

243. *Id.* at 892. *But cf.* Rogers v. Newby, 41 So.2d 451 (1949), discussed in 3 U. FLA. L. REV. 206 (1950), holding that despite emancipatory legislation, the "common-law rule that the husband is liable for the 'pure' torts of his wife still prevails" in that state.

244. While the inter-spousal immunity rule originally obtained in the case of a property tort as well as a personal one (*Id.* at 880), the married women's acts have led to a virtual unanimous agreement among the courts that suits between the spouses are permitted where they are based on an alleged tort to their respective *property* interests. *Id.* at 881. Though the immunity with regard to personal injury suits continues in most jurisdictions, the same conduct for which the right to sue civilly is denied may often constitute a ground for divorce.

245. *See* p. 36 *supra*.

246. *See. e.g.*, Ensminger v. Campbell, 242 Miss. 519, 134 So.2d 728 (1961); Ritter v. Ritter, 31 Pa. 396 (1858).

247. *See, e.g.*, Apitz v. Dames, 205 Ore. 242, 287 P.2d 585 (1955); Self v. Self, 58 Cal.2d 632, 26 Cal. Rptr. 97, 376 P.2d 65 (1962).

248. *Cf.* Bogen v. Bogen, 219 N.C. 51, 53, 12 S.E.2d 649, 651 (1941), wherein

the court states, "whether a man has laid open his wife's head with a bludgeon, put out her eye, broken her arm, or poisoned her body, he is no longer exempt from liability to her on the ground that he vowed at the altar to 'love, cherish, and protect' her. We have progressed that far in civilization and justice."

249. This has been recognized by the Louisiana courts in holding that in direct actions against the insurer, permitted by statute in that state (L.S.A.—Rev. Stat., Tit. 22, § 655 (1959)), the insurer is foreclosed from asserting defenses, such as coverture, normally available to the tortfeasor. Edwards v. Royalty Indemnity Co., 182 La. 171, 161 So. 191 (1935).

250. *See* Newton v. Weber, 119 Misc. 240, 196 N.Y.S. 113 (1922) in which this possibility is specifically recognized.

251. Comment, *Conflict of Laws—Interspousal Immunity*, 68 W. Va. L. Rev. 407, 408 (1966). (Footnotes omitted.)

252. *See* Green, *Relational Interests*, 29 Ill. L. Rev. 460 (1935).

253. Smith v. Nicholas Bldg. Co., 93 Ohio St. 101, 112 N.E. 204 (1915).

254. *Id.* (Emphasis supplied.)

255. Acuff v. Schmit, 78 N.W. 2d 480, 481 (Iowa 1956). "Consortium" includes "not only conjugal fellowship of husband and wife but also services as a prominent, if not the dominant factor; not so much the services resulting in the performance of labor or the earning of wages as the services which contributed and assisted in all the relations of domestic life."

256. West v. City of San Diego, 54 Cal.2d 469, 6 Cal. Rptr. 289, 353 P.2d 929 (1960).

257. *See* Acuff v. Schmit, 78 N.W.2d at 483. *But cf.* language of Lord Campbell in Lynch v. Knight, 9 H.L.C. 577, 589, 11 Eng. Rep. 854. 859 (1861): "Nor can I allow that the loss of *consortium*, or conjugal society, can give a cause of action to the husband alone. . . . But the loss of conjugal society is not a pecuniary loss, and I think it may be a loss which the law may recognize, to the wife as well as to the husband."

258. 365 S.W.2d 539 (Mo. 1963).

259. *Id.* at 540. (Emphasis supplied.)

260. *See, e.g.,* Guy v. Livesey, 1 Crow. 501, 79 Eng. Rep. 428 (K.B. 1618).

261. *See* Note, *Judicial Treatment of Negligent Invasion of Consortium*, 61 Colum. L. Rev. 1341, 1343, note 10 and cases cited therein (1961).

262. 3 W Blackstone Commentaries* 142-43; *see also* Turner v. Heavrin, 182 Ky. 65, 68, 206 S.W. 23, 24 (1918) (dictum).

263. *See* Simeone, *The Wife's Action for Loss of Consortium—Progress or No?*, 4 St. Louis U.L.J. 424, 426 (1957).

264. *See, e.g.,* Feneff v. New York Central & H. R. R. Co., 203 Mass. 278, 89 N.E. 436 (1909).

265. *See e.g.,* Goldman v. Cohen, 30 Misc. 336, 63 N.Y.S. 459 (1900).

266. *See, e.g.,* Patelski v. Snyder, 179 Ill. App. 24 (1913).

267. Ekalo v. Constructive Service Corporation of America, 46 N.J. 82, 215 A.2d 1 (1965), discussed in Comment, *Loss of Consortium—Wife's Action—Injury to Husband Caused by Negligence of Third Party*, 4 N.Y.L. Forum 704 (1965).

268. *See* p. 36 *supra.*

269. *See* Feinsinger, *Legislative Attack on "Heart Balm,"* 33 Mich. L. Rev. 979 (1935), reprinted in Essays on Family Law 750.

270. Eschenbach v. Benjamin, 195 Minn. 378, 263 N.W. 154 (1935).

271. Pratt v. Daly, 55 Ariz. 535, 104 P.2d 147 (1940).

272. Flandermeyer v. Cooper, 85 Ohio St. 327, 98 N.E. 102 (1912).

273. *See* Annot. 23 A.L.R.2d 1378, 1385 (1952).
274. Hitaffer v. Argonne Co., Inc., 183 F.2d 811 (D.C. Cir. 1950).
275. *Id.* at 819.
276. Simeone, *supra* note 263, this chap., at 433-441.
277. PROSSER, TORTS 918 (3d ed. 1964).
278. *See, e.g.,* Ripley v. Ewell, 61 So. 2d 420 (1952).
279. *See, e.g.,* Kronenbitter v. Washburn Wire Co., 4 N.Y.2d 524, 151 N.E.2d 898, 176 N.Y.S.2d 354 (1958); Neuberg v. Bobowicz, 40 Pa. 146, 162 A.2d 662 (1960.)
280. PROSSER, TORTS 918 (3d ed. 1964).
281. *See, e.g.,* Ekalo v. Constructive Service Corp. of America, note 267 *supra,* this chap.
282. PROSSER, TORTS 918-919 (3d ed. 1964).
283. *See, e.g.,* Commonwealth v. Donoghue, 250 Ky. 343, 347, 63 S.W.2d 3, 5 (1933); Krulewitch v. United States, 336 U.S. 440, 447 (1949). (Mr. Justice Jackson, concurring.)
284. *Id.* (Emphasis supplied.)
285. Even where husband and wife are held incapable of conspiring with one another to commit a crime, it has been held that they can be convicted if they join with third persons in a conspiracy. *See, e.g.,* Thompson v. State, 166 Ga. 758, 144 S.E. 301 (1928).
286. People v. Miller, 82 Cal. 107, 22 P. 934 (1889); see also Note, *Criminal Law—Interspousal Conspiracy Doctrine—Husband and Wife Cannot Claim Immunity from Prosecution for Conspiracy Between Themselves,* 34 U. CINN. L. REV. 407 (1965).
287. People v. MacMullen, 134 Cal. App. 81, 83, 24 P.2d 794, 796 (1933).
288. *Id.*
289. People v. Pierce, 61 Cal.2d 879, 40 Cal. Rptr. 845, 395 P.2d 893 (1964).
290. *Id.* at 881, 40 Cal. Rptr. 847, 395 P.2d at 895.
291. *Id.* at 882, 40 Cal. Rptr. at 848, 395 P.2d at 896.
292. *Id.* at 880, 40 Cal. Rptr. at 846, 395 P.2d at 894.
293. United States v. Dege, 364 U.S. 51 (1960).
294. *Id.* at 52. An approach that is inconsistent in spirit, if not technically, with that taken by Justice Frankfurter in Goesart v. Cleary, 335 U.S. at 466, that "the Constitution does not require legislatures to reflect sociological insight, or shifting social standards . . ."
295. *Id.* at 52-53.
296. *Id.* at 53.
297. HAWKINS, 1 PLEAS OF THE CROWN 192 (4th ed. 1762).
298. 364 U.S. at 58.
299. *Id.* at 57-58.
300. *Id.* at 58.
301. *Id.*
302. *Id.*
303. Dalton v. People, 68 Colo. 44, 189 P. 37 (1920).
304. People v. Martin, 4 Ill. 2d 105, 122 N.E.2d 245 (1954).
305. Marks v. State, 144 Tex. Crim. 509, 164 S.W.2d 690 (1942).
306. Mawje v. Reginam [1957], All E.R. 385; Kowbel v. The Queen, 110 Can. Crim. Cas. Ann. 47 (1954).
307. State v. Struck, 44 N.J. Super. 274, 129 A.2d 910 (Essex County Ct. 1957).
308. Commonwealth v. Allen, 24 Pa. County Ct. 65 (1900).

309. 134 Cal. App. 81, 24 P.2d 794 (1933).
310. United States v. Dege, 364 U.S. 51, 58 (1960). (Warren, Ch. J., dissenting.)
311. Comment, *Developments in the Law: Criminal Conspiracy*, 72 HARV. L. REV. 920, 950 (1959).
312. In some jurisdictions, the common law rule has been rejected by statute. *See, e.g.*, REV. CODE OF WASH. §9.22.010 (1961).
313. O'Donnell v. State, 73 Okla. Cr. 1, 117 P.2d 139 (1941).
314. *Id.* 117 P.2d at 141.
315. 4 BLACKSTONE, COMMENTARIES* 28.
316. PERKINS, CRIMINAL LAW 800 (1957).
317. PERKINS, CASES AND MATERIALS ON CRIMINAL LAW AND PROCEDURE 574 (1959).
318. *Id.*
319. *Id.*
320. PERKINS, CRIMINAL LAW 796-805 (1957); *see also* Perkins, *The Doctrine of Coercion*, 19 IOWA L. REV. 507 (1934).
321. KOESTLER, REFLECTIONS ON HANGING 13 (1956).
322. PERKINS, *supra* note 320, this chap., at 798.
323. *Id.*
324. *Id.*
325. *Id.*
326. *Id.* at 799.
327. People v. Stately, 91 Cal. App. 2d Supp. 943, 206 P.2d 76 (1949).
328. King v. City of Owensboro, 187 Ky. 21, 218 S.W. 279 (1920).
329. Note, *Husband and Wife: The Common Law Presumption of Coercion*, 3 OKLA. L. REV. 442, 443-444 (1950).
330. State v. Ready, 251 S.W.2d 680 (Mo. 1952).
331. State v. Cauley, 244 N.C. 701, 94 S.E.2d 915 (1956).
332. Doyle v. State, 317 P.2d 289 (Okl. Cr. 1957).
333. For a summary of other jurisdictions that have either accepted or rejected the rule, *see* Annot., 71 A.L.R. 1116 (1931) and supplements thereto.
334. People v. Stately, 91 Cal. App. 2d Supp. 943, 948, 206 P.2d 76, 81 (1949).
335. CAL. PEN. CODE §26.
336. 91 Cal. App. 2d Supp. 948, 206 P.2d 81. (Emphasis supplied.)
337. PERKINS, *supra* note 320, this chap., at 802.
338. Where *"compulsion"* would be recognized as a defense to a crime, however, with regard to the mental relationship between compeller and compellee, the defense should be available to a wife who was compelled to commit certain crimes, as under threat of death for her disobedience, though the compeller were her husband.
339. *Cf.* MICH. COMP. LAWS §780, 401 (1948).
340. PERKINS, CRIMINAL LAW 28 (1957).
341. N.M. STAT. ANN. §40A-2-4(7) (1953) (Repl. 1964). (Emphasis supplied.)
342. TEXAS PENAL CODE art. 1220 (VERNON'S 1961): "Homicide is justifiable when committed by the husband upon one taken in the act of adultery with the wife, provided the killing takes place before the parties to the act have separated. Such circumstance cannot justify a homicide where it appears that there has been, on the part of the husband, any connivance in or assent to the adulterous connection." The statute has been interpreted as not justifying a husband in killing his wife found in adultery. Billings v. State, 102 Tex. Ct. 338, 277 S.W. 687 (1926).

343. UTAH CODE ANN. §76-30-10 (5) (1953):
Homicide is also justifiable when committed by any person in either of the
following cases:
. . . (5) when committed in a sudden heat of passion caused by the attempt of the deceased to commit rape upon or to defile the wife, daughter,
sister, mother, or other female relative or dependent of the accused, or
when the defilement has actually been committed.
This has been interpreted as permitting justifiable homicide to be found when
a husband kills another man found committing adultery with his wife. State
v. Williams, 49 Utah 320, 328, 163 P. 1104 (1917). Note that word "husband" is
conspicuously absent from statute's enumeration of possible victims of the deceased's defilement.

344. MADDEN at 256-257.

345. KEEZER, MARRIAGE AND DIVORCE 297 (3d ed. Moreland 1946).

346. JACOBS & GOEBEL, DOMESTIC RELATIONS 337, 338 (4th ed. 1961).

347. MADDEN at 259.

348. *Id.*

349. JACOBS & GOEBEL, *supra* note 544 at 412.

350. For many years South Carolina was the only state which did not grant
absolute divorces. In 1949, however, South Carolina "joined the Union" in this
regard. See S.C. CODE ANN. § *et seq* (1962).

351. *But cf.* CAL. CIV. CODE §128, "A divorce must not be granted unless the
plaintiff *or defendant* has been a resident of the state one year, and of the
county in which the action is brought three months, next preceding the commencement of the action." (Emphasis supplied.)

352. NEV. REV. STAT. §125.020 (e) (1957).

353. The United States Court of Appeals, Third Circuit, did so hold in
Alton v. Alton, 207 F.2d 667 (3d Cir. 1953), and the Supreme Court granted
certiorari in that case. Later, however, the Court dismissed the proceeding as
moot after learning that one of the spouses had procured a divorce in another
jurisdiction. 347 U.S. 911 (1954).

354. Williams v. North Carolina, 317 U.S. 287 (1942).

355. N.M. STAT. ANN. § 22-7-1 (8) (1953).

356. N.Y. DOM. REL. LAW § 170. The additional divorce grounds were added
by N.Y. Laws 1966, ch. 254 § 2, and took effect on September 1, 1967.

357. *See* Rosenstiel v. Rosenstiel, 16 N.Y.2d 64, 209 N.E.2d 709, 262 N.Y.S.2d
86 (1965); Wood v. Wood, 16 N.Y.2d 64, 209 N.E.2d 709, 262 N.Y.S.2d 86 (1965).

358. 2 VERNIER, AMERICAN FAMILY LAWS 8 (1932).

359. *See* AMERICAN WOMEN 248-251 (Mead & Kaplan ed. 1965), indicating
that 30 states make a husband's failure to support his wife a ground for absolute divorce.

360. Arkansas and North Dakota permit a husband to be granted a divorce
upon his wife's failure to support him "under certain circumstances." *Id.*

361. See note 31, chap. 2, *supra.*

362. *See, e.g.,* McAllister v. McAllister, 71 Tex. 695, 696, 10 S.W. 294, 295 (1888).

363. *See, e.g.,* Prendergast v. Prendergast, 146 N.C. 225, 59 S.E. 692 (1907).

364. KY. REV. STAT. §403.020 (1963).

365. Kentucky law provides, however, that either spouse not in fault may be
divorced where the other is "*living* in adultery." KY. REV. STATS. §403.020 (2)
(b) (1963). (Emphasis supplied.) This apparently refers to a continued course
of open cohabitation with a third person. But § 403.020 (4), listing causes for
which a husband may be granted a divorce, includes in subdivision (c) "adul-

tery by the wife, or such lewd, lascivious behavior on her part as proves her to be unchaste, without actual proof of an act of adultery." Section 403.020 (3), stating special grounds for which a wife may obtain a divorce does not include adultery by the husband as last defined.

366. ALA. CODE tit. 34, § 21 (1958).

367. *See, e.g.,* GA. CODE ANN. §30-102 (5) (1952). "Pregnancy of the wife, at the time of marriage, unknown to the husband." Unlike statutes of other states, this Georgia provision does not expressly preclude a premarital pregnancy of the wife caused by the husband himself.

368. IOWA CODE §598.9 (1962).

369. *Id.* (Emphasis supplied.)

370. *See* AMERICAN FAMILY LAWS 49 (1932).

371. *See* pp. 13-15 *supra.*

372. KY. REV. STAT. §403.020 (3) (a) (1963).

373. KY. REV. STAT. §403.020 (4) (b) (1963).

374. KELSEN, WHAT IS JUSTICE? 3 (1957).

375. Breitel, *Criminal Law and Equal Justice,* 1966 UTAH L. REV. 1 (1966). (Footnotes omitted.)

Chapter 4. Title VII of the 1964 Civil Rights Act and the Equal Pay Act of 1963.

1. Margolin, *Equal Pay and Equal Employment Opportunities for Women,* N.Y.U. 19TH CONF. ON LABOR 297, 302 (1967).

2. *Id.*

3. Reynolds v. Mountain States Tel. & Tel. Co. [1965-1968 Transfer Binder] CCH EMPL. PRACT. GUIDE ¶ 8111, at 6184, (Ariz. Civ. Rgts, Comm'n 1966).

4. *Id.*

5. *See* chap. 3, *supra.*

6. Waldman, *Marital and Family Characteristics of Workers,* 90 MONTHLY LAB. REV. 29, 27, 30 (1967).

7. In June, 1966, Congresswoman Martha Griffiths of Michigan stated, based on BUREAU OF THE CENSUS, CURRENT POPULATION REPORTS, SERIES P-60, No. 47 (1964), and BUREAU OF LABOR STATISTICS, SPECIAL LABOR-FORCES REPORT, that "the median earnings of white men are $6,497, of Negro men $4,285, of white women $3,859, and of Negro women $2,674. This adverse differential exists in spite of the fact that white females in the labor force have 12.3 years of education on the average as compared to 12.2 years for white men; and nonwhite females have 11.1 years of education to 10 for the nonwhite males. The unemployment rate is highest for the nonwhite female. The same disparities exist when we examine the data for all workers, including temporary as well as full time." 112 CONG. REC. 13055 (1966).

8. This economic condition evoked a limited legislative response in some states. Although, until 1919, none went as far as requiring women employees to be paid the same wages as men performing equal work, many states now cover women but not men in their minimum wage legislation. Representative Martha Griffiths has noted that "the drive for these state protective laws was distorted

for several reasons into laws applying solely to women." Statement of Congresswoman Martha W. Griffiths at Hearing of the Equal Employment Opportunity Comm'n [EEOC] Concerning Proposals to Amend the Commission's Regulations on Sex Discrimination 3 (May 3, 1967). The principal reasons were the United States Supreme Court decisions in which a New York statute limiting working hours of male and female bakery employees to 10 hours a day was invalidated, Lochner v. New York, 198 U.S. 45 (1905), and Oregon's 10-hour a day limitation on working hours for females only was upheld, Muller v. Oregon, 208 U.S. 412 (1908). Statement of Congresswoman Griffiths, *supra* at 3. Although the United States Supreme Court upheld governmental regulation of all employees' wages, hours and working conditions in the 1940's, Darby v. United States, 312 U.S. 100 (1941), the result of the earlier decisions was to convince the state legislatures that half a loaf was better than none, leading to widespread passage of protective legislation for women only. Statement of Congresswoman Griffiths, *supra* at 3-4. *See also* text accompanying note 126 *infra*, this chap., discussing the United States Department of Labor's interpretation of the 1963 federal Equal Pay Act as requiring the extension to males of a state minimum wage applicable only to women whenever that minimum is higher than what the federal law requires. 29 C.F.R. § 800.161-2 (1968).

9. *See, e.g.*, Goesart v. Cleary, 335 U.S. 464, 467 (1948).

10. That the generally higher earnings and employability of male attorneys over female attorneys is the result of sex discrimination rather than other potential factors is persuasively demonstrated in White, *Women in the Law*, 65 MICH. L. REV. 1051, 1070-87 (1967).

11. *See* Opinion Letter of General Counsel, EEOC, July 21, 1966, CCH EMPLY. PRACT. GUIDE ¶ 17,304.04 (1966), discussing a collective bargaining agreement prohibiting employment of female bartenders. *See also* the separate male and female seniority lists in the collective bargaining agreements in Local 12, United Rubber Workers v. NLRB, 368 F.2d 12, 14 (5th Cir. 1966), *cert. denied*, 389 U.S. 837 (1967); Bowe v. Colgate Palmolive Co., 272 F. Supp. 332, 335-36 (S.D. Ind. 1967).

12. *See e.g.*, CAL. BUS. & PROF. CODE § 25656.

13. *See, e.g.*, State v. Hunter, 208 Ore. 282, 300 P.2d 455 (1956) (discussing statutory prohibition against professional female wrestling).

14. *See, e.g.*, Goesart v. Cleary, 335 U.S. 464 (1948); *cf. In re* Carragher, 149 Iowa 225, 128 N.W. 352 (1910) (discrimination founded on public policy, and not merely arbitrary, is not invalid). The prospects for future constitutional attacks on laws that discriminate on the basis of sex are considered in chap. 6, *infra*.

15. Montana and Michigan were the first states to enact equal pay laws in 1919. Twenty-four years later, in 1943, Washington became the third state to do so. Eight states—California, Connecticut, Illinois, Massachusetts, New Hampshire, New York, Pennsylvania, Rhode Island, and Alaska—were added to the list between 1944 and 1949. *See* STATE LEGISLATIVE RESEARCH COUNCIL OF SOUTH DAKOTA, STAFF BACKGROUND MEMORANDUM OF EQUAL PAY LEGISLATION 7 (1965). But as of July, 1968, 36 states had equal pay laws. CCH EMPL. PRACT. GUIDE ¶ 1875. For a reference to the applicable statutes, see *id.*

16. Margolin, *Equal Pay and Equal Employment Opportunities for Women*, N.Y.U. 19TH CONF. OF LABOR 297 (1967).

17. Exec. Order No. 10980, 3 C.F.R. § 201 (1961) (establishing the President's Commission on the Status of Women).

18. *Id.*

19. The Committee name had been changed from the "Committee on Government Contracts."

20. PRESIDENT'S COMMISSION ON THE STATUS OF WOMEN, REPORT OF THE COMMITTEE ON PRIVATE EMPLOYMENT 5 (1963).

21. *Id.* at 6.

22. A dissenting opinion was expressed by Committee Member Caroline Davis of the United Automobile Workers Union, protesting the proposed Executive Order's basic reliance "upon a voluntary program for an indeterminate period." *Id.* at 17.

23. *See* the section on the "peculiar legislative history" of Title VII's prohibition against sex discrimination in employment discussed in text accompanying note 24 *infra*, this chap.

24. 110 CONG. REC. 2720 (1964).

25. *See* Miller, *Sex Discrimination and Title VII of the Civil Rights Act of 1964*, 51 MINN. L. REV. 877, 880 (1967).

26. 20 CONG. Q. 344 (1964).

27. 110 CONG. REC. 2577 (1964).

28. *But see* text following note 58 *infra*, this chap. for how "sanctions" operate under Title VII.

29. 110 CONG. REC. 2577 (1964).

30. Representative Smith has since denied that the purpose of the amendment was to delay voting. *See* Miller, *Sex Discrimination and Title VII of the Civil Rights Act of 1964*, 51 MINN. L. REV. 877, 883 n.34 (1967). But evidence to the contrary seems overwhelming. *Id. See also* chap. 2 *supra;* Note, *Classification on the Basis of Sex and the 1964 Civil Rights Act*, 50 IOWA L. REV. 778, 791 (1965), where it was said that "[t]he fragments of legislative history dealing with the unprecedented sex provision of the Civil Rights Act indicate that the inclusion of the term 'sex' in the bill was promoted by forces that were not primarily concerned with equality for women as a class." *But cf.* Waters, *Sex, State Protective Laws and the Civil Rights Act of 1964*, 18 LAB L.J. 344, 346 (1967), where it is stated that "[t]he amendment on 'sex' was offered by Rep. Howard Smith (D. Va.) on February 8, 1964. This may have been prompted for 'political' reasons since Rep. Smith had opposed its passage. It may also have been an 'afterthought' as a result of the letter he had previously received from the National Women's Party."

31. *Cf.* Cooper v. Delta Airlines, Inc., 274 F. Supp. 781, 782-83 (E.D. La. 1967), where Judge Comisky remarked that "the addition of 'sex' to the prohibition against discrimination based on race, religion, or national origin just *sort of found its way* into the equal employment opportunities section of the Civil Rights Bill." (Emphasis added.)

32. 110 CONG. REC. 2581 (1964).

33. *Id. See also* remarks of New York's Representative Emmanuel Celler; "I think the amendment seems illogical, ill timed, ill placed, and improper." *Id.* at 2578.

34. Miller, *Sex Discrimination and Title VII of the Civil Rights Act of 1964*, 51 MINN. L. REV. 877, 881, *quoting* Letter to Representative Celler from the Women's Bureau of the U.S. Department of Labor (opposing the proposed "sex" amendments of Title VII) .

35. "Sex as a basis of discrimination is charged in 33.7 per cent, 2,031, of the cases. This is a large jump from the figure of approximately 20 per cent which held constant for the first half of the year." Release of EEOC, July 2, 1966, [1965-1968 Transfer Binder] CCH EMPL. PRACT. GUIDE ¶ 8076 (1966).

36. Blumrosen, *The Individual Right to Eliminate Employment Discrimination By Litigation,* in 19 Proc. Indus. Research Ass'n 1 (1967) (annual winter meeting).

37. *Id.*

38. 390 U.S. 400 (1968).

39. *Id.* (Emphasis added.) The Court's analysis of Title II's attorneys' fees provisions would appear to apply equally to Title VII actions based on sex discrimination—especially since the wording of the special attorneys' fees section of Title VII, 42 U.S.C. § 2000e-5 (k) (1964), closely follows that of the section construed in *Newman.* Attorneys and litigants will both therefore be encouraged to bring Title VII sex discrimination suits by the prospect of an award of attorneys' fees as an alternative to the contingent fee or other financial arrangement. *See also id.* § 2000e-5 (e), permitting the court to appoint an attorney for a complainant upon his application "in such circumstances as the court may deem just."

40. These have taken the form of legal interpretations of the Act's language as well as the decisions of the Commission. The Act does not give the Commission power to enforce its decisions directly, its enforcement efforts being limited to "the informed methods of conference, conciliation and persuasion." 42 U.S.C. § 2000-5 (a) (1964). Nevertheless, the Commission's determination that reasonable cause exists to believe that an unlawful employment practice has been committed will be useful to either the aggrieved party who is authorized to sue on his or her own behalf, or by the U.S. Attorney General as intervenor in the aggrieved person's suit, or as an original suitor, *id.* §§ 2000e-5 (e),—6 (a).

41. On February 21, 1968, the EEOC decided by a vote of 3-1 that an airline that refuses to hire and employ members of a particular sex for the position of flight cabin attendant—whether he or she be called a purser, hostess, steward or stewardess—violates the Act. 33 Fed. Reg. 3361 (1968); *cf.* Kaiser Foundation Hosp. v. Local 399, Bldg. Service Employees, [1965-1968 Transfer Binder] CCH Empl. Pract. Guide ¶ 8166 (1967), where it is held that a hospital did not violate Title VII by refusing to permit two male licensed nurses to work in the Licensed Vocational Nurse (LVN) classification where a routine requisite of such employment was "intimate care of female patients." Although this result may have been correct, the award ignored the common practices of permitting male doctors to examine intimately female patients and of allowing female nurses to perform "sensitive personal care" for male patients. *See also* Ward v. Firestone Tire & Rubber Co., 260 F. Supp. 579 (W.D. Tenn. 1966), rejecting a male plaintiff's claim of union and employer discrimination in denying him permission to transfer to a job reserved for women and men with physical disabilities. Even had the plaintiff shown that he would derive tangible benefits from the transfer, noted the court, he could not claim discrimination because the employer "acted with honest purpose and within reason," since "sex and physical disability were bona fide occupational qualifications for the job." *Id.* at 581.

42. Exec. Order No. 11,256, 3 C.F.R. § 320 (1968).

43. Pub. L. No. 90-130 (Nov. 8, 1967). This law has been described as amending Titles "10, 32, and 37 of the United States Code to remove the provisions that limit the career opportunities available to women officers so that on the basis of merit they may have the same promotion and career tenure opportunities as male officers in similar circumstances." S. Rep. No. 676, 90th Cong., 1st Sess. 1 (1967).

44. HAWAII REV. LAWS § 90A-1 (Supp. 1963).

45. WIS. STAT. ANN. §§ 111.31-.32 (5), 111.36 (3)- (4) (Supp. 1964) .

46. Arizona (1965); District of Columbia (1965); Idaho (1967); Maryland (1965); Massachusetts (1965) ; Missouri (1965); Nebraska (1965) Nevada (1965); New York (1965); Utah (1965); Wyoming (1965).

47. State laws are considered herein only to the extent that they assist in interpreting the federal law.

48. 42 U.S.C. § 2000e (b) (1964).

49. *Id.* 2000e (c)

50. *Id.* 2000e (d).

51. *Id.* § 2000e-2 (a).

52. *Id.* § 2000e-2 (b).

53. *Id.* § 2000e-2 (c): "It shall be an unlawful employment practice for a labor organization—

(1) to exclude or to expel from its membership, or otherwise to discriminate against, any individual because of his race, color, religion, sex, or national origin;

(2) to limit, segregate, or classify its membership, or to classify or refuse to refer for employment any individual, in any way which would deprive or tend to deprive any individual of employment opportunities, or would limit such employment opportunities or otherwise adversely affect his status as an employee or as an applicant for employment, because of such individual's race, color, religion, sex, or national origin; or

(3) to cause or attempt to cause an employer to discriminate against an individual in violation of this section."

54. *Id.* § 2000e-2 (e) .

55. For a further consideration of these problems, see text following note 79 *infra,* this chap.

56. *See* note 41 *supra,* this chap.

57. 29 C.F.R. § 1604.1 (1968) (sex discrimination guidelines).

58. 42 U.S.C. § 2000e-5 (f) (1964).

59. *Id.* § 2000e-5 (e).

60. *Id.*

61. *Id.* § 2000e-5 (g).

62. *Id.* § 2000e-5 (i).

63. *Id.* § 2000e-6 (a) .

64. *Id.* § 2000e-5 (a) provides in part: "If the Commission shall determine, after such investigation, that there is reasonable cause to believe that the charge is true, the Commission shall endeavor to eliminate any such alleged unlawful employment practice by informal methods of conference, conciliation, and persuasion." The Commission's function has been characterized as "providing an arbitration clearing house for alleged employment discrimination." Air Transport Ass'n v. Hernandez, 264 F. Supp. 227, 228 (D.D.C. 1967).

65. 42 U.S.C. § 2000e-5 (e) (1964). However, in Hall v. Wertham Bag Corp., 251 F. Supp. 184 (M.D. Tenn. 1966), it was held that the filing of a complaint with the Commission was sufficient for administrative exhaustion under 42 U.S.C. § 2000e-5 (1964). Thus, "a person who [has] made resort to the Commission has exhausted administrative remedies and may sue even though application to the Commission was unsuccessful in that the Commission took no action." Reese v. Atlantic Steel Co., 282 F. Supp. 905, 906 (N.D. Ga. 1967). *But cf.* Choate v. Caterpillar Tractor Co., 274 F. Supp. 776, 779 (S.D. Ill. 1967), where these decisions have been characterized as being "consistent in holding

that resort to the remedy of conciliation is a jurisdictional prerequisite to the right to file a civil action." Dent v. St. Louis, S.F.R.R., 265 F. Supp. 56 (1967). *See also* Quarles v. Phillip Morris, Inc., 271 F. Supp. 842 (E.D. Va. 1967); Mondy v. Crown Zellerbach Corp., 271 F. Supp. 250, 264 (E.D. Ill. 1967); Evenson v. Northwest Airlines, 268 F. Supp. 29 (E.D. Va. 1967).

66. 42 U.S.C. § 2000e-5 (c) (1964).

67. *Id.* § 2000e-5 (b).

68. *See generally,* Rosen, *Division of Authority Under Title VII of the Civil Rights Act of 1964,* 34 GEO. WASH. L. REV. 846 (1966). Since only a minority of states outlaw sex discrimination in employment, initial recourse to a state or local agency would not be required with respect to charges arising in most states.

69. *See* Blumrosen, *Processing Equipment Discrimination Cases,* 90 MONTHLY LAB. REV. 25 (1967).

70. U.S.C. § 2000e-5 (a) (1964).

71. *Id.* § 2000e-12 (b).

72. Air Transport Ass'n v. Hernandez, 264 F. Supp. 227, 229 (D.D.C. 1967). Notwithstanding the broad language in the *Hernandez* case, their effect as law should be limited to cases in which the Commission has ruled that a particular course of conduct would not violate the Act. A Commission opinion that particular conduct does violate the Act would not dispose of the issue in any case.

73. Several bills introduced in the First Session of the 90th Congress would have authorized the Commission to conduct hearings and issue remedial orders to the same extent as is now done by the National Labor Relations Board. The Senate Labor Committee approved such a bill in mid-1968. 36 U.S.L.W. 2724 (May 21, 1968). Shortly thereafter, the threat of a filibuster made the chances for passage in that session very dim. 68 L.R.R.M. 79 (1968).

74. *Cf.* Cooper v. Doyal, 205 So. 2d 59 (La. 1968) .

75. In Local 12, United Rubber Workers v. NLRB, 368 F.2d 12, 14 (5th Cir. 1966), an NLRB determination that the breach of the duty of fair representation constitutes an unfair labor practice under section 8 (b) (1) of the National Labor Relations Act, where separate seniority rolls (white male, Negro male, and female) had been maintained and the local union had summarily refused to process grievances of its Negro members based on improper application of those seniority provisions was approved. Though the unfair labor practice charges were filed by eight Negro employees in the unit, and the case therefore deals with acts of racial discrimination, no reason appears why a comparable result could not be reached where the complainants charge sex discrimination. Dictum in the *Rubber Workers* case suggests, moreover, that this result would obtain despite the alternative remedies available under Title VII. *Id.* at 24.

76. Pioneer Bus Co., 140 NLRB 54, 55 (1962); *cf.* American Mfg. Co. v. St. Louis Cordage Mills Div., 168 NLRB No. 135 (1967) (to be ineffective as a bar, the contract must show sex discrimination on its face).

77. *See* Comment, *Jurisdictional Conflicts in Minority Employment Relations: NLRB and EEOC,* 2 U.S.F.L. REV. 149, 154-55 (1967) ; *see also* M. SOVERN, LEGAL RESTRAINTS ON RACIAL DISCRIMINATION IN EMPLOYMENT 98 (1966).

78. *See* pp. 31-34 *supra.*

79. 42 U.S.C. § 2000e-2 (e) (1) (1964).

80. 29 C.F.R. §§ 1604.1 (b), (c) (1967).

81. *Id.* § 1604.1 (c) .

82. *Id.* § 1604.1 (b).
83. Oldham, *Sex Discrimination and State Protective Laws,* 44 DEN. L.J. 344, 349 (1967).
84. 35 U.S.L.W. 2137 (1966).
85. CCH EMPL. PRACT. GUIDE ¶ 16,900.001 (1968).
86. *See, e.g.,* Mengelkoch v. Industrial Welfare Comm'n, CCH EMPL. PRACT. GUIDE ¶ 9129 (C.D. Cal. 1968), where the court abstained from a decision on an alleged conflict between California's maximum hours law for women and Title VII; Ward v. Luttrel, Civil 67-1622 (D. La., filed Nov. 6, 1967), where there is a challenge to Louisiana's maximum hours law as being in conflict with the 14th amendment and Title VII; Roig v. Southern Tel. & Tel. Co., Civil Action No. 67-574 (D. La., filed Apr. 20, 1967), where damages and injunctive relief were sought for an employer's refusal to accept plaintiffs' bids for the position of test deskman because the job required hours of work in excess of those permitted by Louisiana hours law. Plaintiffs asserted that the hours law did not apply to the job they sought and that if it did it violated the due process and equal protection clauses of the 14th amendment. *See also* Weeks v. Southern Bell Tel. & Tel. Co., 277 F. Supp. 177 (S.D. Ga. 1967), in which an employer's refusal to hire a woman for the job of switchman because it requires lifting more than 30 pounds, in contravention of Rule 59 of the Georgia Department of Labor, was upheld; Bowe v. Colgate Palmolive Co., 272 F. Supp. 332 (S.D. Ind. 1967), where it is held that even in the absence of a state weight-lifting law, employers did not violate Title VII by not allowing women to bid on jobs requiring the lifting of more than 35 pounds; Rosenfeld v. Southern Pac. Co., Civil Action No. 67-1377-5 (Cent. D. Cal., filed Aug.-Sept., 1967), which involved possible conflict between Title VII and California's legislation restricting women's working hours and weight-lifting in employment; Dixon v. Avco (S.D. Ohio, filed Feb. 13, 1968), where it was alleged that there was a denial of promotion in violation of Title VII, while the company claimed the job required lifting over 25 pounds in violation of Ohio law.
87. *See* Weeks v. Southern Bell Tel. and Tel. Co., 277 F. Supp. 177 (S.D. Ga. 1967); Bowe v. Colgate Palmolive Co., 272 F. Supp. 332 (S.D. Ind. 1967). These results were each based in part upon the EEOC's own interpretation of Title VII's bona fide occupational qualification exception as applied to this area. "[R]estrictions on lifting weights will . . . [be honored] except where the limit is set at an unreasonably low level which could not endanger women." 29 C.F.R. § 1604.1 (3) (b) (1968). It should be noted that the factors that are relevant to weight-lifting restrictions—general physical limitations of women and other sex-based differences in physical strength—are not necessarily present when the subject of maximum hours legislation is in question. Moreover, even with respect to weight-lifting ability, some women are possessed of "extraordinary strength and stamina"—a fact that the federal court in *Bowe* found too difficult for employer ascertainment to impose this duty upon him. Bowe v. Colgate Palmolive Co., *supra* at 357.
88. Mengelkoch v. Industrial Welfare Comm'n, CCH EMPL. PRACT. GUIDE ¶ 9129 (D.C. Cal. 1968).
89. CAL. LAB. CODE § 1350.
90. Since chap. 6, *infra,* on the constitutional aspects of sex-based discrimination deals with the equal protection argument in *Mengelkoch* and other cases, the present discussion is limited to Mengelkoch's disposition of the alleged conflict between the state law and Title VII.

91. *See* 28 U.S.C. § 2281 (1964).

92. *See* Miller v. Wilson, 236 U.S. 373 (1915); Muller v. Oregon, 208 U.S. 412 (1908); *In re* Miller, 162 Cal. 687, 124 P. 427 (1912).

93. Mengelkoch v. Industrial Welfare Comm'n, CCH Empl. Pract. Guide ¶ 9129 (D.C. Cal. 1968).

94. *Id.*

95. *Id.*

96. Judge Stephens' dismissal of the federal proceedings, rather than staying them until state court determination of the state issues would reveal whether a decision on the federal question was still necessary, appears to violate what the Supreme Court has characterized as the "better practice." Zwickler v. Koota, 389 U.S. 241, 244 n.4 (1967); *see also* Wright, Federal Courts 171 (1963). Characterizing a potential conflict between state and federal law as essentially a state question is also of doubtful validity—but in view of the considerations discussed in the text this approach may appear beguiling to other federal courts. At the same time, Judge Stephens suggested that a "good case can be made for re-examination" of the constitutional precedents as applied to this situation, in view of the 1967 amendment adding section 1350.5 to the California Labor Code, which limited hours of women working in interstate commerce to 10 per day, while other women working on the same job were limited to 8 hours per day. This "makes suspect the true present purposes of the limitation of working hours for women. Are these restrictions truly based upon a concern for the public health and walfare, a determination to restrict the number of women in industry in favor of male employees, or to protect women against the competition of men?"

97. *Cf.* Coon v. Tingle, 277 F. Supp. 304 (N.D. Ga. 1967), dismissing plaintiff's action seeking to have Georgia Code § 58-1062, which provides that "No female shall be allowed to work in any liquor store as hostess, bar maid or in any manner whatsoever," declared violative of the 14th Amendment and in conflict with Title VII. Though the dismissal in *Coon* was based upon various procedural defects in the complaint and the non-applicability, on jurisdictional grounds, of Title VII, the court also observed that even if these procedural defects had not been present, "the Court would not have reached the constitutionality of the statute under attack . . . because of the doctrine of abstention, the exercise of which seems appropriate here . . . ." *Id.* at 307.

98. *See* text at note 84 *supra,* this chap.

99. Mengelkoch v. Industrial Welfare Commission, CCH Empl. Pract. Guide ¶ 9129 (D.C. Cal. 1968).

100. The Missouri Attorney General has held, without extensive discussion, that Missouri law limiting women's overtime and other "special protection laws . . . have been enacted for the public interest, specifically the protection of the working woman, [and are therefore] a bona fide occupational qualification within the meaning of Section 703 (e) of Title VII of the Civil Rights Act of 1964." [1965-1968 Transfer Binder] CCH Empl. Pract. Guide ¶ 8136 (1967). By contrast, the Arizona Civil Rights Commission, noting that Arizona's eighthour day and forty-eight hour week limitation on women's working hours "does not prevent a woman from working [excess hours] provided that the excess time is spent working for a second employer," has held that state's hour limitation for women to be in conflict with Title VII. Reynolds v. Mountain States Tel. & Tel. Co., [1965-1968 Transfer Binder] CCH Empl. Pract. Guide ¶ 8111, at 6184 (Ariz. Civ. Rgts. Comm'n 1966). Though persuasive, these determinations are not dispositive of the question even within

their own states, and are cited as limited authority for their respective positions.

101. 272 F. Supp. 332 (S.D. Ind. 1967).

102. 277 F. Supp. 117 (S.D. Ga. 1967).

103. *Id.* at 118; Bowe v. Colgate Palmolive Co., 272 F. Supp. 332, 364 (S.D. Ind. 1967); *see* note 109 *infra,* this chap.

104. Note, *Classification on the Basis of Sex and the 1964 Civil Rights Act,* 50 IOWA L. REV. 778 (1965).

105. Bowe v. Colgate Palmolive Co., 272 F. Supp. 332 362 (S.D. Ind. 1967).

106. *See* text accompanying note 120 *infra,* this chap.

107. However, the extension of the rule to men as well as women, along with an interpretation requiring both to satisfy a burden of proof that they can perform the job with little or no harmful effects, would have the virtue of equalizing the rules, with males generally being able to satisfy the burden more often and more readily than females.

108. *See* references in Bowe v. Colgate Palmolive Co., 272 F. Supp. 332, 355 (S.D. Ind. 1967), to the maximum permissible weight limits for women in industry of between 33 and 44 1/10 pounds, set by an I.L.O.-authorized study in 1964, and the 1965 Bulletin of the U.S. Secretary of Labor, recommending essentially the same limits with further qualifications concerning the compactness of the package and the height to which it may be lifted.

109. *Id.* at 356.

110. In *Bowe* the Court found that "it was not [and is not] practical or pragmatically possible for [Colgate], in the operation of its plant, to assess the physical abilities and capabilities of each female who might seek a particular job as a unique individual with a strength and a stamina below average or above average or to consider special female individuals as uniquely qualified among women in general as suited to the performance of certain . . . general labor jobs [which she might seek] . . . by means of her preference sheet." *Id.* at 332. The approach suggested in the text would also conform to the EEOC position, stated in the Commission Guidelines on November 22, 1965, CCH EMPL. PRACT. GUIDE ¶ 17,252.04, that "the principles of nondiscrimination in employment requires that applicants be considered on the basis of individual capacities and not on characteristics generally attributed to a group."

111. Although the following discussion deals with the possible effects of Title VII upon state laws limiting the hours a woman may work in the course of a day or of a week, it may also be applicable to many other types of state "protective" labor laws for women only, such as requirements that women be provided seats at work, *e.g.* COLO. REV. STAT. ANN. § 80-2-13 (1963), rest periods for women only, *e.g.,* WYO. STAT. ANN. § 27-218 (1957), and even weight-lifting restrictions for women workers.

112. *See* note 7 *supra,* this chap.

113. *See, e.g.,* Law of Mar. 12, 1943, ch. 160, 44 Del. Laws 495 (repealed 1965); Law of Apr. 18, 1935, ch. 214, 40 Del. Laws 759 (repealed 1965); Law of Mar. 22, 1917, ch. 230, 29 Del. Laws 714-42 (repealed 1965); Law of Mar. 20, 1913, ch. 175, §§ 25, 4, 6, 7, 8, 27 Del. Laws 425-27 (repealed 1965), which *had* provided, *inter alia,* for maximum hour limitations for females 16 years of age and older in certain establishments as well as meal and rest periods; VA. CODE ANN. § 40-35a (Cum. Supp. 1968), exempting businesses meeting the requirements of the Fair Labor Standards Act from the 9-hour day, 48-hour week limitation on women's working hours. *See also* Law of June 30, 1909, No. 285, § 9, [1909] Mich. Pub. Acts 646 (repealed 1967), which had set a

54-hour per week, 10 hour a day, absolute limitation on working hours of women of all ages and minors below the age of 18 of both sexes. In those states distinguishing maximum hours for women in accordance with whether they are covered by the Fair Labor Standards Act, a constitutional challenge alleging arbitrary discrimination may also be feasible. See discussion of *Mengelkoch* decision, text accompanying notes 87-97 *supra*, this chap.

114. Lochner v. New York, 198 U.S. 45 (1905).

115. *See* cases cited in note 86 *supra*, this chap. Since the above was written, federal district Judge Ferguson has ruled from the bench that the California law limiting women's working hours violated Title VII. *L.A. Daily Journal,* Sept. 17, 1968, p. 1, col. 6. Significantly, this was the result sought by the EEOC itself in that case, Rosenfeld v. Southern Pacific Co. et al, Civil Action No. 67-1377-F, U.S. Dist. Ct., Central District of California, in the *amicus curiae* brief it filed therein. The Commission's efforts to completely invalidate such laws rather than to seek to extend them to men is regrettable, and in a fundamental sense contrary to what is intended by Title VII. The EEOC made the same error, I believe, in its guideline issued in February 1968 (33 Fed. Reg. 3344; 29 C.F.R. 1604.31) which stated that "a difference in optional or compulsory retirement ages based on sex [in pension or retirement plans] violates Title VII." The effect of this guideline was that, if an existing retirement plan gave women employees the option of retiring at age 62, but withheld this option from men until they reached 65, the inequality would be "cured" by requiring women to work until 65. It is submitted that it would have been within the EEOC's statutory power to remedy the situation by requiring the lowering of the optional retirement age for men—subject of course to actuarial factors limiting what can be done to plans now in force. That its earlier ruling may have been an unwelcome development for many women has recently been impliedly conceded by the Commission's general counsel in an opinion on September 13, 1968, permitting "continued early retirement for *current* female employees of *certain ages,* depending on the specific pension and retirement plan under consideration." (News Release, EEOC, September 16, 1968. Emphasis supplied.) This too is an unsatisfactory answer to the long-range problems created by the EEOC's earlier ruling. The Commission and the courts should extend the benefit of an early optional retirement age to male employees, rather than to take it away from female employees, in plans that presently distinguish between the sexes in this area. On August 1, 1968, the Senate Finance Committee reported out H.R.2767, with an amendment that would *permit* sex discrimination in pension and retirement plans. Representative Martha Griffiths has ably demonstrated the danger such an enactment would create for Title VII. CONG. REC. E 7894 (Daily ed., Sept. 12, 1968).

116. This was the employer's position in Mengelkoch v. Industrial Welfare Comm'n, CCH EMPL. PRACT. GUIDE ¶ 9129 (D.C. Cal. 1968).

117. 42 U.S.C. § 2000e-7 (1964).

118. *Id.*

119. Oldham, *Sex Discrimination and State Protective Laws,* 44 DEN. L.J. 344, 370 (1967).

120. 29 U.S.C. § 206 (d) (1) (1964).

121. *Id.* § 218.

122. 29 C.F.R. § 800.161 (1967).

123. *Id.* § 800.162.

124. "In one case 11 men employees of a bank in San Francisco benefited by obtaining overtime compensation which had been paid only to women pur-

suant to the requirements of a California state law. In another instance men checkers in a grocery store had been paid 35 cents less than women." Margolin, *Equal Pay and Equal Employment Opportunities for Women,* N.Y.U. 19TH CONF. ON LABOR 297, 310 (1967).

125. The EEOC, in an Opinion Letter of its General Counsel, has taken the same position, stating that "Where an employer pays a certain wage to employees of one sex in order to comply with a minimum wage law, he must also pay the same wage rate to employees of the opposite sex for equal work." Opinion Letter of General Counsel, EEOC, Mar. 1, 1966, CCH EMPL. PRACT. GUIDE ¶ 17,252.07 (1966).

126. The jurisdictional reach of Title VII is much greater than that of the Equal Pay Act. The latter, being part of the Fair Labor Standards Act, is riddled with exemptions. 29 U.S.C. § 213 (1964). The Equal Pay Act specifically provides that employers who are in violation of the Act shall not comply by reducing the wage rate of any employee. *Id.* § 206 (d) (1). This has no bearing, however, on the validity of extending state minimum wage laws to men, or with respect to the suggestion in the text that other laws be similarly extended under Title VII. In at least one state, however, an Attorney General's Opinion has interpreted the state's own equal employment opportunities statute, which prohibits sex discrimination, as not allowing male employees to avail themselves of state statutory provisions for "minimum wages, food and lodging, maximum hours, meal periods, rest periods, when seats must be provided, uniforms, and certain other working conditions designed for the benefit of female employees, [since males] do not come within the class sought to be benefited, *i.e.,* female employees." Nevada Attorney General's Opinion No. 458, Nov. 13, 1967, CCH EMPL. PRACT. GUIDE ¶ 8207 (1967). This result can be characterized only as question-begging, since the basic problem in such cases is whether the statute involved requires or permits the extension of women's employment benefits to males. It is significant that the article from 13 AM. JUR., *Labor* § 763 (1958), relied upon in the Nevada Attorney General's Opinion, dealt with the constitutional right of the legislature to pass laws safeguarding the health of female employees, and that none of the lawsuits challenging such laws appear to have been brought by male employees seeking to have their benefits extended to them.

127. Of course, some exceptions could be made in the statutes for emergency situations, provided that "emergency" was precisely defined and it was not permitted to become a means of circumventing the basic purpose of the laws to restrict working hours for both sexes.

128. *See* text following note 138 *infra,* this chap.

129. The same approach could be taken with some other laws, see note 111 *supra,* this chap., but would not be feasible, of course, with respect to laws providing, for example, certain benefits in the event of pregnancy.

130. Further support for this approach can be garnered from Section 708 of Title VII, 42 U.S.C. § 2000e-7 (1964) which in effect relieves persons from any duty, liability, etc. provided by any law "which purports to require the doing of any act which would be an unlawful employment practice under this title." *See* text accompanying note 119 *supra,* this chap. When this is coupled with the fact of Congressional approval of the amended bill that prohibited sex discrimination, over the objection of Congresswoman Green on the floor of Congress that passage of the sex provisions would create "new problems for business, for managers, for industrial concerns [which] should be taken into consideration before any vote is made in favor of the amendment without any

hearings at all on the legislation," 110 Cong. Rec. 2584 (1964) , EEOC extension of state protective laws to men, wherever feasible, appears consistent with the spirit and tenor of the basic legislation

131. Mengelkoch v. Industrial Welfare Comm'n, CCH Empl. Pract. Guide ¶ 9128, at 6514 (D.C. Cal. 1968). (Emphasis added.)

132. In its August 19, 1966 policy statement, the EEOC noted that "over forty states have laws or regulations which . . . limit the maximum daily or weekly hours which women employees may work." 35 U.S.L.W. 2137 (1966).

133. Even these do not actually prevent women from working in excess of the "limit" as long as the excess time is spent working for a second employer. Reynolds v. Mountain States Tel. & Tel. Co. [1965-1968 Transfer Binder], CCH Empl. Pract. Guide ¶ 8111 (Ariz. Civ. Rgts Comm'n 1966).

134. 29 U.S.C. §§ 207 (a) (1), (2) (1964) .

135. *Cf.* Citizens' Advisory Council on the Status of Women, Task Force on Labor Relations Report 41 (1968) [hereinafter cited as Task Force Report].

136. *See, e.g.,* Continental Oil Co., 165 NLRB 95 (1966), wherein the NLRB upheld the discharge of an employee for refusal "to work on two Saturdays."

137. *See, e.g.,* collective bargaining agreement construed in Chapman Bait Co., 68-1 CCH Lab. Arb. Awards ¶ 83-16, at 4,085 (1968).

138. Lochner v. New York, 198 U.S. 45 (1905); *see also* Task Force Report 56.

139. *See* text accompanying notes 120-30 *supra,* this chap.

140. Ariz. Rev. Stat. § 23-281 (B) (8) (Supp. 1968); *see also* Nebr. Rev. Stat. § 48-203 (Supp. 1968), which permits women to work up to 12 hours a day and 60 a week on permit from the Commissioner and provided that the "female consents to" additional hours. This is a limited expression of the voluntary overtime principle, being voluntary for women and not for men, and therefore perpetuating sex-based inequality in another form.

141. *Cf.* Task Force Report 58. This distinction in the Arizona law may also make it vulnerable to constitutional attack as an arbitrary discrimination. *See* discussion of Mengelkoch decision in text accompanying notes 87-97 *supra,* this chap.

142. The Task Force on Labor Standards has also endorsed the principle of "voluntary overtime," but its recommendations appear to emphasize the development of private employer-employee agreements on the subject, rather than legislative treatment of the problem. It is also unclear whether the Task Force contemplates that the principle of voluntary overtime shall apply to men employees as well as women. Task Force Report 29-30.

143. Mengelkoch v. Industrial Welfare Comm'n, CCH Empl. Pract. Guide ¶ 9128, at 6514 (D.C. Cal. 1968).

144. 29 U.S.C. § 157 (1964).

145. *See* Consumer Credit Protection Act, Pub. L. No. 90-321, § 304 (May 29, 1968): "(a) No employer may discharge any employee by reason of the fact that his earnings have been subjected to garnishment for any one indebtedness; (b) Whoever wilfully violates subsection (a) of this section shall be fined not more than $1,000, or imprisoned not more than one year, or both."

146. M. Sovern, Legal Restraints on Racial Discrimination in Employment 110 (1966).

147. pp. 31-34 *supra.*

148. Goesart v. Cleary, 335 U.S. 464 (1948).

149. *Id.* at 466.

150. *See* text following note 105 *supra,* this chap.

151. CCH EMPL. PRACT. GUIDE ¶ 17,304.04 (1966).

152. *See* text following note 84 *supra,* this chap.

153. CCH EMPL. PRACT. GUIDE ¶ 17,304.04 (1966).

154. *See, e.g.,* Section A, subd. 14, 19 N.Y.C.R.R. § 205.15. *Cf.* Hesseltine v. State, 6 Ill. 2d 129, 126 N.E.2d 631 (1955).

155. 286 N.Y.S.2d 510 (1968).

156. *Id.* at 515.

157. *Cf.* Hill v. Florida, 325 U.S. 538 (1945), holding that a state statute providing criminal penalties for "business agents" who were not licensed by the state was invalid as being in irreconcilable conflict with the employees' full freedom in collective bargaining envisioned by Congress in the National Labor Relations Act. Thus it would also appear that a wrestling promoter or a woman wrestler who rely upon an EEOC opinion letter that a state prohibition against woman wrestlers is "unlawful" should be able to invoke that ruling as a complete defense to any criminal prosecution for "violating" the state statute. The same result would obtain, moreover, even without an EEOC ruling if a court should hold the state rule "unlawful" in the light of federal or state policy.

158. *See, e.g.,* ARIZ. REV. STAT. § 23-261 A (1956); COLO. REV. STAT. ANN. § 92-10-2 (1963); UTAH CODE ANN. § 34-4-1 (1953).

159. *See* text preceding note 110 *supra,* this chap.

160. TASK FORCE REPORT 32.

Chapter 5.   The Relationship Between the Equal Pay Act of 1963 and Title VII.

1. *See* Legislative History of the Equal Pay Act of 1963 (printed for use of Committee on Education and Labor) S. REP. No. 176, 88th Cong., 1st Sess. 687 (1963). Indeed, it has been suggested that the legislative history of the Equal Pay Act may bear "on the legislative intent or objectives of the 'sex' amendment to Title VII." Margolin, *Equal Pay and Equal Employment Opportunities for Women,* N.Y.U. 19TH CONF. ON LABOR 297, 301 (1967). There can be no quarrel with this suggestion if it means that many members of Congress voted for inclusion of the sex provisions in Title VII because they were informed, directly or indirectly, of the facts about employment discrimination against women that had emerged in the hearings and debate on the Equal Pay Act. But it is difficult to believe that the specific legislative history of the Equal Pay Act can be used to interpret the meaning of difficult provisions in Title VII—especially since the one reference in Title VII to the Equal Pay Act, if interpreted mechanically, may lead to results that are destructive of Title VII's basic promise of equal employment opportunity for women workers. See text following note 61 *infra,* this chap.

2. 29 U.S.C. § 206 (d) (1) (1964).

3. *Id.* § 206 (d) (2).

4. Equal Pay Act of 1963, § 4, 29 U.S.C. § 206 (1964).

5. Portal-to-Portal Act of 1947, 29 U.S.C. § 255 (1964).

6. 29 C.F.R. § 800.166 (b) (1968).

7. 29 U.S.C. § 216 (c) (1964).

8. *Id.* § 216; *see* 29 C.F.R. § 800.166 (1968), for additional remedies under the FLSA.

9. 42 U.S.C. § 2000e-2 (h) (1964).

10. *Id.* The significance of this provision is explored below at text accompanying note 50 *infra*, this chap.

11. 29 C.F.R. § 1604.7 (a) (1968).

12. *Id.* § 1604.7 (b).

13. Opinion Letter, October 12, 1965, CCH EMPL. PRACT. GUIDE ¶ 17,252.09 (1966).

14. *See* text at note 59 *infra*, this chap.

15. 29 C.F.R. § 800.114 (1968).

16. *See* text at note 3 *supra*, this chap.

17. *See* note 4 *supra*, this chap.

18. 29 C.F.R. § 800.106 (1968).

19. Murphy v. Miller Brewing Co. [1965-1968 Transfer Binder]. CCH EMPL. PRACT. GUIDE ¶ 8069 (1966).

20. WISC. STAT. ANN., §§ 111.31-.37 (1961).

21. Note 19 *supra*, this chap.

22. *Id. See also* Wirtz v. Rainbo Baking Co., 54 LC ¶ 31,884 (E.D. Ken. 1967). Though the wage differential held unlawful in that case was contained in a collective bargaining agreement, the union does not appear to have been made a party defendant in the action. *Cf.* Bowe v. Colgate Palmolive Co., 272 F. Supp. 332, 358 (S.D. Ind. 1967), where, in a Title VII charge against an employer and a union, the court observed that even if a technical basis existed for imposing liability on the union, it "has been most assiduous in seeking to protect the rights of the [plaintiff women employees] and to secure relief for them. Although named as a defendant by the plaintiffs, it has been aligned with them and against the defendant Colgate. Under these circumstances a judgment requiring the Union to recompense the plaintiffs, or to indemnify Colgate for the very actions which the Union has protested [maintenance of separate male and female seniority lists to which the union had originally agreed in a contract] would not be warranted." *Id.* at 358.

23. *See* text accompanying note 2 *supra*, this chap., for a more complete text of 29 U.S.C. § 206 (d) (1) (1964).

24. 29 C.F.R. § 800.104 (1968). (Emphasis supplied.)

25. CCH EMPL. PRACT. GUIDE ¶ 1624 (1965).

26. 29 C.F.R. § 800.114 (1968).

27. 42 U.S.C. § 2000e-2 (h) (1964).

28. *Id.*

29. *See* note 41 *supra,* chap 4.

30. *See* text at note 74 *supra*, chap. 4.

31. *See* text accompanying note 2 *supra*, this chap., for more complete text of 29 U.S.C. § 206 (d) (1) (1964).

32. *Id.*

33. *See, e.g.,* Wirtz v. Meade Mfg. Co., 55 LC ¶ 31,936 (D. Kan. 1967) (occasional greater physical demands of job no basis for higher pay for males); Wirtz v. Rainbo Baking Co., 54 LC ¶ 31,884 (E.D. Kan. 1967) (occasional heavy lifting no excuse for wage differential based on sex); *see also* Wirtz v. Basic, Inc., 256 F. Supp. 786 (D. Nev. 1966) (though male employees may be paid shift differential for night work, this does not justify a higher rate for males than females on day shift); 29 C.F.R. § 800.122 (1968): "Insubstantial or

minor differences in the degree or amount of skill, or effort, or responsibility required for the performance of jobs will not render the equal pay standard inapplicable."

34. 55 LC ¶ 31,919 (D. Mass. 1967).

35. 262 F. Supp. 561 (M.D. Fla. 1966).

36. *See also* Wirtz v. Wheaton Glass Co., 36 U.S.L.W. 2705 (D.N.J. 1968).

37. The problem of "effort" is considered in the text accompanying note 46 *infra,* this chap.

38. 42 U.S.C. § 2000e-2 (h)   (1964).

39. An analogy to this technique can be found in the practice of ignoring a Statute of Limitations where a cause of action is pleaded defensively as a counterclaim or a set-off. *See e.g.,* King Bros. Prod., Inc. v. RKO Teleradio Pictures, Inc., 208 F. Supp. 271 (S.D.N.Y. 1962).

40. 379 US 306 (1964).

41. Walker, *Title VII: Complaint and Enforcement Procedures and Relief and Remedies,* 7 B.C. IND. & COMM. L. REV. 495, 519 (1966).

42. 280 F. SUPP. 719 (1968).

43. *Id.* at 728.

44. 110 CONG. REC. 7213 (1964).

45. *Id.* (Emphasis supplied.)

46. 29 U.S.C. § 206 (d) (1)   (1964).

47. 29 C.F.R. § 800.142 (1968). (Emphasis supplied.)

48. Such a result would appear to be consistent with what the New York courts have done in two cases, in requiring special promotional examinations to be given to policewomen who, because of an earlier policy of sex discrimination, had been bypassed in favor of policemen when promotional opportunities had arisen. Shpritzer v. Lang, 13 N.Y.2d 744 (1962) ; Schimmel v. City Civil Service Commission, *reported at* CCH EMPL. PRACT. GUIDE ¶ 9029.

49. *See* text at note 106 *supra,* chap. 4.

50. Though the Department of Labor has interpreted the word "effort" as being "concerned with the measurement of the physical or mental exertion needed for the performance of a job," 29 C.F.R. § 800.127 (1968), the present discussion is concerned only with the matter of physical exertion—since differences in mental exertion that may be required on a job are subject to the same analysis employed above with respect to skill, responsibility, etc.

51. *Cf.* Wirtz v. Dennison Mfg. Co., 55 L.C. ¶ 31, at 919 (D. Mass. 1967).

52. Opinion Letter, January 18, 1966, CCH EMPL. PRACT. GUIDE ¶ 17,252.21 (1966).

53. 29 C.F.R. § 800.131 (1968).

54. *See* text accompanying note 37 *supra,* this chap.

55. *See* note 50 *supra,* this chap.

56. 29 U.S.C. § 206 (d) (1)   (1964); *see* 42 U.S.C. § 2000e-2 (h)   (1964), for a similar exception to sex-based wage discrimination.

57. *See* text at note 10 *supra,* this chap.

58. *See* text accompanying note 11 *supra,* this chap.

59. *See* text accompanying note 15 *supra,* this chap.

60. 29 C.F.R. § 800.163 (1968).

61. *See* 109 CONG. REC. 9196 (1963) (remarks of Representative Thompson): "Thus, among other things, shift differentials, restrictions on or differences based on time of day worked, hours of work, lifting or moving heavy objects . . . would also be exempted under this act."

62. S. REP. No. 176, 88th Cong. 1st Sess. (1963).

63. *See* text accompanying note 80 *supra*, chap. 4.

64. *See* text accompanying note 60-61 *supra*, this chap.

65. 29 U.S.C. § 206 (d) (1) 1964).

66. 29 C.F.R. § 800.142 (1968).

67. EEOC Guidelines, Nov. 22, 1965, CCH EMPL. PRACT. GUIDE ¶ 17,252.04 (1966).

68. *See* text following note 60 *supra*, this chap.

69. *See* text accompanying note 38 *supra*, this chap.

Chapter 6. Constitutional Aspects of Sex-Based Discrimination in American Law

1. Chaps. 2 and 3 of this book sought to identify some major areas of sex-based discrimination in American law and considered whether such discriminations should, as a matter of policy, be preserved. Necessarily assumed in such an approach was the absence of constitutional impediments to the continuance of such policies. The present chapter seeks to determine whether that assumption is warranted.

2. CCPR 36-37.

3. Other discussions of the constitutional aspects of sex-based legal discrimination appear in Crozier, *Constitutionality of Discrimination Based on Sex,* 15 B.U.L. REV. 723 (1935); Note, *Sex, Discrimination, and the Constitution,* 2 STAN. L. REV. 691 (1950); Note, *Classification on the Basis of Sex and the 1964 Civil Rights Act,* 50 IOWA L. REV. 778, 778-88 (1965); Murray and Eastwood, *Jane Crow and the Law: Sex Discrimination and Title VII,* 34 GEO. WASH. L. REV. 232, 235-42 (1965).

4. "The citizens of each State shall be entitled to all privileges and immunities of citizens in the several States." Art. *IV*, Section 2, Par. 1, *Constitution of the United States; see also* Amendment *XIV*, Section 1: ". . . No State shall make or enforce any law which shall abridge the privileges or immunities of citizens of the United States."

5. ". . . [nor shall any State] deny to any person within its jurisdiction the equal protection of the laws." Amendment *XIV, Constitution of the United States.*

6. ". . . nor shall any State deprive any person of life, liberty, or property without due process of law. . . ." *Id., see also* Amendment *V, Constitution of the United States:* "nor [shall any person] be deprived of life, liberty, or property, without due process of law."

7. In re Mahaffey's Estate, 79 Mont. 10, 254 P. 875 (1927).

8. Carrithers v. City of Shelbyville, 126 Ky. 769, 104 S.W.744 (1907).

9. Minor v. Happersett, 21 Wall. 162, 22 L. Ed. 627 (1875).

10. People v. Jemnez, 43 C.A.2d Supp. 739, 121 P.2d 543 (1942); In re Carragher, 149 Iowa 225, 128 N.W. 352 (1910).

11. Hall v. State, 136 Fla. 644, 187 So. 392 (1939); Commonwealth v. Welosky, 276 Mass. 398, 177 N.E. 656 (1931) *cert. denied* 284 U.S. 684 (1932).

12. UTAH CONST. Art. *IV*, § 1 (1953).

13. Salt Lake City v. Wilson, 46 Utah 60, 69, 148 P. 1104, 1107 (1915). Only rarely in the past have some courts been moved to hold that a sex-based discrimination violated constitutional principles. Thus, though the principle of

sex-based inequality of punishment for the same or similar crimes had been frequently sustained (*See, e.g.,* Ex Parte Gosselin, 141 Me. 412, 44 A.2d 882 (1945); Ex Parte Brady, 116 Ohio St. 512, 157 N.E. 69 (1927); Platt v. Commonwealth, 256 Mass. 539. 152 N.E. 914 (1926); State v. Heitman, 105 Kan. 139, 181 P. 630, 8 A.L.R. 848 (1919); In re Dunkerton, 104 Kan. 481, 179 Pac. 347 (1919)), the Indiana Supreme Court, as long ago as 1913, held as violative of the equal protection guarantee a statute prescribing different treatment for males and females *acquitted* of crime on the ground of insanity. Morgan v. State, 179 Ind. 300, 101 N.E. 6 (1913).

14. People v. Jemnez, 49 C.A.2d 739, 121 P.2d 543 (1942); *cf.* Hargens v. Alcoholic Beverage Control App. Bd., 263 A.C.A. 663, (1968); *But see* People v. Gardner, *reported at* 53 L.C. ¶ 9015, wherein the Los Angeles Municipal Court, affirming a conviction on the basis of judicial precedents, at the same time expressed its view that the restriction on female bartenders was unconstitutional and urged defense counsel to perfect an appeal in the case. But in 1968, the California legislature adopted A.B. 1749 (Ch. 1144) which permits female employees to dispense beer or wine behind a bar of a licensee operating a bona fide public eating place, licensed only with an on-sale beer and wine license.

15. Bradwell v. the State, 16 Wall. 130 (U.S. 1872). The court also invoked the common law contractual disabilities of married women and the difficulties clients might have in enforcing contracts with a married woman attorney as an additional reason for upholding the State Court's barring of women from the practice of law.

16. *Id.* at 141. *See also* Ex Parte Lockwood, 154 U.S. 116 (1893) reaffirming the principle of the *Bradwell* case that the right to practice law in the State courts was not a privilege or immunity of a citizen of the United States and that a State court could construe its statutes to determine whether a woman was entitled to be admitted to practice law in that State. There is no indication that the equal protection clause was invoked in either case—although, given the Court's view on the role of women in society, it is likely that an argument based upon that clause would have been equally unsuccessful. *See* discussion of Muller v. Oregon on pp. 152-154 *infra*.

17. 208 U.S. 412 (1908).

18. 198 U.S. 45 (1905).

19. 208 U.S. at 419.

20. *Id.* at 422. In the employment field, a number of State laws enacted in the early part of this century provided special protection to women, in recognition of the differences in the physical capacities of the sexes and of the general weaker bargaining position of women in the labor market. Here too, the Supreme Court has upheld such laws on the general ground that sex is a reasonable basis for classification, although in each instance factors other than the mere sex of the protected employees were present. *See, e.g.,* West Coast Hotel Co. v. Parrish, 300 U.S. 379 (1937); Radice v. New York, 264 U.S. 292 (1924); Bosley v. McLaughlin, 236 U.S. 385 (1915).

21. 208 U.S. 412, 421-22 (1908). (Emphasis supplied.)

22. Murray and Eastwood, *supra* note 3, this chap., at 237, citing Commonwealth v. Welosky, 276 Mass. 398, 414, 177 N.E. 656, 664 (1931), *cert. denied,* 284 U.S. 684 (1932) (jury exclusion); Quong Wing v. Kirkendall, 223 U.S. 59, 63 (1912); People v. Case, 153 Mich. 98, 101, 116 N.W. 558, 560 (1908); State v. Hunter, 208 Ore. 282, 288, 300 P.2d 455, 458 (1956) (licensing of occupations); Allred v. Heaton, 336 S.W.2d 251 (Tex. Civ. App.) *cert. denied,* 364 U.S. 517

(1960); Heaton v. Bristol, 317 S.W.2d 86 (Tex. Civ. App.), *cert. denied,* 356 U.S. 230 (1958).

23. Murray and Eastwood, *supra* note 3, this chap.

24. *Id.* at 241.

25. It is "desirable that there be early review by the U.S. Supreme Court of the validity under the Fifth and Fourteenth Amendments of laws and official practices discriminating against women so that the principle of equality will be firmly established in our constitutional doctrine." CCPR at 37.

26. For further discussion of the proposed equal rights amendment and the "Hayden rider," see pp. 192-196 *infra.*

27. "No female shall be required or permitted to lift any burden of 30 pounds or carry any burden in excess of 15 pounds." *Industrial Commission of Utah, Welfare Regulations for Any Occupation, Trade or Industry,* effective September 14, 1937, cited in CCH STATE LABOR LAWS, UTAH ¶ 45, 525 (1968).

28. CAL. LAB. C. § 1251.

29. *But see* pp. 120-124 *supra,* suggesting that Title VII of the 1964 Civil Rights Act may require employers covered by the Act to permit women employees to prove that they can, without harmful effects, lift weights in excess of a limit imposed by state law.

30. *See* U.S. v. Carolene Products Co., 304 U.S. 144, 152-53, n. 4 (1938); *see also* Cahn, *The Firstness of the First Amendment,* 65 YALE L.J. 464 (1956); Mason, *The Core of Free Government, 1938-40: Mr. Justice Stone and "Preferred Freedoms,"* 65 YALE L.J. 597 (1956).

31. 316 U.S. 535 (1942).

32. *Id.* at 541.

33. *Id.*

34. 388 U.S. 1 (1967).

35. *Id.* at 12.

36. *Id.* at 11.

37. *Id.*

38. 281 F. Supp. 8 (1968).

39. *Id.* at 14.

40. 210 Pa. Super 156, 232 A.2d 247 (1967).

41. 391 U.S. 68, 70 (1968); *see also* Griswold v. Connecticut, 381 U.S. 479, 497 (1965): "In a long series of cases this Court has held that where fundamental personal liberties are involved, they may not be abridged by the States simply on a showing that a regulatory statute has some rational relationship to the effectuation of a proper state purpose. . . ."

42. *Cf.* various opinions in Adamson v. California, 332 U.S. 46 (1947).

43. *Supra* note 41, this chap. (Emphasis supplied, footnotes omitted.)

44. *See* pp. 113-115 *supra.*

45. *See* pp. 80-85 *supra.*

46. 260 F. Supp. 820 (D.C. Mich. 1966).

47. *Id.* at 821.

48. 3 Ohio Misc. 167, 207 N.E.2d 398 (1965).

49. *Id.* at 171, 207 N.E. 2d at 400. *See also* Umpleby v. Dorsey, 10 Ohio Misc. 288, 227 N.E.2d 274 (1967) in which a second Ohio Court of Common Pleas followed the *Clem* case.

50. 34 Wis. 2d 542, 150 N.W.2d 137 (1967); *see also* Black v. United States, 263 F. Supp. 470, 480, n. 33 (1967).

51. Moran v. Quality Aluminum Casting Co., 34 Wis. 2d 542, 551, 150 N.W.2d 137, 141.

52. WISC. STAT. ANN. § 6.015 [now § 246.15], provides in part: "Women shall have the same rights and privileges under the law as men in the exercise of suffrage, freedom of contract, choice of residence for voting purposes, jury service, holding office, holding and conveying property, care and custody of children, *and in all other respects*. . . . (Emphasis supplied.)

53. Seagrave v. Legg, 147 W. Va. 331, 337-38, 127 S.E.2d 605, 608 (1962).

54. *Cf.* Reitman v. Mulkey, 387 U.S. 369 (1967), invalidating a state constitutional provision, adopted by a majority vote of the electorate, on the grounds that it violated the United States Constitution; *see also* American Federation of Labor v. Watson, 327 U.S. 582 (1946).

55. Krohn v. Richardson-Merrell, Inc., 406 S.W.2d 166 (Tenn. 1966). The United States Supreme Court denied certiorari in *Krohn* on March 20, 1967, 386 U.S. 970 (1967), which does not of course mean that the Supreme Court approves the result in that case. Rather it signifies at best that less than four members of the court were willing to review it. *See, e.g.,* Brown v. Allen, 344 U.S. 443, 489-97 (1953).

56. Miskunas v. Union Carbide Corp., 399 F.2d 847 (7th Cir. 1968).

57. *Id.* at 2047.

58. *See* p. 82 *supra.*

59. *See* p. 157 *infra.*

60. *Id.*

61. 247 Md. 95, 231 A.2d 514 (1967).

62. *Id.* at 106-07, 231 A.2d at 520.

63. *Id.* at 115, 231 A.2d at 525.

64. *Id.* at 113, 231 A.2d at 524.

65. *Id.* at 107, 231 A.2d at 521.

66. *Reported at* 37 U.S.L.W. 2046 (1968).

67. *Id.*

68. 391 U.S. 68 (1968).

69. Millington v. Southeastern Elevator Co., *supra* note 66, this chap., at 2046.

70. Levy v. Louisiana, 391 U.S. 68, 70. (Emphasis supplied.)

71. *See* p. 3 *supra.*

72. Levy v. State, La., 192 So. 2d 193 (1966), *cert. denied,* 250 La. 25, 193 So. 2d 530 (1967).

73. Owen v. Illinois Baking Corp., Inc., 260 F. Supp. 820, 821 W.D. Mich. (1966).

74. Seagrave v. Legg, 147 W. Va. 331, 336, 127 S.E.2d 605, 608 (1962): *See also* Casey v. Manson Construction and Engineering Co., 428 P.2d 898, 906, n. 7 (Ore. 1967). Perhaps the most extensive consideration of the matter thus far appears in the *Krohn* case which rejected the constitutional challenge. That is not saying too much, however, since the only reasons advanced by the Tennessee Supreme Court for its decision in *Krohn* were the unelaborated statement that "many and obvious differences between what, by legal logic, is recoverable by the male spouse for injury, on the one hand, and the female spouse on the other may be conceived of" (406 S.W.2d at 168-69), and the resulting conclusion that the Tennessee rule was therefore based on a "practical and logical classification" (*Id.* at 169), rather than working a "discrimination." *Id.*

75. This has been done on policy grounds in some jurisdictions. *See, e.g.,* Gearing v. Berkson, 223 Mass. 257, 111 N.E. 785 (1916).

76. *See* pp. 157-158 *supra.*

77. *Levy v. Louisiana, supra,* note 41, this chap.
78. *Id.*
79. *See* p. 164 *supra.* Even on the assumption that the right to sue for loss of consortium involves an area of economic activity, rather than a "basic civil right," at least one court has held that the discriminatory consortium rule violates the equal protection guarantee, since it is entirely without basis in reason. Karczewski v. Baltimore and Ohio Railroad Co., 274 F. Supp. 169 (1967).
80. *See* pp. 157-158 *supra.*
81. *See* pp. 161-162 *supra.*
82. 210 Pa. Super. 156, 232 A.2d 247 (1967).
83. PA. STAT. ANN. tit. 61, §566 (1964).
84. See statutes upheld in Ex Parte Gosselin, 141 Me. 412, 44 A.2d 882 (1945); Ex Parte Brady, 116 Ohio St. 512, 157 N.E. 69 (1927); Platt v. Commonwealth, 256 Mass. 539, 152 N.E. 914 (1926); State v. Heitman, 105 Kan. 139, 181 P. 630, 8 A.L.R. 848 (1919).
85. PA. STAT. ANN., tit. 61, § 566 (1964).
86. 210 Pa. Super. 156, 160-161, 232 A.2d 247, 251-252 (1967).
87. *Id.* at 161, 232 A.2d at 252.
88. *Id.* at 162, 232 A.2d at 253. (Hoffman, J., dissenting.)
89. *Id.*
90. *Id.* at 163, 232 A.2d at 254.
91. *Id.* at 164, 232 A.2d at 255. (Emphasis supplied.)
92. *See, e.g.,* Ex Parte Carey, 57 Cal. App. 297, 305, 207 Pac. 271, 274: "The state . . . has undertaken to take forcible charge of this class of unfortunates [women convicted of prostitution] and extend to them a home, education, assistance, and encouragement in an effort, otherwise hopeless, to restore them to lives of usefulness. The state combines both altruism and self-preservation." In the same case, the court disposed of the claim that sentencing to the State Farm for Women was, under the circumstances, "cruel and unusual punishment," by noting that "the detention provided for in the statute is not, within the purview of the constitution, punishment at all." 57 Cal. App. at 302, 207 Pac. at 273.
93. 387 U.S. 1 (1967).
94. Commonwealth v. Daniels, *reported at* 37 U.S.L.W. 2063 (1968).
95. At this writing only fragments of the Pennsylvania Supreme Court's opinion in *Daniels* are available in *United States Law Week, supra* note 94, this chap., and I have assumed that the portions of the opinion excerpted therein contain its essential rationale.
96. 37 U.S.L.W. at 2063.
97. *Id.* at 2064.
98. *Id.* at 2063.
99. 281 F. Supp. 8 (D.C. Conn. 1968).
100. CONN. GEN. STAT. ANN. § 17-360 (1960).
101. 281 F. Supp. at 12, n. 28.
102. *Id.* at 14.
103. *Id.* at 15.
104. *Id.* at 17.
105. *See* note 34 *supra,* this chap.
106. 281 F. Supp. at 14.
107. *Id.* (Emphasis supplied.)

108. 208 U.S. 412 (1908).

109. 335 U.S. 464 (1948).

110. 368 U.S. 57 (1961).

111. 281 F. Supp. at 13 (citations omitted).

112. *Id.* at 16.

113. It has been noted that because the decision in *Robinson* was issued in a *habeas corpus* proceeding, it applied only to that case and did not invalidate the statute for all present and future inmates. O.E.O., *Law In Action* (vol. 3, no. 1, May, 1968, p. 4). However, if the lower court decision, which has been appealed by the state, is upheld, the Connecticut Attorney General could release other inmates held under similar circumstances. At least 43 of the 118 present inmates of the State Farm, it has been reported, could benefit from the *Robinson* decision. *Id.*

114. The constitutionality of such statutes has been upheld in the cases cited *supra* note 84, this chap.

115. *See* note 123 *supra*, chap. 2.

116. *See* pp. 160-167 *supra*.

117. *See* pp. 7-13 *supra*.

118. Loving v. Commonwealth of Virginia, 388 U.S. 1, 12 (1967).

119. Application of Gault, 387 U.S. 1, 28 (1967).

120. Professor Foster has already suggested that *Loving,* the anti-miscegenation case, "opens up new areas and issues for attacks upon the constitutionality of particular regulations of the marriage relationship," Foster, *"A Basic Civil Right of Man,"* 2 FAMILY L.Q. 90, 93 (1968), but apparently does not include sex-based age discrimination as one of the potential areas. As suggested above, however, this result might be achievable by combining the decisions in *Loving* and *Gault.*

121. *See, e.g.,* ILL. ANN. STAT., ch. 3, § 131 (Smith-Hurd Repl. 1961).

122. *See* pp. 18-25 *supra*.

123. Jacobson v. Lenhart, 30 Ill.2d 225, 195 N.E.2d 638 (1964).

124. *See* note 121 *supra,* this chap.

125. ILL. ANN. STAT., ch. 83, § 22 (Smith-Hurd Repl. 1961).

126. 30 Ill.2d at 226, 195 N.E.2d at 639.

127. *Id.* at 227, 195 N.E.2d at 640.

128. *Id.* at 228, 195 N.E.2d at 640.

129. ARIZ. REV. STATS. § 13-377 (1956). Interestingly, this statute was involved in the landmark U.S. Supreme Court decision extending certain procedural safeguards to Juvenile Court delinquency proceedings, Application of Gault, 387 U.S. 1 (1967). In that case, Gerald Gault, a 15 year old boy, had been adjudged and committed as a juvenile delinquent for having allegedly made obscene and lewd telephone calls "of the irritatingly offensive, adolescent, sex variety" (387 U.S. at 4) which, had they been made by an adult, would have constituted a misdemeanor pursuant to the above cited section of the Arizona Criminal Code. Since ARIZ. REV. STATS. § 8-201 (b) (1956) defines a "delinquent child" as including " (a) A child who has violated the law of the State or an ordinance or regulation of a political subdivision thereof," a finding that Gerald had violated that law was necessary for a determination of delinquency on that ground. The "law" which the juvenile violates must of course be one that is constitutionally valid. If, as is suggested in the text, serious constitutional questions are raised by this and similar laws, an alternative or additional approach in *Gault* might have been to seek reversal of Gerald

Gault's adjudication of delinquency by challenging that provision of the Arizona Code. This point was not briefed in *Gault*, however, either by the appellant or by any of the *amici curiae* (Legal Aid Society and Citizens' Committee for Children of New York, Inc.; Ohio Association of Juvenile Court Judges; and the American Parents Committee)—a failure probably explained by the parties' preoccupation with the procedural due process questions and by the possible validity of the statute as applied to the particular facts of the *Gault* case. For a reasonable distinction might be drawn between "obscene" utterances made *to* a person and those made in a person's *presence*—although distinctions drawn between the sex of the hearers would still appear vulnerable to equal protection challenge.

130. *See, e.g.*, Ginzburg v. United States, 383 U.S. 463 (1966); Mishkin v. New York, 383 U.S. 502 (1966); Roth v. United States and Alberts v. California, 354 U.S. 476 (1957).

131. *See* pp. 39-40 *supra*.

132. *See, e.g.*, Ginsberg v. State of New York,—U.S.—88 S. Ct. 1274 (1968); *but cf.* Interstate Circuit, Inc., v. City of Dallas,—U.S.—,88 S. Ct. 1298 (1968).

133. 335 U.S. 464 (1948).

134. *Id.* at 466.

135. *Id.*

136. Hoyt v. Florida, 368 U.S. 57, 61 (1961).

137. American society tolerates the expression "sexual intercourse," but its hackles are raised by a four letter equivalent whose linguistic roots can be traced to an earlier Anglo-Saxon word, and which is etymologically related to and sounds like a Danish word currently in use as the socially acceptable word to express the idea of sexual intercourse.

138. A related legal doctrine was once embodied in a Texas statute, TEX. REV. CR. STAT. § 1248 (1925), repealed by TEX. ACTS. 1927, ch. 274. As characterized in State v. Grugin, 147 Mo. 39, 47 S.W. 1058, 1064 (1898), the former Texas Statute reduced "a homicide to manslaughter where insulting words are used to or concerning a female relative, [if] the killing . . . occurs as soon as the parties meet after the knowledge of the insult." This statute was enacted to counteract the common law rule that "provocative words are not recognized as adequate provocation to reduce a wilful killing to manslaughter. . . ." PERKINS, CRIMINAL LAW 49 (1957). Similarly, in *State v. Grugin, id.*, the Missouri Supreme Court held that in some circumstances *"words do amount to a provocation in law,"* relying on cases from other jurisdictions which like the principal case itself involved words suggesting that a female relative of the accused was unchaste or had committed adultery. "In this connection," noted the court in *Grugin (Id.* at 1062), "it must not be forgotten what a high estimate the *men* of all nations have placed on the chastity of their women and on the inviolability of their persons." (Emphasis supplied.) By contrast, no cases appear in which homicide by a female has been reduced to manslaughter though perpetrated in response to words impugning the chastity or indicating adulterous conduct of close male relatives. See also material on the "unwritten law" defense in chap. 3, *supra*, pp. 92-93.

139. Miss., 187 So. 2d 861 (1966).

140. 251 F. Supp. 401 (1966).

141. 187 So. 2d at 863.

142. *See* pp. 104-105 *supra*.

143. *See* text at note 90, chap. 4 *supra*.

144. Mengelkoch v. Industrial Welfare Commission, *reported at* CCH EMPL. PRACT. GUIDE ¶ 9129 (D.C. Cal. 1968).

145. On October 28, 1968, the U.S. Supreme Court decided it had no jurisdiction to entertain the appeals in *Mengelkoch* in that case's present posture—leaving open the possibility that it would hear the case should it come to the Court from the Court of Appeals. Mengelkoch v. Industrial Welfare Commission,—U.S.—, 89 S. Ct. 61 (1968).

146. Since July 2, 1968, persons having fewer than 25 employees, though they are engaged in industries "affecting" commerce have not been covered by Title VII of the 1964 Civil Rights Act. Coverage of the FLSA's equal pay provisions, added by the Equal Pay Act of 1963, is subject to the FLSA's numerous exemptions (29 U.S.C. § 213) as well as that Act's stricter requirements with respect to "interstate commerce." *See, e.g.,* 29 U.S.C. § 206 (a) and (b), and minimum dollar amounts in sales or business volume for most enterprises, in the case of enterprise coverage as opposed to individual employee coverage. *Id.* § 203 (s).

147. 335 U.S. 464 (1948).

148. *Id.* at 467. (Emphasis supplied.)

149. *See* pp. 157-158 *supra.*

150. The premise that the "right to work" is basic does not mean that any state or federal legislation having the effect of limiting job opportunities would be *ipso facto* invalid. It would simply signify that the burden of justification, as I have called it, would be greater than otherwise. Thus it would be possible to continue to sustain the validity of the National Labor Relations Act's implied authorization of union shop agreements, see proviso to § 8 (a) (3) of the Act, on the ground that the general requirements of labor peace and the maintenance of satisfactory working conditions and wages satisfies this greater burden. It should also be noted that the NLRA does not *require* union shop agreements, but merely permits them. Where they exist, they are the products of private contractual arrangements between employers and labor organizations. By analogy with the principles of Shelley v. Kramer, 334 U.S. 1 (1948), however, state action would be present in suits to enforce such agreements, and in such situations their alleged unconstitutionality could be raised. As indicated in the text, however, holding that the right to procure a job is "basic" would not invalidate legislation or court action in aid of various union security arrangements.

151. 388 U.S. 1 (1967).

152. 335 U.S. 464, 466.

153. 391 U.S. 68, 70 (1968).

153a. 239 U.S. 33 (1915).

153b. *Id.* at 41.

154. *See* note 145, *supra* this chap.

154a. *See* note 145 *supra,* this chap.

155. *See* note 8, *supra* chap. 4.

156. 312 U.S. 100 (1940).

157. *Cf.* United States v. South-Eastern Underwriters Association *et al,* 322 U.S. 533 (1944), in which the Supreme Court held that Congress, in enacting the Sherman Act, asserted its power over the business of insurance notwithstanding that it failed to do so expressly and despite the fact that the Supreme Court, starting with Paul v. Virginia, 8 Wall. 168, 183 (1869) had repeatedly held that the business of insurance was not in commerce. Again it must be emphasized that this recommendation in the text is limited to the maximum

hours and minimum wage areas, and that different considerations would dictate alternative approaches with respect to statutes barring women from certain types of employment or imposing weight-lifting restrictions.

158. 347 U.S. 483 (1954).

159. *See* note 41, *supra*, this chap.; *see also* Glona v. American Guarantee & Liability Insurance Co., 391 U.S. 79 (1968), holding as violative of the equal protection guarantee a state's denial to mothers of illegitimate children the right to sue for the latters' wrongful death while providing such relief for mothers of legitimate children.

160. *See* note 49, *supra*, this chap.

161. *See* note 46, *supra*, this chap.

161a. Railway Company v. Whitton, 80 U.S. 270, 286 (1871).

161b. Markham v. City of Newport News, 292 F.2d 711 (1961). (Emphasis supplied.)

161c. *See, e.g.,* the Uniform Time Act of 1966, P.L. 89-387, 80 Stat. 107, 15 U.S.C. § 260 *et seq.,* establishing uniform dates for the commencing and ending of daylight saving time in all states and jurisdictions where it is observed. At the same time, the Act allows each state through enactment of state law to exempt itself on a statewide basis from the daylight saving time provisions of the Act. 15 U.S.C. § 260a. In enacting this legislation in this manner, Congress appeared to be cognizant of the phenomenon discussed in the text. It could have merely adopted a joint resolution extolling the virtues of a uniform daylight saving time system, and exhorting the states to enact such laws. But that would have required the exercise of state initiative. In effect, what Congress then did was to say to the states that if you do not think you can live with this uniform system, then you must exert the initiative to opt out.

162. *See e.g.,* IND. STAT. ANN. § 40-134 (1965 Repl.).

163. 29 U.S.C. § 201 *et seq.* (1965).

164. *See* U.S. DEPT OF LABOR, WOMEN'S BUREAU, ANALYSIS OF COVERAGE AND WAGE RATES OF STATE MINIMUM WAGE LAWS AND ORDERS *passim* (Bulletin 291, August 1, 1965).

165. *See* note 124, chap. 4 *supra*.

166. *See* note 125, chap. 4 *supra*.

167. Cases are collected at 39 A.L.R.2d 740 (1955).

168. *See, e.g.,* Holcombe v. Creamer, 231 Mass. 99, 120 N.E. 354 (1918); Williams v. Evans, 139 Minn. 32, 165 N.W. 495, 166 N.W. 504 (1917).

169. 261 U.S. 525 (1923).

170. *Id.* at 552-53.

171. *Id.* at 553.

172. 300 U.S. 379 (1937).

173. *Id.* at 391.

174. *See, e.g.,* Holden v. Hardy, 169 U.S. 366 (1898).

175. *See* cases cited in *Parrish,* 300 U.S. at 393.

176. 312 U.S. at 125. (Emphasis supplied.)

177. 300 U.S. at 398; *see also id.* at 394-99.

178. *Id.* at 400.

179. *Id.* at 411-12.

180. *Id.* at 400.

181. All this, of course, without taking into consideration the effect upon this area of effective and extensive representation by trade unions.

182. *See, e.g.,* National Labor Relations Board v. Jones & Laughlin Steel Corp., 301 U.S. 1 (1937); Porter v. Investors Syndicate, 286 U.S. 461 (1932).

183. Not all the recent developments in this area have been examined in this chapter. *See, e.g.,* Clarke v. Redeker, 259 F. Supp. 117 (1966), rejecting the claim of a male student at the University of Iowa School of Law that he was unconstitutionally discriminated against by a University regulation which had the effect of according resident status, and thus lower tuition fees, upon non-resident females who married resident males, while not according this privilege upon non-resident males, such as himself, who married resident females. *See also* Matter of Shpritzer v. Lang, 17 A.D.2d 285, aff'd 13 N.Y.2d 744 (1962) holding that policewomen, otherwise eligible, were not barred by reason of their sex, from competing for promotion to the position of sergeant. *Cf.* Schimmel v. City Civil Service Commission of the City of New York, *reported at* CCH EMPL. PRACT. GUIDE ¶ 9029 (1966).

184. *See* note 12, chap. 1 *supra.*

185. CCPR 32.

186. *See* S.J.R. 54, 90th Cong., introduced March 13, 1967, and H.J.R. 22, 90th Cong., introduced January 10, 1967.

187. CCPR 32.

188. In a rough sense, a similar problem was implied in the determination in Baker v. Carr, 369 U.S. 186 (1962) of the relationship between the Fourteenth Amendment's equal protection clause and the "guaranty clause," Art. IV § 4 of the U.S. Constitution.

189. *See, e.g.,* 1945 testimony of Frank Donner for the CIO, that the Equal Rights Amendment "can have no other effect but of repealing protective labor laws for women written into our statute books only after years of bitter struggle. In exchange for an illusory and doctrinaire equality it discards advantages which have taken years to accumulate," Hearings on the Equal Rights Amendment, 79th Cong., 1st Sess., before Subcommittee of the Senate Judiciary Committee, 81 (1945).

190. Salt Lake City v. Wilson, 46 Utah 60, 63, 148 P. 1104, 1107 (1915) (construing a *state* constitutional provision).

Chapter 7.   *Summary and Conclusions*

1. Note 365 *supra,* chap. 3.

2. *See* note 371 *supra,* chap. 3.

3. N.Y. Family Court Act § 712 (b) defines a "person in need of supervision" as "a male less than sixteen years of age and a female less than eighteen years of age who is an habitual truant or who is incorrigible, ungovernable or habitually disobedient and beyond the lawful control of parent or other lawful authority."

4. *See, e.g.,* Gott v. Berea College, 156 Ky., 161 S.W. 204 (1913).

5. *See* County of Kern v. Coley, 229 Cal. App.2d 172, 40 Cal. Rptr. 53 (1964). Professors Lewis and Levy, commenting on the "man-in-the-house" rule, have observed that practically speaking, "the 'community property interest' of the needy children's mother in her *mate's* income represents nothing more than the choice she must make when seeking AFDC between severing the relationship or maintaining the relationship and having his income counted as family resource. If he is unwilling to share his income to the extent it reduced an AFDC allotment, *she has a financial incentive to sever the relationship.*" Lewis & Levy, *Family Law and Welfare Policies: The*

Case for "Dual Systems," 54 CALIF. L. REV. 748, 758-759 (1966). (Emphasis supplied.) As suggested in the text, however, no male recipient is put to that choice or provided with a financial incentive to sever an illicit sexual relationship with a female, regardless of her potential wealth. Since the above was written the United States Supreme Court has invalidated the "man-in-the-house" rule via the statutory construction route, rather than on constitutional grounds. King v. Smith,—U.S.—, 88 S. Ct. 2128 (1968). The equal protection argument advanced by the plaintiffs and concurred in by Mr. Justice Douglas in a separate opinion,—U.S. at—, 88 S. Ct. at 2142, did not consider the unequal treatment between male and female welfare recipients, but concentrated rather on the distinctions drawn between "moral" and "immoral" mothers. It is submitted, however, that sex-based discrimination is present here and should be dealt with by the Court at the earliest opportunity.

INDEXES

Author Index*

* The reference in parentheses is the page number of the annotated citation from the Notes at the end of the volume.

Case Index*

* The reference in parentheses is the page number of the annotated citation from the Notes at the end of the volume.

Subject Index*

* Of text only.

198